CONNECTIONALISM

VOLUME 1

UNITED
METHODISM
AND
AMERICAN
CULTURE

CONNECTIONALISM

ECCLESIOLOGY
MISSION AND
IDENTITY

Russell E.
Richey
Dennis M.
Campbell
William B.
Lawrence
Editors

Abingdon Press
Nashville

UNITED METHODISM AND AMERICAN CULTURE, VOLUME 1
CONNECTIONALISM: ECCLESIOLOGY, MISSION, AND IDENTITY

Copyright © 1997 by Abingdon Press

All rights reserved.

This book is printed on acid-free, recycled paper.

Library of Congress Cataloging-in-Publication Data

Connectionalism / edited by Russell E. Richey, Dennis M. Campbell, William B. Lawrence.
    p. cm. — (United Methodism and American culture: vol. 1)
    Includes bibliographical references.
    ISBN 0-687-02189-8 (alk. paper)
    1. United Methodist Church (U.S.)—Government. 2. United Methodist Church (U.S.)—History. 3. Methodist Church—United States—History. 4. Church and culture—United States. I. Richey, Russell E. II. Campbell, Dennis M., 1945- . III. Lawrence, William Benjamin. IV. Series.
BX8331.2.C65 1997
262'.076—DC21   97-38665
                                      CIP

97 98 99 00 01 02 03 04 05 06— 10 9 8 7 6 5 4 3 2 1

MANUFACTURED IN THE UNITED STATES OF AMERICA

Contents

Preface
United Methodism and American Culture

This volume is one of a series of publications deriving from research, conslutations, and conferences undertaken under a major grant from the Lilly Endowment, Inc. This five-year study has been based at the Divinity School of Duke University and directed by Dennis M. Campbell and Russell E. Richey, with William B. Lawrence as Project Associate, and with the counsel of an advisory board composed of Jackson W. Carroll, also of Duke and Director of the Ormond Center; Rosemary Skinner Keller, Dean of Union Theological Seminary, New York; Donald G. Mathews, Professor of History, University of North Carolina, Chapel Hill; Cornish R. Rogers, Professor of Pastoral Theology, Claremont; and Judith Smith, Associate General Secretary, Office of Interpretation, General Board of Higher Education and Ministry.

The project began under a planning grant that made it possible for the principals to engage in exploratory conversations with a wide array of church members, including board and agency leaders, bishops and district superintendents, clergy and laity, United Methodist faculty, and researchers in other Lilly-sponsored studies. From the counsel received through such exploratory discussions, the project came to pursue three primary objectives:

(1) to provide a careful, fresh estimate of the history of Methodism in America, with particular attention to its twentieth-century experience,
(2) to attempt a portrait of United Methodism at the dawning of a new century, and
(3) to explore policy issues, with a view to the church's effective participation in American society and the world in the future.

We pursued those objectives through sponsored research, through dialogue with the several commissions, committees, and projects studying United Methodism which were launched during the 1992–96 quadrennium, and through a series of conferences and consultations. In the latter process, approximately seventy-five church leaders, scholars, and researchers participated, each working on a specific aspect, theme, or issue from the comprehensive task. From their efforts, we are pleased now to share some of the results in the first of what will be three volumes of essays.

These three studies, organized thematically, will touch on all three of our objectives for the "United Methodism and American Culture" project but focus on the first two. A sampling of insights from these studies appeared in the November 1996 issue of *Circuit Rider*. The third objective we addressed in a series of *Leadership Letters*, widely distributed among United Methodists, explicitly raising policy issues for the church. A related, policy-oriented volume, also to appear from Abingdon Press, will address questions facing the church at the dawn of the new century. Much of the research undertaken as part of this project could not be accommodated in these few volumes and will appear in the future in *Quarterly Review, Circuit Rider, Methodist History,* and other media.

From the start of this project, Abingdon committed itself to be the "publisher of record" and to make the results appropriately accessible to United Methodism. As part of that commitment and this project, Abingdon has already published *The Methodist Conference in America* (Richey) and will publish a two-volume collaborative effort (also involving Richey), *The Methodist Experience in America*, one volume of which will be narrative, the other a historical sourcebook. These two volumes and perhaps others are currently slated to appear also in CD-ROM form.

The project will culminate in three synthetic "statements." One of these, like this volume, will address the church's leadership and be most appropriate for clergy and clergy-to-be. A second will be aimed at the adult laity of the denomination. A third will be in video form and be usable in an even wider set of contexts.

Through these "publishing" efforts we seek to open conversations about the future of our church and its role locally and globally in the decades and century ahead.

Introduction

Russell E. Richey

Commentators on the American scene sometimes speak of churches as connectional. With that term they differentiate denominations with strong corporate, centralized, or hierarchical authority systems from those with systems that are self-consciously or operationally congregational, independent, or free church.[1] Although the word lacks precision, it handily marks off episcopal and presbyterial from congregational polities. So the Roman Catholic, Lutheran, Episcopal and Presbyterian churches are connectional, while Baptist, Congregational (UCC), Christian, and Mennonite churches are not.

Connectional communions, if Protestant, by and large derive from the Magisterial Reformation and often have enjoyed privileged status as state or established churches. By contrast, many, though not all, of the non-connectional churches have roots or affinities with the Radical Reformation and a free-church ecclesiology.[2] The latter fit comfortably within American social and legal patterns, where voluntarism, separation of church and state, localism, and individualism hold sway. The former have had episodic clashes with the courts or with popular opinion, which presume that churches are local bodies "owned" by trustees. To a public, and even a membership, that "knows" religion to be voluntary, connectional churches have had to explain themselves. This burden has been borne most heavily by the Roman Catholics, but virtually all connectional churches can recall some moment of conflict around connectionalism.[3] It is, perhaps, this angularity of connectionalism with respect to American values and practice that puts it forth as a term for distinction.

Methodist Connectionalism

United Methodism and many other American Methodist communions would certainly place themselves among the connectional churches. Our connectionalism, most Methodists would know, does not derive from the Magisterial Reformation or privileged status as a state church. United Methodism and other episcopal Methodisms do owe

1

much to Anglicanism. However, it was John and Charles Wesley, and preeminently John, who defined our connectionalism.[4] The term has a very special meaning for Methodists, a meaning which this collection explores.[5] Wesley's connectionalism was decidedly enriched both by elements of Anglican ecclesiology and practice and by American organizational experience, the latter a concern of the essays by Richard Heitzenrater, Thomas Frank and William Everett, Kenneth Rowe, Charles Zech, and Penny Long Marler and Kirk Hadaway. For some, it is these later accretions that most define connectionalism, accretions like apportionments and corporate bureaucratic boards and agencies that spend the apportionments. And when Methodists reshape the church through mergers, these later accretions tend to preoccupy the architects of the new order, as Robert Sledge shows.

Apportionments vividly convey certain notions of connection and connectionalism. They image the claim, for every charge or church, that centralized authority, program, board, and agency make: the claim that comes as an "obligatory" budgetary asking. To the typical United Methodist, connectionalism means taxation, begrudged even for the pension and salary portions that she understands. Connectionalism has always had its fiscal dimension. Indeed, one might argue that connectionalism had its foundation in the collection of 1742 that inaugurated the class system. Being in connection with Mr. Wesley thereafter had its price. Certainly, early American Methodism depended entirely on the collections brought to quarterly conference, the quarterage equally shared among itinerants, presiding elders, and bishops. Nor is this the first generation of Methodists who have chafed over collections that supported far-off ministries.

However, though impossible and unthinkable without its fiscal dimension, connectionalism has always meant more than sharing a financial burden and indeed has been bearable as a financial burden because it was embraced—and celebrated—for its multiple values. To recall those multiple values helps us to understand why we speak of ourselves as a connectional church and why we simply must think of more than apportionments when we think "connection."

The remainder of this essay explores those multiple values. First, I look at the theological principles that undergird or are latent in Methodist connectionalism. Then, I explore Methodism as a changing covenant, noting the different forms or styles of connectionalism that have emerged over the history of American Methodism.

Connectionalism: A Practical Divinity

At its best, Methodist connectionalism has been more than a form of corporatism, more than a polity, more than a classificatory term. Connectionalism has been a Wesleyan precept, an ecclesial vision, a missional principle, a covenantal commitment, an ethic of equity and proportionality, a tactical stratagem, an elastic and evolving standard, a theology in praxis. Only if these richer meanings are grasped can one appreciate why we give them fiscal expression.

First, connectionalism is a Wesleyan precept, a first-order affirmation, an identifying statement, a recognition of Wesley's authority and that of his successors in the apostolic superintendency. To be Methodist, as Richard Heitzenrater's essay demonstrates, has been to locate ourselves within a system that evolved around and through John and Charles Wesley. To be Methodist has meant singing our hymns, accepting our doctrines, reading our literature, knowing our story, recognizing the Methodist way as a full and adequate expression of the Gospel witness, and accepting our place within a set of gracious relations. The acceptance of our acceptance into class, society, conference gave connection its form by tying those fleeing the wrath to come into bond with one another and with Mr. Wesley. Americans first named themselves Methodist by precept, "Preachers in connexion with the Rev. Mr. Wesley."[6] Connectionalism makes a statement, a statement about authority, a statement about identity. Taking up these matters are the first and last essays in this collection, those by Richard Heitzenrater and by Penny Long Marler and Kirk Hadaway.

Second, connectionalism appeals to an ecclesial vision. Indeed, connectionalism represents a/the distinctive Methodist manner of being the church, a multifaceted, not simply political, mode of spirituality, unity, mission, governance, and fraternity that Methodists lived and operated better than they interpreted, the latter point a central concern of Thomas Frank's and William Everett's chapter. Methodists came closest to articulating this vision in what they said, and more important, what they did, with conference. The same might be affirmed of the United Brethren and Evangelical Association.

In "The Large Minutes" Wesley recognized "Christian conference" as one of five "instituted" means of grace. That designation and the character of the other four—prayer, searching the Scriptures, the Lord's Supper and fasting—suggest how very central to the Christian life and the Methodist movement Wesley placed "conference." The reference here was not specifically to the annual or to the quarterly Methodist meetings or conferences but rather to the mode of engagement, discipline, purpose, and structure that they shared with all serious Christian encounter and that characterized all the Methodist structures. Conference was the way Wesley sought to conduct his affairs with his people.

The "connexion" of preachers became a family headed and governed by John Wesley; it was a monastic-like order held together by affection, by common rules, by a shared mission, and by watchfulness of each member over one another; it functioned as a brotherhood of religious aspiration and song; it served as a quasi-professional society which concerned itself with the reception, training, credentialing, monitoring, and deployment of Wesley's lay preachers; it became a community of preachers whose commitment to the cause and one another competed with all other relationships; it was a body whose resources provided for the wants and needs of its members. When one of its members died, it constituted the agency of memorial and memory. It served as the spiritual center of Methodism; it was multivalent.

This gracious vision, this notion of structure as grace, characterized all dimensions of connection, not just conference. The several structurings of the Wesleyan spirit had emerged in stages and in relation to entities named as the occasion suggested—societies, bands, classes, stewards, trustees, circuits, connexion, conference, quarterly meeting. These were the spatial *and* temporal outworking of a set of religious impulses, never fully integrated into theory, but nevertheless characteristic of a peculiar Wesleyan style of organization, unity, mission, reform, spirituality. Constituting the Wesleyan economy, these features and practices expressed Wesleyan spiritual and religious emphases, the accent on the priesthood of all believers and the insistence on the mutual interdependence of all parts of the body of Christ. They cohered because Methodism cohered, because they belonged together in the religious experience and administrative style of John Wesley, because they possessed a center in him, because Wesley envisioned Methodism as an integrated connection.

Third, connectionalism actualizes a missional principle, a principle expressed perhaps best by itinerancy and general superintendency. Itinerancy has meant that the connection has first claim on itinerants and the connection makes its claim on behalf of its purpose, namely "to reform the Continent, and spread scriptural Holiness over these Lands." Connectionalism and itinerancy constitute the church as missionary by nature, a point developed explicitly by Richard Heitzenrater and Mark Wethington in their essays. Ministers are sent, and they are sent where most needed. A certain amount of consultation always went on—even before the *Discipline* so required—but such conversation served to guide the appointing authority to the wisest decisions for the whole. So ministers are ordained in conference because the call is not to some locale but to mission, to the connection, to the world. The missional principle inherent in itinerancy belongs, however, to the whole people. We all are sent, commissioned, missionaries, as Sarah Sloan Kreutziger shows.

Perhaps it is because connection is missional that we have had such difficulty in making it function as a formal ecclesiology. When we think ecclesiologically, we revert rather automatically to the language of the Articles of Religion—"a congregation of faithful men in which the pure Word of God is preached, and the Sacraments duly administered according to Christ's ordinance."[7] We don't mine our connectional pattern, practice, and heritage for their ecclesiological implications because we have other resources and because, if we do reflect about connection in other than polity terms, we do so soteriologically. Connection belongs for us to doctrines of salvation, the Christian life, and mission, not to Christology or ecclesiology. If Methodists were to structure their theology systematically around the creed, discussion of connection might well come up, not when talking about Christ and his Body or in expounding upon the holy catholic church or the communion of saints, but rather when discussing forgiveness, resurrection, and life everlasting. Connection might well be treated under soteriology.[8] It makes a statement about how we will effect the salvation of souls and the redemption of the world. It speaks about our mission.

Fourth, connectionalism expresses a covenant to carry through on the missional commitment. That covenant has often been spoken of in relation to those "in full connection," whose membership in conference put them in covenant relationship with one another, with all the people whom they committed to serve and, of course, preeminently with God. But Methodism initially treated all members in the same fashion, holding them to their disciplinary obligations, expecting them to care for their neighbors, pressing on them the counsels of perfection, issuing tickets to those in good standing for the love feast, and excluding those whose walk diverged from the Methodist way. Such a larger covenantal bond, in principle, continues to this day. It is one of the resources for our renewal, a point developed in different ways by William B. McClain, Sarah Sloan Kreutziger, Mark Wethington, and Penny Edgell Becker.

Fifth, connectionalism, as a covenant, necessitated an ethic of equity and proportionality. That always took fiscal form. Those who had much paid more to support the shared ministry than those who had little. That sharing according to means is especially obvious in the early collections of American Methodism and is accessible today in the records of early conferences. For instance, in the early-nineteenth century the Baltimore circuits constituted something like 12% of the Baltimore Conference but delivered more than twice that percentage in its collections. But equity and proportionality applied across the board, not just fiscally. In appointments, bishops, and cabinets sent itinerants (who were paid equally) where the connection needed them. Today, when the reverse potential holds sway—the gifted are sent, not to where the need is greatest but to where the reward is greatest—it is worth recalling that salary differentials initially emerged so that persons with families and individuals sent to higher cost, urban areas would not suffer. The essays by Mark Wethington and Charles Zech explore financial policies and the ethic of connectionalism, but in quite different ways. Wethington urges United Methodism to bring its expenditures in line with its true mission. Zech explores financial dissent from mission not understood or appreciated on a congregational level.

Sixth, connectionalism was a tactical stratagem. It worked. Methodism, with its principles of itinerancy and connectionalism, elaborated a national, frontier-oriented, ministry-delivery-system.[9] With its orientation to the whole, to continent and world, Methodism early adopted new mechanisms that took or brought the Gospel to those who needed it. Methodists pioneered, literally in forest and plain, but also with camp meetings, Sunday schools, newspapers, women's organizations, church extension, Freedmen's Aid, missionary organization, and eventually corporate structures. The stages in this pioneering are outlined below. A different schema for reading that pioneering is undertaken by William Everett and Thomas Frank in the second chapter. Suffice it to say here that the boards, agencies, and apportionments that now seem to some a burden ironically emerged and were, at first, enthusiastically embraced for their ability to carry the Methodist message. They connected Gospel with need.

Seventh, as just implied, connectionalism has been an elastic and evolving principle and pattern. It has permitted, indeed needed, innovation, creativity, fresh starts, some break from the denominational norm. By such new ventures, connectionalism found new expressions of itself. John Vincent, as Kenneth Rowe shows, experimented with Sunday schools, his innovations earning him leadership of the denomination, as head of the Methodist Episcopal Sunday School Union and, eventually, bishop. He then guided Methodism and much of evangelical Protestantism into the international lesson, training institutes for teachers, standard curricula—a new educational connectionalism. As his example indicates, innovation led to new commonalities and sharing, to new norms, to consolidations that served the whole.

This novelty-to-connectional-norm is strikingly exemplified in Methodist institution-building. First with colleges, then with seminaries and universities, next with hospitals, then with homes, orphanages, camps, and retirement facilities, Methodist laity and clergy ventured daringly in new enterprise, confident that the institution would serve the connection and hopeful that the Methodist people shared the vision. Often the people did. The essays by Bradley Longfield and Robert Monk document such vision and enterprise with respect to universities and campus ministry respectively. The story of risk-taking makes the narratives of our nationally renowned Methodist universities and hospitals truly inspiring, a claim made for Duke as for many of our schools. But the larger picture also includes false-starts, missteps, and failures. And today, some of United Methodism's greatest institutions seem less than attentive to their heritage and the constituency they were created to serve. Nevertheless, they have stood, if they don't always stand today, as icons of connectionalism.

Eighth, then, connectionalism rests on just such institutional outworkings of the faith. Connectionalism constitutes a Wesleyan theo-logical style, a practical theology, an experimental divinity. As for other aspects of our praxis, connectionalism's theological dimension has not been sufficiently developed systematically and formally. Still, connec-tionalism has served to express, give shape to, choreograph, structure our notions of who we are, what we affirm, and what we are called upon to do. Connectionalism displays our theological system, a programmatic and operational statement of the Wesleyan theology of praxis. We live our theology. Connectionalism expresses it.

Connectionalism: A Changing Covenant

In living their theology, Methodists gave connectionalism different form in different periods. They held themselves together, undertook their mission, defined their identity, communicated with one another, and structured governance in styles appropriate for the day. Each style had its own grammar and rules touching form, substance, procedure, and structure. Seven different styles seem distinct enough to warrant mention and brief characterization. They are Wesleyan (episcopal), popular, voluntary, corporate, federal, professional, and post-corporate. I have arranged them here in roughly chronological order, though the first two emerged at virtually the same time, the federal has been in the process of development over the whole of our history, and several others have also evolved over long periods of time. Further, they all live on. One style does not disappear after its period of dominance but instead remains to find altered place in the successive style. So these seven styles represent continuing options for Methodist self-understanding, definition of mission, and connectional shaping. They function as historical generalizations, as a typology, as models.

Oral/Aural Connection

How did American Methodism connect itself over the course of its history? Of what did its connectionalism consist? How did it structure and display its theology?[10] In its first decades, American Methodism depended upon the connectional, missional, and disciplinary provisions that Wesley had made, provisions enriched and decorated after 1784 with the episcopal features taken over from Anglicanism.[11] The character and look of this formative connectionalism Heitzenrater well describes in the first chapter. Conferences, itinerating general superintendents, a national itinerant ministry, and classes for the Methodist peoples gave voice to Methodism's Arminian and gracious word. Connection had a preeminently *oral* character (a style every bit as characteristic of the United Brethren and Evangelical movements as of the Methodist Episcopal). Preaching mediated a Wesleyan reading of scripture, hymns instilled our doctrines, class meetings translated promise into practice, love feasts expressed the joy that young and old, rich and poor, white and black, English and German had *heard* and *experienced*. Methodist connectionalism *voiced* itself and measured its effectiveness by the quality, intensity, and volume of its utterance. Did one preach with "liberty"? elicit tears? demand or produce shouts and cries? Virtually any journal or diary of this period attests and assesses this voiced connectionalism. For instance, Jesse Lee noted for late 1783 and for 1784:

> [Dec.] Saturday 31st, I preached at Mr. Spain's with great liberty to a good congregation, and the Spirit of the Lord came upon us, and we were bathed in tears—I wept—and so loud were the people's cries, that I could scarcely be heard, though I spoke very loud. I met the class—most of the

members expressed a great desire for holiness of heart and life, and said they were determined to seek for perfect love.

> Sunday 1st of February, I preached at Coleman's with life and liberty, to a weeping congregation. When I met the class, we were highly favoured of the Lord, with a comfortable sense of his love shed abroad in our hearts; the brethren wept, and praised God together. . . .
> Saturday 14th.—We held our quarterly meeting for Amerlia Circuit, at old father Patrick's—we had a good meeting for the first day. One Sunday morning we had a happy love feast; at which time I wept much, and prayed earnestly that the Lord would take every evil temper and every wrong desire out of my heart, and fill my soul with perfect love. I felt the pain of parting with my friends in that circuit. . . .[12]

By preaching, singing, and testifying early Methodists voiced their love for one another and so quite literally heard themselves together. And in connecting themselves to one another and to their mission, they heeded the variety of rubrics, practices, and offices that Wesley had given them. Connectionalism had a specifically Wesleyan grammar and vocabulary. And the rules were those taken over from Wesley and adjusted to the American scene and episcopal governance in what Americans called a *Discipline*. In its thirty pages[13] or so, Methodists found guidance for spreading scriptural holiness. So Methodism connected itself through an itinerant general superintendent (and specifically Asbury), annual and general conferences, and a nationally itinerant traveling ministry (itinerants and presiding elders whom Asbury appointed across conference lines and on a national basis, reinforcing his own itinerant general superintendency with an itinerant general ministry). The ministry, the episcopacy, and the conferences constituted a particularly important and underappreciated connective voice. Methodism hung together in hearing a common Arminian gospel.

Connected by Event

A second form or style of connectionalism, which requires more elaboration, also derives from the earliest phases of Methodism and is so intertwined with the first as to be infrequently distinguished. Everett and Frank do isolate and name it, describing it as popular public assembly. This designation contextualizes early Methodist gatherings—crowds taken outside for preaching, the quarterly meeting and love-feast, the camp meeting, the assemblages around conference—in the long tradition of Christian (and secular) popular gatherings. I prefer a more regional understanding, namely as the religious counterpart to the event-based community of the upper south and lower middle states.[14] Like elections, musters, dances, horse-races, Methodist community was event, defined less by space or place than by time, something that occurred. Connectionalism *occurred—by appointment*. It was *event*.

Its event character was well captured by the admonition, "Don't disappoint an appointment!" Of the events constitutive of and connectional for Methodism, that most important and expressive was the quarterly meeting. In it the ecclesial dimensions of conference, outlined above, came most fully alive. One key to the quarterly conference's connective role came from an early change in design and length. In 1780 the American conference recommended that quarterly meetings be a two-day affair and a weekend event, whenever possible.[15] From that point, the quarterly meeting quite literally brought the connection together, as this account indicates:

> I went next morning to brother Hobb's. Next day, was our quarterly-meeting, and a great many people came out; here I met brother Whatcoat and brother Morrell; one of them preached, and the other exhorted. Next day, brother Whatcoat opened the love-feast; and after the bread and water were handed round, divers young converts spoke very feelingly of the goodness of God, and his dealings with their souls: we had a precious time. There was a large congregation, and one of our brethren preached, and the other gave an exhortation: we had a solemn, and I trust, a profitable time to many to souls.[16]

The next account, for 1818, is particularly interesting because it comes from a British Methodist and describes the American quarterly meeting as something novel. The observer describes the whole event and captures a common feature of the quarterly meeting, namely its gathering preachers, as well as people, from far and wide, connecting Methodists within and beyond the circuit.

> I had an opportunity of attending a quarterly meeting on Redding circuit; and as it was the first I ever attended, I will describe it as faithfully as I can. . . . The place where the quarterly meeting was held, was Weston. The presiding elder was Ebenezer Washburn. The preacher in charge was James M. Smith, brother of Eben, and his colleague was Theodosius Clark. Beside these the other preachers present were Hawley Sandford, Samuel Bushnell, Cyrus Silliman, and Oliver Sykes. The exercises began at eleven o'clock on Saturday. The presiding elder preached the sermon, and the preacher in charge exhorted. After this a call was made to know how many persons wanted places of entertainment; that point being ascertained, another call was made to know who would entertain them. On this point there was no backwardness on the part of the people. One said, I can take

four, another *six*, another *eight*, &c. The preacher then made the distribution accordingly. The members of the quarterly conference tarried for business, which was soon disposed of, as there were no complaints, no appeals, no licenses to be renewed, no applications for recommendation for deacon's or elder's orders, or for admission into the traveling connection, no reports to be acted upon, and not a great deal of money to be divided among the preachers. The presiding elder had lost his horse, and a handsome sum was made up by the members of the conference toward purchasing another.

In the evening there was a general prayer-meeting at the Church. I did not enjoy it much. There was, according to my judgment at that time, too much noise by far. To some, probably, it was a good meeting, but my ears had not become accustomed to such lively singing and loud praying. The next morning the love-feast commenced at nine o'clock, and closed at half-past ten. After the love-feast the sacrament of the Lord's supper was administered. One probationer was publicly admitted into full membership; one who had been expelled was read out; and the bans of marriage published for one happy pair. The presiding elder preached again on Sabbath, and brother Sykes administered a startling exhortation, during the delivery of which some cried and screamed aloud. . . . I had never witnessed anything like such manifestations of feeling, either in London or elsewhere, and was therefore unprepared to judge whether the excitement proceeded from the depths of penitential distress, or from an ecstasy of joy. The sermons both days were sound, orthodox, and powerful; but the exhortations seemed to be based upon a principle which I had not, as yet, considered to be the correct one—namely, that the greatest noise does the greatest good.[17]

The event-based character of Methodist connectionalism displayed itself most extravagantly in the institution that housed warm-weather quarterly meetings, namely the camp meeting. Camp-meetings, as events, oriented the Methodist connection towards its mission, namely redeeming individuals and society. This engagement with the world and the worldly gave them their storied character. Order seemed always perilous. But then conquests over the worldly, the melting of the stony heart, the conversion of the recalcitrant spouse seemed the more momentous. Camp meetings and even quarterly meetings as popular assembly gradually waned as Methodism put down roots in place, traded preaching houses for proper churches, stationed pastors, circumscribed community by space, and slowly transformed the camp meetings themselves into spas and the quarterly conference into a congregational business meeting. The holiness protests of the Civil War era endeavored to return Methodism, not just to perfection, but also to event-based community. So they created a new connection, a national organization devoted to camp meetings, the National Camp Meeting Association for the Promotion of Holiness. Recollections confirm the holiness assessment, making clear how important the institutions of quarterly and camp meetings had been and that they no longer retained that importance.

> The old quarterly meeting conferences and love-feasts! what was more characteristic of practical Methodism than they? The horses and carriages, and groups of men, women, and children plodding the highways on foot, for twenty miles or more, as on a holy pilgrimage; the assemblage of preachers, traveling and local, from all the neighboring appointments; the two days of preaching and exhorting, praying and praising; the powerful convictions, and more powerful conversions; and especially the Sunday morning love-feast, with its stirring testimonies and kindling songs; its tears and shoutings—how precious their reminiscences! Alas, for the changes which are coming over us![18]

What would connect Methodism—connect Methodists to one another, voice their common affirmations, and give expression to their mission—as event (camp meetings) and orality (the shout) waned? Itineration increasingly occurred within conferences. Multiple bishops lacked the cohesive and connective power that had been Asbury's and the bishops soon began itinerating by region. General conferences, as we will note below, became, especially after the 1808 provisions for constitutional status and delegation, the important legislative connection.[19] But general conferences met only every four years. Who or what would connect, day-to-day, week-to-week, as had Asbury and his lieutenants? How would Methodism hear a common Word?

Connection by Press and Voluntary Society

The *printed page* gradually assumed the connecting, mediating, grace-delivering, missional role previously carried by the spoken word, and *voluntary association* replaced much of what had been provided through the large popular event. Under the leadership of Joshua Soule, book agent/editor (1816–20), and particularly his successor, Nathan Bangs, the Book Concern became the most innovative and connecting force in Methodist life (a role clearly increasing in importance during the preceding decade). The publishing enterprise developed in a number of directions but none more important than the establishment of media for regular communication. *The Methodist Magazine* (1818) and the *Christian Advocate* (1826) provided the church with a clear voice, one that could convey across the connection complicated and complex ideas in coherent fashion, one that could get through with a uniform message despite itinerants' varying efforts in and enthusiasm for the published wares. The magazine for clergy, and more important, the weekly paper for the whole church, focused the entire church's efforts for nurture and outreach. (The United Brethren published the *Zion's Advocate* from 1829 to 1831 and followed with the paper that lasted till union in 1946, *The Religious Telescope*, a bi-weekly and an English-language venture from the start. The Evangelical Association launched its journal, *Der Christliche Botschafter*, in 1836. Initially a monthly, it lasted as a German paper till the union but gradually was upstaged by the English paper, *Evangelical Messenger*, begun in 1848.) Connection came through paper, tract, hymnbook, discipline, and Bible. Every itinerant peddled for the Book Concern. Regional *Advocates*, their editors also elected by General Conference, came eventually to nuance Methodism's written word for our many audiences. Through them, Methodism transmitted its "word" to its many publics. Through them Methodists heard one another across the entire connection.

Also keeping Methodists, United Brethren, and Evangelicals on the *same page* were the new *voluntary* societies that focused the common faith towards concerted witness. The Missionary Society of the Methodist Episcopal Church was formed in 1819/20 and the Sunday School Union in 1827 (counterpart organizations for the Evangelicals and United Brethren formed in 1838 and 1841 [missions] and roughly 1820 and 1835 [Sunday schools]). These two programmatic associations came to have great connective power across the Methodist peoples, drawing them into local and conference associations and drawing these associations into action on behalf of the cause. They prospered (as did voluntary movements across American Protestantism) because the church threw its shoulder behind this re-organization and because the new media from the Book Agency reinforced the organizational efforts. Popular literature, particularly for Sunday schools, made the program of the church available to every Methodist community.

Nathan Bangs saw the importance of these new institutions within the larger Methodist connectional system. After commenting on classes, stewards, exhorters, local preachers, itinerants, conferences, and bishops, he noted:

> In addition to this regular work, in which we behold a beautiful gradation of office and order, from the lowest to the highest, there is the book establishment, which has grown up with the growth of the church, and from which are issued a great variety of books on all branches of theological knowledge, suited to ministers of the gospel, including such as are suited to youth and children, as well as those for Sabbath schools, and a

great number of tracts for gratuitous distribution by tract societies, Bibles and Testaments of various sizes, a quarterly review, and weekly religious papers. This establishment is conducted by a suitable number of agents and editors, who are elected by the General Conference, to which body they are responsible for their official conduct, and, in the interval of the General, the New York Annual Conference exercises a supervision of this estimable and highly useful establishment.

In the last place, we may mention the Missionary Society of the Methodist Episcopal Church, which was organized in 1819, and has since spread itself, by means of auxiliary and branch societies, all over the United States and Territories, and, by means of its missionaries, has extended its operations among the aboriginal tribes of our wildernesses, among the descendants of Africa in the south, the new and poorer white settlements of our country, and also has sent its living heralds to Africa, to South America, and to the Oregon Territory. May its boundaries continually enlarge![20]

Both Sunday School and Missions channeled Methodist lay imagination and energies into the building of great networks of loosely-related societies, male and female, zealously committed to evangelization of youth and the "heathen." Methodists still connected with oral testimony and the written word but increasingly channeled their witness through societies with a missional or programmatic purpose. They did so by joining, and joining with others. The program of the church ran with *voluntary* societies.

Programmed and Corporate Connection

By the 1870s, such societies, in the case of the MEC including the Missionary Society, the Church Extension Society, the Board of Education, the Sunday-School Union, and the Tract Society, as well as the more loosely related Freemen's Aid Society and Book Concern, not to mention temperance organizations, preachers' aid societies, and various others, had become too successful, General Conferences thought, to be allowed to run themselves, compete with one another, and remain self-governing. So in 1872 and 1874, the MEC and MECS took action to make the boards elective and thereby accountable to General Conference, thus turning voluntary societies into national, corporate denominational boards. The magnitude of the change, A. J. Kynett explained in relation to his own agency four years later, noting that previously:

> Although organized by order of the General Conference, the corporate body was, by the terms of its Constitution and Charter, a "Society"

composed of such members and friends of the Church as might contribute to its funds the sum of one dollar per annum, or twenty dollars at one time. These had the legal right to elect its managers; but only such as could be present at the annual meetings in Philadelphia could share in the exercise of this right. It was, therefore, clearly beyond the reach of the Church government, and equally beyond the reach of all contributors to its funds, except only a portion of those who resided in the city of Philadelphia.[21]

The change effected in 1872 was structural and legal, as indicated in the enabling report:

> The special Committee "appointed to consider and report concerning the relations of our various benevolent societies to the authorities of the Church, and whether any action is necessary, and if so what, to place them under the full control of the General Conference," has considered the subject stated. . . .
> With respect to the Missionary Society incorporated by the New York Legislature, it noted "To place this corporation under the control of the General Conference, it will be proper to procure an act of the Legislature to amend the charter so as to provide that the Board of Managers shall be elected by the General Conference."[22]

At last, connectionalism had a denominational-structural expression, *a corporate structure.* Agencies proved remarkable connectional delivery systems, serving missional, identity-providing, communicative, and governance functions. These roles and their operation on a national level Everett and Frank detail with some care in their essay. Rowe shows how the corporate structure imprinted itself as well on local levels. Local Methodists, conference committees, and national boards embraced corporate structure for what it facilitated: effective programs. And programs expressed Methodist ideals and ideas in missions, education, witness, and reform.

Until 1939 or so, the boards and agencies were surrounded with other bodies, also active on a national level, that bound the connection together and worked programmatically. These included the college or board of bishops and general conferences but also other national organizations (women's, youth, reform, temperance, etc.), national papers, clergy magazines, the seminaries (particularly Boston for the north and Vanderbilt in the south), and the publishing houses.

Federal-Style Connection

Ironically, the union of 1939 (MEC, MECS, MPC), in the endeavor to create a more national church, tore much of the connectional fabric— dropping power and authority into jurisdictional conferences, including particularly the power to elect; making bishops regional rather than general superintendents;[23] bloating general conference by intention and regionalizing seminaries and other teaching agencies by accident; consolidating boards into even more significant bureaucracies and empowering those boards to select their professional staff. The net effect of these changes was to leave the agencies as *the* connecting power nationally *and* to undo the accountability that 1872 had achieved. In the union of 1939, rather than that of 1968, lie many of the concerns that trouble agency critics today.

The actions of 1939 also consolidated within Methodist *governance* patterns and practices that had long characterized American politics, in particular:

—separation of powers and distinct legislative, executive, and judicial agencies;

—provision for judicial review;

—delimitation of national authority and reservation of powers and prerogatives to regional bodies (jurisdiction and conference);

—construal of Methodist conference structures at all levels as representative bodies and therefore to be inclusive of laity as well as clergy in accord with principles of equity and proportionality.

(For elaboration of these points and of this rubric of *federalism*, see the essay by Frank and Everett.)

Concern to make Methodist polity behave according to American precept had begun when the first conferences convened. It had been made operative by Asbury's call for a general conference, and an elected episcopacy. It had found expression in the 1808 constitution and provision for delegated representation. It had animated the reform efforts of African Methodists, Republicans, Methodist Protestants, Wesleyans, Free Methodists, and Nazarenes. It had encouraged women and Blacks in their quest for representation, ordination, episcopal orders. Yet while Methodists accommodated themselves to American political practice over the course of their history, only in 1939 did they accord American civil theory full disciplinary status. The reunion of 1939 made *federalism*, political rights, representation, and separation of powers into Methodist principle. The linchpin in this federalism is the jurisdictional conference, an accommodation to Methodist racism and (Southern) regionalism.

Professional Connections

Decisions in 1939 probably disguised, though by no means discouraged, another long-term trend in Methodist connectionalism, namely its reliance upon professions, professionalism, and professional association. What the merger of 1939 disguised with the new jurisdictional structures and its ratification of full laity representation was the way in which conference structures, particularly annual conferences, had evolved into professional organizations.[24] Conferences increasingly functioned for clergy the way the state bar did for lawyers. They set standards, reviewed credentials, admitted to practice, guarded prerogative, pressed for compensation, contracted for health-care, maintained pensions, and oversaw professional ethics. Ironically, conference professionalism continued and grew even as conferences became representative and laity were included. Professional interests and concerns lodged themselves in boards or committees, particularly Ordained Ministry, executive sessions, and various clergy-only affairs.

Professionalism was by no means limited to conference. Indeed, many sectors of Methodist leadership gradually developed professional patterns. Sarah Kreutziger shows how urban missions, settlement houses, urban volunteers, and deaconesses were affected by professionalism and how these prophetic actions yielded the new profession of social work. Robert Monk notes that campus chaplaincy gradually took on a professional aspect. The same might even more readily be demonstrated for other forms of chaplaincy, military and hospital especially. Each role or vocational niche in the church seemed to acquire a professional aspect; persons in that calling gathered together in regional and national meetings; once organized they sought denominational recognition and/or relation to some board or agency. New offices and old created new professional or quasi-professional associations, new networks that connected the church to offer or receive the special expertise and counsel. So, various church professionals—Christian educators, lay workers, evangelists, missionaries, information officers, large-church pastors, musicians, fiscal officers, church and society persons, and, after 1968, council directors—gathered from across the country in annual, professional or professional-like meetings. And what they sought was comparable to what other professional groupings sought when assembled—how to become more effective in the particular service to which they had been called, how to be better leaders, how to offer the church the guidance or counsel which they alone could give. The connection was well-served by such professionalism. *And* the church was connected through these professional networks, connected by the service they offered for the whole, connected in their very existence as the religious counterparts to the webs that held American society together, professional association.

The servant-character of Methodist guidance gives to Methodist professionalism and religious professionalism generally an ambiguous, even self-contradictory character. Professionals exert influence and lead out of expertise, specialized skills, and privileged knowledge. The church at one moment honors and requires such human elitism and in the next moment reminds itself of the priesthood of all believers, the sinfulness of all, and the gifted nature of truly gracious leadership. It is charisma and dependence upon God, not professionalism alone, that characterize the true servants of God. Ambiguity and even conflict over professional expertise underlie some of the strains in connectional affairs, beginning in the late-nineteenth century and continuing throughout the twentieth century. Bradley Longfield exposes some of the ambiguity over professionalism by exploring the tensions over Methodist higher education. So does Robert Monk, describing how campus ministry dealt with the growing professionalism of campus ministry, the eager advocacy and interventionism of student leadership, and the uncertainty of the church at large over both. The 1960s and 1970s brought campus ministry and its politicized connections—indeed, Methodist connectionalism as a whole—into crisis.

Post-Corporate Connectionalism

The three dominant styles of twentieth-century connectionalism—corporate, federal, and professional—are under siege. The attacks on agencies, centralized governance of any sort and elitism are not Methodist-specific but are paralleled in other denominations, in large-scale business enterprise, and in government at all levels. Americans have apparently tired of working in, under, and through corporate, bureaucratic structures, tired of having the shots called at national or even conference headquarters, tired of kowtowing to experts. They protest in various ways—tax-payer revolts, rebellions against headquarters, voting the rascals out, dropping out.

Organizations respond by down-sizing, aping Japanese organization, adopting total quality management, and resorting to new measures of influence—regulation, grant-making, franchising, consulting, credentialing—tactics that do work, at least in the short run. Virtually every one of these tactics has found its way into denominational repertoire. So United Methodists find themselves offered various franchise opportunities by boards and agencies, Disciple Bible Study being the most dramatic instance. The few successful ventures in franchising, grant-making, and consulting do not "redeem" the boards and agencies but instead seem to dissociate themselves from agency programs and so undercut rather than bolster goodwill towards the connectional structures.[25] And other tactics in organizational vogue, particularly those that are more controlling, intrusive, accountability-prepossessed, and regulatory, do not meet with such favor. Indeed, they both foster and function with an enervating suspicion. Their efforts to make the system work and to command the funds necessary for effective functioning are met with hostility and suspicion. Boards, committees, commissions, and task forces function in an atmosphere where accountability is the first order of business, where every slate is immediately assessed for its representativeness, where suspicion reigns that money is not being equitably or properly expended, where leadership is experienced only as power. Balkanization reigns in church, as in American politics.

Disquiet over United Methodist agencies belongs within the larger cultural traumas and the desperate quest for new modalities of community, cooperation, labor, and governance. In finding such new modalities of connection, Methodists can and should lead. It is a Methodist specialty. And Methodists are leading. Experiments in connection abound: in the caucuses, in media ministries, in new and old efforts at discipleship, in listening groups, in Council of Bishops initiatives, and in Disciple Bible Study and Emmaus Walks. Such experiments have not solidified into a new paradigm of connection. Instead, what haunts connectional gatherings and efforts to put up new connectional fabric are calls for *accountability* and hermeneutics of suspicion. Any new ventures now face the immediate challenge as to whether all constituencies have been properly represented. Reformers find it difficult to move through and beyond the politics of accountability to discerning, much less addressing, the missional ends that connection should serve. To term these quests for connection a new style, overstates their functionality and acceptance. Our category "post-corporate connectionalism" indicates a point of departure rather than an arrival.

Conclusion

This essay has been crafted to assist the reading of the chapters that follow. In the first section, I noted what essays by Charles Zech, Penny Becker, and Penny Marler and Kirk Hadaway observe, namely that Methodism behaves in certain ways like other connectional churches. Shared, for instance, are the crises, uncertainties, and inner turmoil outlined immediately above as "post-corporate connectionalism." Methodism, however, has, at least in its better historical moments, understood its connectionalism as something different from a mere polity classification, something more than just a strong corporate, centralized, or hierarchical authority system, something complex and variegated.

The second part of this essay explored those multiple values, identifying theological principles that undergird or are latent in Methodist connectionalism. Connectionalism has been, I suggested, a Wesleyan precept, an ecclesial vision, a missional principle, a covenantal commitment, an ethic of equity and proportionality, a tactical stratagem, an elastic and evolving standard, a theology in praxis. The several essays in the volume develop or illustrate each of these points, and I call attention to the fuller discussions.

In the last section, I treated Methodism as a changing covenant, noting the different forms or styles of connectionalism that have emerged over the history of American Methodism. Seven forms of connectionalism, I argue, each with its distinctive organizational style, have emerged and, for their day and for the Methodism of their day, have been judged as appropriate measures in enunciating and achieving corporate purposes:

Wesleyan (episcopal)	oral/aural
popular	event
voluntary	printed page
corporate	program
professional	guidance
federal	governance
post-corporate	accountability

In its own way, each style sought to define corporate praxis (a piety and ecclesiology), to provide mechanisms for collective hearing (our doctrine), to delineate an organizational language (an ecclesial vision), to orient Methodists towards goals (a mission), and to call forth effort (covenant and ethic). Some of these served better and more faithfully as theology in practice, as practical divinity, than others. And none, at this point, seems quite adequate, including particularly the style we have awkwardly labelled "post-corporate."

As we ourselves think and act towards a new connectional vision, this collection, and perhaps this essay, might help us get our bearings.

～ Richard P. Heitzenrater ～

This essay by Richard Heitzenrater belongs first in the collection for chronological reasons. It examines the emergence and gradual evolution of connectionalism (and itinerancy) and the meaning they had for John Wesley and his associates. The essay belongs first also because it addresses a concern that shapes the volume, and indeed this entire project. Connection, association or fellowship with Wesley, Heitzenrater indicates, had fundamentally to do with the mission or calling that Wesley understood as God's. Mission constituted the essence of connectionalism. Connectionalism emerged for and was governed by its purposes. An orienting commitment, connection with Wesley meant accepting God's calling, placing oneself in an ordered community (conference, class or band), covenanting with other members, accepting "our" doctrines, committing oneself to a disciplined life, and responding to the expectation of (or to) leadership, in order to be fully led by the Spirit. Itinerancy actualized this multi-faceted connectional purpose by deploying leadership on behalf of the whole and appointing leaders (traveling preachers, in particular) where they were most needed for the spreading of scriptural holiness. Would American Methodists, Heitzenrater queries, hold to these forms and their missional purposes, both challenged from the start? Do they today? Do current efforts at reordering the connection honor both form and purpose? To what extent do proposals for new structures or policies reflect the multifaceted connectionalism that Heitzenrater discerns? How Wesleyan is connectionalism today?

Connectionalism and Itinerancy: Wesleyan Principles and Practice

Richard P. Heitzenrater

Introduction

In the present day, Methodists often equate "connectionalism" with denominational apportionments and "itinerancy" with frequent moving of clergy. While these may now appear to be obvious associations in United Methodism through long practice, the early Wesleyan principles that gave rise to a polity characterized by these two phenomena do not necessarily engender our present understanding or application of these concepts.

In order to discover these principles, we need to look again at the Wesleyan tradition in the eighteenth century in terms of the formulation and development of connectionalism and itinerancy.[1] In particular, we will look carefully at the historical rationale behind (1) the development of a dynamic network of Methodist societies in eighteenth-century Great Britain (and subsequently America) and (2) the understanding of ministry that undergirded the deployment of leaders among those societies. Such an examination may lead to insights as to how the principles behind the traditions of connectionalism and itinerancy might be appropriated in the contemporary church in fresh ways that recapture some of the vision and vitality of early Methodism.

Connectionalism

The connectional model in eighteenth-century Methodism is defined by the voluntary association of evangelical leaders (mostly lay preachers) with John Wesley, and his acceptance of them, bringing them "into connection" with him and thereby with his understanding of God's purpose for the movement—the mission to reform the church, to spread scriptural holiness across the land.

23

"Connectional" is not a term that was used by the Methodists during Wesley's lifetime. As we have come to know it, however, the root of the idea is present and is evident in the frequent use of the term "connection" (orig., "connexion") as the movement developed in its middle and later years. Itinerancy, as we will come to see, has an inherent relationship to the concept of connectionalism. Of course, itinerancy is a practice that preceded Wesley, was adopted quite early by Wesley, and is evident throughout the life of the organized movement.

The idea of connectionalism is nothing more than a specific application of the more general idea of the *connection* between two or more things. "Connection" can, of course, have several meanings itself. It can refer to (1) the act of connecting, (2) the state of being connected, (3) a set of things that are connected, or (4) something that does the connecting or provides the connection. Wesley uses the term in the second general sense (that has implications for the later, more particular usage) in 1748 in a letter to Vincent Perronet when he talks about "Christian connection" in the sense of "fellowship": "Are not the bulk of the parishioners a mere rope of sand? What Christian connexion is there between them? What intercourse in spiritual things? What watching over each other's souls? What bearing of one another's burthens?"[2]

Wesley's concern for this sense of fellowship between what he called "true Christians" is what led to the Methodist revival and to the growing network of groups and their leaders that could provide such nurturing fellowship. Before many years had elapsed, Wesley was beginning to talk about those preachers who were "in connexion" with him. In order to understand the political and doctrinal significance of this terminology, one must understand the nature of the Methodist organization in the early days of the revival.

As Methodism began to grow and spread across Great Britain from its beginnings in Oxford, London, and Bristol (leaving Georgia aside for this discussion), it took on the character of a network of groups (societies) that is generally familiar to most of us. What is not so readily recognized, however, is that, in addition to those groups that may have been started directly by the Wesleys, there were many societies that were started by other people and became part of the movement through their association with Wesley. In some cases, individual leaders such as William Darney had started local revivals and established a whole "round" (circuit) of societies which then became associated with the Wesleys. Many of Wesley's personal friends from his earlier days in

Oxford and London started groups which then became related to the Methodist revival and to the Wesleys.

Part of this story of a growing amalgam of groups started by a disparate set of leaders is not only the intense common sense of evangelical purpose felt by these leaders who associated with Wesley, but also the clear manifestation of theological diversity among those leaders who were inclined to come into the Wesleyan network. As early as 1739, Wesley and some of his evangelical clergy friends (mostly former Oxford Methodists) decided to benefit from their similar experiences by conferring regularly in London—annually on the eve of Ascension Day, and three other times during the year if possible. In the meantime, they agreed to circulate among themselves monthly accounts of what they were doing in their own particular stations. At the same time, they expressed the hope that they might recruit other friends to join their endeavor (and even drew up a list of prospects).[3] These intentions were apparently never fulfilled, since it appears Wesley had a falling out with Gambold before the date of their first intended conference.

The agreement among these Methodists to confer about their ideas and activities, however, represents the first manifestation of an organizational connection among those leaders of the revival. In the following months and years, theological tensions developed between the Wesleys, whose Anglican theology generally had an Arminian slant, and many of these associates, especially those who were Calvinist or Moravian in their orientation. John Wesley had a well-documented split with Whitefield the Calvinist in the late 1730s as well as with the Moravians in the early 1740s. He tried very hard, as the movement developed, to keep his preachers, especially the lay helpers, informed and restrained within a proper theological framework. He was especially concerned about the threat of antinomianism that might result from Calvinist or Moravian thinking, namely predestination and stillness.[4]

In August 1743, John took a major step in order to overcome the potential fragmentation of the revival (especially along theological lines) and thus in effect to challenge the incursions of Calvinist and Moravian thinking among the Methodists. Calling together a group of those persons associated with, or influential among the Methodists, he chose those who he thought would benefit from a discussion of the doctrine and structure of the revival. Wesley understood Christian **conference**, or religious conversation, to be an instituted means of grace, a channel by which God can act in significant ways.[5]

Leaders from among the Calvinists and Moravians (Whitefield, Spangenburg, and Hutton) were invited to this conference, as were John Nelson (Methodist preacher) and Charles Wesley. The first three did not appear, but the other three had a good discussion for a day or so. The following week, Wesley put in writing what was on his mind at the time and produced a short treatise that outlined the problems inherent in three major doctrines of Calvinism—unconditional election, irresistible grace, and final perseverance. Although somewhat irenic in outward tone, this work was substantially a definition of Wesley's own theological position and presented a line of demarcation with the Calvinists.[6]

The next summer, Wesley again called a conference but this time did not invite the leaders from the other two parties. He did include, however, persons who were aligned with him and the Methodist revival but who were still inclined toward the Calvinist or Moravians positions.[7] On the eve of this conference, Wesley wrote a letter to the Moravian Church in England. In similar fashion to his memorandum on the three dangers of Calvinism the previous year, he outlined the three categories of problems he saw in the Moravians—universal salvation, antinomianism, and quietism. He concluded by pressing the Moravians to change in three areas: doctrine, discipline, and practice.[8] As he met with the preachers in June 1744, therefore, his mind was quite clear as to the main distinctions between his own wing of the revival and those who were inclined toward Calvinism or Moravianism.

This conference, now remembered as the first annual conference, represents a crucial step in the emergence of a group of preachers and clergy who were publicly identified as part of the Wesleyan branch of the revival. Those leaders were willingly committed to Wesley's views on doctrine, polity, and mission. As the conference became an annual affair, the sifting of participants was partly done by Wesley—he decided whom to invite (in many cases, apparently, those who needed instruction or correction). A further sifting was done by those who were invited—they could choose not to come, and thereby indicate a desire to dissociate from the Wesleys rather than be instructed by them. What was becoming clear was that the Wesleyan movement was increasingly delimited by the list of who willingly associated with John and Charles Wesley—those who were in fellowship with them. Before long, these were referred to as those who were "in connection with" the Wesleys, as distinguished from those who were in connection with Whitefield or others.

Unity, if not uniformity, was one of the primary desiderata in the Wesleyan scheme, not unlike the approach of his Anglican heritage. Diversity was a given part of the situation (or of the problem, in some sense), not a desirable goal.[9] The great need was for stating guidelines and boundaries that would fix the essential core of doctrine and discipline and define the limits of acceptable preaching and activity within the Methodist mission to spread scriptural holiness. The amalgamated nature of the revival as it began to develop a series of networks, and the eventual eagerness of some "strangers" to preach in the Wesleyan societies, made it necessary for Wesley to "regularize" his own "sons in the gospel"—that is, to provide for uniformity through rules (*regula*). From the Rules for Bands in 1738, to the General Rules in 1743, to the various lists of Rules for Helpers, Rules for Visitors, Rules for Reading, etc., Wesley provided guidelines for the regulation (regularization) of the movement. The discussions at the annual conferences were primarily intended for guidance of the preachers and were recorded in the minutes *(Minutes of some late Conversations between the Rev. Mr. Wesleys and others)* in question and answer form—on matters of doctrine and polity, both the questions and the answers basically originated with Wesley himself.

This whole relationship between Wesley and the preachers is not unlike the development of Charlemagne's regulation of the expanding Holy Roman Empire. The latter sent out assistants called *missi dominici* ("sent of the lord") who were expected to take the emperor's regulations to the furthest corners of the empire, enforce them in the emperor's stead, and bring back word of how things were going so as to inform the development of further regulations. It is a not uncommon means of promoting unity, if not uniformity, among a disparate and diverse set of followers. Wesley often used the terms, "messengers of God" and "sent of God" to indicate his apostolic view of the Methodist scheme of deploying preachers in a mission to spread scriptural holiness.

In this process within Methodism, Wesley was the "connection" in the sense of "something that does the connecting or provides the connection." There are, of course, many ways in which the Carolingian comparison does not hold up. One of those is the great effort that Wesley made to keep in personal contact *in situ* with the preachers and the societies. During the months of good weather, Wesley traveled about the countryside to the various societies, which (especially at the beginning) were widely scattered, visiting all the preachers and leaders he could,[10] helping to inform and encourage them, enforcing the rules, and (if necessary) expelling those who would not abide by the regulations.[11] During the winter months, he generally stayed close to London, but did try to correspond with every preacher he had not been able to visit personally the previous year. When Wesley talked about preachers being "in connection with" him, he took the matter seriously and worked very hard to maintain that connection closely.[12]

Part of Wesley's penchant for this close connection with the preachers came about, of course, of necessity. His preachers were mostly an uneducated, fairly rough lot, and the Wesleys felt compelled not only to develop a probationary period ("on trial") before their preachers were "set apart," but also, even after they were brought in to "full connection," a means of yearly examination to ensure that they continued to manifest the gifts and grace that were necessary to their task. John felt that grace was the primary prerequisite; Charles was more concerned about gifts. During one especially difficult spell in the 1750s, Charles (who had been put in charge of these examinations) took great pride in expelling a number of preachers who he did not think had the requisite gifts. In this great purge, Charles was very clear about his unhappiness with John's looser standards. He told John Bennett, "A friend of ours [brother John] (without God's counsel) made a preacher of a tailor; I, with God's help, shall make a tailor of him again."[13] Nine preachers were laid aside that year, including William Darney, who kept singing hymns ("doggerel") of his own composition and continued to preach perseverance of the saints, against the expressed order of the Wesleys. In spite of the purge, John managed to keep nearly forty preachers, the number he felt was necessary to keep the connection intact at that point (1753).

This close control of the preachers also extended to any interlopers, not in full connection, who wanted to preach in the societies. Written permission from Wesley or his Assistant was necessary for such people to preach in a given local area. These persons were not recognized as preachers in the connection, but were still personally controlled by Wesley. One such preacher, Sarah Mallet, was the only woman we know to have gained this specific written approval for preaching in a local society. And Wesley continued to give her specific advice from time to time, such as the admonition never to scream while speaking to the people since it not only is "disgustful to the hearers" but also is "offering God murder for sacrifice."[14]

Those preachers who passed muster were given a copy of the latest edition of the "Large" *Minutes*, inscribed with the following notation:

> So long as you freely consent and earnestly endeavour to walk according to the following rules, we shall rejoice to acknowledge you as a fellow-labourer.
>
> JW

Being in connection with John Wesley meant consenting to and trying to follow his rules, and thereby acknowledging oneself as his "son in the gospel."

In the midst of the difficulties of the 1750s, Wesley came to realize that this sense of connectedness of the preachers to him should also be strengthened by an explicit expression of covenantal relationship among themselves, who in one instance are referred to by Wesley as the "connected brethren."[15] He was aware of the danger of becoming as "a rope of sand," the apt metaphor mentioned in his earlier letter to Perronet referring to the lack of Christian fellowship among most congregations. Therefore, a covenant was drawn up in 1752 in which the preachers declared that they would speak and act in union with each other.[16] Wesley was particularly concerned about maintaining the connection among the preachers after he himself was dead. As long as he lived, he felt that he would be "a centre of union to all our traveling as well as local preachers."

In 1769, he again suggested a method whereby to preserve a firm union among the preachers. This plan included their meeting together in conference, their seeking God by fasting and prayer, and their drawing up articles of agreement, to be signed by those who chose to act in concert. His suggested "Articles of Agreement" had three points to which the preachers subscribed:

1. to devote ourselves entirely to God;
2. to preach the old Methodist doctrines and no other;
3. to observe and enforce the whole Methodist discipline.[17]

In essence, Wesley suggested that the Conference, through its leadership, should anticipate becoming the locus of the authority that he held while alive, including the power to propose preachers, fix appointments, and decide the time of conference. This was not the eventual form of these arrangements, which took final shape in the Deed of Declaration in 1784, but the plan exhibits his concern for those elements of the connection that he thought were central: conference of the preachers, covenant of the preachers, a sense of calling, a commitment to doctrines, the maintenance of discipline, a zest for the mission, the careful selection of leaders, and the leading of God's spirit.

Eventually, the concept of "connection" expanded beyond the tight relationship between Wesley and his preachers to include the membership as well. References to the "Methodist connection" often have the more delimited sense, referring simply to the preachers. But on occasion the phrase also implies the whole movement. Wesley was early concerned for a sense of unity among the whole structure. At the 1749 Conference, Wesley expressed concern for "a general union of our societies throughout England . . . firmly united together by one spirit of love and heavenly mindedness." Among other things, he developed a centralized list of members, arranged in four categories (awakened, seekers, justified, sanctified). He developed an organization that could nurture the spiritual life of the people, through the bands, classes, and societies with their various leaders and activities, and that could also support a program of opportunities throughout the connection beyond what any local society could do—helping feed and house the poor, educate the children, build new preaching-houses in remote areas, provide for preachers' widows and children, assist with legal fees, furnish medical help.

The combined resources of "the people called Methodists," poor as they were, enabled a number of significant ministries throughout the British Isles. The method of collection and disbursement of funds included a number of voluntary offerings, mandatory penny subscriptions, and other collections that were made by local stewards, sent to the circuit stewards, and transmitted to the stewards of the London society who distributed the proceeds of the various funds for the intended purposes.[18] At times, a portion of the money collected was sent back to the local society for specific projects. Through these collections and funds, the Methodists were able to develop a mission that reached the needy and disenfranchised throughout the three kingdoms in ways that they could not otherwise have done.

There was a spiritual as well as an organizational and financial aspect to this movement-wide sense of unity. Among other things, Wesley encouraged the preachers to circulate accounts of conversions and holy deaths, anticipating one important feature of his *Arminian Magazine*, started in the late 1770s. The Wesleys produced an extensive list of publications, many of them inexpensive or even free, for the edification and nurture of the people. To further their common spiritual life, the societies also had letter days, at which time correspondence that described religious experiences was read aloud to the group.

These attempts to develop and share a common Methodist experience give rise to a sense of general connection among the people. In one instance late in his life, Wesley talked disparagingly about "half-Methodists"—those who might frequently have heard Methodist preaching but are in no further connection, or those who had once been (but were no longer) "in full connection," a term otherwise rather consistently reserved for full-time traveling preachers.[19] Just a year before he died, Wesley wrote to the people of Trowbridge, saying "I have only one thing in view—to keep all the Methodists in Great Britain one connected people."[20]

Central to that aspect of connection was Wesley's power of appointing and stationing the preachers. The previous quotation arose in the context of one of many disputes with local trustees of Methodist societies who wanted to exercise the power of displacing preachers that had been sent to their society by Wesley. The deed upon which the preaching houses were to be settled stipulated that the trustees would accept the preachers appointed by Wesley. And the trustees, in fact, were responsible for seeing to it that those preachers expounded proper Methodist doctrine—"no other doctrine than that contained in Mr. Wesley's Notes upon the New Testament and four volumes of Sermons."[21] But some of the trustees refused to use such a deed, and others refused to abide by it. Wesley saw this as a threat to the basic plan of the Methodist connection, which centered upon the concept of itinerancy.

Itinerancy

The Wesleyan model of itinerancy was designed to allow the central authority (Wesley) to deploy leadership resources to best advantage in order to effect the mission of the movement (in terms of place—putting people where they were most needed; in terms of people—allowing for various talents, changing of preaching). "Traveling preachers" were those fully committed to the Methodist mission and discipline by their covenant to submit to Wesleyan appointment wherever and whenever they were needed.

Itinerancy of the Methodist preachers, beginning with John Wesley himself, was the result of Wesley's principle that he should preach wherever he could do the most good.[22] Or, to state it another way, he should preach wherever there was a need, and especially where the need was greatest.[23] The result was both a disregard for parish boundaries (should the incumbent clergy not be fulfilling his commission to preach the gospel) and a constant shifting of location (as there were continually new opportunities for ministry opening up).

As a practical matter, the Methodist movement in the 1740s resulted in the establishment of more societies than could be supplied with full-time preachers. For a time, the lay preachers were allowed to preach on a part-time basis while they continued to maintain their previous employment (of all kinds—barber, butcher, farmer, tailor, veterinary medicine vendor, etc.). Very soon, however, Wesley began to expect the preachers to be full time. His "sons in the gospel," beginning in the early 1740s, were to spend all their effort in "the work of saving souls" and received an allowance from the stewards within the Methodist connection. At times, "half-itinerants" did come back into the picture (full-time for only part of the year, or part-time for all of the year),[24] but the full-time requirement was an important element in Wesley's control of the connection, even though it often jeopardized the ability of the movement to have enough preachers to supply all the circuits.[25] Local preachers, who did not travel (i.e., itinerate), could take up some of the slack, of course, but they were not considered to have the same authority as the full-time itinerants who were "in full connection."

It became necessary therefore to develop a system whereby the leadership could be spread throughout the connection to provide the optimum effect.[26] The resultant program of itinerancy was quite different, of course, from the typical ecclesiastical mode of supplying parish churches with priests who usually stayed in one parish (or set of parishes) for many years. Wesley recognized that many people liked some aspects of the stability that such a pattern exhibited: "It is certain many persons both in Scotland and England would be well pleased to have the same preachers always."[27] But as he always pointed out, "That is not the Methodist plan," the plan of itinerancy that he felt God had blessed over the years.[28] In many instances, he had seen the societies decline and stagnate from even the slightest variance from strict itinerancy. In one instance, a society of one hundred and sixty persons had shrunk to about fifty. In Wesley's analysis, "Such is the fruit of a single preacher's staying a whole year in one place!"[29] And of course, on more than one occasion he admitted that even he could not keep a congregation alive week after week if he stayed in one place for as much as a year:

> I myself may perhaps have as much variety of matter as many of our preachers. Yet, I am well assured, were I to preach three years together in one place, both the people and myself would grow as dead as stones.

Indeed, this is quite contrary to the whole economy of Methodism: God has always wrought among us by a constant change of preachers.[30]

One form of the principle behind moving the preachers is stated by Wesley in the early *Minutes*, answering the question "What is a sufficient call to a new place?" with, "A probability of doing more good by going thither than by staying longer where we are."[31] The point of moving about was to search out the "wanderers from God," for certainly, Wesley said, such wanderers could not be expected always to search out the preachers.[32] As the organization developed and circuits or rounds of societies were formed, the movement of preachers was among as well as within circuits. At first, preachers were moved to a new circuit every three months at a minimum. The maximum stay eventually became two years.[33]

And Wesley did not want the preachers hanging about within the circuits: "We totally reject the thought of a preacher staying a fortnight together in one place."[34] Not only was this immobility liable to bring monotony of preaching (the same preacher at least twice a day), or perhaps worse, a reduction in preaching from the minimum expected standard of twice a day, but also such a situation failed to take advantage of one of the positive strengths of the itinerant plan:

> We have found by long and constant experience that a frequent change of preachers is best. This preacher has one talent, that another. No one whom I ever yet knew has all the talents which are needful for beginning, continuing, and perfecting the work of grace in an whole congregation.[35]

Perhaps the strongest reason for supporting the itinerant plan, in Wesley's mind, was the fact that it was the greatest reinforcement to the strength of the connection as such. One of the threats to the movement was the potential fragmentation through doctrinal or political fragmentation. The strength of the connection was its ability to effect its mission to an extent and in a manner that was greater than any local congregation or sum of local congregations acting autonomously could effect. And thus any attempt at local control over the itinerant system was seen as a danger to the effectiveness of the whole Methodist plan.

This problem was frequently manifest in the attempts by local trustees to control their society's property. Wesley even suggested that the preaching houses be built "plain and decent," because otherwise the necessity of raising money would make them reliant upon rich people: "But if so, we must be dependent upon them, yea, and governed by them. And then farewell to the Methodist discipline, if not doctrine too."[36]

But even more dangerous, in Wesley's way of thinking, was the attempt by some local trustees to dismiss, or refuse to accept, preachers appointed by Wesley at the Conference. Wesley minced no words when he entered into the fray on these occasions: "If the trustees of houses are to displace preachers, then itinerancy is at an end."[37] In his mind, itinerancy and the connection could be preserved no other way than to have the appointment of preachers vested in him while he lived, and in the Conference after he died.[38] The purpose of the Model Deed and the control of the preaching-houses was not to accumulate property rights. The dispute amounted to one issue: "What I claim is the right of stationing the preachers." He saw the direct consequences of any other system of appointment: "If itinerancy is interrupted, [ancient Methodism] will speedily come to nothing."[39] The double danger was pointed out in a treatise concerning a dispute over the preaching-house at Birstall:

> Whenever the trustees exert their power of placing and displacing preachers, then, (1) Itinerant preaching is no more. When the trustees in any place have found and fixed a preacher they like, the rotation of preachers is at an end—at least till they are tired of their favourite preacher, and so turn him out. (2) While he stays, is not the bridle in his mouth? How dares he speak the full and the whole truth, since whenever he displeases the trustees he is liable to lose his bread? How much less will he dare to put a trustee, though ever so ungodly, out of the society?[40]

In trying to protect the Methodist mission to spread scriptural holiness, Wesley could control the itinerants, but enforcing Methodist doctrine and polity among the local trustees was quite another matter.

The variation in length of time that preachers stayed in an appointment (from three months in some cases to three years in other, exceptional cases) highlights another important point with regard to itinerancy. How long one stayed in one area was not as important as how long one was fulfilling the needs and providing the needed mission and ministry (of the connection) in that area. Or, to look at in another way, how *soon* one moved was not so important as to recognize just *when* there was a greater need somewhere else for that the person to meet. These were the kinds of questions and decisions that Wesley thought he was best suited to make (a function taken over by a committee of the Conference at his death). And the basic issue concerning the itinerancy of the full-time preachers was not the necessity of every preacher to move every so often, but rather the sincerity of their commitment to the mission of Methodism as evidenced by their *willingness to move* at the direction of Mr. Wesley.

All of this has the ring of autocracy and hierarchy. That is true. Wesley was no friend to democracy. The cry of "liberty" in his later life became associated in his mind with the libertinism of the French, and the various threats to the monarchy gave him pause when anyone suggested a more democratic form of legislative authority within the Methodist movement. "We are no Republicans" was his response to requests for the Conference to decide issues by popular vote while he was still alive. Democracy was, in his understanding, not a source of real religious or civil freedom or liberty, and the idea that power derives from the people (a principle being tested in France and America in his day) he felt was in reality a cunningly-devised fable.[41] And to those who cried for wider theological leeway in the English scene, he could say, "Anyone who bawls for more religious liberty must be totally void of shame and can have no excuse but want of understanding."[42]

Summary

Connectionalism is the covenantal association of preachers committed to a united mission to spread scriptural holiness (and to abide by the doctrine/discipline of the organization designed to implement that mission) under the direction of John Wesley and the conference.

Itinerancy is a method for deployment of preachers who are willing to be placed in stations where and when they are needed most (as decided by John Wesley and the conference) in order to further the Methodist mission to spread scriptural holiness.

One way to distill the principles of connectionalism and itinerancy is to ask the question, Why? Why did Wesley feel that the connectional model was essential? The concept of preachers in connection with Wesley provided a centralized and united framework for developing and effecting a common mission. The vision that gave shape and impetus to the whole resided in Wesley, the "centre of union," and he was assisted primarily by preachers who were recognized as being "connected" to him and through him to the Church of England. This unity was manifest through various covenants that expressed shared vision and responsibility. Various rules and examinations provided for enforcement of uniformity; discipline and expulsions exhibited the desire for conformity in order to protect and enhance the mission of the movement.

Why did Wesley feel that itinerancy was essential? As far as he knew, the itinerant plan was the best method for the deployment of resources to enable the Methodist mission (among and within the circuits). It took advantage of the variety of leaders' talents; it minimized the effect of individual limitations (preaching, education, etc.); it gave the Methodists an ability to spread resources over a broader area (unattractive areas, remote circuits). Itinerancy was the primary means of embodying full-time commitment to the connectional mission.[43] By this means, the Methodists could promote mission interests that might transcend the interests and prejudices of the local population or congregation. The itinerants represented the whole connection (in and to the Church) in each local area, and their centralized deployment helped overcome local inequities and prejudices. This plan allowed for both direction and accountability. And through this means, Wesley was convinced that they could thereby protect Methodist doctrine and polity, two basic expressions of the mission.

Together, these traditions of connectionalism and itinerancy both speak to the covenanting of preachers to a common mission to spread scriptural holiness, connected by a vision of God's purpose for human-kind as represented by John Wesley. Fundamental to an understanding of these traditions is a full view of their purpose with regard to the mission. To maintain the form without the purpose would be comparable, to use a favorite Wesleyan quotation, to having the form of godliness without the power thereof (cf. 1 Tim. 3:5). In terms of the Methodist tradition itself, the forms of connectionalism and itinerancy arise out of the purpose for which they were developed—to spread scriptural holiness. Either to lose sight of the purpose or to do away with the forms is to disregard an essential feature of the Methodist tradition, and perhaps thereby become disconnected from the tradition itself. Wesley himself feared that if this should happen, Methodists could cease to exist, either in Europe or America. At the very least, he pointed out, they would undoubtedly become a "dead sect" unless they held fast "the doctrine, spirit, and discipline with which they first set out."[44]

Epilogue

This Wesleyan understanding of connectionalism and itinerancy met severe challenges in American Methodism and underwent significant changes in practice as the years passed. Wesley's understanding of polity fit well within his political understanding that a limited monarchy was not only the best form of government but also the most favorable toward true religious liberty. All power, in his view, derives from God; there is an inherent hierarchical framework in the body politic, which includes the Church. His view of the Church would easily be more amenable to the concept of a theocracy than to the context of a democracy.

Wesley was certainly not averse to the idea of an established Church, though such a prospect had little support among the American patriots. As he grew older, however, he did grow to accept the need for dissenting groups and denominations in certain contexts. The ecclesial model of a denomination/church as a voluntary *gathering* of like-minded spirits, nevertheless, does not fully satisfy Wesley's apostolic model of the church as a divine *sending* of those called by God to the mission (from the Latin, *missio*, "the act of sending") of spreading scriptural holiness. It is no accident that Wesley constantly harkens back to the apostolic days and specifically sets the American Methodists at liberty "to follow the Scriptures and the Primitive Church." He also frequently refers to Methodist preachers as "extraordinary messengers of God." The circuit rider comes to epitomize this concept of those "sent of God," the church in mission. A fully balanced Wesleyan scheme, then, would include both the traditional ecclesial model of the fellowship of believers gathered for Word and Sacrament, and the active apostolic model of the mission of that same band of spiritual pilgrims, sent into the world to transform it with a faith that acts through love.

Beginning with Francis Asbury's decision to have the body of preachers vote on Wesley's scheme for setting up a Methodist denomination in America, the Wesleyan model of how the church organizes itself for worship and mission began to face significant challenges. Issues of authority, structure, representation, and rights burst into the open, the year after Wesley's death, at the Methodist conferences of 1792 in England and America. The name of the "Republican Methodist Church," established by James O'Kelly and his associates at that point, would have seemed an oxymoron to Wesley. And yet, many of the principles and particular issues of that gave rise to that denomination have continued to challenge Methodism through the succeeding generations.

The inherent tension between Wesley's understanding of the Methodist connection and the American understanding of popular democracy has resulted over the years in many issue-oriented battles as well as a continuing struggle for self-identity. It could be argued that such a tension brought a healthy vitality to American Methodism in the nineteenth century, even at the cost of a muddled ecclesiology. But even as we continue to struggle with clarity in the self-identity, we would be well-advised never to lose sight of the principles that sent us on our way. Tradition does not bind us to the past, but, by reminding us of who we were and whose we are, constantly leads us to a fuller appreciation of our possibilities for the future. And such a vision is necessary in a denomination that is still working toward defining a unified view of its nature and mission as a church.

∼ William Johnson Everett and Thomas Edward Frank ∼

In the previous essay, Heitzenrater raised questions about the viability and vitality of our connectionalism from the vantage of Wesley's England. William Everett and Thomas Frank pose issues that emerge from United Methodism's current efforts to interpret its ecclesial nature in American courtrooms, particularly in the face of liability suits, and to construe its "connectionalism" so as to minimize its exposure to attorneys and claimants probing for deep pockets. They insist that "Pacific Homes" and similar cases have quite literally put United Methodism's connectionalism on trial, as have also recent struggles for organizational reorganization and even efforts at Christian unity. In its flight or fight for juridical cover, in its efforts at reform, in its ecumenical endeavor will Methodism remain true to its connectional heritage? That question, they note, is complicated by the fact that over the course of its history Methodism has drawn from various sources—not just Wesley—in conceptualizing and structuring itself. They argue that three models or theories of order have proved particularly important: "public assembly," "federalism," and "corporatism." The first, Methodists share with American society generally, indeed with most free societies; the second, with the American political order; the third, with corporations and other centralized bureaucratic agencies. With respect to none of these, the authors suggest, has Methodism thought very deeply, theologically, or biblically. The recent challenges, then, represent an opportunity for ecclesiological self-reflection. The church can and should draw out the best of the political and theological potential of these several traditions, particularly that of public assembly. Would that point find common consent? Are the several models Frank and Everett develop adequate and appropriate expressions of Wesleyan connectionalism?

Constitutional Order in United Methodism and American Culture

William Johnson Everett
and
Thomas Edward Frank

United Methodists are deeply engaged with questions about their organizational forms and purposes. Amid calls for new paradigms and more effective organizational systems, the church's General Conference has taken up numerous proposals for structural reform. These address a wide range of fundamental elements of the church's polity, such as the nature and role of episcopacy, annual conferences, and congregations in the overall governance of the church.

Debates about reform and restructuring, however, have suffered from a lack of critical discussion of the ecclesiology underlying them. Like other contemporary institutions, the church needs to address with greater clarity the elements that constitute it as a body and the nature of the authority that enables those elements to work together toward a unified purpose. In particular, as United Methodism considers a covenant with other Protestant bodies to bring together catholic, evangelical, and reformed ecclesial traditions in a Church of Christ Uniting (COCU), it must clarify its expectations of the constitution of such an ecclesial covenant as well as the distinctives of Methodist tradition that are its unique contribution to emerging forms of church.[1]

The ferment over denominational forms as well as conversations about ecumenical relationships present United Methodism with an opportunity, then, to address polity issues in a fresh way. However, ecclesiological proposals must be formulated in critical engagement with the organizational forms prevalent in the larger society as well as in the church's own traditions.

Methodism grew up within a new nation deeply imbued with the voluntary ethos of associationalism. The nation sought to become a democratic republic that would be fertile ground both for economic enterprise and for associational life. Methodism as it became fully a denomination was profoundly shaped by these commitments. Indeed historian of American religion Nathan O. Hatch has argued that Methodism "invented the American denomination, making obsolete the European reality of church at the cultural center and sect at the periphery."[2] Neither established churches nor sects set apart from society, denominations became America's unique form of ecclesial voluntary association for authorizing ministries and supporting missions.

Methodism's rapid growth during the formative period of American political institutions led to heated debates. For some, especially Methodist Protestants, a church in which bishops appointed pastors and in which conferences assembled clergy but excluded laity was out of keeping with the emerging democracy. For others the crucial issue was the balance of powers between the episcopacy and the General Conference in an organization of growing resources and influence. These debates revealed both the diversity of traditions within an emergent Methodism and their tensions with the developing republican order of the nation.

Eclecticism and pragmatism were native to Methodist ecclesiology and polity. In their episcopal greetings introducing the 1939 *Discipline*, the bishops of the newly formed Methodist Church explained that:

> The Methodist Discipline is a growth rather than a purposive creation. The founders of Methodism did not work with a set plan, as to details. They dealt with conditions as they arose. . . .[3]

This disposition to "deal with conditions" and to let the church's discipline grow from efforts to advance people's spiritual life is fundamental to the character of United Methodism and its predecessor bodies. Methodism's central historic purpose has been to invite people to the disciplines and practices of Christian life and action, whatever their circumstances. Consequently, United Methodist polity is an exercise in practical theology—the interplay of theological reflection upon contexts and situations of ministry and actions of witness and service to the Gospel. What has been lacking, however, is adequate theological reflection on the relationship of the church's institutional forms with the models of governance projected by other major institutions in American culture.

Since the heady days of nineteenth-century growth the church has devoted little debate to the constructive task of defining more precisely its nature as an ecclesial body. In a twentieth century marked by world wars, economic depression, and the expansion of a global market, the church has had to address vast issues of social change. In its continuing response to new contexts and needs, the church has tended to borrow elements uncritically from diverse forms of ecclesiology, corporate business, and civil polity. These have been woven together in a largely oral tradition about its ways of getting things done.

In popular discourse Methodists have often expressed what they see as connections between church order and American institutions. For instance, parallels are drawn between United Methodism and the three branches of United States government. The first generations of Methodists were especially eager to show that their polity was not incompatible with ideals of the new republic. Thus they pointed to the church's division of powers, with the conferences as the legislative branch, the episcopacy as the executive branch, and a judiciary function lying in a special committee of the General Conference. After the 1939 union, of course, Methodists could argue that their legislative bodies were now fully and equally delegated by both clergy and laity, and that the judiciary was now located in a separate Judicial Council parallel to the United States Supreme Court.

In fact, however, this is a strained and misleading analogy, not only because United Methodism is not solely an American denomination but also because federalism is only one of at least three principles of organization in the church. Models of public association and corporate organization have also played a major role in the formation of the church's polity. We need to pursue a much more critical analysis of the way various models of organization are brought together with theological commitments to shape the church's ecclesiology.

Critical engagement between ecclesial and civil constitutional forms must undergird the search for an appropriate ecclesiology for United Methodists today. The church has an opportunity to constitute itself anew in a polity that more fully incorporates congregations and conferences as constituted assemblies, and that advances a broader sense of episcopacy. We believe that reflection on how elements of public assembly, federalism, and corporatism are brought together in a coherent ecclesiology can also be indispensable for wider institutional reforms in the society.

We shall first explore the meaning of these three major principles of organization and their impact on the development of Methodist polity. We shall then turn to a case study of the Pacific Homes litigation in the late 1970s, which revealed fundamental problems of church order in relationship to American legal culture. Finally, we shall take up a critical examination of the key issues illuminated by this case that require careful attention in the current ecclesiological debates.

Elements of Public Assembly

The victorious American colonies constituted themselves as a federal republic. As a republic, they sought to govern themselves through congresses, assemblies, and conventions rather than through the paternal guidance of a monarch. Though the United States Constitution of 1787 presumed this lush proliferation of councils and assemblies, it did not articulate their presence constitutionally. Only the First Amendment ensured their vital place by protecting freedom of religion, of public assembly, and of communication. The right of assembling in publics, whether religious or civil, became the core of the people's constitutional liberty.[4]

What then are the key dimensions of this "publicity" intrinsic to American constitutionalism? First, public assembly is a form of *participation* in power and authority. It is a mode of self-governance. People have a right to participate in the structures of authority that hold them in common obligations with others. They have a right to be in direct communication with others who participate in the powers of governance.

The religious echoes of this right to public participation were already manifest in the open public preaching of revivals, in which itinerant Methodist preachers played a central role. In the ecstatic gatherings of camp meetings people found their own voices—slaves and free citizens, women and men, people of all ages. The revivalist temper found its way into the wider political culture, and into the societies and churches of Methodism in particular. Many United Methodist local churches have functioned primarily as indoor camp meetings—assemblies for preaching, singing, and conversion—with affiliated organizations for education and missions. They have also been a center for public life in many towns and cities across America.

This congregating in public assembly, fundamentally dependent on the unpredictable work of the Spirit, always has an ephemeral character. It cannot be sustained by law but only by will and inspiration. Both civilly and ecclesially, the maintenance of the public assembly so crucial to governance has been very difficult. Neither the congregational life of United Methodism nor the popular assemblies of the republic have been able to find explicit constitutional recognition and legitimation. Meanwhile in contemporary market culture, invocations to participate fall on the deaf ears of hurrying commuters and exhausted weekend couch potatoes. The spirit of the assembly soon becomes the object of bureaucratic programming.

Second, public assemblies are modes of reasonable *persuasion*. While people act and agree on the basis of many sinister as well as altruistic motives, non-coercive persuasion according to reason is the benchmark that legitimates the decisions of the public. This is why non-violence is so crucial to the existence of a public. Moreover, the criteria of persuasion require a rough economic and social equality among the participants in order to strengthen their immunity from external coercion.

Here again, the emerging idea of a republic found common chord with the religious impulses of evangelical Christianity. In the conversations and arguments of meetings, societies, congregations, and conventions, believers had to hammer out common agreements in order to build and sustain the often isolated congregations of an expanding commonwealth. Without hierarchical guidance people had to live by persuasion in order to form a largely cooperative order in the church as well as in civil society.

The work of persuasion in both churches and general publics has had to swim against the tide of subliminal advertising and media sound bites that seek instant impact over sustained argument. One-way communication, whether by preachers or by mass media, stultifies the habits of dialogue. Decisions by majority vote cut off the requirement for persuasion and the creating of consensus in both church and civil assemblies. How to cultivate the arts of persuasion is a major challenge for any institutions committed to public life.

Third, a public always appears as a *plurality* of strangers who need conversation and argument in order to create understanding and agreement. In a public of persuasion the multiplicity of opinions requires public testing and evaluation. The task of a constitution, as James Madison understood it, was to translate the many natural factions and interests of society into the measured opinions of a public argument for the sake of governance.[5]

Similarly, by placing such a high premium on personal experience, evangelical Christianity also created the conditions for religious pluralism—of congregations, movements, denominations, and associations. Sometimes all these religious interests could be held together under a common tent of conversation, but at other times people set out to build their own tent, only to find a plurality of groups emerging within its folds. United Methodism, as it has expanded among a diverse population, has struggled with how varied ethnic, cultural, racial, and interest groups can share fully in the various publics of the church. How to honor our commitments to the particular sources of our faith experience as well as maintain commitments to the welfare of the whole has remained a key issue both in ecclesiology and in civil governance.

Finally, a public can sustain itself only if it can find sufficient points of *commonality* in which to ground its efforts at persuasion. A cultural world of common reference offers the benchmarks people need in order to reach a conclusion accessible to public reason. In the civil order this is constituted by common history, language, geography, shared values and visions, mutual interests, and the like. Sustaining this commonality is a critical cultural task for any republic that cannot rely on the single inheritance of a monarch who purports to be kin (and king) to all.

Much evangelical Christianity has sought to resist the fissiparous effects of ecstatic experientialism by appeal to Scriptures as the sole necessary commonality of the Christian people. Methodism's theological commonality by contrast has focused less on doctrinal propositions about Scripture than on a method and process for theological reflection. In order to resist the dogmatic schisms arising from different interpretations of Scripture, Methodism both held onto its Anglican ecclesial heritage and invoked the varied commonalities of creeds, Wesleyan roots and history, statements, resolutions, and its *Book of (Doctrines and) Discipline*. Around this cultural core a host of stories, customs, and traditions have gradually entwined themselves.

These four elements of public assembly—participation, persuasion, plurality, and commonality—are only partially realized in any public. Yet they offer a framework for examining the principle of public assembly that has so deeply shaped both the civil and ecclesial forms of American constitutional culture. They can serve as a checklist with which to look at the character of any assembly, whether religious or civil.

Most Methodists know the church through the public gatherings of the local congregation. They soon discover, though, that their local congregation occupies a politically complex and often ambiguous place within the wider church. The question of denominational life is how these local assemblies are linked together in the wider church. Federalism is a major way this constitutional question has been answered in American government and society.

Elements of Federalism

Federalism, like public assembly, has direct affinity with concepts and practices rooted in our religious heritage as well as political experience. Historically it is rooted not only in classical political theory but even more deeply in the covenantal polity of ancient Israel.[6] Concepts of a promissory God, of life according to a higher law, and of relationships of mutual consent in making covenants and mutual reconciliation in their violation have deeply permeated our religious consciousness. Many people see the American Constitution as a covenant-like document indebted to this heritage, and conversely, many church members have viewed denominational polity as a form of federal government.[7]

An examination of six key elements in federalism shows both how United Methodist polity accords with federalist order and how it departs from classic federal conceptions. First, a federal order entails a *constitutional definition of mutual rights and responsibilities among its constituting entities.* United Methodism was in this sense brought into being by a formal constitution in 1968.[8]

Division One of the 1968 Constitution puts forward the general provisions for the church, beginning by declaring the union of The Evangelical United Brethren Church and The Methodist Church (Art. I). Divisions Two and Three clearly establish conferences and episcopacy as United Methodism's constitutive elements, as they have been from the beginning of Methodism. As the constitutional historian of an earlier period, John J. Tigert, wrote,

> Since 1744 the two constant factors of Methodist polity, (1) a superintending and appointing power, and (2) a consulting body called the Conference, have been continuously operative. These two factors are constitutional or elemental in the government of Methodism . . . the former chiefly executive and the latter chiefly legislative.[9]

To state the case more broadly, United Methodism comprises an unsettled, often unreflective, yet remarkably creative blending of two constitutive principles: republican democracy and episcopacy.

First, the principle of republican democracy essential to free societies and voluntary organizations has been constitutive of United Methodism most visibly through its conferences. While these assemblies have their origin in the organization of Methodism as a voluntary society in the Church of England, they took on a distinctly American form in parallel with the legislative assemblies and political conventions of the emerging republic in the nineteenth century.

Wesley gathered conferences of Methodist preachers to consult with him, but they were never decision-making bodies. In the American context, however, from the moment the "Christmas Conference" of 1784 voted to accept Francis Asbury and Thomas Coke as general superintendents, the preachers collectively became the fundamental legislative body of the new church.

In fact, one could argue, with the weight of constitutional opinion in the late-nineteenth century, that "the body of traveling elders," that is, all the ordained preachers collectively, were the "original or primary constituency" that brought the Methodist Episcopal Church into being. In addition to electing their general superintendents, they voted on changes to the *Discipline* each year in annual conference, created a quadrennial general conference of all ordained preachers in 1792, and in 1808 made it a delegated General Conference with restrictions on its powers. In a genealogical sense, then, both the conference system and the episcopacy hold their charter from this original body—the "traveling preachers" of this one unbroken "traveling Connection."[10]

Nearly a hundred years passed before laity had any representation in the conferences at all, and fifty more years before they gained equal participation. Yet it was still this primal body of ordained preachers who had to vote to amend the constitution to include lay representation. This expanded and continuous aggregation of all clergy and corresponding lay members of all annual conferences are the electors who must vote on any amendments to the Constitution.[11]

The Constitution names the annual conferences as "the basic body in the church." One way this is true is that they elect delegates to general conferences. On the other hand, the General Conference is the only body in the church with legislative powers over the connection as a whole. It defines and fixes the powers of all other units, including the bishops, clergy, laity, annual conferences, and "connectional enterprises of the Church" in missions, education, and other ministries.[12] It is given powers even over the annual conferences whose delegates constitute it.

These powers are not unlimited, however. Beginning in 1808 the General Conference of the Methodist Episcopal Church built in certain checks on the delegated body it was creating. The "restrictive rules" have continued in force in mainly the same form ever since.[13] Most important from a polity standpoint, the restrictive rules make it very difficult for the General Conference "to do away with episcopacy or destroy the plan of our itinerant general superintendency."[14]

Episcopacy is the second constitutive element of United Methodism. However, because United Methodism is a synthesis of varying polities, this episcopacy is, in the laconic words of Bishop John L. Nuelsen, "an episcopacy that the Christian church ha[s] not yet seen."[15] The bishops in council are charged by the Constitution with planning "for the general oversight and promotion of the temporal and spiritual interests of the entire Church."[16] Though bishops are elected to office by lay and clergy delegates in Jurisdictional or Central Conferences and their presidential duties are limited to the bounds of those conferences, they are to practice a general superintendency.

In some ways United Methodist episcopacy is kin to its Anglican and Roman Catholic forebears. The Constitution grants bishops the power to appoint ministers to the charges in consultation with the district superintendents, who are extensions of the episcopal office.[17] The Constitution also gives bishops life tenure. These are both features associated ecclesiologically with a monarchical episcopacy, that is, an episcopacy understood as rule-rooted in a hierarchy of personal statuses and apostolic succession.

Yet while United Methodist episcopacy was initiated by Wesley, Coke, and others steeped in the Anglican heritage, it differs significantly from the episcopacy of that heritage. In Anglican ecclesiology, the bishop is the unit of church and presides over a diocese. Parishes are local expressions of the episcopal diocese. Clergy are the representatives of the bishop in a local place. The bishop visits each parish to perform confirmations, because all parishioners are members of the bishop's extended congregation.

Little of this applies in United Methodist episcopacy. Oddly, the Constitution fails to specify even that the bishops have authority to ordain the clergy—this is listed as one of the "presidential duties" in a later legislative paragraph[18]—much less that they share other aspects of an Anglican model such as the authority to confirm new members. The sacraments are not mentioned either, which means that in United Methodism bishops are not understood as a distinct order retaining sacramental authority that is then delegated to clergy as extensions of the bishop when they are ordained elder.[19] Though the Constitution does not state this explicitly, later legislative paragraphs make clear that bishops remain part of the body of elders as well as the itinerancy, receiving their assignments from the jurisdictional conference.[20]

Thus United Methodist episcopacy constitutes the church in a functional way through the bishops' legislatively defined roles of oversight and superintendency. Bishops are called to a broad mandate of oversight. In one of the *Discipline*'s simplest and most compelling phrases, they are asked "to lead"—"to lead and oversee the spiritual and temporal affairs of The United Methodist Church."[21] The generality of this duty is also its strength. Bishops are given wide latitude to speak, intervene, encourage, preach, evangelize, to put themselves on the line. As with their ancestor Asbury, their constant travel and omnipresence make the connection tangible. The bishops have also had wide influence in the missional activism of the church. They serve on and preside in general agencies and boards of trustees of church-related institutions. Their energy and experience are in such demand that they have had to be wary of becoming mere program promoters and "sales managers."[22] The conferences—fleeting moments of assembly—would never be enough to sustain the connection without the itinerant superintendency. Little wonder, then, that many voices in United Methodism today call for stronger episcopal leadership—not authoritarianism or autocracy, much less monarchy, but a leadership of presence and vision that will give the connection its coherence for the future.

The persistent ecclesiological question, however, is in what sense the tasks of teaching, evangelism, and mission constitute "church." The traditional Methodist privileging of preaching and mission activism over sacramental order results in enduring ambiguities for the *episkopoi* of this church. The Restrictive Rule protects "the *plan* of our itinerant general superintendency" [emphasis ours]—that is, its role in advancing the church's mission—more than any inherent authority.

The episcopal prerogatives of appointment-making and life tenure have been challenged repeatedly—in the 1820s, 1890s, and 1970s. The word "episcopal" was dropped from the denominational name when The Methodist Church was formed in 1939, in part to make the Methodist Protestant partners to the union more comfortable in accepting ecclesial life with bishops, whose appointive authority had been one source of their protest in the 1820s. Moreover, many twentieth-century United Methodists have complained of the association of episcopacy with patriarchy and an outmoded culture of deference and paternalism. All this unrest indicates that for lack of a firm ecclesiological basis, the functions of bishops depend far more on "the consent of the governed" than on organic roots in the traditional understanding of episcopacy. At the same time, it must be said that the church continues to depend on the episcopacy for much of its coherence and continuity.

The second element in federalism is provision for a *balance or division of powers between the constituting units*. Federalist theory harbors suspicion of any concentration of power and authority. Instead of an organic theory for differentiating functions within a unitary whole, it posits a dynamic equipoise among equal powers bound together in an overarching common covenant. The constituting entities must consciously come to agreement about major decisions.

Thus the Tenth Amendment of the U.S. Constitution states that "the powers not delegated to the United States by the Constitution, nor prohibited by it to the States, are reserved to the States respectively, or to the people." In United Methodism annual conferences retain "such other rights as have not been delegated to the General Conference under the Constitution."[23] At first glance the breadth of General Conference powers would not seem to leave much room for "other rights." The Constitution grants General Conference "full legislative power over all matters distinctively connectional," which includes determining the duties and powers of annual conferences.[24] But at the same time, the annual conferences constitutionally retain the sole right to vote "on all matters relating to the character and conference relations of [their] ministerial members"—their historic, primary function. It should be noted, however, that this constitutional function belongs only to the clergy session of the conference, not to the lay members. Each annual conference can also develop its own program initiatives and raise its own money to support them as long as it does not financially obligate any other organizational unit of the church.[25] Moreover, as we have already pointed out, annual conference members collectively vote on constitutional amendments as the final power over all such changes.

Another way in which the church has attempted to achieve some balance among the constituting powers has been through the creation of jurisdictional and central conferences. "Jurisdiction" is both a geographic and a legal term. As a name for a geographic area it carries with it the intention of adapting United Methodism to regional cultures. In this sense it served well to enable the Methodist Episcopal Church South to sustain many of its customs and relationships after the 1939 union with the larger, more centralized, and more national Methodist Episcopal Church (north). The jurisdictional system also allowed the denomination to preserve racial segregation in a Central Jurisdiction based not on region but on race. This accommodation to racial patterns had the effect of modifying the "plan" of general superintendency. Mainly in order to prevent black bishops from presiding at white conferences, the Constitution restricted bishops' powers of "residential and presidential supervision" to their own jurisdiction. The restriction remains, even in the absence today of the racial jurisdiction.

As a legal term "jurisdiction" indicates the limits of power of various agents. The designers of this system intended it to create a balance or distribution of powers throughout the connection. Membership of the general agencies would be elected by jurisdictions. The work of general agencies would be shared by jurisdictional auxiliaries. Jurisdictional conferences would be responsible for and in many cases actually own the educational and mission institutions within their boundaries. Moreover, they would have power to determine the boundaries of the annual conferences within their own territory.[26] A survey of current jurisdictional conference journals, however, shows clearly that these hopes were never realized.[27] Only the Southeastern Jurisdiction—the region of the old MECS—has any significant level of staff and budget for program. In fact, all the institutions that technically are jurisdictionally owned relate in various ways to the entire connection.

Thus, the jurisdictional conference remains a constitutional anomaly originally invented to accommodate a social and cultural difference. All the duties assigned to it by the Constitution historically belonged to the General Conference. In effect, jurisdictions are simply regional derivatives of the General Conference and do not have a fundamental role in constituting the church.

This is not in any way to dismiss the primary political function of jurisdictional conferences—the electing and consecrating of bishops—only to make clear that the function derives from the General Conference. The episcopacy in the United States is constituted by the jurisdictional conferences; that is, the conference elects and the college of bishops consecrates by the laying on of hands. But the number of bishops is determined on "a uniform basis" set by General Conference, and once bishops are elected their membership resides in the Council of Bishops.[28]

Central conferences have powers and duties parallel to the jurisdictional conferences, but in a distinctive context that makes them in practice much more constitutive of the church in their regions. Since they exercise those powers in nations outside the United States, the Constitution grants them the power "to make such rules and regulations for the administration of the work within their boundaries"—this in common with jurisdictional conferences—but also the power to make "such changes and adaptations of the General Discipline as the conditions in the respective areas may require."[29]

Central conferences may not make changes "contrary to the Constitution and the General Rules of The United Methodist Church,"[30] but this still leaves wide range for encouraging local churches and annual conferences to organize in the most suitable fashion, and for churches of a region to adapt their ministry, worship, and other practices to the local or national context.

Third, federalism requires a *balance of powers within its governing units*. For instance, legislation passed by Congress must be signed by the President and may be reviewed by the Supreme Court, and major presidential proposals must be considered by Congress. In United Methodism this balance of powers is perhaps most explicit in the division of rights and duties between the conferences and the episcopacy. The General Conference has sole legislative power over the *Discipline* while annual conferences have the sole right to admit clergy to membership. Unlike the President of the United States or the governor of a state the bishops individually or collectively do not make specific legislative or budgetary proposals. They do not manage agencies charged with carrying out legislation and are in no sense executive administrators of the conferences. Bishops are members of no conference and have no voice except as presiding officers. In particular, they have no voice in the admission of clergy to an annual conference.

On the other hand, bishops retain the sole right to ordain and to appoint pastors to their charges. They are also individually and as a council charged with two broad duties: (1) "general oversight and promotion of the temporal and spiritual interests of the entire Church," and (2) "carrying into effect the rules, regulations, and responsibilities prescribed and enjoined by the General Conference."[31] The possible conflict between these two duties is further evidence of the delicate balance of power between bishops and the General Conference.

Fourth, federalism requires an *independent judiciary* to interpret the constitution. This prevents either legislative or executive powers from defining basic rights and responsibilities, and thus is a critical element in balancing their powers. In the Constitution of the United Methodist Church, Division Four constitutes a Judicial Council to make final determination of "the constitutionality of any act of the General Conference." This helps to limit the powers of the General Conference, which cannot—as it once did in the Methodist Episcopal Church— judge the constitutionality of its own acts. The Council also has the authority to review and "pass upon decisions of law made by bishops in Annual Conferences."[32] Thus, while bishops are given the constitutional mandate of making decisions of law in their presiding role in conferences, thereby acting as a judiciary, the Judicial Council is equally mandated to review their rulings.

Judicial powers fully exercised become constructive interventions in the government of the body. The very act of interpreting church law also contributes to the church's self-understanding and certainly affects its practices. As in civil polity, though, the judiciary has no means for enforcing its own decisions. It depends entirely on the legitimacy granted it by the constitutive units.

Fifth, federalism requires that the *constituting units have representation in the wider governing assembly.* While the exact forms and proportions of representation may vary, the principle itself is critical to a republic pursuing democratic values. That is, all citizens must have access to some public, which then delegates some of its members to participate in more general publics. These delegates then represent their electors in this wider assembly, and in that assembly must also consider the interests of the whole federation.

The United Methodist Constitution guarantees these representative rights to the annual conferences, who elect by a formula of proportionality their delegates to jurisdictional, central, and general conferences.[33] Throughout Methodist history annual conferences have been the locus of membership for the clergy. Because they alone have the power to admit clergy to the ordained ministry, the conference is the body to which "all the ordained ministers [are] bound in special covenant."[34]

Laity are now members of annual conferences as well, but not on the same basis. Their church membership remains in their local church, and they are excluded from the core function of voting on clergy relations. Their membership in annual conference is not based on proportional representation of the lay members of the local church, but is tied to the pastoral charge (one lay member per pastor appointed to a charge). Thus, the congregation as such is not represented in the wider polity of the church. Indeed, congregations are not in any way self-constituting within this system. They are governed not by annual meetings but by a charge conference called and presided over by a district superintendent. In United Methodist practice they are known primarily as "local churches"—the local manifestation of the "connection" in a particular place—and as "pastoral charges"—a name referring to the pastoral appointment by the bishop which may include one or more local churches.

Thus, while all United Methodist conferences—General, jurisdictional, central, and annual—are equally lay and clergy, the delegated bodies can hardly be called fully representative, since the basis of representation is already skewed toward the clergy in the annual conferences. Moreover, the formula for General Conference is based equally on the number of clergy and the number of church members in each annual conference, which does not adequately account for the fact that in regions with many large congregations (currently the Sunbelt of the United States) clergy may serve on average far more members than in areas with smaller congregations.[35] This problem is addressed by the practice of bicameral legislatures in civil polity, but United Methodism lacks such a solution.

Finally, in federalism *each citizen stands within the jurisdiction of two or more of the governing partners in the federation.* In the United States a citizen votes, enjoys representation, pays taxes, and receives services from municipal, county, state, and federal governments. In the United Methodist Church, while there is no popular vote for representatives or referenda on conference actions, each church member belongs not only to the local church but to the whole connection.[36] Each member has a right to petition General Conference, to study and accept or reject conference resolutions, and of course, to "vote" with financial donations as well.

A review of these six principles of federalism shows that they have indeed been a formative influence in United Methodist polity. The very fact of the church's having a formal constitution, combined with its concerns for defined and balanced powers and rights of representation, indicates a federal model. At the same time, however, because United Methodist polity embodies elements of several ecclesial traditions and has developed as a growth in varying circumstances, a closer examination of its constituting units exhibits many ways in which it varies from federal principles. This departure is due not only to internal ecclesiological considerations but also to the presence of yet a third mode of organization—the corporation.

Elements of Corporatism

A third major influence on the formation of United Methodist polity is the understanding of corporations in American—and now global—society. Corporations provide a means of organizing large and complex enterprises around defined purposes. They rationalize authority, distinguish and specialize functions bureaucratically, and institute chains of decision and command that facilitate action. At the same time, they tend toward hierarchy and centralization of power in a single "head" of the corporate "body."

Corporatism, like public assembly and federalism, has deep theological roots. The very notion of the church as the body of Christ generated the idea of an immortal institution distinct from its transient human members. Paul's image of this body as an organic interdependency of functions (Rom. 12:4–8; 1 Cor. 12:12–31; Eph. 1:22–23, 4:11–16) has exerted extraordinary power within ecclesiology as well as Western society. Without it, modern society probably would not have the cultural base to legitimate the corporation.[37]

Corporatism is most visible in United Methodism in the General and annual conference agencies of the denomination. Administrative and programmatic units tend to be organized bureaucratically and to reflect and reinforce trends in business management. While they have been effective in organizing large enterprises such as missions, publishing, and pensions, they have also drawn the church into structural forms in tension with United Methodism's wider ecclesial character.

Two basic principles constitute corporatism.[38] First, *corporations generally organize themselves bureaucratically through the differentiation and specialization of functions.* This "rational" form of organization enables them to coordinate a complex set of tasks toward a clearly defined goal. It encourages the development of specialized knowledge and employment of persons with expert skills in particular kinds of work. Bureaucracy usually divides the practice of these skills from the setting of general policy, thus creating a hierarchy of control. A central body or head, represented in a chief executive officer (CEO), takes responsibility for making policy, which subsidiary offices then carry out. Internal controls systematize the acquisition and use of funds and channel initiatives into structures for evaluating personnel and program.

United Methodism has utilized this principle of corporatism in a variety of ways over the past hundred years. The denomination began to elaborate a bureaucracy in the 1870s.[39] Both the Methodist Episcopal Church and Methodist Episcopal Church South exerted increasing control over independent associations for education, evangelism, and mission. These were centralized, housed in specially built office buildings, and funded by coordinated budgets. By 1972 the plan for restructuring the agencies of the new church—promising greater efficiency and coordination—created more centralization by consolidating the church's efforts in everything from children's educational materials to agricultural missions into four program boards.

Moreover, the portfolios of these boards, along with other specialized initiatives expressing the church's commitments, such as standing commissions on Christian unity, religion, and race, and on the status and role of women, were mirrored in all organizational "levels" of the church. The General Conference mandated that local church congregations as well as annual conferences carry out parallel functions preferably in similarly specialized units. This would provide for the most efficient and effective communication throughout the connection.

All program initiatives were to be coordinated by councils on ministries (COMs), thus providing the General and annual conferences as well as local churches with means of central control. In many annual conferences the COM represented the first centralized bureaucracy ever attempted, with the COM director acting like a CEO of conference program.

Many critics in church and management challenge classical hierarchical views of the corporation. At the same time new forms of corporatism such as total quality management, chaos theory, and other organizational development schemes drawn from corporate life continue to shape the reform of church organizations.[40]

Second, while corporations are collective enterprises involving any number of people, *for legal purposes they are single bodies or fictional persons*. Corporate entities can acquire property, assume debt, and risk liability. They can sue and be sued in courts of law. Moreover, the CEO is normally the public face of the fictional corporate person, embodying both the enterprise itself and its action in the public sphere.

United Methodism has donned the corporate mask in order to acquire property, employ personnel, and manage funds. Most local church congregations and all annual conferences and general agencies are legally incorporated with trustees or boards of directors. Particularly in the general agencies, the general secretaries function most clearly as the CEOs who represent the enterprise as a whole. In local churches and annual conferences, the church has continued to borrow the corporate legal fiction while trying to avoid the corporate consequence of the single executive head.

As legal issues surrounding liability and personnel actions have proliferated, bureaucratic controls have become more elaborate. Policies and procedures govern virtually every aspect of corporate action. The chief administrative units for finance and administration and for pensions have become indispensable to the church's life.

However, unlike the modern corporation, there is no single "head" of the United Methodist Church. The bishops in particular are not recognized as heads of the church, whether as CEOs or chairs of the board, even though they carry out very important functions within the ecclesial body. Neither are agency executives heads of anything more than their clearly defined organization. Theologically, only Christ is the head of the church and exercises this headship through many forms—individual disciples, assemblies, conferences, agencies, and bishops. Such a conception of religious corporation, however, eludes the typical practices and conceptions of economic corporations and civil courts alike, as the Pacific Homes cases revealed in painful particularity.

Principles on Trial: The Pacific Homes Case

Any reforms in civil or ecclesial governance need to take into account these three primary modes of constitutional order in American culture. Principles of public assembly, federalism, and corporatism all play a necessary role in American political and organizational culture. In appropriating these organizational forms the church needs to be guided by its own deepest theological and ecclesiological commitments. An appropriate integration requires awareness of the three modes as well as attention to the actual historical dynamics of their implementation. To gain greater critical awareness of this historical context we turn now to the complex litigation which embroiled the United Methodist Church in the late 1970s and brought many of these issues to the surface.

Beginning in 1912, church organizations which later became part of the United Methodist Church sponsored a number of nursing and retirement homes in southern California as part of their charitable mission.[41] These homes, including seven residential centers and seven convalescent hospitals, had by 1975 come to serve about 1700 people under the corporate name of Pacific Homes, a non-profit corporation created in 1929. The board of directors of Pacific Homes was elected annually by the Pacific and Southwest Annual Conference of the United Methodist Church.

In the late 1960s Pacific Homes began to encounter severe financial difficulties because the costs of care steadily exceeded the funds generated by the "life care" payment system, according to which retirees prepaid their lifetime care with a lump sum fixed on entry into the Homes. Increase in longevity of the population and sharp inflationary increases made this arrangement increasingly impossible. The Annual Conference arranged and guaranteed several loans for the Homes and finally appointed a "crisis management team" to reorganize the Homes and convert to a pay-as-you-go system over an extended period of time.

By 1976 the Conference agreed to subsidize the Homes in the amount of $5 million over a nine-year period to bring them through this reorganization. However, the State of California, where the Homes are incorporated, refused to approve this conversion plan. As a result Pacific Homes had to declare bankruptcy in 1977. Although 91% of the residents voted to accept a bankruptcy plan proposed by the management team to enable Pacific Homes to regain viability, two class action suits brought on behalf of approximately 150 of the residents blocked this arrangement. These two suits sought to hold not only the Pacific Homes corporation but various United Methodist entities and "The United Methodist Church" itself responsible for claims totalling $366 million. Subsequent suits against not only United Methodist-related entities but also individuals involved in the administration of Pacific Homes brought the total to over $600 million.

Even though there is no legally incorporated body called "The United Methodist Church," plaintiffs sought to sue it as an "unincorporated association." California law gives legal personality to groups who act like an incorporated association if they have a common purpose and function under a common name under circumstances where fairness requires the group be recognized as a legal entity. Fairness includes those situations where persons dealing with the association contend their legal rights have been violated.[42] By breaking down the distinction between formally incorporated and unincorporated groups, courts had enabled people to sue labor unions, political parties, clubs, lodges, and churches with greater ease. Indeed, under the California definition the mere allegation of legal injury seemed to be enough to establish this corporate persona for an association.

As noted in various documents related to the case, no religious denomination as such had ever been held to be a jural entity liable to suit apart from its various incorporated units. Not even the Roman Catholic Church, with its purported hierarchy of command from the Vatican to the local parish, had been so treated. Because of the landmark character of the case, the National Council of Churches filed a brief *amicus curiae* with the defendants and the case received extensive national coverage.

The Trial Court: Free Exercise of Religion
vs. Ecclesial Corporality

At the first stage of litigation, the California trial court held that the United Methodist Church was not a jural body that can be held liable for the acts of its purported agents. The Court accepted the church's argument that there is no central representative for "The United Methodist Church," much less a chief executive officer who could be a principal directing the activities of United Methodist Church "agents" around the world. The court held that the United Methodist Church was a "spiritual confederation" held together by shared beliefs. The many entities holding this common name and sharing adherence to the United Methodist *Book of Discipline* did not compose either a single jural body or an unincorporated association amenable to suit. Most important, treating churches like the United Methodist Church as simply another corporate body would abrogate First Amendment protections for religion. Any evaluation of the church's internal structure would violate this shield protecting the church's freedom to practice its faith through the design of its institutional life.

Arguing from the standpoint of religious free exercise, the trial court judge, Ross G. Tharp, wrote:

> A contrary ruling would effectively destroy Methodism in this country, and would have a chilling effect on all churches and religious movements by inhibiting the free association of persons of similar religious beliefs. If all members of a particular faith were to be held personally liable for the transgressions of their fellow churchmen, church pews would soon be empty and the pulpits of America silent.[43]

In short, Constitutional protection of religion took precedence over the ordinary claims of corporate liability.

The Appeals Court: Market Fairness vs. Freedom of Religion

The Fourth District Court of Appeals in California then reversed this ruling, holding that such First Amendment protection gave churches an "unfair" advantage in "commercial affairs" such as nursing homes.[44] This claim rested on the courts' previous development of a doctrine of "neutral principles" by which to treat the "secular" aspects of religious and non-religious corporations and contracts alike. In applying these "neutral principles" to the United Methodist Church the court argued that the church did not differ significantly from other corporations carrying on the same activities. To give the church special consideration might even violate the First Amendment's prohibition of the establishment of religion. Upon removing this veil of protection for the church, the Court then went on to examine its internal organization to find that it was indeed a corporate hierarchy which could be sued as a "principal" responsible for the actions of its "agent," in this case Pacific Homes, Inc.

To make this case for hierarchical agency, the court argued that "the Council of Bishops is equivalent to the board of directors of the United Methodist Church." Quoting the church's own newly-minted language from the 1976 *Book of Discipline*, the court singled out the statement: "[the] Council of Bishops is thus the corporate expression of episcopal leadership in the Church" overseeing "the spiritual and temporal affairs of the whole Church."[45] In line with this reasoning the plaintiffs had indeed served their court summons and complaint to a former president of the Council, who then claimed that he could not speak as a representative of the United Methodist Church—something only the quadrennial General Conference can do. Since this General Conference, as a legislative body, does not exist between sessions, the court looked to the Council of Bishops as its interim executive representative, in short, as its "board of directors," despite *The Book of Discipline*'s distribution of powers to a variety of bodies and agents.

Drawing on corporate analogies, the court said in addition:

> It [UMC] is hierarchical; the 43,000 local churches and 114 Annual Conferences are governed through the structure described by the Book of Discipline of the United Methodist Church (Discipline). In United Methodism "the local church is a part of the whole body of the general church and is subject to the higher authority of the organization and its laws and regulations."[46]

The Appeals Court's argument thus drew on corporate models of executive authority to construe both the conferences and the episcopacy. It could then assert that the various parts of the whole United Methodist Church were agents of each other and mutually liable. To do otherwise would be unfair to similar corporate actors. In the court's view, any preferential treatment to religion, especially to treat it differently in civil law because of its own religious self-understanding, would do more injury to the establishment clause than to the free exercise clause. Moreover, it would provide a shield under which unscrupulous and fraudulent operators could seek religious immunity from lawsuits. The Pacific Homes case did not present any religious activities to the court but only commercial activities conducted by a religious body. Such secular activities had to comply fully with ordinary civil law.

Church defendants appealed to the United States Supreme Court to render a final verdict on its suability, but the Court refused to do so on technical grounds. Fearing an even more ruinous siege of litigation the Conference and related defendants settled with the plaintiffs out of court for $21 million, not to mention legal costs of over $4 million to the Conference and national agencies of the church also involved in the suits. Various conferences and agencies of the United Methodist Church loaned the Conference funds to make these settlement payments.

As a result every entity within the United Methodist connection had to take steps to establish "firewalls" to limit the liability of the entities comprising the entire denomination for the actions of its constituent parts.[47] Such firewalls called into question the nature of "connection" among conferences, agencies, and local churches.

One of the most striking effects of the Pacific Homes cases was to lead the church's General Conference in 1984 to change the *Book of Discipline* so that the Council of Bishops, rather than being the "corporate" expression of episcopal leadership in the church, as cited by the Barr court, would now be the "collegial" expression of that leadership.[48] The language of corporate unity was replaced by that of cooperation among independent superintendents overseeing the work of the ministers—something that may have been more congenial to Wesley's intention and historic Methodist practice but nevertheless marked a change of course from the conception of episcopacy toward which United Methodists had been trying to move.

The California Appeals Court ruling presently stands as an anomaly, and the United States Supreme Court has never issued a ruling which would settle the underlying Constitutional issues. While courts in at least nine states subsequently dismissed suits brought against the denomination as a whole, legal actions of this kind continue to plague religious organizations.[49]

The Issues in Light of the Three Modes of Constitutional Order

This complex and costly legal battle serves as a stethoscope which can enable us to hear deep internal dynamics in the relationship between civil and ecclesial constitutional forms in American culture. The litigation itself revolved around questions of establishment and free exercise of religion, the suability of churches, and the degree to which civil courts can construe questions of church law and ecclesiology.

United Methodist authorities had argued the church's case not only on the grounds of sheer organizational structure but also as a case of autonomy and free exercise for religious groups whose organizational self-understanding should be protected from re-interpretation by a civil court. Such an insulation of internal church decisions was well grounded in Constitutional law. A long series of legal precedents had confirmed that civil courts cannot interfere in internal church disputes, even when it appears that church authorities have acted in violation of their own established procedures.[50] There simply is no "higher court" to adjudicate theological matters.

However, this legal tradition was carved out largely in the face of governmental intrusions on religion. Liability suits now force the court to use these traditions in a radically different direction—a new context of consumer protection and marketplace performance. A church's dealings with an external marketplace are quite different from internal relationships historically insulated from court interference. In external matters the Appeals Court and in a related case the United States Supreme Court, held that its arm of adjudication can be long indeed.[51] This change demands not only legal reinterpretation but ecclesiological rethinking as well.

The churches now face a new legal context in which to approach questions of ecclesiology. This new context affects the way we think about questions of association and federal order within religious organizations, of the unique character of publics as distinct from markets within the society and the church, and the nature of corporate liability in an ecclesial setting. How then can our awareness of the three modes of constitutional order help us illuminate the key issues facing the church in this situation?

Church as Corporation or Church as Public Assembly

The Pacific Homes cases revealed a deep tension between the perspectives of assembly and federalism on the one hand and those of corporation on the other, both in ecclesial and civil realms. The trial court argued from traditions of public assembly and saw the case in terms of religious freedom. The appeals court argued from the perspectives of corporations and markets and saw the case as a question of corporate liability for marketplace derelictions. The Church was caught in the middle because it engaged in many corporate practices without a clear ecclesiological understanding of the differences between federal and corporate order and of the role of public assembly in defining the nature of the church.

A. The Church as a Corporate Entity

Indeed, the church has a profound tradition that understands the church in a corporate way. The church is seen as "the body of Christ" in two ways—as a spiritual or mystical body, with its unity in the resurrected Christ, and as a temporal body in which it is institutionalized for ordinary life among other worldly institutions. Both constitute the one "body of Christ." Within this tradition, the Methodist "connection" could not be merely otherworldly. It had to have real presence in the world of human action. But, the church argued, the real presence of this connection did not necessarily have an ordinary legal form. There is a real arena of human activity—indeed, the most important kind of public activity—that exists prior to and apart from civil law. The appeals court, however, followed the logic of a corporatist interpretation in another direction—toward the marketplace of hierarchical business corporations rather than the republic of church and state.

Indeed, many of the arguments in this case agreed on the use of language of body and corporation to describe the organizational issues at stake. The *Discipline* for a short time drew on this language in describing the Council of Bishops as "the corporate expression of episcopal leadership in the church."[52] In United Methodist theological tradition, this language refers to the way Christ is really and truly present through the teaching and general pastoral oversight (the root of the word "episcopal") of the bishops. It is the way the mind of Christ really has a body among us. But the control of this body through the episcopal representative is essentially a matter of persuasion seeking the assent of faith rather than a command seeking automatic obedience. However, the appeals court seized on this corporal language within the framework of contemporary business enterprise to argue that therefore the Council of Bishops, with its president, is the chief executive organ of the church.

Drawing on corporatist language in the *Discipline* and seeing in the term "connectional" a hierarchical principal, the Appeals Court agreed with the plaintiffs' claim that the United Methodist Church was a hierarchical denomination with a central principal agent, to which all subordinate agents were responsible. To do so, it drew upon a long-standing legal precedent which reduces a church's ecclesiology to a choice between "hierarchical" and "congregational" forms. This simplistic distinction derives from an 1872 ruling by the United States Supreme Court in *Watson v. Jones* concerning a dispute over church property.[53]

In that case the Court first identified three forms of church order relevant to legal cases. In the first form church property is held in a trust which specifies the intent of the original donor(s). Those who administer that trust most closely in accord with the trust's original intent then have rightful claim to the property. The problem with such an approach is that it draws the courts into theological examinations in order to assess the meaning of the original trust. Such a theological function for the court would eventually erode the distinction between civil and religious spheres. Republican governance, with its inherent plurality of all kinds of expression, ought not go down that road, argued the Supreme Court.

The United Methodist Church, however, in keeping with the English trust tradition and adapting it to the American civil environment, has explicitly construed its entire property arrangement in terms of *trusts*. All property under the United Methodist name is held "in trust for The United Methodist Church" to "be used, kept, and maintained as a place of divine worship of the United Methodist ministry and members of The United Methodist Church."[54] Such a web of trusts is what many Methodists mean by calling their church a "connectional" church. Because American civil law since *Watson v. Jones* largely has chosen not to pursue the trust arrangement for settling church disputes, the courts have not developed any understanding of the intricate meanings of this trust connectionalism.[55] What indeed does it mean to hold property "in trust" for the United Methodist Church if such a person, real or fictional, has no address and cannot appear in court? Furthermore, how can a court use "neutral principles" to separate out the theological and the "secular" meanings of the trust?

The second form cited in *Watson v. Jones* involves congregations which are "strictly independent of other ecclesiastical associations" and owe "no fealty or obligation to any higher authority." Such cases can be resolved "by the ordinary principles which govern voluntary associations"—majority vote of the members or other procedures previously defined by association. Because of the seemingly clean character of this ecclesial type within American law it actually functions as the normative case.[56] Just as entrepreneurial corporatism is the normative type of American business, so congregationalism is the norm in religious associations. To go beyond pure congregationalism for the sake of the spiritual unity of the church universal as the body of Christ is to risk unceasing lawsuits in a litigious world.

The third form is one in which the conflicted group "is but a subordinate member of some general church organization in which there are superior ecclesiastical tribunals with a general and ultimate power of control more or less complete in some supreme judicatory over the whole membership of that general organization." In this case, the decisions of the highest judicial organ must be respected by the court.

The court in *Watson v. Jones* did not in fact use the term "hierarchy." It focused on the judicial appeals process within a religious organization rather than its line of executive command. In this sense, it was working within the world of federalism more than corporatism. However, by the time we reach the Pacific Homes cases we find that the term "hierarchy" has been used to define such third types, possibly because of the use of that term in the context of priestly governance in cases involving the Orthodox Church.[57] Moreover, this "hierarchy" concerns not merely judicial appeals within a church but control over employment as well as property. In short, it is the hierarchy of a bureaucratic corporation. If the church is "congregational" then liability stops with the congregation. However, if it is "hierarchical," then liability touches all "levels" of the organization, conceived in corporatist terms.

This presents the churches with a critical problem. When "hierarchy" becomes conflated with the corporate forms of organization typical of American business firms, and when "non-profit" organizations are interpreted in terms of for-profit organizations, then depiction of a religious organization as "hierarchical" leads the courts to treat churches the same as other organizations engaged in commercial affairs—all of this in the name of "fairness" and justice with regard to the claims of persons against church-related agencies. Here we have moved from disputes between factions within churches to disputes between church authorities and their "customers" or "clients," conceived in terms of business life. The power of this business or market model of religion has worked to overturn the historic immunity to suit enjoyed by religious and charitable organizations. No longer do they represent a public or transcendent purpose rooted in a people's common good. They are treated like one interested party among others, all competing for the allegiance of free individuals in the marketplace.

Within this context of claims by "customers" and "clients" against church agencies, the formulation of *Watson v. Jones* becomes a question of who possesses liability within a complex church organization rather than whether church disputes should be settled within the church or in the civil courts. This collision of two worldviews—an ancient spiritual tradition and a modern commercial-legal positivism—lay at the heart of the multimillion-dollar Pacific Homes dispute.

B. Federal "Connection" or Episcopal Hierarchy?

Over against the courts' conceptions of corporate liability the church posed its own terminology of connection, which draws in a complex way on its roots in practices of assembly and federalism as well as its theological understanding of the church as the body of Christ. However, on this central term in United Methodist ecclesiology church spokespersons could find little agreement. Neither the court nor the church could turn it into a useful organizational or legal concept. The reason for this confusion is embedded not only in Methodist origins, principally in its reconstrual of episcopacy, but in the way Methodism engaged the corporate and legal forms of trusteeship.

The "connexion" originally referred to the personal relationship between Mr. Wesley and his preachers. It was not a connection of congregations or agencies but a relationship among preachers who were seeking the regeneration of individuals through class meetings and societies, and a spreading of holiness through the world. Wesley preferred to call his oversight of the connexion a superintendency, not an episcopacy, since the term bishop referred to Anglican prelates of the established church. The functional bias of superintendency stood in sharp contrast to the corporate notion of the Bishop as a representative of the church as the body of Christ.

As Methodism developed in America it adopted the organizational patterns around it, and it proved difficult to maintain Wesley's original conception of connection within a world Wesley could neither imagine nor desire. Connectionalism had to be accommodated to the forms of association known to American business and law. From a legal standpoint, connection became equated with trust deeds for holding property. As the itinerant preachers began to settle into stations, their preaching "charges" began to become congregations. When Methodists adopted bureaucratic organization toward the end of the nineteenth century, they inevitably assumed the corporate forms that made this possible in law. This is the leading edge of hierarchy and corporate liability that the Pacific Homes court and plaintiffs engaged.

In the course of this development Methodists could not clearly articulate what is "connected" and how these parts are connected to each other. Since congregations, conferences, and councils were not the original units of connection, they could not fit the original spiritual and ministerial meaning of Wesley. Yet these were the connections the court and the plaintiffs were looking for. They therefore took the theological language of the Wesleyan tradition and attached it to places totally unforeseen and even unimaginable to Wesley—and indeed to his present heirs in the leadership of the United Methodist Church.

In the pleadings and affidavits presented to the Pacific Homes courts we find a variety of interpretations of the church as a "connection." The United Methodist Church, claimed one church brief, is a "spiritual 'connection'" whose units—"churches, conferences, boards, agencies or institutions"—operate "within a loose, non-authoritarian confederation pursuant to the *Book of Discipline*."[58] In an important affidavit to the court the distinguished United Methodist sociologist of religious organizations Murray Leiffer put it this way:

> The general United Methodist denomination is a voluntary religious movement and connectional network of millions of persons, known as 'members,' and literally thousands of units, denominated as local churches, conferences, boards. . . . [This] connectional religious denomination and movement [is] structured around two fundamental church units, namely, (a) the local Charge, with its local congregation or congregations and (b) the Annual Conference.

However, Leiffer noted, these fundamental units may not act as agents for other units nor "bind or obligate them in any way." He concluded that the

> United Methodist Church is not a single entity. . . . It is not a unified corporate body, but in actuality is an international religious faith and denomination which constitutionally declares itself to be a branch of the Church universal and the ministry of Christ.[59]

On the one hand, Leiffer wanted to stress the autonomy of the various "units" in order to resist court intrusion on liability issues, which require relationships of agency and mutuality. On the other hand, he wanted to preserve the organic sense of the universal body of Christ. The exigencies of the situation pressed him to a "loose confederation" of "autonomous units"—a kind of corporate congregationalism. In the process, almost unnoticed, the United Methodist connection moved, again under the impact of civil law, from being a relation of superintendents with ministers to being a relationship among "churches," "conferences," "units" and "members." Rather than the deep mutuality and accountability characterizing

Wesley's relationship with his ministers, the meaning of "connection" brought before the court emphasized the autonomy of "spiritually confederated" groups.

C. Recovering the Church as Assemblies in Covenant

The problem with approaching a concept of church from the standpoint of business models of incorporation is that corporate models have little room for the independent initiative and extra-organizational activity that struggles to articulation in the confusions of the Methodist statements about "connection." While the corporate analogies draw on important strands of theological tradition, they cannot grasp the peculiar mix of effervescence and order which characterize not only Methodism but mainline American religion. This peculiar mix is also embedded in the rich tapestry of publics that generated the original American Constitutional order.

The spontaneous mass meetings, revivals, camp meetings, and conferences driving the engine of personal revival in the early American Republic did not fit the corporate understandings of established Christianity. Rather, they brought to mind the ideas of assembly, congregation, convention—ideas resonant with the root word *ekklesia* and the ideas of public in the republican theorists of the day.

While a small number of theologians were able to grasp this eruption of religious experience in the early-nineteenth century as a fundamental ecclesiological change (or renewal, if you will), most people understood these "great awakenings" as matters of individual experience—a psychological revolution. Thus, it was difficult to interpret the ecclesiological shift as an issue both for theology and society. Individualism rather than a sense of the total system of organized relationships carried the day. The meaning of these new understandings of organizational relationships—a shift from the hierarchy of command to a covenant or compact of distinct but related publics—was overwhelmed by individualistic concepts of personal experience.

Like these religious assemblies, the public meetings, conventions, and conferences typical of the early republican movement also have no ongoing corporate form. They are not "constituted" in the United States Constitution and have an ambiguous status in American society despite the veneration they receive. Yet they are the ecstatic moments of inspiration without which a republic cannot be sustained. Without these "effervescent" moments[60] the ordinary barriers of family, race, class, geography, and even language cannot be bridged to create a wider republic. As a part of this republican development, American Methodism is an effort to sustain such peculiar publics within a culture which generally speaks the language of commercial individualism and legal positivism. Spontaneous publics and the "connections" that sustain them are neither real nor legally responsible. Whether this crucial reality can be sustained in such an environment is the challenge facing not only the United Methodism of the Pacific Homes case but republican orders in general.

In response to the Pacific Homes case we need to step back from the language of corporation and hierarchy and reclaim the language of assembly that energized the original Methodist movement. We then need to examine the language of "connection" more closely in the light of federalist theories. From that point we might move to an ecclesiology that can be in critical conversation with federal republican theories and practices.

How, then, might we reconstrue connection in a way that avoids misplaced corporatism as well as a fragmented congregationalism? The federalist language contains not only a heritage of political wisdom for safeguarding the vitality of republics but also leads us to its roots in the biblical notion of covenant, both of which may assist us here.

In the court case we have examined, all parties referred continuously to the *Discipline* as in fact the body of commitments constituting the connection. Indeed, it is the *Discipline* which defines the mutual accountability of the various units—including ministers, bishops, conferences, and agencies—constituting United Methodism. In that sense it is the covenant of this federal ecclesial order. However, "covenant" is not part of Methodism's original vocabulary, largely because of Methodism's origins, even though its practices are thoroughly immersed in the republican effervescence and lawlike mutual accountability typical of the covenantal tradition and its federalist expressions. If anything *is* the "connection" it is the institutional form constituted by this covenant-like document. The *Discipline* is the interim authority, rather than any bishop, president, or council, between the periodic conferences which guide the organization.

In these respects United Methodism rehearses, perhaps more explicitly, tensions and deficiencies within the American polity itself. The more one presses an emphasis on the centrality of the spirited public assembly as the practical center of the church or of a society, the more one moves to some notion of covenant as the connecting bonds within and among those publics. The more one stresses the bodily functionality of a group as a stable organism, the more one moves to some notion of headship as the connecting and representative bond. Methodism exhibits both this covenantal "connection" and this corporatism—tendencies which we see in American society generally. Its inability to give clear voice to its basic self-understanding within this tension reflects American disputes over federal order and public freedom as well as offering some illuminating points of entry into a critical engagement with them.

A federalist vision of United Methodist ecclesiology can save it from a reductionist view of connection as a corporate hierarchy and renew the role of public assembly in its ecclesiology. In this vision a vital federalism is not a pyramid of representation and command but a web of crosscutting accountabilities among a variety of publics. But these constitutional relationships are always interrupted, as it were, by the overarching commitments of the people making up the total church. Bishops interrupt to teach. Evangelistic movements offend and even bypass congregations to affect conferences. Conferences establish agencies which make demands on local congregations. This vital mix of spontaneity and order—of assembly and covenant—continuously presses the participants to articulate anew the fundamental covenant informing their constituted federal order.

Conclusion

In the many legislative changes of the past century the United Methodist Church has largely ignored fundamental issues of ecclesiology and polity. In particular the connectional covenant by which United Methodists agree to live together needs major attention from the laity, clergy, and scholars of the church. In that regard the statement "The Journey of a Connectional People" added to the *Discipline* in 1988 made a beginning, but more in the direction of exhortation than as a coherent formulation of the constitutional order of the church.[61]

We believe that an analysis of the three modes of constitutional order described above can help the church sort through some of these major ecclesiological and polity issues. We can only illustrate this with a few examples here.

First, the principles of public assembly within a federal framework require that we look at the local congregation as a participatory assembly rather than as an audience of individuals gathered for evangelistic preaching and mission activism. An ecclesial sense of assembly within a federal framework of covenantal responsibility can enhance the congregation's sense of being the fullness of church in each place through the recognition and exercise of the members' baptismal gifts. The people gathered together can then become the subject rather than the object of ministry and mission. One implication of this would be to base representation of congregations in the annual conference on the number of lay members in a congregation rather than on the number of clergy assigned to a pastoral charge.

Second, a reconstituted understanding of corporatism in ecclesiology would lead us to see the episcopacy not as an executive representative of the church but as a prophetic overseer seeking to bring to bear the mind of Christ in the midst of the people's life and faith together. As the trend continues toward the merger of annual conferences with each bishop presiding at only one conference, it will become increasingly difficult to distinguish between the bishop as executive manager of conference programs and the bishop as general superintendent assigned to a particular area within the whole connection. The integration of corporatist principles with those of assembly and federalism would enable the church to embrace more fully a model of episcopacy centered on proclamation, teaching, sacramental leadership and spiritual guidance, in short, prophetic oversight of the United Methodist people.

Third, a reformulation of the corporatist aspects of the church within a framework of assembly and federalism can also help us rethink the church's understanding of "service." While service (*diakonia*) is a fundamental practice of Christian faith, many church leaders, agencies, and programs are encouraging the church to adopt marketplace understandings of the "service industries." Thinking about the church as a service provider with clients and customers obscures the baptismal citizenship of believers as participants and actors with responsibility for their own assemblies. It also subjects the church unnecessarily to practices of corporate law whose main purpose is to protect corporations from liability in the marketplace. An ecclesiology rooted more in assembly and federal connection sees the church as an assembly of assemblies within an overarching covenant—a "political" movement anticipating God's ultimate order of governance more than a business corporation providing services within a limited market segment.

Finally, within this perspective the church must take the *Book of Discipline* itself more seriously as its primary constituting covenant. This will require that much greater care be given to the consistency between constitutional order and specific legislation within the *Discipline*. As matters stand now, few United Methodists engage the Constitution in their deliberations. Meanwhile legislative paragraphs are full of inconsistencies and uneven attention to their place within the whole. They are the record of a series of General Conference actions but not the fabric of a coherent covenant of interlocking responsibilities. When no connection is made in the *Discipline* between the chapter on the ministry of all Christians and the paragraphs on church membership, or when one looks in vain through the entire chapter on episcopacy for an ecclesiology to support the United Methodist plan of superintendency, it becomes obvious that the church has simply taken for granted some of its most basic elements.

The church needs to achieve clarity about its underlying ecclesiology for its own internal good order, but also for defining itself effectively over against the implicit ecclesiologies present in the way other institutions, especially those of law and business, view the church. Constitutional confusions within the *Discipline* spring from the effervescence of the church's numerous assemblies. We believe, however, that the time has come to attend to these dimensions of ecclesiological order, so that the church can maintain its integrity as it addresses the powerful institutions of American culture.

~ William B. McClain ~

Connectionalism requires commitment to the whole, to the larger mission, and to the center where the parts intersect and unite. Reflection on connectionalism therefore naturally focuses on polity and corporate purpose, as the two prior essays indicate. However, like a chain, the connection has been no stronger than its weakest link. Therefore to understand connectionalism also requires focusing on "links" away from the center, and particularly on Methodism in its local expression and in its resolve to live out its mission and identity. William B. McClain explores a link or set of links that seemed ever at risk, namely the attachment to Methodism of its African American membership. McClain discerns among Blacks a complex fidelity rooted in early Methodism's radical witness against slavery, its gospel of free grace, and its willingness to embrace slave as well as free, poor as well as rich, within a new communal order, but a fidelity mindful of the steady retreat that Methodism made from that witness, gospel, and community. Given Methodism's compromise of its principles, its embrace of slavery and segregation, and its toleration of injustice, why, asks McClain, did African Americans remain Methodist and why did so many stay within the Methodist Episcopal and Methodist Protestant folds? McClain indicates that they stayed to be a strong link to Methodism's better instincts and to be a witness to principles that the church as a whole so easily sacrificed. McClain concludes by asking what it would mean for United Methodism to reconnect with the African Methodist communities, who in linking themselves to Methodism's better instincts and its higher principles had been forced to disconnect themselves from white domination and intransigence. What indeed might such reconnection mean for Methodism's understanding of its purposes, for its mission, for its agenda in North America and across the globe? And what do Methodism's efforts with biracial community indicate about connectionalism? What today constitute the ethical and social expressions of connectionalism? In United Methodist self-presentation? In actuality?

African American Methodists: A Remnant and a Reminder

William B. McClain

From the earliest days of the advent of Methodism—with its peculiar and promising proclamation of the prevenience of grace—to the present, the descendants of Africa in this country have embraced Christianity as preached by the Methodists. The continued presence of African Americans in Methodism throughout its checkered career in matters of faith and practice, its acts of courage and cowardice in matters of race and justice, and its schisms and mergers as a Christian Protestant denominational body is an anomaly. African American Methodists are both a remnant of hope and a reminder of the ideal for *their* church to match its practice with its proclamation.

The Africans and Their Fierce Fidelity to Methodism

On a Sunday in April of 1787, the history of Methodism in this country would change forever. On that date, Richard Allen, Absalom Jones, and a small group of African Americans walked out of St. George's Methodist Episcopal Church in Philadelphia. The exact details of the precipitating incident are not completely clear, but seem to involve members of that group being asked to leave their places of prayer around the altar to return to the racially segregated balcony. As humiliating and painful as the departure proved to be, Allen was candid and clear in his commitment: "As for me, I could never be anything but a Methodist . . . and I am thankful that ever I heard a Methodist preacher." Allen, of course, would go on to establish and become the first bishop of the African Methodist Episcopal Church, and Absalom Jones would be the first African American Episcopal rector in America.

When Allen was asked in 1791 by his fellow members of the Free African Society, a mutual-aid, "self-improvement" association that he had helped to organize in November of 1787, to form them into an Episcopal Church, he acknowledged the honor but politely and definitely declined, using the same words: "As for me, I could never be anything but a Methodist. . . . I am glad that ever I heard a Methodist preacher." Allen, a Delaware ex-slave, had been converted under the Methodist preaching, was later licensed to preach, and had traveled the various Methodist circuits in Delaware, Maryland, and New Jersey with Richard Whatcoat, Irie Ellis, and Peter Morratte. He enthusiastically engaged in these preaching missions to spread the simple gospel of grace by which Methodism was so clearly and closely identified, and which he so personally had experienced.

No doubt Allen moved many by sharing the details of his own dramatic conversion and exhorting others to seek what he had himself found—albeit lost and found:

> I was awakened and brought to see myself, poor, wretched and undone, and without the mercy of God must be lost. Shortly after, I obtained mercy through the blood of Christ, *and was constrained to exhort my old companions to seek the Lord*. I went rejoicing for several days and was happy in the Lord, in conversing with many old, experienced Christians. I was brought under doubts, and was tempted to believe I was deceived, and was constrained to seek the Lord afresh. I went with my head bowed down for many days. My sins were a heavy burden. I was tempted to believe there was no mercy for me. I cried to the Lord both night and day. One night I thought hell would be my portion. I cried unto Him who delightest to hear the prayers of a poor sinner, and all of a sudden my dungeon shook, my chains flew off, and, glory to God, I cried. My soul was filled. I cried enough for me—the Saviour died. Now, my confidence was strengthened that the Lord, for Christ's sake, had heard my prayers and pardoned all my sins.[1]

There is little wonder what his response to the African Free Society would be when they sought to become Episcopalians and to make him their pastor:

> I cannot be anything but a Methodist, as I was born and awakened under them . . . for their plain and simple gospel suits best for any people; for the unlearned can understand, and the learned are sure to understand; and the reason that the Methodists are so successful in the awakening and conversion of the colored people is the plain doctrine and having good discipline.[2]

In spite of Allen's refusal to form the Free African Society into an Episcopal church, the Society proceeded to vote to become Episcopalians and to use the building that Allen and Jones had secured subscriptions to build as "The African Church," albeit with the clear intention of remaining within the Methodist relation. When the M.E. church rebuffed Allen by refusing to supply a minister, he proceeded to move an old blacksmith shop to a lot he owned and renovated it to become a place of worship—*a Methodist place of worship.*

Allen adds later in his recounting of the situation and his view about the offer: *"I was confident there was no religious sect or denomination that would suit the capacity of the colored people as well as the Methodists,* for the plain and simple gospel suits best for any people. . . ."[3]

Richard Allen's staunch loyalty to Methodism, and his tenacious commitment to the Wesleyan particular and peculiar understanding and expression of the Christian faith, is but one dramatic example of the fierce fidelity and the extraordinary bond that has characterized his and so many millions of other African Americans' devotion to the Methodist Church from its inception. Although he left the Methodist Episcopal Church to found an African Church, the new church was thoroughly Methodist in its doctrine, polity, theology, and practice.

What was true of Allen was to be so of other African Americans who departed at later times: James Varick and Peter Williams from John Street Church in New York to form the African Methodist Episcopal Zion Church a few years later, and the black Methodists who petitioned the General Conference meeting in New Orleans in 1866 after the Civil War to form a Colored Methodist Episcopal Church. The latter church was formed in 1870 in Jackson, Tennessee, and changed its name to Christian Methodist Episcopal Church in 1954.[4]

American Methodist Faith and the African Presence

Just as can be said of their presence in the Christian Church when it was born at Pentecost (see Acts 2), Africans have been a part of the Methodist Church in the United States from its very beginning. In fact, the two Antiguans Wesley baptized at Bristol in 1758—I have elsewhere called them the "Holy Nameless Two"[5]—can be credited with being the first Methodists in North America. These two were so moved by the simple gospel of grace John Wesley preached that they went home and converted their master, Nathaniel H. Gilbert, then returned to Antigua to establish the first Methodist Chapel in this hemisphere, in the West Indies.

When Methodism had its beginning in the United States, Annie Sweitzer was there at Sam's Creek in Frederick County, Maryland, with Robert Strawbridge, in the first meeting of the first Methodist society in colonial America. Two years later, Black Bettye was there as one of the five people in New York when Philip Embury held the first Methodist service at Barbara Heck's house. Several black subscribers were on the roster of membership paying their part when the John Street Church built the first meeting house in 1768. Margaret, Rachel, and several other African servants were on the list of contributors to the fund for building the John Street Chapel.[6]

The Prominence of Harry Hoosier

Richard Allen and Harry Hoosier were at Lovely Lane in Baltimore, Maryland when the Christmas Conference was convened to organize the Methodist Episcopal Church in 1784, although they were there as lay preachers—as were so many others. In fact, "Black Harry," as he was familiarly known and referred to by his associates, had gone up and down the East coast with Coke and Asbury spreading the news of the impending organizing Christmas Conference.

Harry Hoosier, born a slave near Fayetteville, North Carolina, around 1750, heard the eminent British Methodist preacher, Francis Asbury, preach and was converted. He was soon licensed to preach. Although he could neither read nor write, he refused to allow Richard Allen to teach him. He reportedly told Allen: "I sing by faith, pray by faith, and do everything by faith; without faith in Jesus Christ I can do nothing."[7]

Many of those who were quite literate in his day testified to Harry Hoosier's utterly amazing eloquence and ability, and to what his professed faith apparently enabled him to do. Abel Stevens, in his first volume of *History of the Methodist Church*, quotes one of those learned observers' commendation of his "preaching abilities, complete command of his voice, aptness in language, and free delivery, as to Scripture and doctrinal truth."[8] Dr. Benjamin Rush, a noted physician of Philadelphia and one of the signers of the Declaration of Independence, a leading abolitionist and friend of African Methodists, heard him preach and made the comment about Hoosier: "Making allowances for his illiteracy, he was the greatest orator in America."[9] Bishop Thomas Coke paid the highest tribute of all to Hoosier: "Any story of the beginning of Methodism in America which does not give a prominent place to Harry Hoosier, familiarly called 'Black Harry,' is inadequate. Surely he deserves a place in Methodism's Hall of Fame."[10]

African American Methodists: A Staunch Loyalty

By the time the Civil War split the nation into northern and southern fragments with the church divided into corresponding regional parts, there were over 200,000 African Americans who claimed fierce loyalty and utter devotion to the southern Methodist church. That number was reduced to a little more than 78,000 in 1866, owing to the numbers of black Americans who defected to the "African" churches as the Union Armies opened up new territories for the northern African Methodist evangelists to crusade and urge these black Methodists to join the independent churches as a badge of their freedom.

But even in the face of the implications and the contradictory realities, they remained in the church, both North and South, and probably would have all said as Richard Allen had said seventy-five years earlier: "As for me, I could never be anything but a Methodist. . . . And I am thankful that ever I heard a Methodist preacher." It was a part of that group whose descendants are the African American constituency of the contemporary United Methodist Church, the heirs of Harry Hoosier and the makers of Zoar, the loyalists and the remnant, who became "a church-within-a-church."

My colleague at Vanderbilt University, the historian Lewis Baldwin, has made the point many times in his work and writings that of the several black preachers active in the early Methodist movement who traveled the circuits, preached at the Methodist meetings, and provided spiritual leadership for their people—Richard Allen, Daniel Coker, Henry Evans, Absalom Jones, Christopher Rush, Abraham Thompson, James Varick, Harry Hoosier—all except Absalom Jones remained Methodist in some form.[11]

The Appeal of Methodism to African Americans

Why were these African Americans drawn to Methodism in the first place? What was the appeal of this nascent communion? The *Discipline of the United Methodist Church*, attempts to account for their response in its discussion of "Black People and Their United Methodist Heritage." In summary it cites (1) the Methodist tradition's evangelistic appeal; and (2) the church's attitude toward slavery.

There is little question that the simple gospel as preached by the Methodist itinerants appealed to the slaves as it did to poor white farmers, coal mine workers, and others who were the outcasts and the déclassé masses. Great numbers flocked to hear the good news, and they expressed their feelings with cries, screams, shouts, tears, prostrations, physical convulsions, and other physical and emotional responses, including sometimes fainting and falling insensibly. John Thompson, born as a slave in Maryland in 1812, draws the clear distinction between this revivalist preaching and the more ritualistic and staid approach of the established church:

> My mistress and her family were all Episcopalians. The nearest church was five miles from our plantation and there was no Methodist Church nearer than ten miles. So we went to the Episcopal Church, but always came home as we went, for the preaching was above our comprehension, so we could understand but little that was said. But soon the Methodist religion was brought among us, and preached in a manner so plain that the wayfaring man, though a fool, could not err therein. This new doctrine produced great consternation among the slaveholders. It was something which they could not understand. It brought glad tidings to the poor bondsman; it bound up the broken-hearted; it opened the prison doors to those that were bound, and let the captives go free. As soon as it got among the slaves, it spread from plantation to plantation, until it reached ours, where there were but few who did not experience religion.[12]

But as Donald Mathews has pointed out in so much of his careful writing and research, "Methodist ideology was also a collage of sound, symbol, and act. It was style and mood evinced in oral communication."[13] Some people who observed it and opposed its expression called it noise. One such man in New Bern, North Carolina, in 1807 makes his feelings especially clear, but also gives us a picture of the scene of this *communitas*, which he condemned and called "farcical":

> About a week past there was a methodist conference in this place which lasted 7 or 8 days & nights with very little intermission, during which *there was a large concourse of people of various colors, classes and such*, assembled for various purposes. Confusion, shouting, praying, singing, laughing, talking, amorous engagements, falling down, kicking, squealing and a thousand other ludicrous things prevailed most of the time and frequently of nights, all at once—In short, it was the most detestable *farcical* scene that ever I beheld.[14]

The initial strong stance the Methodists took against slavery is well known. The fact that the church compromised its principled position is even better known and has had more serious consequences. My late colleague at Wesley Theological Seminary, Clarence Goen, in a book that has not received the reading it deserves, called it *Broken Churches, Broken Nation*.[15] But the church initially was ardent in its anti-slavery posture, and that hardly escaped the African slaves' attention.

Perhaps the clearest evidence of how the slaves felt about the Methodists and their stance on slavery is seen in the account of the Gabriel Prosser slave revolt in Virginia. Prosser, convinced on religious grounds—perhaps the influence of the evangelical Methodists—that slavery should be overturned, and that he had been chosen by God to be a deliverer of his people, planned a rebellion. His plan was to destroy Henrico County and to establish a new black kingdom in Virginia, killing whites and looting the treasury at Richmond, taking all necessary arms and artillery. In Gabriel's testimony we find him a serious student of the Bible, twenty-five years old, with unusual physical strength and impressive mental capacities. It was a well-planned revolt in which Gabriel said he had ten thousand men ready to go into battle. The plot failed because of logistical problems, frightened and fearful slave informers, and a serious storm. And Gabriel, along with several other slaves, was hanged. But central to our point here was Gabriel's instruction concerning the two groups of Christians he believed to be on God's side against the evil and un-Christian practice of slavery: "All Methodists and Quakers were to be spared."

Clearly, Gabriel knew of the Methodist stance against slavery. And some would maintain that it was through the itinerant Methodist ministers who went back and forth from circuit to circuit that information was transmitted to the insurgents. The point here is that the Methodists were known for their stance against slavery, and even though the church was to compromise later, the slaves were won over by this stance and encouraged by the church's opposition to slavery. John Wesley had expressed it in 1743 in the original *General Rules*, and the Christmas Conference of 1784 had adopted this strong position against the institution of slavery.

Such early Methodist preachers as Francis Asbury, Freeborn Garrettson, Thomas Rankin, Ezekiel Cooper, and Thomas Coke were inspired by the moral claims of John Wesley against slavery, and took rather seriously Wesley's mandate and answer to the question of what could be expected of Methodists: "to reform the nation, and especially the church, and spread scriptural holiness throughout the land."

These circuit riders were evangelically enthusiastic in their commitment to preach the principles of free grace available to all and freedom from slavery, in spite of the pressures of social and economic realities. Lewis Baldwin cites an important grievance of Asbury, who, in one of his journal entries, complained that Methodists often had serious problems gaining access to slaves because "their masters are afraid of the influence of our principles."[16]

At first it was the English-born Methodist preachers such as Asbury, Rankin, and Coke who led the vigorous anti-slavery struggle, but then preachers who were born on American soil came along and took up the charge against slavery. For example, on the Delmarva Peninsula there was Joseph Everett, a Methodist preacher who not only preached against slavery, but also refused to eat with slaveholders until they freed their slaves. In a study of Methodism in that region, William H. Williams, a history professor at the University of Delaware at Georgetown, has discovered:

> In 1797, an Episcopal rector in Talbot County [Maryland], observed that the Methodist preachers "relish the manumitting subject as highly as the Quaker preachers and spread the evil far and wide." In Somerset County, in 1801, a circuit rider told his congregation to assume that "the clouds of vengeance are collecting over the heads of the inhabitants of this country for their cruelty to the poor distressed Africans."[17]

In addition to these two factors, I think there were some others: namely, (3) the style of preaching and worship appealed to the slaves; (4) slaves were allowed to serve as lay preachers and exercised considerable influence among Blacks and Whites, despite the restrictions on their movement, function, and opportunities for leadership; and (5) Methodism was adaptable enough to fit their own unique situation so that they could make it their own. I will not amplify these any further in this essay. I have discussed these in earlier writings, and at considerable length in *Black People in the Methodist Church: Whither Thou Goest?*

The Romance Between African Americans and Methodism

Our question at the moment is not why they *came*, but why African Americans have *stayed* in what is now the United Methodist Church throughout this checkered history of dealing with the issues of race and justice. Why would a people continue to be part of a church that compromised its principles on slavery to the developing American culture and to a strange economic system that incorporated manifest destiny? Why did they remain when, in a pernicious plan unworthy of Machiavelli, they were officially segregated into a separate "church-within-a church" for the first time in their almost 175-year long history associated with Methodism? Why did African Americans endure the demeaning institutional machinery set in motion to effect this humiliating "church-within-a-church" contrivance? Why have African Americans remained Methodists when the church they love so often puts convention above conscience, is so often more concerned about unity than about uniqueness, and is more willing to conform than to create? Why have they remained faithful to a church when what they perceived as a genuinely decorous romance has so often been made into a sordid affair—unrequited and contemptible? What have African Americans contributed to this romance and to this church—a church whose history is so filled with missed opportunities to be uniquely Christian, a world church in America, and whose failures in one period have so often negated its success in another? And what of United Methodism's future as we close a century that Methodism began with the rather correct, if dubiously-based claim to be the largest and "most American Church?"

First, it needs to be said that the United Methodist Church is not alone in the problems it currently faces. It is well known, and there is more documentation than we need to review here,[18] that the predominantly white, organized, connectional Protestant Christian bodies in the western world are in the same predicament. They all face aging and declining memberships and a loss of enthusiasm about their unique claims and identity. They listen to straying, struggling, and competing apologists, a call for a more interiorized and privatized form of religion with an attending self-fulfillment ethic, and conflicting and confusing messages about what salvation means—salvation *from* what and *to* what. As they produce fewer zealous youths, the lack of loyalty and support both from so many who are their mainstay and those who are their natural heirs threaten their very existence.

Present Methodism: A Positive Difference

Part of the positive difference for Methodism and the promise for its future may lie in the very perils of its past and its present. Its hope for vision and fulfillment may be inherent in the solutions found to one of *its most pressing present problems—its perspective on and its practice of inclusiveness*. I do not merely offer this as alliterative poetry, but a solid prophetic reality: Methodism is still the most multicultured church in the nation: pluralistic, democratic, and with the means within its particular and diverse theological, historical, homiletic, liturgical, and ecclesial tradition, and the human resources to forge a new and creative history. But, oh the will to face the dilemma! It will need to drink fresh water from old clean springs, and purify those streams from the left and the right that have been polluted and poisoned by a non-yielding, intolerant, contemporary fundamentalism (that is, focusing on non-essential issues of faith with efforts to dominate and control the symbols of legitimacy, while offering non-dialogical, iron-clad theological absolutes). Such fundamentalism becomes even more of an impediment when it is linked to a very conservative political and free-market ideology.

Why Have African Americans Remained in the Church?

But the theological debate is not our primary concern and consideration in this essay. And yet, to be the totally inclusive community which Methodism espouses—in obedience to its Lord—and that church which African Americans have so long dreamed of, hoped for, worked for, and constantly called the church back to, we must be aware of the impediments. To be biblically centered is one thing. To be fundamentalist is another. African American Methodists have not historically viewed Scripture as the fundamentalists do. Rather, they have seen the Bible as the story of divine redemption of the natural and the human realms, a story of God's constant overture to reclaim straying and lost creation, and the expression of God's willingness to get *to* us by getting *with* us. It is not a textbook for science, the chest of rigid moral codes upon which we can structure a society, nor the repository of proof-texts, but the story of human experiences with God in which they can identify. One need only look at the African American spirituals, for example, to see this epitomized. They also are the quintessence of the important role hermeneutics and reading strategies play in appropriating Scripture.

I think that one can safely say that African American Methodists have not too very closely identified theologically with the liberal left or the conservative right, but certainly not ever with the literalists and the fundamentalists. If a label could be placed on them at all, it would probably be that of *evangelical essentialists*. That is to say, they have separated out of the faith that which is essential and substantial from that which is accidental and peripheral. They have dwelt with and accented that which is at the center or the essentials of the faith, and not what is at the edges and the boundaries. For them, Jesus, the liberating Word, the one who brings freedom and justice, the one who identifies with the poor and the disinherited, the one who gives a perspective on sets of facts and makes them truth, is essential.

A Belief in the Gospel They Heard

So, we can say first of all, *the African Americans have stayed because they believe that God is for real in Jesus Christ as revealed both in Scripture and in their experience.* They believe that the gospel of grace, the glad tidings of Jesus—of love, redemption, and release—that they heard from the Methodist preacher, was not merely an enticement to increase numbers or to make them more serviceable, obedient, and subservient to an earthly master, but was instead the very grand and royal invitation of the Word of God to come and accept their God-offered place as valuable creatures, created by a loving God who has made them "a little lower than the angels," and "a little less than God" (Psalm 139). Their dignity, worth, freedom, and identity were bestowed upon them at birth and could be claimed through the complete transaction of God through Christ at Calvary. That was at once humbling and gratifying, freeing and joy-producing, but also obliging and disciplining. But more than anything, it was for certain, "good news, the kingdom's comin'."

Further, they understood that the action of the gospel of grace broke down every barrier that separated, made distinctions, or divided those who recognize and receive that grace. Those first black women at Bristol believed it. Annie Sweitzer at Sam's Creek believed it. Bettye at the John Street society believed it. Harry Hoosier believed it, sang it, prayed and eloquently preached it with faith, power, and passion from the flowering hills of North Carolina to the teeming northeastern shores of the Atlantic in Massachusetts. Millions of African Americans have been in Methodist meetings and continue to come to Methodist churches and offer their fierce loyalty to the church because they heard and believe the promise that the love of God in a crucified and risen Lord welcomes, pardons, cleanses, and relieves. And many now, and many thousands gone, witness to their own experience that those whom Christ frees are free, indeed! As they say so often in words heard in churches and chapels from one coast to the other: "The world didn't give it to me, and the world can't take it away."

To Claim Their Own History and Heritage

Second, *African Americans have remained in the United Methodist Church because they feel that the church is as much theirs as anybody else's.* The history of John Wesley and African Americans begins in South Carolina in 1737 when Wesley sought to instruct the Africans in the Christian faith he met when he crossed over from Savannah to the colony of South Carolina. This pre-dates the first Methodist Society meeting in Frederick County, Maryland by almost 30 years. But as I have indicated earlier, when that society was formed with Robert Strawbridge at Sam's Creek in 1764, Annie Sweitzer, referred to as "Aunt Annie," a slave of the Sweitzer family, was entered as a charter member. That was true of Bettye, an African, at the John Street Society in New York in 1776 when they met at Barbara Heck's house. By 1789, seventy of the 360 members of the New York group of Methodists were African Americans. The African Americans, slaves and free, who joined the movement not only participated in the services, gave to the building funds, and attended and led the class meetings, but these new African American Methodists preached and evangelized. Slaves, ex-slaves, free and indentured servants preached and converted wherever and whenever possible.

Henry Evans, a free African American and an early preacher, established Methodism in Fayetteville, North Carolina, and served that mixed church until he died. Bishop Capers points out that Evans "was confessedly the father of the Methodist Church, white and black, in Fayetteville, and the best preacher of his time in that quarter."[19] He sustained beatings for preaching to Whites until they defended him and urged him to stay and serve them. In his last sermon and his farewell to his congregation, the old man appeared from his quarters. Capers, who had come as his replacement tells the story in reverent detail:

> The little door between his humble shed and the chancel where I stood was opened and the dying man entered for a last farewell to his people. He was almost too feeble to stand at all, but supporting himself by the railing of the chancel, he said: "I have come to say my last word to you. It is this: 'None but Christ. Three times I have had my life in jeopardy for preaching the Gospel to you. Three times have I broken the ice on the edge of the water and swam across Cape Fear to preach the Gospel to you. And now, if in my last hour I could trust to that or to any thing else but to Christ crucified, for my salvation, all should be lost and my soul perish forever."[20]

With such faith and passion, African Americans witnessed to their bonding to Christ and the Methodist Episcopal Church.

Grant Shockley has pointed out that "the thousands of black converts who accepted Christianity as their religion and Methodism as their denomination represented one of the largest non-white accessions to the Christian church in North America."[21] These African American Methodists claimed the Methodist Church as their church and they refused to be "defined out" of Methodism on racial grounds. It is their church. Its failures as well as its achievements are part of their history as well. The choice to stay is as much an exercise of freedom as the choice to leave. And for those African Americans who have stayed, the choice to stay is a more viable option of their freedom. It is their church, their spiritual home. They will witness where they are. And they have chosen to stay and weather the enticements and the embarrassing criticisms, insults, humiliation, taunts, and jibes from other African Americans—sometimes from those well-meaning brothers and sisters, the African and colored Methodists who chose to depart. But as for those who chose to stay, the United Methodist Church is as much their church as anybody else's.

To Be A Missional Presence

Third, the *African Americans have remained because they have felt their presence is required.* Their understanding of the Bible and the meaning of the Christian community is that it is made up of people from every nation and station—just as it was at Pentecost. It is not fortuitous that African American United Methodists *initiated,* and joined with other ethnic-minority theologians (Asian, Hispanic-Latino, and Native Americans) and certain invited Euro-Americans for two quadrennia in, the Roundtable of Ethnic Theologians and issued their report in a publication: *Out of Every Tribe and Nation.*[22]

These ethnic theologians have met to experience the native settings of each other: in a sweat lodge in Arizona, to the accompaniment of mariachis in San Antonio, in a Korean church in Chicago with an Asian ambience, and to the beat of ancient spirituals on black St. Helena Island in South Carolina. To leave would deprive Methodism of this authenticity as the Church of Jesus Christ where people of God of every tribe and nation, every hue and language, from the East and from the West, occidental and oriental gather together around the Word and the Sacraments. To leave would mean an empty seat at the roundtable. To leave would deprive the church of that peculiar voice that is theirs in the conversation about what God's grace means and in making known what God is doing in the world, the reading of the "signs of the times," as seen through their eyes and experienced in their hearts and souls. This group of theologians has resolved to continue to meet. For it is the decided wisdom of the Roundtable that such voices must be heard from every tribe and nation.

But even while African American United Methodists existed in separate congregations, they have been not only a protest but also a testimony that segregation, racism, mistreatment, discrimination, a Central Jurisdiction, or nothing else can dissuade them from, as Shockley puts it: "their bonding to Christ and the church through Wesleyan, as well as Episcopal Methodism. This attitude was not a fleeting one or limited to that [any] generation. It has persisted since the late 1700s to the present."[23] For they believe that "the redeemed of the

Lord ought to say so" by joining with others who "are being saved" for the upbuilding of the church, and as a sign of the presence of the reign of God, and the coming of the "beloved community" of God. Their presence is necessary so that "all flesh shall see it together." They believe that it is a part of their mission and a part of their ability to help the church keep before it what are priorities and what is essential for the church to be the church, lest it allow itself to forge an unholy and unhealthy union with the culture and betray its Lord.

The Primordial Conscience of Methodism

Fourth, *African Americans have remained to be the conscience of United Methodism*. From the very beginning, African Americans have believed that the church would somehow rise above the accidents of race, the ephemerality of station, the changing and shifting political ideologies of the nation, and *be* the church. When that has not been the case, as has happened so often in Methodism's more than two and a half centuries, African Americans have raised again and again the cry: Let the church be the church!

We hear that cry from Richard Allen and those who left with him at Philadelphia. We hear that cry as the church splits into North and South over the issue of slavery. We hear that cry at Kansas City while the white members of the church stand to celebrate its victory of an ultimate compromise to segregation and a Central Jurisdiction for structural unity. We hear that cry now as the church hedges and hesitates to practice its own principled policy of inclusiveness and open itinerary. And that cry is implicitly stuck in the throats of the rainbow-colored Methodists each Sunday morning at 11 o'clock as local churches gather in the most segregated hour of the week—unlike the jobs they go to, the schools where they study, or the sports or entertainment events they have attended during the week.

African American United Methodists have seen many changes take place as a result of their persistent prodding and pushing the church. Their presence in the church has indelibly influenced every decade and development of the church and its life in America and its ability to effect change in the larger society: black bishops elected to serve the whole church, black superintendents to administer districts that include all United Methodists in their region, national boards and agency executives, and annual conference staff personnel (often to avoid appointing well-qualified African Americans to majority-white-membership churches), a few African American pastors serving predominantly white local churches, and a hymnal that includes many songs from the African American tradition that are being sung in churches all over the nation and the world.

A Future?

So, can we now see reflected in the local United Methodist churches the hues of all of the "people who are called Methodists" who reside in those towns and cities? As United Methodists, can we reach out to the *separated* African Americans who call themselves *Methodists* too? Can we restructure the United Methodist Church, alter its attitudes and practices, and say: "Please come back! We are ready to *be* the church?" Will we?

If we cannot do that, what word do we have for other African Americans or the many other persons who people our cities, populate our towns, and live in our rural communities, who are unchurched and languish in doubt, despair, disorder, and unfreedom? What hope can we offer for reconciliation, a restored people, a redeemed world, the beloved community? What word do we have for the brothers and sisters who have no faith, no confidence, and no interest in the church or the Christ it represents? That is the challenge to Methodism as we turn to another millennium. That reaching out, restoring, reclaiming, and proclaiming may be the real future of Methodism in America. The growth, the survival, and even the justification for the very raison d'être of *United* Methodism (certainly a misnomer!) may well depend upon it.

~ Bradley J. Longfield ~

Received historical wisdom credits Methodist growth in American society to connectionalism, and particularly to its effective system of evangelization—itinerancy, appointment, circuit-development, strategic expansion, use of the vernacular, aggressive recruitment of leadership, and reliance on lay offices. Connectional engagement with American society by no means abated when the circuit rider dismounted, as Bradley Longfield shows in this exploration of why the Methodist denomination invested so heavily in higher education, and particularly in the establishment of universities. The university served as both vehicle for and expression of a Methodism that would take a contributing, even leading, place in American society. It emblemmed a new style of connectionalism, one that depended on an educated leadership, that expressed value in monetary terms, that aspired to gentility and cultural respect, that increasingly centralized and nationalized its decision- and policy-making. Such a new connectional agenda some Methodists found objectionable, particularly because of the new distinctions that it drew within. To those lines of distinction and to the increasingly bourgeois perspective with which Methodism operated, the holiness movements protested. But the fault line within Methodism ran deeper, Longfield suggests, than the size of the 'come-outer' population might suggest. So Methodist universities and the church's organization of itself to found and support them become, for Longfield, a useful lens on Methodism's late-nineteenth-century internal war. He finds that war to have had several fronts. To change the image, university-founding posed distinctive futures for the church, whether to be urban or rural, regionalized or centralized, denominational or ecumenical. What ought its identity, its mission, its ecclesial self-expression to be? What was to be lost and what gained by Methodism's investing of itself so lavishly and wholly in educational enterprise? What was to be lost and what gained by closing the door on the educational opportunities? Were there genuine alternatives?

Methodist Identities and the Founding of Methodist Universities

Bradley J. Longfield

Standard treatments of Methodist involvement in higher education point almost unanimously to the lack of college education and antipathy to formal higher education among many early American Methodists.[1] Granted, there is always a nod at the efforts of Coke and Asbury in the opening of Cokesbury College in 1787, but after the school burned, Asbury's comment that, "The Lord . . . called not the Methodists to build colleges," seemed to sum up general sentiment.[2] By 1830 Methodists did begin to join in the college-founding frenzy that those of a more Reformed bent had pioneered, so that by the advent of the Civil War Methodists oversaw 34 colleges, second only to Presbyterians.[3]

Given this comparatively slow start in support of higher education in America, the fact that nine nationally-recognized universities currently claim some relation to the Methodist Church is remarkable.[4] While all mainline denominations claim colleges—some very good colleges—within the denominational family, none comes near the number of universities that the Methodist Church counted or counts as partners. American, Boston, Drew, Duke, Emory, Northwestern, Southern Methodist, Syracuse, University of Southern California, and Vanderbilt—to name only the most prominent—all have Methodist roots. Though some of these schools were universities in name only until well into the twentieth century, the fact that American Methodists, once so averse to higher education, aspired to university-building in the late-nineteenth and early-twentieth centuries is itself evidence that a profound shift in Methodist identity was underway.

While some historians of higher education have investigated the place of religion in higher education in the "age of the university," this concern has been primarily from the perspective of the university. Little has been done to examine the dynamics involved in denominationally-related efforts to found universities. The enormous amount of time and money that some individuals invested in these schools suggests the significant symbolic—not to mention material—importance that many perceived in these institutions. As such, Methodist efforts in higher education provide a largely untapped resource for examining the identity, or identities, of Methodism at the turn of the twentieth century.

A study of Methodist efforts in university-building in the late-nineteenth and early-twentieth centuries reveals significant identity crises within Methodism generated or aggravated by changes in Methodist denominations and American culture in this era. Individuals and the denominations themselves struggled to define themselves in the midst of tensions sparked by growing differences of education, class, geography, and ecclesiology within these denominations and by the changing status of Methodism from outsiders to insiders in the cultural establishment. These tensions existed not simply between but also within individuals and groups as the Methodist Episcopal Church and the Methodist Episcopal Church, South came ever more into the cultural and ecclesiological mainstream.

One key reason for Methodist prominence in university education is that Methodists came of age economically in the era of university building.[5] By the middle of the nineteenth century, Methodists had become not only the largest denominational fellowship in the nation but also the wealthiest, with total assets of almost $15 million.[6] In the years after Appomattox, upwardly-mobile urban Methodists began displaying their wealth by building large, ornate churches in residential areas.[7] In an era when universities—as opposed to liberal arts colleges— were just being formed in the United States, one place that some Methodists decided to put their new-found wealth, in addition to church structures, was in universities.[8] But given the fact that it took large sums of money to create and maintain a university, the question still lingers as to why universities caught the imagination of Wesley's heirs. While Rockefeller, Stanford, and Vanderbilt certainly provided a model for such philanthropy, rich Methodists did not have to follow suit. Except in the case of Princeton, which was never administratively linked to the Presbyterian Church, Presbyterians, for example, did not work to transform their colleges into major universities or to build new universities in this era. Part of the difference, it seems, may be attributed to the changing status of Methodists from outsiders to insiders in the Protestant establishment in the nineteenth century.[9]

Insider vs. Outsider

The university seems to have had an especial allure for Methodists, not least because, as Donald Marti has suggested, they had been criticized for so long by educated Reformed Protestants who looked askance at the dearth of formal education among Methodist pastors.[10] As cultural and religious insiders, Presbyterians, for example, did not feel the need to establish their own universities in the late-nineteenth century. After all, by this time they had been the educational establishment in America for over a century.[11] But some Methodists, as historical outsiders in the world of education, felt a particular compulsion to establish landmarks of education, cathedrals of learning, at least in part to demonstrate their arrival among the cultural elite.[12] Thus, in 1891 Henry Buttz, president of Drew Theological Seminary, cited the schools, colleges, and theological seminaries of the Methodist Episcopal Church as key evidence that the church was a "great Church," "one whose success . . . has been such as to lead to its general recognition as an important factor in the world's progress."[13]

Historian Richard Bushman has drawn the connection between humble Methodist beginnings and its later preoccupation with ornate church structures and an educated clergy. In *The Refinement of America* he claims, "The plebeian beginnings of the Methodists . . . made the construction of tasteful churches all the more urgent for a later generation of cultivated members. . . . Methodist churches came to be made up of well-dressed worshippers, sitting in beautiful structures, listening to educated ministers."[14] For many Methodists by the late-nineteenth century, a college degree, no less than dignified church architecture and genteel dress, served as a crucial emblem of the arrival of Methodism in the cultural mainstream.

As such, when, in 1867, the trustees of the Biblical Institute in Concord, New Hampshire, moved the school to Boston, talk of building a university around the school immediately began to surface as a means of boosting the educational, social, and professional status of Boston Methodists.[15] This was the era when, as E. Digby Baltzell has noted, "club and educational affiliations, rather than family position and accomplishment alone" established one in the upper classes.[16] Isaac Rich, Jacob Sleeper, and Lee Claflin, three Boston Methodists who had earned fortunes but nevertheless felt like outsiders among the Boston elite, gave generously to Boston University as one means of separating themselves from the hoards of new immigrants and emphasizing their "Protestantism and their Yankee heritage."[17]

Part and parcel of this concern to establish Methodist credentials was the desire to influence the culture. When the Methodist Episcopal Church, South, was struggling to maintain its control of Vanderbilt in the early-twentieth century, Bishop Warren Candler argued that the struggle provided the "opportunity to save . . . in a measure, the entire South from the ruinous effects of secularized and godless culture."[18] Likewise, supporters of American University in Washington, D.C., envisioned it as "a powerful ally in the fierce battle which is being waged between skepticism and infidelity on the one hand and the Christian faith on the other."[19]

This concern for higher education as a means of establishing Methodist cultural credentials and cementing Methodist influence in the culture was not, however, reflected in all Methodist circles. Northwestern University, for example, had been founded by Chicago Methodists in 1851 to provide for education in the expanding region. But in 1884, as enrollments at Northwestern dropped, President Cummings reported to his Board of Trustees that Methodists nationally had only one student in college for every 1,000 members. This placed them fifth in the line of mainline denominations, behind Episcopalians, Baptists, Presbyterians, and Congregationalists.[20] Even granted the small percentage of Americans who attended college in this era, Methodists found themselves significantly underrepresented on college and university campuses compared to other mainline denominations.

This stunning disjunction between those Methodists who supported universities and the vast majority of Methodists who were either unwilling or unable to invest time or money in higher education betrays, it seems, a stark division within Methodism as to the importance of higher education in the Christian life. Given that the early-American-Methodist antipathy to higher education persisted among many Methodists through the nineteenth century, a split personality emerged within Methodism as a denomination that at once favored and disparaged education.

Richard Hofstadter, in *Anti-Intellectualism in American Life*, in fact lifts up Methodist attitudes toward education as an "illustration of the divided soul of American religion."[21] As Hofstadter notes, Methodists had, throughout the nineteenth century, held divergent positions on the value of education. While some supported the founding of Methodist academies and an educated ministry, others, such as the renowned evangelist Peter Cartwright, worried that education would lead to an anemic faith and a weakened church.[22] The push for education among Methodists, Hofstadter argues, was strongest in New

England and weakest in the South and on the frontier, leading to ongoing debates about the proper identity of Methodism. He summarizes:

> As Methodism diffused throughout the country, along the frontier and into the South, in a milieu less demanding of educational performance, its original dissent from the respectable, the schooled, and the established kept reasserting itself, but its own success again compelled it to wage a battle against the invading forces of gentility. In a more decentralized church, each locality might have been more free to set its own character, but in a denomination with the formidable centralization of the Methodists, the fight over the cultural tone of the church became general.[23]

These debates over the cultural and intellectual identity of Methodism did not evaporate in the late-nineteenth century. Rather, in the face of the founding of Methodist universities, many Methodists, it appears, simply voted with their feet and failed to attend these schools. In one sense, of course, they were no different in this than the bulk of Americans of the era, who did not pursue higher education. But in another sense, especially in relation to their mainline peers, Methodists did make a statement about their view of the value of universities and the Methodist relationship to the educated, cultural elite. Though increasing numbers of Methodists were, by the turn of the twentieth century, supporting an educated ministry, Methodists in general were clearly not of one mind on the need for or value of higher learning.

Newly-Rich vs. Middle Class

The tension within Methodism between those who would build universities and those who would not or could not use them, was reflected in the support of many Methodists for these schools. In the wake of the renowned separation of Vanderbilt from the Southern Church in 1914, the General Conference recommended that the church should found two Methodist universities, one east of the Mississippi and one to the west.[24]

The choice of Emory as one of these schools—due to Asa Candler's Coca Cola fortune—was nothing short of a foregone conclusion. Bishop Warren A. Candler, former president of Emory, had been named chair of the Educational Commission formed by the General Conference to establish these two schools. His brother, Asa Candler, was also a member of the commission. Shortly after the General Conference the board of Emory College, on which Asa Candler sat, expressed its desire to assist the commission in its work and the Atlanta Chamber of

Commerce, which could hardly ignore the desires of its past president, Asa Candler, pledged $500,000 to lure the Methodist university to Atlanta. Druid Hills, a development financed by Candler, offered seventy-five acres of land. This maneuvering was finally capped by a $1 million pledge on 16 July 1914 by Asa Candler.[25] For all intents and purposes the Candlers bought themselves a university.

Even, however, as the Candler brothers labored to build a university, they ran into a persistent lack of concern for education in the broader Methodist community. In a period of despondency with which probably any university administrator can empathize, Warren Candler wrote, "I seem to have wasted my life—especially during the last four years, during which I have toiled day and night to give the Church a university. . . . But I cannot do it, and it grieves me sorely."[26]

Likewise, when Southern Methodist University was founded in the early-twentieth century, Texas Methodists, though pledging support for the new school, failed to fulfill their promises. It seems that this reflected both lack of enthusiasm among much of the Methodist constituency for a university and unrealistic pledges by numerous small Methodist congregations.[27] The quip of one Methodist Texas cattleman that he knew "nothing about the university and care[d] less," probably reflected the sentiment of many on the range.[28]

Finally, when the Duke family began to support Trinity College and underwrote its move to Durham, North Carolina, in 1892 they expected North Carolina Methodists to follow in their generosity. But significant funds were not forthcoming and the Dukes, in the years ahead, had to plow hundreds of thousands of dollars into the school before J. B. Duke signed his indenture transforming the college into a university in 1924.[29]

While very wealthy Methodists were willing to sink significant money into higher education, Methodists of more modest means failed to support these schools with significant funds. This discrepancy suggests developing class differences within Methodism.

W. Bruce Leslie has recently argued in *Gentlemen and Scholars* that while colleges in the mid-nineteenth century were vehicles of local prestige and ethnoreligious identity, by World War I they catered to members of the growing urban Protestant upper and upper-middle classes as a means of ensuring worldly success.[30] Surveys in the 1920s suggest that family income and parental education were significant factors in college attendance, leading historian David Levine to speculate that "the son of a moderately successful businessman or professional was perhaps more than twice as likely to attend college as the son of a semi-skilled machinist" in that era.[31] Given the social and educational strata of most Methodists at the time, and a significant jump in tuition at Methodist schools in the 1920s, many Methodists probably found the cost of college more than they were willing or able to absorb.[32]

As a result, Ferdinand Lundberg, though likely overstating the case, argued in 1937 that Duke and Northwestern were among the "upper-class schools . . . that . . . cater to the offspring of the upper classes . . . or . . . aim to turn out graduates that will be, regardless of their class origin, of pecuniary value to the upper class."[33] Even given Lundberg's bias, it is clear that the increasingly upper-class tendencies of many universities would not sit well with the largely middle-class culture of American Methodism. This would be especially true in the South where economic growth and urbanization increased class stratification and social distinctions.[34]

In the late-nineteenth and early-twentieth centuries, Methodism was a church agitated by conflicting class identities and values. Many Methodists, especially urban Methodists, rose in wealth, but Methodism was still, as H. Richard Niebuhr noted in *The Social Sources of Denominationalism*, primarily a middle-class church.[35] Different conceptions about the value of higher education, especially university education, and differing abilities to pay for higher education, even if one desired it, reflect growing class differentiations within Methodist circles.

While by the turn of the century some Methodists had arrived among the upper-middle and upper classes, or were determined to make it with the help of higher education, others could see little reason for investing their time or money in universities. "If the well-off want to support universities," many Methodists seemed to say, "that is fine, but don't expect us to send our children or dollars." While Methodists of various economic classes could find a comfortable place within the Methodist tradition, efforts to found and support universities reveal deepening fissures within the church concerning the nature and mission of the church.

Universities as markers of cultural arrival spoke not only for the church, or a part of the church, then, but also to the church. By supporting university education, wealthy Methodists were encouraging their sisters and brothers in the faith to get on board the train to intellectual respectability, cultural influence, and financial security.

These differences in economic class and variant attitudes toward the cultural establishment were aggravated by growing geographic tensions in the church. As some Methodists moved to the cities and built their universities there, friction between urban and rural Methodists—and the question of the geographic identity of Methodism—also came into play.

Urban vs. Rural Methodism

When Asa Candler donated his first large gift to Emory in 1914 he did not make his donation contingent upon the location of the university in Atlanta. But the proper setting of the new school was clear enough to all concerned. Emory had been located in the town of Oxford and the move to Atlanta was an important symbolic proclamation of Methodism's arrival in the city.[36] Indeed, the ties between Emory and Atlanta were so strong that historian David Levine dubbed Emory a "prototype of the urban school."[37]

In the late-nineteenth century, mainline Protestants saw cities as both promise and threat. Cities were a threat because of the teeming urban masses who seemed to be, in large part, indifferent or even hostile to religion—at least to Protestant evangelicalism.[38] But precisely because it was assumed that the city would stand at the center of twentieth-century America, the metropolis provided a great opportunity for religious influence on the nation.[39]

Richard Bushman has argued that in the course of the nineteenth century the terms "city" and "country" became cultural markers of gentility and rudeness, of civilization and barbarism. "The terms," Bushman contends, "divided the world in half, implying refinement and polish in the city and courseness in the country. . . . City and country represented the extremes of two contrasting ways of life."[40] Methodist efforts at university building in the late-nineteenth and early-twentieth centuries highlighted the fault lines between these ways of life within Methodism as urban and rural Methodists contended for the identity of Methodism on the fields of higher education.

In 1850 some Chicago Methodists, convinced that Chicago was to be "the metropolis of the Northwest and a great center of population" resolved to found a "university in the Northwest under the patronage of the Methodist Episcopal Church."[41] Indeed the late-nineteenth and early-twentieth centuries witnessed what one historian has dubbed the "rise of Chicago in Methodism."[42] In 1852 a depository of the Methodist Book Concern was opened in Chicago and shortly thereafter the *Northwestern Christian Advocate* commenced publication.[43]

Evanston, the site of the new school, north of Chicago, was named after John Evans, a prominent Methodist physician, real estate speculator, and future territorial governor of Colorado who had been converted to Methodism by Matthew Simpson.[44] After purchase of the land, development proceeded swiftly, and in 1854 rail connections to Chicago were finished, elevating real estate values and cementing the university's ties to the city.[45]

As Emory's move to Atlanta suggests, the same urban trends were manifest among Methodists south of the Mason-Dixon line. In 1892 Trinity College, a Methodist school, moved from rural Randolph County, North Carolina, to Durham, a growing factory town.[46] The move was inspired by President Crowell's belief that inasmuch as "the main creative forces in modern society" were found in cities, Trinity needed to move to an urban area to join the cutting edge of cultural advance.[47]

A desire to enhance the prestige of Durham and a deep-seated Methodist belief in faithful stewardship had early led Washington Duke and his children, especially Benjamin Duke, to contribute to the welfare of Durham and Methodism.[48] Washington Duke, who had moved to Durham in 1874, and whose tobacco firm helped transform the town into a city, coveted a college for Durham and in 1890 outbid Raleigh for the new home of Trinity.[49] Despite opposition from Methodists in the western part of the state, the trustees decided to move.[50]

Durham, which was not only a stronghold of Methodism, but of growing Methodist wealth, particularly in the persons of Washington Duke and Julian S. Carr, looked to be promising territory for a Methodist college.[51] Durhamites in general and the Dukes in particular were conspicuous in their efforts to demonstrate to the world, and especially to the North, that Durham was fulfilling the promise of the New South.[52] Once the Dukes had brought Trinity to Durham, they could hardly let it fail, for the school's failure would look like the Dukes' failure. Trinity had become, in essence, an extension of Duke enterprises.[53]

Methodist universities marked the urban turn of Methodism not only in their geography but also in the architecture and the architects used for new campuses. The architectural firm selected for the new campuses of Duke University was Horace Trumbauer of Philadelphia, which had designed J. B. Duke's mansion on Fifth Avenue, New York, and Widener Memorial Library at Harvard.[54] For landscaping, Duke hired Olmstead Brothers of Boston, founded by Frederick Law Olmstead, designer of New York's Central Park.[55]

The actual architect for the Duke campus was Julian Abele, who had studied at the Ecole des Beaux Arts in Paris and designed Duke's East campus in Beaux-Arts fashion.[56] The Beaux-Arts system, which became popular at the 1893 Chicago World's Fair, helped inspire the City Beautiful movement, an effort of "middle- and upper-middle-class Americans . . . to refashion their cities into beautiful, functional entities."[57] The Beaux-Arts style was used not only at Duke but at Stanford, the University of Chicago, Southern Methodist University, and Emory.[58]

Despite the strong urban impulse of Methodism manifest in the university locations and architecture, not all Methodists were convinced that Methodists' new-found love affair with the city was an unmitigated blessing. The tension between urban and rural Methodists in Trinity's move from Randolph County to Durham was also a factor in the founding of Syracuse University. In the 1860s many New York Methodists, convinced that the church needed a school in a "more central position," agitated unsuccessfully to move Genesee College from Lima to Syracuse. As a result Syracuse University was chartered as a new school in 1870.[59]

These urban/rural tensions were perhaps most strongly felt in Texas in the events surrounding the birth of Southern Methodist University (SMU). In the years from 1870 to 1910, the population of Texas increased almost five-fold, and Methodism followed suit.[60] Some saw the need for a theological school closer than Vanderbilt, but Southwestern University, a Methodist school located in Georgetown, Texas, appeared to many to be poorly located for a major Methodist academy.[61]

In 1887 the *Texas Christian Advocate*, seeking a more central location, had moved from Galveston to Dallas, in 1899 a branch of the Methodist Publishing House was opened in that city, and in 1903 a medical department of Southwestern University was opened in Dallas, making the city something of a urban center for Texas Methodism.[62] Some, concerned that Methodism needed a university based in a developing urban center, wanted Southwestern to move to Dallas and, in time, Methodist and civic leaders in Dallas and Forth Worth began a bidding war to move the college.[63]

The trustees of Southwestern, fighting, at least in part, for the traditions of rural Methodism, refused to change location, and a plan was thus established to "build a completely new central university" which was finally placed in Dallas.[64] Southwestern remained in

Georgetown but was never to attain the stature of the new university founded in the city.

The battle over the location of SMU, as well as the fact that, as noted earlier, many Methodists did not fulfill their pledges to SMU, would seem to indicate that the stress between urban and rural Methodists amplified tensions between Methodists of different classes. As late as 1916 nearly 90% of Southern Methodists resided in rural areas, and in Texas there was significant animosity between urban and rural dwellers.[65]

One Texas Methodist, worried that the church was focusing too much on urban areas, pointedly asked in 1921, "Shall the church continue its present policy of abandonment of the rural districts and the centralizing of its work in the cities . . . or shall the church change that policy and give to the rural districts their just share of its work?"[66] Methodists from the country or small towns, who had long viewed various small town colleges—such as Trinity, Genesee, and Southwestern—as their schools, were hesitant to send their dollars into the city to the detriment of the rural institutions.

Inherent in these battles was the question of whether Methodism would be primarily an urban or rural denomination and therefore dominated by the perceived differences between urban and rural cultures. Joseph Gusfield, in his study of the American temperance movement, has argued that many rural Protestants supported the Eighteenth Amendment as a means of establishing "the victory of . . . rural over urban, tradition over modernity, the middle class over both the lower and upper strata."[67] Though Gusfield perhaps overstates his case, and though all Methodists supported prohibition, Gusfield's claim does lend support to the belief that the Methodist denominations may well have been agitated by growing friction between rural and urban, as well as middle-class versus upper-class, constituencies.

While many in Methodism enthusiastically embraced the urban turn of the denomination, others reflected a desire to keep the denominational schools, and their children, close to the land. As Bushman noted about Americans in general, "City and country were like social classes, separate but engaged, and the engagement had many moods: resentment, suspicion, envy, awe. The tension between these two poles was an enduring source of conflict and strain that took many twists and turns."[68]

These urban/rural conflicts, while present in all areas of the nation, seemed stronger in the South than in the North. Despite the startling growth of Southern cities after the turn of the century, the South remained overwhelmingly rural. While by 1920 more than half of the national population was urban, in the South three-quarters of the population continued to live in rural areas, giving the Southern church a much more rural cast than its Northern counterpart.[69]

Friction between the urban and rural constituencies of Methodism therefore reflected and aggravated the strain between proponents of the upper class versus middle class and elite versus populist identities of Methodism. Moreover, universities at the turn of the century manifested larger regional stresses within Methodism and the pull between regional and centralizing concerns in the denomination.

Regionalism vs. Centralization

The names of many Methodist universities—Boston, Syracuse, Northwestern, Southern Methodist, University of Southern California—betray a powerful and persistent regional emphasis within Methodism. In the past twenty years historians of higher education, most notably David Potts, have argued that local and regional pride and boosterism were critical in the founding of "denominational" colleges in the early-nineteenth century.[70] What has not been emphasized in this important revisionist trend is that denominations themselves tended to have strong regional allegiances.

In the 1850s, for example, North Carolina Methodists withdrew their support from Randolph-Macon in Virginia in order to support Trinity College.[71] Likewise, when Boston University was founded in 1869, it realized substantial financial benefits from Massachusetts Methodists to the detriment of Wesleyan University in Middletown, Connecticut.[72]

As a rule, Methodist universities conceived of themselves as regional educational centers and frequently sought to dominate the Methodist educational system in their domains. Northwestern University's first president, Clarke Hinman, for example, envisioned his school as "a great central Methodist university in the Northwest" that would receive funds and students from the region.[73] But Northwestern had difficulty overcoming strong local interests in Methodist circles. Despite Northwestern's name, for example, its efforts to solicit funds from Iowans were largely unsuccessful due to the allegiance of Hawkeyes to Iowa Wesleyan.[74]

Likewise, Southern Methodist was founded, as the name implies, with the dream of providing an academic center for those south of the Mason-Dixon line.[75] Indeed, the founders of SMU struggled over a name for the institution, but after Texas Wesleyan, Southland, Trans-Mississippi, and Central were rejected, Southern Methodist was agreed upon, perhaps revealing not a little Texas imperialism.[76] The developers of SMU wanted it to be a capstone school for Texas Methodism and to bring the other Methodist colleges into "one harmonious system" under the control of one governing board. Significantly, the other schools would hear nothing of the plan.[77]

Regional and institutional competition notwithstanding, these universities aspired to be, and for some Methodists functioned as, regional centers of loyalty in much the same way that state schools—especially their athletic teams—now provide a focus for regional allegiance within the nation more broadly.

What is particularly noteworthy, given this regionalism, is a countervailing tendency within Methodism to encourage the use of universities as national denominational centers. Vanderbilt, for example, was founded in Nashville as an effort to provide a central university for the Southern Church.[78] Perhaps the most notable example of this desire for a central university, however, is American University in Washington, D.C.

American University—as the name implies—was conceived with the intent of providing a national Methodist, or broadly Protestant, center for graduate education in the nation's capital.[79] Although it was chartered in 1893, the grandiose plans for the school and lack of popular support delayed its opening until 1914.[80]

Some of the most vocal critics of the plan were the leaders and supporters of other Methodist universities.[81] William Warren, president of Boston University, which probably understood itself to be *the* national university of the Methodist Church, was an especially adamant opponent of the new school at the time, but the eventual battle between John Fletcher Hurst, president of American University, and James Day, president of Syracuse, outdid all others in demonstrating friction within the Methodist educational system.[82]

Much to Hurst's chagrin, Day, it seems, made a practice out of canvassing churches in New York shortly before representatives of American University were to arrive. The competition for Methodist loyalty eventually degenerated into name-calling, Hurst—betraying his ambition that Methodism be perceived as an urban and urbane religion—characterized Syracuse as a "country college," and Day responded by criticizing Hurst's "impecunious" fund raising.[83]

The tension between the regional and centralizing impulses in the church resulted in the 1892 General Conference of the Methodist

Episcopal Church passing resolutions supporting American University in theory but requiring that the university secure $5 million in endowment prior to opening.[84] This requirement was eventually dropped, but opposition to a national university center ensured that the institution would never dominate the national educational network of the denomination.[85]

While the dream of an institutional center for Methodism failed, efforts at administrative centralization succeeded and continue today in the work of the University Senate.[86] In the same year that the General Conference of the Northern Church approved American University, it created the University Senate to standardize and approve Methodist schools, thus bringing a sense of national connectionalism to the church's educational institutions.[87] Presidents of the church's universities, such as William Warren of Boston, James Day of Syracuse, and Henry Rogers of Northwestern, were regular and prominent members of the Senate in its early years and heavily influenced its direction.[88]

The creation of the Senate not only manifested the increasing bureaucratization of the church in the late-nineteenth century, it also demonstrated the major influence of key individuals in the church. For years, editors of denominational papers had become college and university presidents and moved on to become bishops. The leadership of the church—and especially higher education in the church—came from a rather elite and well-networked pool. In the South, more than in the North, it appears, this network was linked by kinship but in both cases major personalities continued to play key roles in the denominations despite increasing bureaucratization.[89]

The Senate seems to have been a successful means of reconciling, or at least controlling, the conflicting tendencies toward regionalism and centralization within Methodism. While allowing individual schools to pursue their regional agendas, the Senate also allowed key educational players in the church a voice in who could represent Methodists in the educational arena and what respectable Methodist higher education entailed.

Even so, the regional and local versus centralizing impulses in Methodist higher education in this era reveal significant tensions surrounding the identity of Methodism as a connectional body. From its earliest years, American Methodism struggled to reconcile competing impulses toward centralization of authority and local or regional autonomy. The Fluvanna Conference of 1779, the O'Kelly schism of 1792, the formation of the Methodist Protestant Church in

1830, and the formation of the Methodist Episcopal Church, South in 1844 all reflected this stress between centralization and freedom.[90] More recently, there have been increasing and articulate calls in the United Methodist Church for decentralization as one response to contemporary church controversies and crises.[91]

In an era of increasing centralization and bureaucratization in the church, Methodist universities well reflected the long-standing tensions in the church about the identity of the church as a connectional body. While many in the church sought to consolidate Methodist educational programs and institutions, others understood Methodism's genius to be most authentically reflected—at least as far as colleges and universities were concerned—in a network of loosely bound institutions.

Denominationalism vs. Ecumenism

Finally, Methodist universities illumine friction within the churches concerning the identity of Methodist denominations as distinctive, even sectarian, bodies and countervailing impulses to emphasize Methodism's broadly Protestant or ecumenical concerns. These tensions reflect aspects of the earlier discussion of Methodists as insiders and outsiders in American culture—and in some sense bring us full circle—but the emphasis here is significant and discrete.

When Asa Candler donated his initial $1 million to found Emory University, he insisted that he did not "seek a sectarian end" but rather trusted his church to use the funds to promote an "evangelical and brotherly type of Christianity" which would "benefit the people of . . . [his] section and country without regard to denominational lines."[92]

At the same time, however, he claimed, as per the requirement of the General Conference of the Southern Church, that Emory University be "secured to the church beyond the possibility of alienation at any time in the future."[93] Candler wanted to have it both ways. While claiming to support a "non-sectarian" school, he insisted that it be under the perpetual control of one denomination.

This was nothing new in Methodism. From early on Methodists had at once denied sectarian intent and voiced denominational loyalty in founding colleges.[94] Indeed, as denominations developed in the United States they lived precisely in the tension between denominational cooperation and rivalry.[95] But as Methodists moved into the "age of the university" this conflict between the specifically Methodist nature of higher education and what might be called the ecumenical nature of these schools took on a new form.

Some historians of higher education have recently argued that in the course of the nineteenth century many colleges became more "denominational" in tone.[96] Depending on how one understands the nature of "denominationalism," there is good evidence for this within Methodism.

The creation of the University Senate in the North, for example, and similar efforts of the Southern Church to tighten the church-college connection in this era, brought schools under tighter administrative control.[97] Moreover, though schools became more urban in orientation, this did not always mean they were more cosmopolitan. Northwestern—for example—denied sectarian machinations as a matter of course, but the town of Evanston and the university were decidedly Methodist in tone.[98] The First Methodist Episcopal Church was the "cathedral church [of the city]," its membership included Evanston's most prominent citizens, and many of the streets of Evanston were named for Methodist saints.[99] Indeed, Frances Willard summed up the tenor of Evanston calling it a "Methodist Cambridge of the prairies."[100]

Additionally, Methodist schools such as Northwestern, Boston, Syracuse, Vanderbilt, and Trinity all became coeducational in the late-nineteenth century.[101] As David Potts has argued, the strong appeal of coeducation in Methodist schools mirrored denominational consideration of the ordination of women in this era. Though the 1880 General Conference of the Methodist Episcopal Church blocked efforts to ordain women, more than a dozen women had received local preacher's licences in the 1870s. The adoption of coeducation by Methodist institutions, contrary to most other schools at the time, thus reflected the expansion of women's roles in the denomination.[102] In significant ways, then, these schools did come under stronger bureaucratic control and reflected denominational distinctives which could point to a growing denominational emphasis.

On the other hand, as Candler's hopes for Emory point out, Methodists sought their universities to be, in a sense, ecumenical institutions, to serve without regard to denominational lines. James Day, for example, while insisting that Syracuse University was Methodist, also claimed that it was "to be far more Christian than denominational."[103]

But as Methodists became more comfortable as custodians of the Protestant establishment, this concern for tolerant ecumenism moved ever closer to a concern for a Protestant America—and thus America—in general. James Day, while claiming that Syracuse was both a

Methodist and non-denominational institution, could also look to the time when the university would be "the center of the educational system of the State of New York."[104]

The most obvious manifestation of this broadly Protestant public mission of Methodist universities is found in American University.[105] Though first dubbed the "American Methodist University," the name, revealing the founders' fear of sectarian labels and growing comfort with the American Protestant and cultural establishment, was shortened to simply "American University."[106] The General Conference, in approving the formation of the school, noted that it was "the imperative duty of the Protestant Church to provide in the city of Washington a University, Christian, catholic, tolerant, and American."[107] True to form, this broad, tolerant, Protestant, American university was to be under the control of the Methodist Church.[108]

The universities reflected perfectly, then, this tension in Methodism between the efforts to maintain distinctive denominational identity and control and the desire to be broadly Protestant—now frequently understood to mean simply American—institutions. Certainly one aspect of this dynamic is, as George Marsden has argued, that "once a college expanded its vision to become a university and to serve a broad middle-class constituency, the days were numbered when any substantive denominational tradition could survive."[109] But these tensions in Methodist higher education also point to varying conceptions of Methodist identity and Methodist relations to the culture at the turn of the century.

For some Methodists, it seems, by the late-nineteenth century, the distinction between denominational, ecumenical, and American identities appeared to have evolved to almost no distinction at all. But inherent differences did remain in some circles. While the founders of American University dropped "Methodist" from the institution's name, the university was to be under the direct control of the church. Moreover, the founders of Southern Methodist University retained the denominational label and Candler insisted that Emory, though non-sectarian, be under the church's direction.

These seemingly countervailing tendencies reflect varying conceptions of the identity of Methodism at the turn of the century and varying conceptions of the proper relationship of Methodism to the broader American culture. Sidney Mead has argued that in the years after the Civil War evangelical Protestantism and "Americanism" joined hands, leading to the "sanctification of . . . the American way of life." "The denominations," Mead claims, "eventually found themselves as completely identified with nationalism and their country's political and economic systems as had ever been known in Christendom."[110]

This may well be the case. Certainly many Methodists were becoming less concerned with denominational distinctives and more comfortable with the society. But at the same time, Methodists wanted these schools to be Methodist schools, or at least under Methodist control, revealing at least a vestigial understanding that the Methodist churches had a distinctive mission in higher education. Even granting the wide variety of motives in Methodist efforts at university building, there was, at this point, still some concern within these denominations about the identity of Methodism in relation to other denominations and American culture more broadly. Methodists wanted to be distinctive yet tolerant, a particular yet inclusive people.

Methodist universities reflected the travail of Methodism as it wrestled with the changing nature of America, and Methodist Americans, in the late-nineteenth and early-twentieth centuries. Close enough to their sectarian past to remember life as outsiders and still smarting from criticism from Reformed Protestants about anti-intellectual tendencies, many wealthy Methodists saw the formation of universities as a means to establish Methodism in the mainstream and to minister to the culture.

But as denominations in transition, within a society in transition, Methodism was riddled with tensions concerning its identity relating to education, class, geography, ecclesiology, and denominational distinctiveness and mission. While some Methodists labored assiduously to provide the church with universities, others reflected an anti-intellectual strain that segments of American Methodism had manifested since its birth. While some Methodists invested millions in new-found wealth to establish Methodist academies, others, from the middle class, bridled at the increasingly upper and upper-middle class nature of these schools and mustered little financial support for such endeavors. While some Methodists gloried in the urban turn of segments of the church, others sought to preserve the agrarian virtues and identity of nineteenth-century American Methodism. While some sought to centralize higher education, either regionally or nationally, others thought Methodist connectionalism—at least for colleges and universities—was best realized in a network of related institutions. While Methodists sought to provide broadly-Protestant or even public institutions of higher education some, even at the same time, wanted to maintain Methodist control or some kind of distinctive Methodist identity.

Russell Richey has recently argued that early American Methodism spoke with four distinct languages that offered Methodists a "range of . . . various identities and choices as to what constituted Methodism."[111] The story of the founding of Methodist universities in the late-nineteenth and early-twentieth centuries demonstrates that the Methodist communions, North and South, continued to contain multiple identities in this era. Such variety, in making room for peoples of diverse classes, education, region, and ecclesiological persuasion, provided strength for Methodism and contributed significantly to Methodism's growth. But this diversity also led to significant tensions within the Methodist communions, as Methodists struggled to determine who they were in the rapidly changing culture of turn-of-the-century America.[112]

~ Kenneth E. Rowe ~

Like a tree, connectionalism must have strong roots to support a full crown. The crown is no more "connectional" than the roots, though it is the crown—the corporate or episcopal connectional center—which commands our attention. A Methodism that expressed itself connectionally in the late-nineteenth century by founding learning centers (universities) and by turning once-voluntary campaigns into denominational boards and agencies also expressed itself connectionally in new church and Sunday-school buildings. Indeed, the two went hand-in-hand. The national boards would have been unthinkable and unworkable without the presence and resources of highly organized, complex congregations. The latter, fashionably accommodated in fine buildings with large sanctuaries, garnered a local membership earlier decentralized into classes, a membership physically together only in quarterly or camp meetings, a membership which far exceeded the cramped quarters of the little preaching houses. And national boards and agencies had local programmatic counterparts in Sunday-school superintendents and members of an official board. In the following essay, Kenneth Rowe examines the architectural program of Methodism, as it was exemplified especially by George Washington Kramer. Kramer guided American architects, by precept and example, in building grand auditorium sanctuaries and in making a new statement about the church through a Sunday-school building. The Akron-plan educational building gave programmatic and spatial expression to the graded class and uniform lesson. It arrayed individual space for each age and class so as to face common space where the Sunday-school superintendent and musician could hold forth. If these were the physical, architectural renderings of late-nineteenth-century Methodism and Methodist connectionalism, what most aptly expressed earlier connectionalism, and what later? What captures the present state of connectionalism, and what its future? And who are the proper architects of our connectionalism?

Redesigning Methodist Churches: Auditorium-Style Sanctuaries and Akron-Plan Sunday Schools in Romanesque Costume 1875–1925

Kenneth E. Rowe

Methodism's centennial era in America (1866–84) coincided with its transformation into a solidly middle-class church. Nothing symbolizes Methodism's new status and social location better than the network of impressive, even monumental, regional Methodist churches that came to dominate the urban landscape during the last quarter of the nineteenth century. An earlier generation of Methodists considered elegant churches to be detrimental to spiritual worship. With the rise of middle-class respectability, however, fine church buildings were seen to demonstrate the authority and influence of the Methodists, as well as the wealth and status of its membership. Mid-century church leaders like Abel Stevens assumed that Methodism's "permanent hold upon its congregations, especially in the larger communities, will depend much upon the convenience and even the elegance of its churches."[1] Within this context, prospective members were seen as "audiences to be wooed, rather than souls to be saved."[2]

The new churches also reflected the hierarchy developing in connectional Methodism, with its accompanying centralization of power. A new generation of upscale churches provided important regional centers of Methodist strength and missionary outreach. In every major city and town, Methodists built large and refined architectural monuments to their spirituality. In smaller cities and prosperous rural districts, Methodists built more limited versions of the same churches.

Whether large or small, the new churches differed significantly from their predecessors in many ways. In the construction of its new churches, Methodism shunned classical architecture, whose imitation of pagan temples seemed an inappropriate way to express Christian faith. Gothic and Romanesque-revival styles, to even the most casual observer, marked both the spiritual and temporal prosperity of the church. The plans often supplied by leading architects and circulated through denominational departments of architecture, not only spread style, but they also marked the elaboration of functions in the modern church. The buildings were adapted to the broader social concerns which were becoming fundamental aspects of church life. Space was set aside for an office for the minister and for meetings of the trustees and official boards, as well as for the growing number of auxiliary organizations associated with the late-Victorian congregation—Sunday schools, lending libraries, women's home and foreign missionary societies, men's brotherhoods, youth fellowships. Often the congregation built an adjoining hall for social and recreational gatherings as well as social outreach ministries.

When Methodism's flagship church in Pittsburgh, Christ MEC, was gutted by fire in 1891, the congregation set out to build a trendsetting church for their city and for their denomination. The sale of the center-city site plus a sizable insurance settlement enabled the congregation to hire the nation's leading ecclesiastical architect, George Washington Kramer.[3] Construction began in May, 1893, and a year and a half later, 13 January 1895, the monumental new church was dedicated by Bishop Charles H. Fowler.[4]

Kramer's plan for the new Christ Church featured both a new exterior style (Romanesque) and a new interior plan (theater-style sanctuary and Akron-plan Sunday school). The massive church, built around a large central tower surrounded by broad transepts with curving, arcaded porticos, was modeled after H. H. Richardson's monumental Trinity Church, Boston, erected in 1877 for one of the era's pulpit princes, Episcopal bishop Phillips Brooks.[5] The rough stone-faced exterior with deep-set, intricately carved openings made a powerful statement. Inside, a broad worship space inspired by the arrangement of the secular theater replaced the narrow Gothic sanctuary of old Christ Church. Galleries surrounded the central pulpit platform on three sides so that every hearer was as close as possible to the preacher. On the fourth side and behind the pulpit area the space was filled with the ranks of the choir, that reinforced the appeal of the preacher with its devotional singing, and on either side of the choir rose the gilded pipes of the organ.[6] Curved pews circled the dominating pulpit, lush carpet covered the sloping floors and radiating aisles, plaster moldings circling walls and ceiling echoed exterior Romanesque carvings, and large Tiffany stained glass windows flooded the interior with delicate hues.[7] Olives and gold predominated in the color scheme. As a building it was wonderfully elegant and highly efficient for its purpose in the days when large crowds regularly hung upon the words of the preacher.

Kramer brought the Sunday school out of the basement where it had been crammed in old Christ Church and gave it as much attention and space as the new sanctuary. Patterned after what came to be known as the Akron-plan, the Sunday school featured two curving tiers of classrooms facing a large central auditorium. The plan efficiently gathered a large number of classes close to and in full view of the superintendent, who led the school in opening and closing worship from a platform at its center, but allowed doors to be slid closed in the interim, accommodating individual class sessions.

The new Christ Church, built at a cost of $275,000 and dedicated debt-free, modeled the dramatic changes being made in the primary spatial components of Protestant churches between 1875 and 1925. Auditorium-style sanctuaries and Akron-plan Sunday schools were built by the thousands across the country.[8] Methodists were among the first to accept the auditorium style for worship use, and the Akron plan was created for a Methodist Sunday school in Akron, Ohio. Methodists were deeply involved in the spread of both plans by their newly-formed denominational departments of architecture.[9] The two plans shaped the interiors of Methodist churches (and other mainline Protestant churches) for fifty years. Much maligned and misunderstood, auditorium-style churches with Akron-plan Sunday schools represent what may be the most common type of Methodist church building still in use today.[10]

Auditorium-Style Sanctuaries

The parallel rise of great preachers and great cities produced both an opportunity and a difficulty that was new to the Protestants. The popularity of the preachers drew city crowds so large that they could not be contained in traditional church buildings. It became necessary to rent auditoriums or theaters to accommodate the people. However, the rental of theaters could only serve as a temporary expedient. Church leaders and architects alike searched for new ways to build churches in forms that followed, if not maximized, function and funding. The more income-producing pew space the architect could squeeze out of the building site, the sooner construction costs could be met and more church income turned to missionary service.

Logic precluded the Gothic plan. Lengthening narrow Gothic naves only added more pews at the back with a poor view and bad acoustics. A plan in the form of wide rectangle, circle or square, on the other hand, could have seats at the back of the main floor or gallery only slightly less desirable [rentable!] than the front seats. The auditorium or theater-plan worship space was seen as a natural means for gathering great numbers of people in structures that were constructed on building lots severely constrained in both size and shape. Efficiency, not aesthetics, was the architectural byword of the day.[11]

Like the Gothic revival before it, the new auditorium church was an urban phenomenon. The earliest known churches to use a theater plan were built for urban pulpit princes. Charles Finney's Broadway Tabernacle in New York City, built in 1836, was one of the first. With the deep galleries in a circular design, Finney's radical plan allowed the speaker to have eye contact with almost everyone in the congregation, and no person was seated more than seventy feet away from the platform.[12] Fourteen years later (1850), Henry Ward Beecher's design for Plymouth Church in Brooklyn included a full complement of features that would blossom in post-Civil War church building: curving pews, radiating aisles, and curved, sloping balcony; semicircular pulpit platform; choir loft and organ behind and above the pulpit.[13] Ten years later the large oval-shaped Metropolitan Tabernacle built in South London in 1859–61 for world-class Baptist evangelist Charles H. Spurgeon seated 5,000 on the main floor and two tiers of galleries.[14] When a large church of similar interior design was built for Dwight L. Moody in Chicago in 1876, the new style became the rage among mainline Protestants, especially Methodists.[15]

The advantages of the new plan were apparent to preacher and trustee alike. Attention to acoustics, sight-lines, seating comfort, and ventilation added to the preacher's ability to communicate the gospel. The comfortableness of the auditorium would make the hearers feel welcome, while the theater-like seating arrangement and prominent pulpit would facilitate the reception of the message.[16] Theater-like churches could also be built with sufficient economy to avoid the burden of debt which hampered many congregations who had built Gothic cathedralettes a decade earlier. The increasing use of the auditorium style was in its own way a response to economic conditions much like the skyscraper that was evolving in New York and Chicago at the same time.

In the early 1870s a small group of iconoclastic architects took the plan of the auditorium-style mega-churches built for the most successful preachers and applied it to the less ambitious, more typical churches being constructed in smaller cities and country towns across America. One of the most important of these architects, George Washington Kramer (1847–1938), of Akron, Ohio, standardized the plan. In his best-selling book, *The What, How and Why of Church Building*, published in 1897 Kramer insisted :

> The auditorium should . . . be provided with seating semi-circular in arrangement, or may be pulled out to the elliptic. On the center of the one side facing the seats should be a platform for the speaker; the seats should rise as they recede from the platform and will form concentric curves, every one facing the pulpit squarely.[17]

Kramer moved his practice to New York City in 1894, and from there he catered to rich and famous mainline Protestant congregations across the country, many of them Methodist, until he retired in 1924. Kramer's eulogizer boasts that he designed more than 2,200 churches in every state of the union.[18]

Church sanctuaries designed by Kramer and a host of other major and minor architects and builders took many shapes, including the circle, oval, ellipse, and even polygon; square and wide rectangle shapes, however, predominated. To improve sight lines and acoustics, floors sloped or bowled, traditional pews curved or individual theater-style seats were installed. To save the cost of the more expensive curved pews or individual seats, less affluent congregations chose straight pews angled toward the pulpit. Whether straight or curved, the new pews and individual seats were a far cry from the stiff-backed pews of the early-nineteenth-century church. Increasingly anatomically designed, Victorian pews were also usually cushioned; some were designed to look like long sofas.[19]

The center aisle was replaced with radiating aisles, which posed no problems for weddings or funerals, as these events were routinely conducted in private residences or funeral homes.[20] Circling the sanctuary in all but the smallest churches was a gallery sufficiently shallow to keep its occupants close to the pulpit and improve acoustics in the pews below.

The pulpit, fashioned of carved wood or scrolled brass, stood at the center of a raised, often semi-circular, platform wide enough to contain several chairs or a large sofa behind it for the platform party. The communion table was small and inconspicuous below the pulpit platform, uncluttered by cross and candles and behind a curved communion rail with cushioned or carpeted kneeler. The Baptismal font was usually small and placed off to one side. Less expensive and more common was a communion basin/bowl kept in a closet and brought out only for Baptisms. The choir and organ console and pipes were usually placed behind and raised above the pulpit platform.

Auditorium churches were brightly lit by large windows, generally confined to the side and rear of the room. Windows behind the pulpit were discouraged because the strong light would strain the eyes of parishioners during the sermon. So-called art glass, consisting of inexpensive glass in shades of white and gold accented with strong blues, greens, and purples, reduced glare while still providing plenty of light. A central dome fitted with skylights using the same kind of glass lit other churches from above. Imitation stained glass, (brightly colored and patterned paper glued to ordinary window glass) made attractive windows available to even the most modest church buildings.[21] Although windows sometimes featured biblical figures or landscapes popularized by Louis Tiffany and other prominent stained glass makers, abstract geometric designs featuring simple Christian symbols were more common.[22] Gas fixtures, later electrified, amply lit the evening services.[23] Coal-burning steam boilers or hot air furnaces kept Methodists warm in the winter. A few churches, notably the 1891 First M.E. Church, South, Birmingham, Alabama, installed an ice-based system designed to ease the sultry summer heat.[24]

Kramer introduced a variation on the standard plan in 1880, the "Pulpit in the Corner Church," where the pulpit, choir, and organ were located in one corner of the auditorium, diagonally opposite the main entrance. This arrangement permitted the seating of the entire congregation within a ninety-degree quadrant from the pulpit. Kramer believed this would maximize the auditorium's focus on the pulpit. It proved especially suitable also for the placement of a Sunday-school area to one side and opening into the auditorium, an arrangement Kramer called the "Combination Church."[25]

As the plan increased in popularity other architects lost no time in making auditorium church designs available by mail by placing advertisements in Methodist annual conference journals. Church plan catalogues were also made available by denominational agencies. In 1875 the Board of Church Extension of the Methodist Episcopal Church created a Department of Architecture, which issued an annual catalog of plans prepared by Philadelphia architect Benjamin D. Price beginning in 1877.[26] Within a decade the Methodist Episcopal Church, South and the Church of the United Brethren in Christ began to issue a version of the same catalogue, which was expanded and modified each year by Price. His early designs consisted of simple wide rectangles which featured straight pews angled forward on each side to keep the cost down. Plan number 38 in the 1885 catalog, an exception, included fully curving pews and matching communion rail.[27] By 1889 Price added three plans (numbers 54, 55, & 56) for churches with a full complement of auditorium-style features including sloping floors, radiating aisles, curved pews and communion rail, items ranging in price from $3,000 to $20,000.[28]

The emphasis on the word at the expense of the sacrament, and all that this implied for public worship and church architecture, was well advanced in the Methodist world at the time Christ Church, Pittsburgh was rebuilt in 1895. Its token Communion Table looked inconspicuous beneath a pulpit that dominated the building. The conversion of the individual was still the major Methodist concern, and the gifted evangelical preacher, the chief instrument. The result was a new conception of the church building as a place where large numbers of people could feel as much at home as in any secular meeting hall and could be brought into the closest possible encounter with the message and personality of the preacher. Instead of a splendid pulpit giving authority and prestige to the sermon, no matter how ordinary the preacher, there now appeared the preacher's desk-set on a large open platform that gave greater scope and visibility to the idiosyncrasies of the preacher. Here preachers could leave the shelter of the pulpit in order to come face to face with their hearers, plead with them person to person, kneel in prayer for them, or walk to and fro as they used all the dramatic arts to convey their appeal. Turn of the century Methodist preachers yearned to preside over a building where the physical arrangement of pews, gallery, and platform combined to concentrate and emphasize the power and centrality of their sermon.

Akron-Plan Sunday Schools

The new auditorium-plan churches reached their most character-istic form in combination with a new kind of architecture for a rival part of the late-nineteenth-century church, the Sunday school. Although Sunday schools were an important adjunct to Methodist preaching from the 1790s, accommodations for them in most Methodist churches had been modest. Sunday schools were usually confined to the corners of the sanctuary.

From the start Sunday-school workers agitated for something better. The sanctuary was unsuitable for educational purposes for several reasons. The placement of pews in the sanctuary, fixed on the floor and facing forward, made it difficult for teachers to gather their young scholars in circles or other formations that would facilitate the teaching process. Partitioning the space to lessen disturbances between class groups was impossible. Theologically/aesthetically, too, the sanctuary was considered an inappropriate place for Sunday-school activity—it compromised the sanctity of the space, yet did not provide the proper educational environment for children. One-room churches had to go!

By the 1850s church architects and planners were advocating a combination lecture room/Sunday-school room alongside of or to the rear of the sanctuary. A less expensive and more popular alternative was to raise the sanctuary thus providing for a full basement in which to house the Sunday school.[29] The Sunday school in old Christ Church, Pittsburgh, was confined to several small rooms and one larger room in the basement.

After the Civil War the Sunday school had grown in both size and importance. Its program of study and recreation expanded to include adults and youth as well as children. And a new curriculum transformed Sunday schools from a single room into a group of rooms arranged in a distinctive formation—the uniform lesson plan, which established a common Scripture lesson for children of all ages in the school. Adopted by the International Sunday-School Association in 1872, the new curriculum required a distinctive sequence of activities during the school session which had important implications for the plan of Sunday-school buildings. Sunday-school superintendents and teachers alike demanded accommodations to match the new curriculum and their expanding program.[30]

Lewis Miller, a Methodist businessman in Akron, Ohio who had grown rich by inventing and manufacturing superior farm machinery and famous by helping found the Chautauqua Association, turned his inventiveness and philanthropy toward the Sunday school.[31] Shortly after moving to Akron, Miller became Sunday-school superintendent of First Methodist Episcopal Church, a position he retained for over thirty five years until his death in 1899. He grieved that the Sunday schedule (church and school meeting at the same time) deprived children of the experience of worship. So he guided them to plan and lead worship for their peers using part of the Sunday-school hour. He also saw the wisdom of dividing the school into grades based on age using a uniform lesson plan. When Akron Methodists decided to build a new church, Miller saw his chance to plan and build the most efficient Sunday-school building possible for the growing congregation.

Tradition says that Miller found his inspiration at a Sunday-school picnic held in a park which contained a natural amphitheater or geological punch bowl.[32] Observing how children naturally grouped in ascending curves, all facing the central spot at the flat base of the incline, he sketched a building to match in the fall of 1866. Advice from Sunday-school leader, John Vincent, father of the uniform lesson plan and later Methodist Bishop—"Provide for togetherness and separateness; have a room in which the whole school can be brought together in a moment for simultaneous exercises, and with the minimum of movement be divided into classes for uninterrupted work"[33]—matched Miller's emerging conception of the Sunday-school plan. Akron architect and fellow church member Jacob Snyder helped Miller perfect the Sunday-school plan and designed the adjoining sanctuary.

The Sunday-school building, erected at the rear of the church sanctuary, was dedicated in 1870, two years before the rest of the church was completed.[34] The brick-faced exterior of both Sunday-school wing and sanctuary remained in Gothic style. The Sunday-school building was two stories capped by a nine-sided, windowed, semi-circular dome. Inside, two tiers of classrooms framed a large, open, semi-circular space dominated by a wide superintendent's platform on the side wall that would later adjoin the sanctuary.[35] On the platform were a lectern and a table, in front was a piano, and behind was a blackboard. Chairs were grouped in semicircles for the youth classes held in the main room.[36]

Classrooms were separated from each other by brick partitions and from the central space by windowed doors. When folded open, the doors gave each class member and teacher a clear view of the superintendent without leaving their seats. The transition from worship to learning could be made quietly and quickly, as Vincent's maxim suggested.

Aesthetic considerations tempered the pragmatic in the decoration of the building's interior. The ceiling of the main room was painted sky blue with wisps of white clouds. Frescoes of "Faith," "Hope" and "Christ Blessing Little Children" were added to the wall above the superintendent's platform. The motto adopted by the school, "And they searched the Scriptures daily whether those things were so," was painted on the wall above the classrooms. At the center of the main room was a large fountain which squirted water on a statue of a boy hugging a fish. The stained-glass windows of the dome above cast a rosy glow on the green carpets that covered the floors of the main room and classrooms.[37]

Delegations from all sections of the country visited Akron to see and be convinced. Considered by most visitors to be a functional and aesthetic success, the plan was much discussed in the religious press. Vincent promoted it as the model Sunday school in his *Sunday School Journal* and later in his 1887 book, *The Modern Sunday-School*.[38] He supervised construction of a Sunday school modeled after it for his home church in Plainfield, New Jersey, in 1888.[39] Standard church-building books soon promoted the Akron plan. Denominational architectural catalogues of the period incorporated the plan into their larger, more costly church designs. No one asked whether children should worship without their parents, their pastor, or their choir. No one asked whether the assembly hall was a good space for worship. No one asked whether cubicles made good classrooms or why half the space stood empty much of the time.

Architects and builders, prominent and obscure, rushed to accommodate the demand. Bruce Price's design for the First Methodist Episcopal Church in Wilkes-Barre, Pennsylvania, (completed in 1877) is said to have been the first use of the Akron plan in the eastern United States.[40] Akron plans were prominent in Stanford White's First Methodist Episcopal Church in Baltimore (completed 1887, now known as Lovely Lane United Methodist Church), Sydney R. Badgley's Epworth Memorial Methodist Episcopal Church in Cleveland (1893, demolished 1920) and George W. Kramer's Union Methodist Episcopal Church in New York (1895).

Like the auditorium style, the Akron plan evolved into a standard type which was fitted with an increasingly sophisticated array of furnishings and equipment—seating designed for each age group, blackboards, sand tables for replicating biblical geography, cabinets for curios from the Holy Land, and a multitude of maps, charts, and pictures. The most remarkable feature of the Sunday school was the partitions. Although curtains placed on horizontal rods were sometimes used to save cost, only wood partitions provided soundproofing. By the 1880s a number of manufacturers produced doors that folded, rolled up or slid to one side. Rolling partitions, resembling roll-top desks then in vogue, were the most popular and practical for large openings. Partitions in some churches, like those in Epworth Memorial M.E. Church, Cleveland, were so large and so heavy that four hydraulic engines were used to lift them.[41]

Credit for popularizing the Akron plan belongs not to John Vincent or Lewis Miller but to the aforementioned architect George W. Kramer. In the early 1880s Kramer joined the Akron firm of Jacob Snyder, which designed the Akron Sunday school, and he quickly became the firm's specialist in church design. His work was so highly regarded that he withdrew from the firm in 1894 to open his own firm in New York City, where he devoted himself exclusively to designing churches until his retirement in 1924. Kramer published his own theories and plans in the 1897 book, *The What, How and Why of Church Building*, which was reprinted in 1901. In 1911 Kramer served as architectural consultant and illustrator for Marion Lawrance's definitive work, *Housing the Sunday School*, published jointly by the Methodist Episcopal Church and the Presbyterian Church for the International Sunday School Association.[42] Kramer supplied designs and plans for moderately priced churches, and his drawings were published by northern and southern branches of the Methodist Episcopal Church.

Standard Akron-plan Sunday schools by Kramer and others called for two curved tiers of classrooms facing onto a central rotunda. Variations on the theme abounded. Urban congestion sometimes forced placing the Sunday school space in the basement beneath the sanctuary. More common and less expensive to build where space permitted was a row of small classrooms on either side of the increasingly popular fellowship hall. The large, high, open room could serve as a theater, lecture hall, concert hall, dining room, gymnasium, and general gathering area as well as the central portion of the Sunday school. In the same way flanking classrooms could also serve as club rooms for the now-popular organizations for women, men, and youth.

Throughout his long career Kramer experimented with the Akron plan, producing a number of variations on the theme. His major innovation was the "Combination Church," which placed the Sunday school beside the sanctuary and separated from it by a movable partition. When opened, the Sunday school became an extension of the sanctuary, often doubling its size for such special occasions as lectures, plays, and holiday and revival meetings. The Sunday school also could spill out into the sanctuary for its major extravaganzas. In a combination church the Sunday school could not be placed behind the pulpit wall, as with the original Akron arrangement. Instead, the school was placed to one side of the sanctuary. This arrangement, combined with Kramer's pulpit in the corner church, would permit the superintendent's platform to be used in the preaching service or revival meeting as an extension of the pulpit platform. Kramer drew out his combination church to its logical conclusion in the building he designed for Bushwick Avenue Methodist Episcopal Church, Brooklyn in 1894. To house "the largest Methodist Sunday school in the world" he wrapped its rooms around three sides of a central pulpit and organ.[43]

By the 1890s the Akron plan had become standard for Sunday schools for all medium-sized or large Methodist congregations. Village or rural churches with smaller schools made do with simpler facilities that consisted of a small suite of rooms not unlike the conventional mid-nineteenth-century arrangement. But the height of ambition for pastors and Sunday-school teachers as the twentieth century dawned was to have a building modeled on the Akron plan.

The growing size of the Sunday school and the increasing sophistication of its operation combined to create a building that came to rival the church proper. It represented the first step toward the multi-purpose church buildings called institutional churches built in the early years of the twentieth century when Sunday-school classrooms were joined by bowling alleys, gymnasiums, and swimming pools as well as fellowship halls, kitchens, and club rooms.

Methodist Romanesque

While appearing like theaters within, combination Auditorium/ Akron-plan churches resembled "traditional" churches on the outside. Victorian Gothic, used by church builders and architects famous and obscure, ran its course for a quarter of a century. When churches began to build again after the Civil War, Gothic was still preferred, until one man of genius in design came to the forefront of American architecture. Henry Hobson Richardson proposed a shift to Romanesque designs. The auditorium style's wide, open, central space was more easily expressed in the curving wall or tall central lantern of the Romanesque. The chief alternative, Gothic, was less accommodating because the required narrow nave and deep chancel were less flexible.[44]

As a young man, Richardson headed for France to study architecture at L'Ecole des Beaux Arts. The Civil War kept him there for five years. He traveled extensively in the south of France, absorbing the power of Gothic architecture's parent—Romanesque design, characterized by rounded arches and low pitch roofs. When Richardson returned to America to open an office in Boston, Phillips Brooks, rector of Trinity Episcopal Church, saw his potential. Brooks led his congregation to build with excellence from 1872 to 1877. He did not want the pretence of a cathedral. Brooks specified that the Lord's Table was to be of wood and the people were to have direct access to it. The Baptismal Font was to stand beside the table in clear view of the congregation. He would preach from a reading desk placed in the middle of the chancel rather than from a lofty and distant pulpit.[45] Richardson responded to Brooks' program with a wide, short nave enlarged by broad transepts and a semi-circular apse, also wide and short.[46] Trinity Church (Episcopal) became instantly famous for the power of Richardson's composition, the skill of his engineering, and the beauty of its decoration, but fellow Episcopalians failed to appreciate the radical thinking that Phillips Brooks had invested in its chancel. That was considered a "Low Church" aberration. But evangelical Protestants, especially Methodists, sought to copy the church on countless corner lots. The breadth and mass (wide naves) of what came to be called "Richardsonian Romanesque" style enabled architects to experiment with semicircular interior designs thought to promote interaction between the minister and the congregation. Internal arrangements gave increasing prominence to the preacher, and platforms that could accommodate visitors and choirs supplanted earlier patterns.

Christ Church, Methodist in Pittsburgh was only one of the impressive new Romanesque Methodist churches. Baltimore's First Methodist Episcopal Church (1884–1887), by celebrated architect Stanford White, is Romanesque in style with Etruscan detailing. Its massive granite walls are enclosed by a conical tile roof and topped by a 225-foot tower with a huge weather vane. Stained glass windows by Louis Tiffany in shades of Pompeian red cast a rosy glow throughout the massive oval sanctuary. Inspired by the starry mosaics of Ravenna, the great vaulted ceiling over the 1,000 seats was painted to show the heavens as they appeared at 3:00 A.M. the day of the church's dedication, with all major stars and planets in their proper positions.[47]

Another early notable Romanesque Methodist design was Weary and Kramer's First Methodist Episcopal Church, South, Birmingham, Alabama (1891). The 1400-seat sanctuary occupied the main body of the building with a gallery extending around three sides and joining with the choir gallery above the pulpit to create a continuous seating space circling the pulpit—the auditorium style drawn out to its logical conclusion. Intricate fresco work and a magnificent chandelier graced the high domed ceiling. Handsome pews, lush carpet, and 142 stained-glass windows complemented the interior.[48]

Other notable Methodist churches in Romanesque style are Cleveland's Epworth Memorial M.E. Church (Sydney R. Badgley, 1893),

Denver's Asbury M.E. Church (Kidder & Humphreys, 1890), Detroit's Cass Avenue M.E. Church (Malcomson and Higgenbotham, 1891), Hartford's St. Paul's M.E. Church (Kramer, 1900), Johnstown, Pennsylvania's First United Brethren Church (Kramer, 1912), Minneapolis's Wesley M.E. Church (Warren H. Hayes, 1891), Nashville's West End M.E. Church, South (1889), New York's Park Avenue M.E. Church (Kramer, 1883), Philadelphia's Union M.E. Church (Haszelhurst and Huckel, 1889); Reading, Pennsylvania's Holy Cross M.E. Church (1893), Scranton, Pennsylvania's Elm Park M.E. Church (Weary and Kramer, 1893), and Washington's Union M.E. Church (Kramer, 1895).

The affinity of the Romanesque Revival with the plan and function of the theater assured the connection of style and plan for many years after the 1890s, when Romanesque style was out of fashion for other public buildings. Auditorium-style Methodist churches dressed in Romanesque costume continued to be built, especially in the north and middle west until World War I.

Conclusion

The middle and later years of the nineteenth century were the heyday of the revival meeting and of the Sunday school. Towns were growing. Newly arrived families had no church home. Preachers and song leaders were brought in to attract sinners who ignored routine services, and choirs dropped denominational divisions to sing together. Overflow crowds flocked in; more space was needed than the church would require at any other season. When an inspired architect like Kramer attached the Sunday-school assembly hall to one side of the sanctuary, he had an instant hit. A rolling wall could separate the two spaces through most of the year but throw them together for the big event. Educators liked classroom space adjacent to assembly space. Evangelists liked sloping floors and semicircular pews to bring the people near and a stage to pace across. Revival choirs left their traditional gallery over the entrance to mount the stage with the evangelist as part of the act. The people settled down in their cushioned pews as an audience settles in the theater, passively, to watch the professionals perform. Form followed function supremely in high-fashion, late-Victorian Methodist churches.

Both auditorium-style sanctuaries and Akron-plan Sunday schools, which had been revolutionary developments in the 1870s, dominated church building by 1900. The form and purpose of their interior spaces embodied the triumph of highly significant developments in denominational programming and ministerial practice as well as building engineering and parish economics. The large scale and fashionable style of the new churches also expressed the ambitions and aspirations of upscale Methodists in late-Victorian America. The monumental exteriors, along with their Main Street, increasingly suburban, locations, reflected the physical and social distance from the urban population that bourgeois congregations strove to maintain.

By the 1920s, however, Methodists were among the first to repudiate both plans actively and officially, promoting instead a long narrow Gothic worship space and a multi-room/public-school-like Sunday school. The congregation of First Methodist Episcopal Church in Akron, Ohio tore down their famous church and Sunday-school buildings in 1914 and replaced them with a traditional sanctuary and a separate public school-like educational building. In the 1950s Christ Church, Pittsburgh, remodeled its sanctuary and old Sunday-school rooms and built a large new education building. Massive auditoriums and Akron-plan Sunday schools were out of fashion. Problematic for their sheer size and bulk, many of the examples that remain experienced a pattern of alteration and neglect that has continued through the present day.

Photo 1: The Interior of Christ Methodist Episcopal Church

Photo 2: Original Chapel and Sunday School

Photo 3: The Exterior of Christ Methodist Episcopal Church

⌣ Sarah Sloan Kreutziger ⌣

Wesleyan connectionalism, Heitzenrater observed, was governed by its purpose, preeminently that which the Americans rendered as "To reform the Continent, and to spread scriptural Holiness over these Lands."[1] In the following essay Sarah Sloan Kreutziger reviews a later stage in the pursuit of that purpose, namely Methodist engagement, and especially Methodist women's engagement, in late-nineteenth and early-twentieth-century ministries to the poor, the displaced, the recently arrived, the unemployed, the homeless, the ill, the untrained. She shows that the Methodist settlement movement grew out of prior connectional endeavor—city missions, freedman's aid, home missions, the institutional church movement, the temperance crusade, training schools.

Further, both the settlement houses and the prior connectional networks constituted a peculiarly female expression of connectionalism. Its form—the structure of home missions for instance—differed perhaps little from its denominational (male) counterpart. But its style, imagery, and vision differed markedly. The women would apply "mother heart" to urban and industrial problems, would remold the church as a larger household of faith, would reshape American society through deaconesses, city missionaries, and volunteers into a homelike place. The women shared with the denomination as a whole goals of perfection for the individual and the kingdom of God for society, contending no less than their male reformer counterparts for a transformed individual and against the structures of evil. But they spoke of motherhood and the home rather than (or in addition to) the brotherhood of man and fatherhood of God. Kreutziger also shows how this female social Christianity evolved through professionalization, secularization, scientific charity, sociology, and the opening of other female careers into professional social work. The social worker took the place of the deaconess, the latter a casualty of the transition from perfectionist practical divinity to pragmatism, social darwinism, socialism, secularization, professionalism.

While social work gained in efficiency, she suggests, it may have lost much— namely the vision, sense of mission, and structured church support that it possessed when undertaken as part of Methodism's connectional outreach. Her story invites nostalgia and regret, particularly over the decline of deaconess. Yet, she also makes clear that the reformist structures of Methodist connectionalism live on, albeit in transformed shape, in the safety net of social service. Her essay invites questions about durability of connectional structures. What happens when the purposes or needs of organizations change?

Her analysis also prompts reflection about the place of initiative in creating connectional program and structure. Her reading also raises questions about male and female in connectional endeavor. How has connectionalism been engendered, given birth, nurtured, and fed? Have there been distinctive male and female roles, patterns, dimensions to connectionalism all along? If so, what shape do they assume today?

Wesley's Legacy of Social Holiness: The Methodist Settlement Movement and American Social Reform

Sarah Sloan Kreutziger

American social reformers at the end of this century, not unlike their counterparts in the church, are hearing the clarion call for action heralded in the familiar convictions of earlier crusaders. In their book, *Unfaithful Angels,* social work educators Harry Specht and Mark Courtney argue that social work has abandoned its original objective of enabling "people to create and use a healthful and nurturing social environment" and has instead opted for secular priesthood in the "Church of Individual Repair" (1994: 7, 12–14). Social work's accommodation to society's preoccupation with the cultivation of self, they contend, has led to a psychodynamically-derived therapeutic approach based primarily on intrapsychic interventions. They propose that the profession return to its defining mission, with its antecedents in the tradition of the settlement house movement, to neighborhood advocacy groups and community associations as major modes of intervention (152–62). This approach is based on early social work's strong belief in the perfectibility of society (7).

The summons for social work's return to the idea of societal perfectibility comes as social work, like the mainline churches that share many of its modern values about social responsibility, digs into its historical and spiritual soil to nurture a vision and mission for the future (see also Lieby 1978: 17; Lissak 1989: 14; Lloyd 1971: 138). Left unrecognized by many social and other reformers in this call is the role that evangelicalism, defined primarily in nineteenth-century America through Methodist values and influence (Ahlstrom 1972: 2.372; Hardman 1983: 108; Hudson 1974: 3–15 and 1981: 180; Kreutziger 1991, Link et al. 1981: 267; Smith 1980: 7–10), played in inspiring that reforming zeal.

The evangelical idea of perfectibility, derived from Methodism founder John Wesley's doctrine of entire sanctification, was the basis for significant female-led social reform movements in the nineteenth century. Entire sanctification was a synergistic concept that required an intense, ongoing personal relationship with God in tandem with service to one's neighbors as necessary for a "perfected" sin-free, holy life. "Going on to perfection" included the notion of progress as holy pilgrimage and embodied the optimistic idea of positive change over time. Tied to the Protestant elevation of the individual will over the authority of the institution, perfectionism lent energy and hope to the emerging sense that one could control one's destiny. Because it gave women permission to venture out in service to others beyond traditional lines of authority, perfectionism had special meaning for early to mid-nineteenth-century women tied in the bonds of "the woman's sphere." Through freely-bestowed grace they could create a perfected America seen as God's hope for a Christian world just as well as men. "To go where the Spirit led" in spite of any temporal or human authority was immensely liberating because it allowed women to operate from the authority of "radical obedience" to Scripture, a stance that was more "likely to make the greater impact on their male colleagues, for their claims [could not] be so easily rejected" (Ruether & McLaughlin 1979: 19).

This "radical obedience" led them into greater realms of influence as members of religious societies that, in time, became fertile ground for national social reform movements. The religious settlement movement was one significant reform effort that came out of this cultural transformation. Although long neglected by church and social-work historians, the religious settlement movement preceded the non-sectarian social settlement movement (Jane Addams' Hull House is its most famous proponent) by at least thirty years. Its work paralleled and intersected the more widely-publicized social settlements and lent energy and ideas to their common mission. Although often disdained by its more famous counterpart, the religious settlements thrived and continue in altered form today.

Beginning in the mid-nineteenth century, this religious reform movement, financed and run mostly by volunteer women, developed programs to reach the poorest inhabitants of the inner-cities. The religious settlers formed Sunday schools, industrial education, bathhouses, kindergartens, nurseries, clubs, loan banks, job bureaus, dispensaries, reading rooms, and legal services, as well as the organizational networks (a very particular strength in Methodism) to support these activities. As such, their tract societies, city missions, institutional churches, and deaconess service laid the foundation and organizational structure for later social reform initiatives.

This chapter examines the Methodist Settlement Movement against the backdrop of American social and religious currents within the context of the settlement movement in general. Special attention is paid to the lives and activities of the women who founded, funded, staffed, and sustained its drive through the peak of its influence in the first two decades of the twentieth century and to the aftermath of their work today.

Early City Missions

The origins of the Religious Settlement Movement in American Methodism began in New York City "on the 5th of July, 1819, [when] 'a number of females' met at the Wesleyan Seminary . . . for the purpose of forming an Auxiliary Society to the Missionary Society of the Methodist Episcopal Church, which had been formed the previous April" (Mason 1870: 82). The first president of the Ladies Home Missionary Society, Mary Mason, was an active worker in New York's first Sunday school. In words similar to those that would be used later by the Society's most famous member, evangelist Phoebe Palmer, Mason declared that the goals of the Society were to "imitate the pious Phoebe who was the servant of the church" as well as to raise money for "our dear brethren who are spending their strength and wasting their health in traversing dreary mountains and pathless forests to carry the glad tidings of the free salvation to the scattered inhabitants of the wilderness" (83–84).

While their founding purpose was to support missionaries to the North American Indians, their work gradually expanded into missionary work closer to their homes. By 1850, Palmer and the "ladies of the mission," united in evangelistic pragmatism, began their work at the Five Points Mission, the earliest city mission in America and the precursor of later settlement homes and community centers in the United States (Leiby 1978: 83; Magalis 1973: 79; Riis 1962: 147).

These women were thoroughly Wesleyan in their vision for the Mission. Their task was no less than the perfecting of America, starting with the part of the city that provided the greatest challenge: the slums of Five Points. With characteristic zeal, the women built the Mission on land that had once housed an old brewery. The Five Points Mission was located in an area surrounded by

> miserable-looking buildings, liquor stores innumerable, neglected children by scores, playing in rags and dirt, squalid-looking women, brutal men with black eyes and disfigured faces, proclaiming drunken brawls and fearful violence. (Ladies of the Mission 1854: 33)

The women set about their task with enthusiasm. Spurred on by Palmer, who reminded them that women were particularly effective in mission work because they could devote their total energies to this cause unencumbered by outside temptations and the "exposure to the storms and combative elements of business or political life" (Palmer 1985: 19), they raised money for a building, appointed a paid missionary, and provided the volunteer energy to conduct church services, Sunday schools, and a nursery for working women.

Over the years, the women opened a reading room for the worker so that "he might lose all taste for the low haunts of ignorance and vice," (Ladies 1854: 87); started a medical dispensary; installed public baths; and provided shelter, clothes, and food for the poor. Their stated goal was to reform and convert those "from the deepest moral degradation into which human beings can sink" into "sons of God and heirs of everlasting life" (74).

Another project of the women at Five Points was rescue work. In 1833, the ladies formed the New York Reform Society to help women who "were victims of sin and shame" to "stay the evil" that the temptations of the city forced upon the young. This Society employed city missionaries who were some of the first professional female social workers. One of their most famous city missionaries was Margaret Pryor. A description of her "walks of usefulness" among the inhabitants of Five Points was compiled into a best-selling book (Ingraham 1844) that did much to popularize and publicize the work of the Mission (36–44).

Pryor's and Palmer's pleas to move into social reform were spoken in the religious language common to what was termed the "woman's sphere of action," and hundreds of women enlisted in the cause. Catherine Booth, cofounder of the Salvation Army (Magnuson 1977: 112–13), Frances Willard, the major leader of the Woman's Christian Temperance Union (White 1986: 97–98), and Hannah Whitall Smith, best-selling author of holiness writings, were directly influenced by Palmer's call to action (Hardesty, Dayton, and Dayton 1979: 235). Other women were equally inspired by Palmer's use of early female Methodist leaders and women of the Bible, as examples of what needed to be done for the promotion of holiness. She declared that women's unused services were "a sort of potter's field where the gifts of woman, as so many strangers are buried" (Palmer 1985: 341). She encouraged her readers to be "visitors" for the work of benevolent societies. They were to gather people for Sabbath school, take care of the poor, and create the kind of communities where individuals, now educated, free from alcohol, and well-fed, could create a global sanctification (212).

The Institutional Church

The Five Points Mission's programs and activities were rapidly duplicated as the country began to face the increasing social problems of the industrial age and the difficulties experienced by the men and women who fueled its labor force.

"Between 1860 and 1900, some fourteen million immigrants came to America and about another nine million, mainly from southern and eastern Europe . . . arrived between 1900 and 1910" (Trattner 1979: 135). This influx of unskilled, poor, often illiterate, non-English-speaking individuals, created massive crowding in the cities. In New York City in 1890, for example, 37,000 people or two-thirds of the population lived in tenements. Chicago, the fastest growing city in the world, had the additional problem of tenement dwellers living with the smells and ill health "back of the stockyards." Gangs and criminals preyed upon the tenement dwellers, and "the urban frontier, like the rural frontier, was a dangerous place" (Seller 1981: 50).

The immigrants often brought political attitudes with them that made them ill-equipped to fight for change (Hofstadter 1955). Many came out of autocratic, feudal societies in which government was primarily an agent of social control and hardship. Their recourse was through old-world political traditions that ensured their immediate needs of survival. In the slums, they turned to the "padrone," the political boss, who could manipulate the system for personal gain in exchange for the immigrants' votes.

The reformer, on the other hand, who based citizenship on self-denial, responsibility, and patriotic civic action, was a stranger to the new American. Reforms such as temperance, women's rights, and moral purity were alien and frustrating. The reformers in turn failed to identify with the immigrants; although they were horrified by the living conditions in the cities and moved by the misery of the new citizens, they saw the newcomers as alcoholic, unsanitary, and unpatriotic purveyors of loose morals and foreign religion—a threat to everything that was decent and ordered in civilization (Hofstadter 1955: 179–82).

The reformers were also concerned about the overall breakdown of traditional religious belief in the larger culture that was causing the

Protestant churches to forget their mission to create a sanctified society. Churches were leaving the inner cities instead of facing its challenges (Dixon 1896). Social activists complained that "continental ideas of the Sabbath," competition from useless pursuits such as reading popular newspapers, books, and magazines, nomadic habits in living, private pews in churches, fancy dress among the affluent, and indifference to the plight of the poor were undermining city evangelization (Strong 1893: 210–11). The solution to these changes was to set up a specialized form of these early city missions in the inner-city churches to hold the line against the onslaught of these evils by changing the environment that produced them. The purpose of these missions was to Christianize the new arrivals into the American way of life by introducing them to the benefits of sanctified living. These citadels of hope were known as industrial or institutional churches.

These expanded city missions were the major precursor of the settlement movement, sectarian and non-sectarian. Programs and activities developed in these "open" or "free" churches, as they were also called, were adopted by the social settlers and others following in their footsteps (Bremner 1956: 61). These churches

> viewed themselves as "institutions" that ministered seven days a week to the physical and spiritual wants of all people within their reach. [They] sponsored clinics, free Saturday night concerts, self-supporting restaurants and lodging houses, woodyards for the unemployed, "fresh air work" for women and children, and "gold-cure" establishments for drunkards. There was a marked emphasis on practical education. Institutional churches sponsored libraries and literary societies and carried on kindergartens, trade schools, and community colleges. (McBride 1983: xi)

Although the Episcopalians and Congregationalists had more known leaders in the industrial church movement, the Methodists were very active in establishing industrial churches as an outgrowth of their missionary and church extension societies. One of their first established industrial churches was Wesley Chapel in Cincinnati, started in a decaying downtown church. Led by J. W. Magruder, it had by 1895, a kindergarten, a day nursery, a ladies' benevolent society, a bureau of justice (forerunner to the Legal Aid Societies), a saving association, and a visitation society (Abell 1962: 158–59; McBride 1972: 97).

The costs of running these churches led ultimately to forming church unions to pay for what Social Gospel leader Walter Rauschenbusch claimed were "voluntary gifts and labor of a few . . . [that] tries to furnish what the entire cooperative community ought to furnish" (1911: 304–5). The Chicago Missionary Society was ultimately the most successful in combining efforts for a united front to the cities' problems. By 1900, it had collected one hundred thousand dollars to build one hundred churches to service one-third of the inner cities' population. Eight years previously the Methodist General Conference had approved the plan under the direction of its National City Evangelization Union. Its leaders were George P. Mains and Frank Mason North, prominent men in the Social Gospel movement. In 1894, the United Church movement encouraged its interdenominationalism with the formation of the Institutional Church League. Six years later, the league represented 173 open and institutional churches in America (Abell 1962: 163–69). This organization was a direct forerunner of the Federation of Churches, later renamed the National Council of Churches (Hopkins 1940: 303; North 1909: 257).

Although Aaron Abell, historian of the Social Gospel, described the institutional church as similar to the secularized social settlement in its adoption of methods of the "new charity" and educational theories (Abell 1962: 164), there is some evidence that it did not forego its evangelical values. Esther McBride, researcher on the Open Church, argues directly that the primary mission of the industrial churches was evangelism. While their methods and activities were similar to nonsectarian charities, their motivation and philosophy were quite different. Frank Mason North's writings (1909) support this. North spoke often of "radical Christianity" as the employment of the drive for Christian mission "in the sanctification of life," an effort to turn Christianity into a movement for reform (264–65). The ultimate purpose of North's work was to see "these communities of men . . . transformed into the City of God" (267).

For Methodist women who supported industrial churches as part of their city mission work, the primary purpose of industrial churches was city evangelism. Although missionary society workers over the years did adopt some of the methods of the new social science and technology that the organized charities used, the women insisted that the ultimate purpose for their work came from Scripture. They were to feed the hungry, care for the sick, and clothe the poor (Tatum 1960: 241). In Methodism, any secularization of the institutional church happened in opposition to the wishes of its organizing and primary fund-raising agency, the Woman's Home Missionary Society.

The home missionary societies were composed of mostly middle-class, Methodist women, increasingly better educated and freed from domestic labor by the same industrial revolution that was creating the massive social problems in the cities and towns. While other Protestant denominations were interested in ministering to the poor and unskilled, the Methodists were among the most zealous, committed, and well organized. By 1844, when the Methodist Episcopal Church separated into the southern and northern branches over the question of slavery, there were three-hundred and sixty missionaries in the United States and one mission in Liberia supported primarily by local missionary societies (Norwood 1974: 330).

In time these groups banded together through the connectional system to set up national organizations in the two branches. The northern church established its missionary societies in 1869 to aid foreign missions; the Methodist Episcopal Church, South organized its first foreign missionary society in 1878. The Women's Home Missionary Society of the northern church, established in 1880, was the forerunner of the southern Methodist church's Home Mission Society, established in 1890. Methodism's connectionalism continued to be present in these women's groups despite the division of the church's structure. The missionary work of the North, in fact, grew out of its mission to the South (*Woman's Home Missions* 1930: 3).

Jennie Culver Hartzell and her minister husband, Dr. Joseph Hartzell, were sent to the South from the northern Methodist Episcopal Church (MEC) in 1869. Dr. Hartzell was to be the Presiding Elder for the MEC of the New Orleans District. Both of them, but especially Mrs. Hartzell, were interested in working with African Americans. Out of her interest came eight sewing schools that served over five hundred girls with manual training, prayer, and religious instruction; thirteen small mission schools which served as training laboratories for the historically black New Orleans University; three common schools for girls and women; and five industrial schools (Barclay 1957: 3.149–51).

Although the 1880 General Conference of the MEC did not approve of Hartzell's request to have her mission work incorporated into the larger structure of the church, it did approve a report officially connecting this work to the Freedman's Aid Society, an organization set up by the northern church after the Civil War to help African Americans in the South. Within a week, the Woman's Home Missionary Society was organized with Hartzell as recording secretary. Lucy Hayes, wife of American President Rutherford B. Hayes, was its first president (Davis 1890: 45). Their first three projects included the work begun by Hartzell; an additional program in South Carolina that included Sunday schools, temperance societies, and home visitation; as well as similar work among African Americans at Clark University in Georgia (Barclay 1957: 3.152). In 1884, the General Conference recognized and adopted the Woman's Home Missionary Society's work (*Discipline of the MEC* 1884: 152–53). By 1895, it had organized 2,500 local societies, welcomed 65,000 members, and collected almost a million dollars ("Board of Missions Report" in Barclay 1957: 3.157).

The Church of the United Brethren in Christ, one stem of Methodism's German branch, began its local organization of missionary work in 1869 in the Ohio German Conference under the urging of missionary D. K. Flickinger. Despite the lack of enthusiasm from many women and opposition to the group's forming an autonomous organization instead of functioning as an auxiliary to the general missionary society, the women succeeded at the General Conference in 1877 in becoming a fully authorized board of the church. Theirs was the first group in American Methodism to join the foreign and home missions into one agency. In 1946, by the time of the union of the United Brethren Church in Christ with the Evangelical Church (who had organized their mission work in 1883), the women had built several mission churches, three schools, and two medical centers (Letzig 1987: 6–8).

Missionary organization began in the Methodist Protestant Church in 1879, with reluctant General Conference approval in 1880. The Movement, however, did not produce the numbers or influence of the much larger Methodist Episcopal Churches.

For the Methodist Episcopal Church, South, official adoption of missionary work in the United States came at about the same time as it did for the German branches. Originally named the Woman's Department of Church Extension in 1882, the first Woman's Home Missionary Society function was to raise funds for homes for frontier ministers and their families (McDowell 1982: 6). Its first general secretary, Lucinda B. Helm, expanded its work despite opposition that broadening the work would limit parsonage building. In 1890, the General Conference amended the constitution to permit the Woman's Department of the Board of Church Extension to be renamed the Woman's Parsonage and Home Mission Society. In 1898, the department was changed to the Woman's Home Mission Society and placed under the Woman's Board of Home Missions. In 1910, it become the Woman's Missionary Council (McDowell 1982: 12). Initial work included education for the poor and unchurched among the Cuban immigrants in Florida and the mountain people in Appalachia, and an orphanage in Tennessee. Shortly afterwards, schools were opened for Oriental newcomers on the Pacific Coast (12–15).

Much of the mission work of the Home Missionary Societies in the South and in the North came from the evangelical view that placed women in the position of moral guardians of the home. In the North, missionary society members organized under the banner of "evangelical domesticity" (Lee 1981), the notion that women's spiritual superiority gave them the right to protect their homes and children from the influences of evil. Women, in effect, became "evangelists for the home" (113–16). Frances Willard's national political temperance platform was organized under the Prohibition Home Protection Party (Willard 1889: 382). The journal of the Home Missionary Society in the Methodist Episcopal Church, South was called *Our Homes* (Alexander 1898: 134–35). Countless women echoed the belief that "in every well-regulated family their [*sic*] mother is the potent influence in molding the little ones committed to her sacred guidance" (*Woman's Missionary Society of the Methodist Episcopal Church, South* 1884: 4). This concern was especially great for the homes "among the godless inhabitants of this land" (Alexander 1898: 91). A sanctified society required sanctified mothers. As such, much of the reform activity was directed toward other women and their children. As the first president of the Woman's Home Missionary Society stated at an annual meeting:

> In conclusion, may we not sum up the whole matter in these few words? America is the "cradle of the future" for the world. The future of America is in her homes and her homes depend on the mothers of America. Hence the value and importance of missionary societies whose work is done by women in the homes of our beloved country. (Hayes, quoted in Davis 1890: 96)

The southern branches of the missionary societies, at least in the middle decades of the nineteenth century, faced other problems. The War between the States had left the South devastated and poor (Fish 1969: 31–35). For white women in the South, the "plantation system" that had previously enslaved their black sisters held them in bondage as well. This rigid, tightly-knit social order where tradition, custom, and lines of authority were paramount assigned women and children to roles of obedience and submissiveness. As a result, religious activity for women centered around individual piety and submission to male authority. Women were urged to lead ideal Christian lives that stressed an inward personal holiness, obedience, and perfection, instead of the more communal "social holiness" of evangelical service that their northern sisters were channelling into abolition, women's rights, and other reforms (Thompson 1972: 24–86; Scott 1970: 4–21).

Despite the devastation of the Civil War and its aftermath, the abolition of slavery and the loosening of the severely controlled system that supported it produced a liberating spirit of reform activities that had previously been denied southern women. The aimlessness that "saps the springs of power and sulls the finest soul" (Kearney 1900: 45) was poured into work within "their appointed sphere": the churches. The churches' connectional structure, in turn, allowed women to go beyond their regional boundaries and take the leading role in the organization of national benevolent societies. Over time, the wives, sisters, and daughters of former slave holders and their northern Methodist counterparts came together to establish agencies and groups that promoted racial harmony and solidarity and reinforced the cause of women's suffrage in the process (Hall 1979: 62–106, Scott 1984: 190–211). A major product of there work was the outgrowth of settlements houses from their early mission projects.

The Religious Settlements

The settlement houses in the Methodist Episcopal Church began as an expanded mission project of the Woman's Home Missionary Society (WHMS), the Chicago Training School for City, Home, and Foreign Missions (CTS), and several independent associations, as a way to focus the talents and energies of Methodist women into a more concentrated, personalized effort to counter the massive social problems resulting from the negative effects of industrialization. While the objective of the leaders of the religious settlement movement was still the perfectibility of society through the changed hearts of individuals, living in the poorer neighborhoods revealed an even greater impediment to their vision: societal evil. Going on to perfection began to include a systematic attack on society as "an organic whole," as reflected in the emerging theology of the Social Gospel. The incorporation of these liberalized beliefs into the "Mother Heart," the religious metaphor that city missionary leader Lucy Rider Meyer used to express the feminine side of God embodied in evangelistic domesticity, would change the nature of religious cause and mission as it drew closer to the same currents of social thought that were molding the beginnings of professional social work.

Settlement houses in the Methodist Episcopal Church, South were begun for the same ideological reasons as the settlements in the North. The populations they served, however, were more often poorer black and white Americans than European immigrants. Nevertheless, their leaders followed similar pathways into professional work with similar results.

Building the Structure

Methodist settlement houses started by missionary societies, deaconess homes, and training schools often began as child care facilities for working mothers and expanded into kindergartens, sewing clubs, domestic service classes, homemakers clubs, rescue work for women, boys' athletic clubs, classes in cooking, play grounds, and religious services. Although they also included reading rooms, public baths, English classes, night schools, dispensaries, lectures, concerts, music classes, bookkeeping and banking classes, military drills, gymnastics, milk stations, penny savings, libraries, and "improvement clubs for men," they were primarily geared to the needs of mothers and children (Woods and Kennedy 1911: 6, 8, 74, 80, 90, 92, 133, 149, 151–53, 239, 258, 291–92, 294–95, 298).

Volunteers from the missionary societies and churches along with a few paid city missionaries initially ran many of the early mission settlements, but the demand for further training for this expanded work prompted missionary society leaders such as Lucy Rider Meyer, Jane Bancroft Robinson, and Belle Harris Bennett to advocate for biblically-trained women who would live in the neighborhoods among the disadvantaged, much like missionaries did in foreign lands. After a great deal of pleading for monies from Methodist women, hard work, and planning, their efforts paid off in the formation of a new version of the city missionary: the deaconess.

Deaconesses were distinguished from the city missionaries by the costumes they wore, their communal living arrangements, their formal connection to the church, and their unsalaried service *(Deaconess Advocate* February 1901: 11). Just as in the ordained ministry which was closed to women at that time, deaconesses would "minister to the poor, visit the sick, pray for the dying, care for the orphan, seek the wandering, comfort the sorrowing, [and] save the sinning . . ." (Thoburn and Leonard, quoted in Lee 1963: 37). Despite opposition from some ministers about "hen-preachers" (Horton 1928: 187), deaconesses, with the biblical deaconess Phoebe (Romans 16:1) as their example, went into the American mission field in the inner cities of the North and the factory towns and rural communities of the South as part of the twentieth-century vanguard for the religious settlement movement. In the first thirty years of the Methodist diaconate, the

Chicago Training School founded by Meyer sent nearly 4,000 deaconesses and city missionaries to work in hospitals, schools, settlements, rescue homes, and churches; forty of which had been started by its graduates (Brown 1985: 24, 27). Due to the tremendous influence of Meyer and other leaders in the northern mission societies in the founding of settlements plus pioneering work in city missions from such leaders as Laura Haygood (Brown and Brown 1904), religious settlement work in the South was predominately Methodist. When the listing of the National Federations of Settlements (Woods and Kennedy) appeared in 1911, Methodist settlements constituted anywhere from 30% to 100% of the total settlements named in the southern states. Southern Methodist settlements which served white populations were called Wesley Houses because the term, "settlement," was offensive to church leaders who equated the word to "something non-evangelical and even non-Christian" (Tatum 1960: 242). Settlements that served the African American communities were known as Bethlehem Houses.

While most of the southern settlements served white American cotton mill employees, others served French-Acadian families and Italian immigrants in Louisiana; African American farm workers in Tennessee and Georgia; Central European seafood workers in Mississippi; and Hispanic migrant workers in Texas and Florida (Nelson 1909: 7–68; Tatum 1960: 242–81). Many of these settlements were headed by deaconesses who resided in the neighborhoods among the people they served. In 1910, the "peak" year of the deaconess movement according to deaconess historian Mary Agnes Dougherty, there were six training schools, and 90 social agencies staffed by 1,069 deaconesses (Glidden 1988: 10).

The office of deaconess was recognized by the General Conference of the Methodist Episcopal Church in 1888, three years after Meyer had begun the Chicago Training School. In 1903, in the Methodist Episcopal Church, South, they were organized under the sponsorship of the Woman's Home Missionary Society. An outgrowth of their work was the South's first deaconess school, the Scarritt Bible and Training School, established by the Woman's Board of Foreign Missions in 1892 (MacDonell 1928: 64).

Deaconesses were recognized in the Methodist Protestant Church in 1908. German Methodists organized in 1868 in Germany, the country where the modern diaconate had begun in 1820 under a Lutheran pastor named Theodore Fliedner (Golder 1903: 35; Meyer 1892: 3). The

German-American deaconesses were organized separately from the Methodist Episcopal Churches under the name of "Bethesda Society."

Another separate Methodist deaconess order was begun in Ohio in 1891 by Isabella Thoburn and businessman James N. Gamble (cofounder of Procter and Gamble Corporation), as the Elizabeth Gamble Deaconess Association. This small society was responsible for the founding of Christ Hospital in Cincinnati; a three-year nurses' training program; a Bible training school; a home for the aged; several missions; and the Cameron Church for the Deaf, the first of its kind in the nation. By 1962, 372 deaconesses had worked within this independent organization (Lee 1963: 40–46).

All of the Methodist Episcopal Church deaconess groups were united in the merger of the northern and southern churches in 1939 into the Methodist Church where they were placed in the jurisdiction of the Bureau of Deaconess Work under the direction of the Woman's Division of Christian Service of the Board of Missions (Lee 1963: 71–72; Letzig 1987: 32). The other groups joined in 1968 with the merger of the Evangelical United Church and the Methodist Church into the United Methodist Church. At that time, the Woman's Division of the Methodist Church was restructured by transferring the Department of Work in Home Fields and Department of Work in Foreign Fields to the Division of National Missions and the Division of World Missions. This transfer meant that all administration of women's mission institutions were moved to the General Board of Global Ministries with the safeguard that funding for the administration of these programs would come from the Woman's Division (Stevens 1978: 87).

While these shifting structures often created problems among the disparate deaconess associations such as the "thirty years war" that pitted Meyer and the CTS against Bancroft and the WHMS over the origins and control of the deaconess movement in its early years (Horton 1928: 190–97; WHMS 1911: 6; Robinson 1930: 4), there was little disagreement over the reasons for their work. Deaconess, as representative of the caring, nurturing side of God, the Mother Heart, were called to serve God's less fortunate children "for Jesus sake" (Horton 1928: 151).

The Mother Heart as Metaphor for Evangelism

The religious ideation that formed the beliefs and values of the deaconess "Protestant sisterhood" came out of the same perfectionistic spirit that nurtured the volunteer participants of the missionary societies. Deaconess leaders publicly declared that their goal was the salvation of the larger "household of faith": American society. This huge "household" was seen as a giant field for mission. The *Deaconess Advocate*, the journal of the CTS, the largest and best known deaconess training school in America, regularly carried stories of poor widows, children in rags, drunken parents, and dying men in need of conversion. Deaconess ventures into the city mission field were to lead individuals into God's kingdom, which they saw in terms of America's spiritual manifest destiny (*Deaconess Advocate* May 1889: 1). The evils of unchurched people, drunkenness, pauperism, and foreign influences could be wiped out with a return to Christian values based on the earlier promise of God's covenant with America. This heavenly pattern, imprinted on America, would ensure the salvation of other countries as well. As deaconess leader Belle Horton declared, the deaconess battle cry became "we must 'save America for the world's sake'" (1904: 41).

According to deaconess reasoning, justification for women's entry into the noble and ambitious endeavor for worldwide salvation came from the Bible and church tradition as expressed through the Mother Heart. The Mother Heart was the nurturing, caring, feminine side of God which women naturally understood and possessed. Under this banner, deaconess and city missionaries fought to strengthen families and purify their neighborhoods so that they could become part of a sanctified society.

The image of a larger household of faith was reenforced by the living arrangements of the deaconess community. Although the later part of the nineteenth century ushered in a more secularized society somewhat unrecognized, the American home was still considered the bulwark against the evils of the world and the cradle for Christian training and virtue. Because of the perceived encroachment of a more vulgarized world into these sacred citadels as well as the strong currents of perfectionistic drives still operating, women "used the culture of the home to crusade out into the male 'world' to press their issues of woman's rights and social reform" (Ruether and Keller 1986: xx). As a result, "the women's sphere now seemed to harbor two contradictory impulses: domestic outreach, embodied in social settlement work, and domestic retreat, embodied in the bourgeois family" (Hunter 1984: xiv). The deaconess tried to encompass both. By offering a safe, homelike atmosphere to women from rural America who were often frightened of urban life, they paved the way for women to move into the larger world (Dougherty 1979).

In the first issue of the *Deaconess Advocate*, Meyer wrote that the object of the Chicago Training School was "to furnish a true home, under Christian and missionary influences, for our students" (1886: 1). Other deaconess homes reflected this same idea. Scarritt's program stressed that "Christian home making, and the day-by-day life at the school [were] intended to be a model of ideal home life" (Cobb 1987: 20). The superintendent of the home was a "housemother" who supervised the "motherhouse." Her job was to "emphasize the home idea by many simple devices that will occur to the Mother Heart" (Lunn 1895: 5). Residents were "sisters" "with the superintendent taking the place of mother or directing older sister" (Meyer 1892: 70). It was a place where all of the "daughters of Methodism" would be taught the values of "Mother Church" (Horton 1897: 10).

The Mother Heart was broad enough to provide both a home and a mission for all women unmarried or widowed. The deaconess community was a place for a woman without natural family or life goals since it provided a position for those with "empty hands and [a] vacant life" (Bancroft 1890: 253). This home atmosphere transformed the group into a family strong enough to enable deaconesses and other women to venture out into the world to fight "unbelief, disease, and all other forms of sin" (Wheeler 1889: 288). Deaconesses' devotion and love for each other emanating from their unity in Christ (Bancroft 229; Gibson 1928: 87; Wheeler 1889: 288) created a united front, it was claimed, to fight the social problems in the community. It was an easy step for deaconess leaders to extend the home metaphor to include the world in a specifically feminine version of the deaconess' place in the Social Gospel.

The Mother Heart and the Kingdom of God

Leaders of the Social Gospel had modified Wesleyan-evangelical values by liberalizing the doctrine of entire sanctification at its theological center. Wesley taught that entire sanctification was delivered through God's grace separately to each individual. Social Gospel theoreticians drew from these religious roots as well as Darwinian theory to enlarge the concept to include this deliverance as an "organic" or institutional whole. This "whole" was a new society built around communal values of the "brotherhood of man" under the "fatherhood of God." America, in accordance with its spiritual manifest destiny, could become one large sanctified family as part of the earthly kingdom of God. Additionally, methods derived from "social" science, which was now part of the "universal" front against societal sins, would be used in the struggle for societal perfection as part of God's progressive will.

Deaconesses, whose values were already centered around Christian mutuality and sisterhood reinforced by communal living and church connectionalism, readily integrated the holistic Social Gospel tenets and their scientific methods of service delivery into their ideological center (Dougherty 1979). Since building the kingdom of God required the sanctification of each home to usher in the new age, it was important to include the work of those whose specific mission was the care of God's "unmothered" children. Because the special province of deaconesses was home evangelization, it was easy for them to conclude that the Mother Heart, the feminine nature of God's love, held great significance for their work in the building of the kingdom. This allowed the deaconesses, and by extension, women, greater authority to become ministering women in the whole of society.

This reasoning permitted Meyer and other deaconess leaders to justify deaconess' demands for equal access and authority to become "ministers" in a church long unbalanced because of its lack of female leaders, who naturally carried the feminine side of God's care in their work. Meyer's use of familiar religious symbols and language in her writings and talks enabled her to enlist other evangelical middle-class women in the fight for equal rights for women and other liberal reforms she and other deaconess leaders championed (Bancroft 1890: 252; Crist 1980: 368; *Deaconess Advocate* January 1901: 6; January 1891: 6; January 1895: 3; Horton 1928: 221; MacDonell 1928: 246–47; Wheeler 1889: 300).

The Social Gospel leaders, along with the Methodist deaconesses and other mainline religious reformers, however, helped sow the seeds of a new rationalized order for social reform in America with these liberal values. This transformation of Wesleyan perfectionism and other religious tenets into beliefs consistent with utilitarian liberalism and other positivistic philosophies to meet the challenges of a rapidly changing world eventually led to the transformation of the Social Gospel and those movements that followed its lead. As social historian James Turner explained:

> religion caused unbelief. In trying to adapt their religious beliefs to socioeconomic change, to new moral challenges, to novel problems of knowledge, to the tightening standards of science, the defenders of God slowly strangled Him. (1985: xiii)

In other words, the more that social reformers tried to mold religious values and doctrines, including Wesleyan perfectionism, into contemporary standards and practices that were increasingly drawn from science and technology, the easier it became for religious progressives to accept universalistic, humanistic values and ideas as part of the solution to build a better society. The deaconesses and other religious settlers over the first two decades of the twentieth century increasingly drew their educational methods and service delivery from the techniques of positivistic-scientific utilitarianism touted as "scientific charity" from the emerging field of "social" science as they sought solutions to the intractable problems they faced in the neighborhoods they served and as they competed for students and workers in the emerging "professionalism" of social work.

Perfectibility, Practical Divinity, and Professionalism

For the deaconesses and city missionaries, the application of Christian principles to everyday problems and concerns was a way of ushering in the manifest destiny of God's kingdom. The first steps of the journey had been taken in the earlier religious awakening, particularly in the revivals which had echoed Wesley's admonition: "there is no holiness but social holiness." Wesley had also urged his followers to remember that they did not live as "solitary Christians" in isolation from society and its politics (Hudson 1981: 30; Wesley 1986: 14.3211). He was the first to see that the church's major task could be mission to others (Schmidt 1976: 88). The work of the Methodist social reformers was an embodiment of that legacy, carried out in the name of the Methodist Church. Methodism's inherent pragmatism which gave a plan or method to religious experience and created the ideological climate of "practical divinity," had a sympathetic familiarity to utilitarian ideas and practices that were becoming part of American's excitement with the industrial age. As time went on, words like "scientific charity" and "social Christianity" were used more and more in American culture to denote the mixing of scientific and business practices with religious mission. It was an easy and uncritical step, then, for deaconesses and other religious workers to begin using the same terms and methods in their training and work.

Frances Willard, Methodist leader of the Woman's Christian Temperance Union, predicted in her introduction to Meyer's first book (1892) that the deaconesses would provide a generalized "practical element" in religion. Other deaconesses agreed with that assessment

(Golder, Meyers Papers). Deaconess journals were replete with injunctions to expand God's work with "practical effort[s]" (*Deaconess Advocate* June 1893: 16) to "organize, organize" for the waves of a "thousand foreigners a day [who] land on our shores" (May 1893: 2). This population would be the focus for "testing the tentative proposals of practical philanthropists" working in the name of Christ (1890: 7). Even the Bible was studied practically in order to promote "practical kindness and institutions of mercy" (*Deaconess Advocate* September 1901: 7; July 1904: 9). The present world needed

> a practical religion. . . . And if their convictions as to Christian truth are to be reviewed they must be approached in practical methods. Hence the rise and development amongst us of what is called Social Christianity. (Stephenson 1902: 10)

The practical religion of Wesley would provide practical methods for practical solutions to concrete problems. What was disappearing in the equation was the Wesleyan grounding of practical service in tandem with personal holiness within a larger transcendental relationship with God. Without that spiritual foundation, it was a short step to the acceptance of any scientific theory and method offered in the name of progress and practicality, especially as deaconesses worked more and more with other social reformers.

Deaconesses, city missionaries, and volunteers who staffed the religious settlement institutions were on the front lines of the city mission field. The early city missions, as part of the religious settlement movement, had provided the model for early neighborhood involvement in the lives of the dispossessed for non-sectarian settlements and associated charities that followed just as they had for the sectarian settlements. As such, there was a great deal of exchange of information, speakers, ideals, and services among the leaders and workers in the three parallel reform movements as they moved from their religious origins into an increasingly non-sectarian orientation.

Meyer was a friend of social settlement leader Jane Addams, and each was involved with the other's work. Deaconess Irva Brown, a friend of both, said that Addams helped Meyer select the site for the original school and was involved in Meyer's early plans (Brown 1985: 6; *Bulletin* 1945: 9). In fact, Meyer had wanted to put Addams on the Chicago Training School's Board of Trustees in 1892, but was voted down. According to one historian:

> Hull-House was just then drawing the fire of the churches because it had been thought necessary to eliminate any direct religious teaching from its

program and one or two members of the Training School Board protested against the presence of this "UnChristian enterprise." (Horton 1928: 182)

Addams wrote of this experience in *Twenty Years at Hull-House*, describing Meyer as "the open-minded head of the school" and adding her "sympathy for the embarrassment in which the head of the school was placed" (Addams 1981: 72). Addams also admitted her sympathy for Meyer's efforts when she stated that the "actual activities of a missionary school are not unlike many that are carried on in a Settlement situated in a foreign quarter" (49). Their friendship continued throughout their careers, and Meyer frequently spoke of Addam's work through the *Deaconess Advocate*.

Shortly before Addams began her work at Hull-House, Meyer had proposed a deaconess settlement apart from the deaconess home along the lines of the social settlements which were being set up in several large cities at that time. In 1889, she wrote about "Our Bit-of-Heaven-House," a proposal to put a nice home in the middle of the slums staffed by six deaconesses. She wanted a "cadet corps of young women living there with open parlors for singing and reading each night" (*Deaconess Advocate* June 1889: 2). This became a reality in 1891 when "Bit-of-Heaven" opened in an Italian section of Chicago. Although deaconesses visited, nursed the sick, established a "poor closet," and held weekly Bible meetings, the venture was unsuccessful because of lack of support from the church (*Deaconess Advocate* March 1891: 9; Horton 1909: 154–57). Meyer persisted. In 1898, an old parsonage on Wabash Avenue offered itself for this purpose and Meyer worked diligently for a year to keep it going. She apparently was unsuccessful in her efforts. By 1905, however, the *Deaconess Advocate* reported that there were at least four settlements being run by deaconesses in Chicago, Denver, Cleveland, and Washington (March 1902: 13; May 1903: 12; April 1905: 12).

Despite opposition from the church members who opposed the non-sectarian atmosphere of the social settlements, social settlement leaders continued to lecture regularly at the Chicago Training School, and the students' field work included living as residents at Hull-House and other social settlements (Brown 1985: 9). Meyer used noted settlement advocates George Herron, Josiah Strong, Jacob Riis, and Robert Hunter as Social Gospel/social work authorities in the *Deaconess Advocate* (December 1895: 5; July 1902: 7; April 1905: 12). Articles from the social settlement journal, *The Commons*, and talks from the National Conference of Charities and Corrections were reviewed and critiqued in the *Deaconess Advocate* as well (May 1902: 6; July 1902: 70). By 1913,

Meyers had supplemented the religious social work lectures with textbooks by charity-organization pioneer social workers Edward J. Devine and Amos Warner (*Bulletin* January 1914: 13; Meyer Papers, File I, Garrett Evangelical Theological Seminary Archives, Chicago). By 1918, her students were working in the United Charities and Juvenile Protective Associations as "visitors" (*Bulletin* December 1918: 19) and learning to be participants in the codified, "scientific" methods of the "new charity," touted by Charity Organization Society (COS) leader Mary Richmond as "the ambulance corps in the army of civilization . . . social physicians and nursers . . . skilled in relief and prevention of distress" (Richmond 1930: 115).

"Scientific charity" became part of the deaconess curricula by the mid-1890s. Course objectives included giving "general information concerning the missionary fields, including statistics and a knowledge of the habits, customs, and religions of the people" (*Announcement* 1895: 7). By 1899, sociology was added (14). Six years later, industrial work included "personal investigations and study of philanthropic and religious institutions in the city" (*Bulletin* July 1905: 22). During the four-month course, scientific temperance was also part of the schedule, with lectures from Mary McDowell (a Methodist) from the University of Chicago Settlement, Anna Gordon, vice-president of the Woman's Christian Temperance Union, and W. A. Evans, who served as Chief of the Department of Health (pamphlet, Meyer Papers).

Although religious language continued to be used to inspire and motivate deaconesses, city missionaries, and their followers, "practical divinity" increasingly referred to the John Dewey-inspired pragmatism of the social settlements or the "scientific charity" of the COS theoreticians, both of which reenforced pragmatism's encouragement of the substitution of fixed, normative standards with a relativistic, utilitarian definition of truth as a consequence of one's actions and beliefs. These instrumental values tied to the prevailing Social Gospel/Darwinian concepts of organic wholeness and progressive change over time, as well as an unbounded faith in democratic interrelatedness, created a climate of universalistic faith. This universalism crept into the thinking of the religious settlers. As such, practical divinity was less and less tied to the more specific foundation of Wesleyan evangelical theological doctrine as practicality took on the more universal meaning of doing good for others in the name of a less normative "Force" discerned from internal consciousness (Carson 1990: 45–46, 106–7; Dewey 1970: 33; James 1987: 522; Marty 1986: 82).

This reinterpreted meshing of practical divinity and scientific study was not lost on the students. The class essay of 1895 declared that "we are living in an essentially sociological age. . . . Earnest souls everywhere are concentrating every energy into the great work of the renovation and purification of society" (*Deaconess Advocate* June 1895: 5). These students carried these beliefs into the field. In time it would become more difficult to distinguish the ideology and practice of students who graduated from deaconess schools and those who graduated from the university-based schools of social work. As deaconess training and values became less and less distinguishable from the values and methods of early professional social work, deaconess organizations began to lose the sponsorship of the church and other financial backers and the deaconess training schools were merged into schools of theology (Tatem 1960: 35; Nola Smee, telephone interview, 22 July 1995) or schools of social work (address by Walter Athern, 26 April 1926, Boston University School of Theology Archives).

Nevertheless, the deaconess movement as part of the religious settlement movement, had paved the way for religious women to move into society as trained, paid professionals. Wesleyan perfectionistic beliefs, altered to be sure, moved with these women into the new field of nonsectarian social work, which was rapidly displacing its earlier evangelical mission with the methods and ideology of what social work historian Roy Lubove (1965) calls "the professional altruist." Increasingly, societal perfection would be couched in terms such as "social engineering" and "ethical culture" (Carson 1990: 17–19).

Professional Pressures

The transition of social work from an evangelically-based organization of religiously motivated individuals into a secular organization of professionals had far-reaching results. "The spontaneous will to serve," so evident in earlier volunteer social reform efforts, according to Lubove, was subverted as social work moved into professional status. The authority to interfere in the lives of clients by virtue of technical competence rather than the moral and class superiority that had served early social workers became the vehicle for the legitimation of early professionals. The establishment of "in groups," professionally trained specialists who because of their expertise were invited to become part of a subculture of professional associations and organizations, was the primary method used to facilitate this transformation (Lubove 1965: 118–56). Previous values that had stressed compassion, emotional involvement, vigorous love of humanity were "educated out," he claims, in preference for a "scientific trained intelligence and skillful application of technique" (122). This new climate of professionalism drastically changed the relationship between helper and those helped. Agencies became bureaucratic rather than evangelical, more contractual than spontaneous, and more removed from their clients (164).

While this movement toward scientifically trained intelligence and skilled techniques was certainly a major thread in the education of religious settlers and other mission workers, Methodist settlers for a time were able to balance the effects of this encroachment because of their earlier grounding in evangelical teaching reenforced by their continued ties with churches not as ready to move into the more liberal theology of the day. With time, however, it became more and more difficult to balance the models of individual investigations established earlier in missions and settlements by "friendly visitors" with the larger vision of reforming society through the establishment of social institutions and national associations for community action. This trend became more pronounced after World War I when the Community Chest, organized by business leaders for a more equitable distribution of monies, standardized the level of funding to all social agencies and added a level of bureaucratic control. This action quelled the social settlers' ability to rally their neighborhoods for social action and advocacy and the religious settlers' freedom to proselytize for denominational membership. The social and religious settlements were placed in the same position of having to answer to a *new* organizational hierarchy that determined policy and program, which created different dilemmas for both(Trolander 1987: 23).

One of the defining differences and continuing tensions between the sectarian and non-sectarian settlements had been the pressure of the churches on the settlements to continue evangelizing for church growth in the communities they served (Doris Alexander, telephone interview, 22 July 1995; Davis 1967: 15). This pressure caused many of the social settlements started by religious organizations to sever their ties with those organizations in order to solicit community-wide support and to appeal to wealthy industrialists more interested in ecumenical charities (Dubroca 1955: 41; Trolander 1987: 20). With centralized community funding, the social settlers were again forced to answer to an organizational hierarchy that could dictate policy and program. Since religious settlers were already experienced in responding to administrating agencies, this was not as difficult for them as it was for social settlers. The religious settlers' dilemma lay elsewhere. Their challenge was in their reaction to funding guidelines that conflicted with their religious obligations. The net result was less emphasis on controversial community action from the social settlements (Trolander 1987: 23) and increased pressure on the sectarian settlements to move away from evangelizing the community for church membership. Funding from the Community Chest also reinforced the trend to replace sectarian-trained workers with professionals in all the settlements. This had a major impact on the deaconess movement.

The Decline of Deaconess Leadership

The Community Chest, with the image of the expert influencing its leaders, encouraged the use of professionals in place of volunteer community workers. Shell-shocked veterans of World War I and families displaced by the death of soldiers required a more direct approach to health and personal problems than relationships with friendly neighbors. Red Cross social workers treating military personnel and their families discovered that Freudian psychiatry reinforced social casework's emphasis on treatment of the individual. It was an easy step for them to reframe the analysis and collection of facts for social diagnosis and study into newer theories and methods of developmental psychology and mental hygiene. The friendly visitor was becoming the neighborhood therapist as settlements moved more into the role of mental health centers (Leiby 1978: 176–90).

Even the use of groups, the traditional settlement avenue for attracting residents of the surrounding neighborhoods, became psychologized. After World War II and into the 1950s, concerns over juvenile delinquency, coupled with the availability of many more trained social workers, resulted in a large increase of professional staff. These professionals made "social group work" the focus of treatment for groups that had been the mainstay of settlement work for years (Switzer, in Bryan and Davis 1990: 246–50; Trolander 1987: 32–35). To their credit, Methodist settlers saw social group work as a method both for individual development and for "developing the group itself to where it would have some larger social goal and make a contribution to public life" (Farris 1986: 5).

By the early 1960s, the hiring of professional social workers had reached its peak as settlers moved out of the houses. By 1970, many directors of the social settlements had master of social work degrees. This trend led, according to one settlement historian, to greater emotional distancing from the neighborhoods and the earlier settlement reliance on mutual growth and learning. As she explains:

> In place of spontaneity and being available around the clock, [social workers] made appointments and 'treatment plans.' Instead of seeking to do *with* the neighborhood, they sought to do *for* the neighborhood. Their 'profession' detachment from the neighborhood was not only physical, it was psychological. (Trolander 1987: 39)

While Methodist settlements followed similar patterns of hiring practices as the social settlements, there were some differences. For one thing, Methodist deaconesses continued to reside in the settlements until as late as 1986 (Nola Smee, telephone interview, 22 July 1995) which continued the physical as well as the symbolic presence and sense of involvement in the neighborhoods that is part of the settlement legacy. Even when their residencies ended (beginning in the 1960s), it had more to do with changes in the Methodist Church and society than with lack of deaconess dedication. Specifically, the decline of deaconess residence in settlements parallelled the decline of the deaconess movement as a whole, as deaconesses began to retire and fewer and fewer women were willing to expend the level of commitment required. Other reasons for the decline of the deaconess movement are given by Betty Purkey, head of the Deaconess Division under the Board of Global Ministries for the United Methodist Church. They are: the church's opening the door to ordained ministry for women in 1956, the restructuring of the Woman's Division in 1964 with the consequence that deaconesses would no longer be funded by or assigned to ministries from the General Board and agencies, and the lack of recognition and promotion for deaconesses positions by the church. The success of an earlier deaconess crusade, the right of women to full participation in the church's ministry, in other words, contributed to the loss of support for the deaconess position (telephone interview, 24 July 1995).

Discussions with over twenty men and women who have worked or are working in the church's seventy former settlements, now called community centers, reveal a "hodgepodge" of individuals employed in these institutions, including home missionaries, diaconal ministers, ordained ministers, professional social workers, and business people. Currently there are no deaconesses working as directors (Lula Garrett, telephone interview, 20 July 1995). In the absence of deaconess administrators a flexible approach to hiring has been created that takes into consideration the needs of the organization as well as the individuals served. The majority of directors of Methodist social institutions are men with significant representation of minorities.

Another challenge to women's role in the administration of social agencies begun and sustained by their efforts has been the gradual increase in settlement leadership by males. This trend began in the 1960s with the corresponding rise in decentralization of settlement management in favor of local neighborhoods, and with the resulting ascendancy of African Americans and other ethnic minorities to positions of leadership. The rights and responsibilities for these groups has long been intertwined with settlement's history, both religious and social.

The Rise of African American and Male Leadership

Because the Methodist religious settlements in the South had a history of working with African Americans in the Bethlehem Houses, Methodist settlers were often leaders in race relations in that section of the country as well as in the settlement movement as a whole. For example, the salary of Mary DeBardeleben, who was described as "the first missionary to the Negro race in America" (Tatum 1960: 249), was collected by the Woman's Missionary Council in 1911 to begin a "Christian community center for Negroes" in Augusta, Georgia. The Center, named Galloway Hall, became the first Bethlehem House. Under DeBardeleben's direction, the residents organized a Colored Civic Improvement League which established three playgrounds for neglected children, opened clubs, classes, Sunday schools, and a kindergarten (249). The women of Nashville, Tennessee, established a successful center in 1912, and Chattanooga churches started one in 1922 (267–70). Others houses were started in Winston-Salem, North Carolina, and Spartanburg, South Carolina, in the 1930s (262-63).

More significant for the civil rights of African Americans, however, was the acceptance of interracial advisory boards for African American settlements with members selected from the community. These boards laid the groundwork for Methodist settlements to become the first institutions in many cities, especially in the South, to integrate programs in their communities (Doris Anderson, telephone interview, 22 July 1995; David Billings, telephone interview, 25 July 1995).

In the North, however, emigration patterns that turned white settlement neighborhoods into African American ones did not begin until after World War I. At that time, European migrations to America were slowed to a trickle while southern Blacks moved to the North and settled in the neighborhoods that previously had housed the Europeans. The settlements were forced to adjust to this community shift with policies that responded to the differing needs of American-born citizens faced with discrimination based on racism rather than discrimination based on being foreign-born. More important, settlers had to come face to face with their own policies and practices that had systematically excluded Blacks from the "democratic ideal."

Although sympathetic to the plight of the African Americans, social and religious settlers had pasted over the systemic problems caused by racism by building separate facilities for each group (Bryan and Davis 1990: 133–34; Tatum 1960: 242; Trolander 1987: 21–23). By the 1960s, however, with the advent of the civil rights movement, there was a major shift in the direction of full inclusion for all ethnic minorities. According to the records of the National Federation of Settlements, most of the directors of settlement houses from that era were white, despite the fact that most settlements were surrounded by African American populations and half of the social workers serving in the agencies were black. In 1968, with the War on Poverty (WOP) underway and the emphasis of decentralization of advisory boards, with a corresponding increase in representation of community involvement, there was a successful effort to turn the administration of the Federation over to African American leadership. While the action rectified many past injustices, it had the additional effect of changing the leadership from female to male, a pattern that continues today, not only on the national level, but on the local level as well. Since the connotation of the name, "settlement," implied "reference to a building where well-to-do people 'settled' in order to help the poor in the surrounding neighborhood was no longer applicable," the Federation's name was changed to the "United Neighborhood Centers" (Trolander 1987: 217, 216–33).

The Methodist settlements reacted to the changing ideological landscape in much the same way as the settlement movement in general. Methodists had severed their denominational connection over slavery in 1844, and the issues of interracial relationships had continued over the years to be a major source of soul searching and social action within the Women's Division and other missionary activities. During World War II, for example, along with petitioning for world peace, demanding the end of unfair displacement of women in industry, and holding conferences on family and demobilization, the Department of Christian Social Relations was holding interracial workshops and calling for "ways to conserve and strengthen gains for minority families that had accrued from the widening of job opportunity . . . from military service" (Stevens 1978: 29). By the 1960s, the women were sending out resolutions that declared, among other things, that their purpose was to "*unite* . . . efforts with all groups in the church toward eliminating in The Methodist Church all forms of segregation based on race whether in basic structures or institutional life" (91). Institutional works, including the original religious settlements (now renamed community centers), were more and more employing African American directors to work with African American staff in African American neighborhoods.

Despite this decentralization of institutional power, advisory boards for the community centers were still composed of interracial mixes because of the insistence in Methodist circles that a certain number of members come not only from the surrounding communities, but from the Methodist connection and the community at large (telephone survey of 14 Methodist community centers, September 1994 and July-August 1995). This racial (and gender) mixture helped with fund raising since many of the local communities served by the centers were unable to raise significant money to maintain their organizations. It also encouraged continued input and a sense of ownership from others not living in the neighborhoods. This continued representation was important, according to the former center director David Billings, because outside support helped with funding and offered continuing identification in transitional periods. A social center in a changing neighborhood that had not significantly served the needs of ethnic minorities in the past was not as readily embraced by those minorities after its former population had left the area. Until the necessary transition occurred, other support was essential (Billings, telephone interview, 25 July 1995). Today, in many of these centers, an integrated board with dedicated volunteers continues to raise funds, provide needed services, and support these institutions as part of their churches' social ministry. Nevertheless, the community centers have been and are forced to go outside of the churches to seek funding.

The Rise of Governmental Funding

During the 1930s and 40s, with the advent of the depression and New Deal economics, much-needed governmental funding challenged the sectarian basis of the Methodist settlements in ways that directly reenforced professional secularization and made them even more like the social settlements. During the second World War, the Works

Progress Administration (WPA) provided government paid employees to buttress child care activities in the settlements for working mothers who took jobs that the men had left behind as they went to war. Female volunteers became scarce as they too went to work to support the war effort, leaving less supervision for the adolescents who typically had been the beneficiaries for much of the recreational activities that the settlements provided. As a result, the teenagers began to be more disruptive, forcing the settlers further to decrease these activities in favor of greater services to younger children (Trolander 1987: 24–29). The decision to create programs based on governmental funding, justified as they were by the practical needs of the neighborhood and the declining financial support of the churches and individual contributions, set in place a pattern that allowed governmental access into policies and practices that undermined the sectarian settlement's freedom to pursue religious programs and activities in the same manner as a church. Evangelizing of any kind was increasingly out of the question since it now jeopardized agency funding.

This pattern was accelerated in the 1960s with the War on Poverty, when massive amounts of governmental aid were sent into low-income communities. Despite the criticism by community activist Saul Alinsky that settlements no longer spoke for their neighborhoods because they were out of touch with the truly disadvantaged in the communities, WOP funds were given as settlements opened their doors to antipoverty programs, voter registration drives, and educational projects like Headstart. VISTA workers were also added to staffs in large numbers as the young volunteers revived the idea of residency in neighborhoods (David Billings, telephone interview, 25 July 1996; Nola Smee, telephone interview, 22 July 1995; Trolander 200–206). The successful use of semiprofessionals helped to revive the enthusiasm for volunteer work and helped in the decentralization of settlement management since many VISTA volunteers were hired from the neighborhoods.

Federal money continued in the 1970s and 80s because of some of the backlash from the liberal policies of antipoverty programs that had sought to open up new areas of service delivery from nontraditional sources. The failure of these efforts made the neighborhood houses a favorable place to place governmental resources since their long-term stability and ties to organized religion worked in their favor during more conservative times. (David Billings, telephone interview, 25 July 1995; Nola Smee, telephone interview, 22 July 1995). The additional funding, undergirded by church financial help and volunteer resources, allowed the religious centers to return to the settlement legacy of social advocacy long thought to be the sole providence of the social settlers who were not hamstrung, it was believed, by church dogma and control. Many of the newer social reform efforts supplemented by church volunteers and funding came out of religious settlement work. Some of these programs are: alternate schools for dropouts (St. Mark's in New Orleans), voter registration centers (South Side Settlement in Columbus), the American Center for Law and Justice (Bethlehem Center, Augusta), Midnight Basketball (Marcy-Newberry Center, Chicago), Congregations for Children (Moore Community House, Biloxi), and a pilot program that evolved in the 1980s into Atlanta's Habitat for Humanity affiliate (Wesley Center, Atlanta). Ironically, the sectarian ropes that had connected the centers to the church— sometimes uncomfortably—also had provided the needed stability for their survival during the constant changes in funding, staff, and administrations.

Implications for the Future

There is some truth to the observation of social historian Walter Trattner (1979: 137) that the majority of settlements, rather than progressive secular "spearheads for reform," as pictured by their social work advocates, were instead "city mission[s] bent on religious proselytizing, rigorous Americanization, and the imposition of social conformity upon the lower-class clientele" (17). What Trattner and others do not see in their analysis of these "modified missions," which they claim "were of little importance" (Davis 1967: 23), is the narrow lens with which they view the total picture.

Religious settlements have long taken a back seat to the highly publicized work of social settlements such as Hull-House where "St. Jane" and her impressive list of friends turned neighborhood friendliness into national organizations for social reform (Addams 1981; Davis 1967; Leiby 1979: 111–62) despite the fact that the religious values and drive that sent both groups of settlers into inner-city communities were similar. This blind spot has also made it difficult for social historians to compare with any great depth or accuracy settlement work not in the historical spotlight.

Overlooked in their analysis is the national reform effort that built and sustained the religious settlements because of the work of hundreds of women who supported the training schools, sent money, and volunteered their time and energies in a unified effort to serve those who they perceived needed their help and care. Whether these women are seen as agents of social control or societal transformation (Lissak 1989: 5) depends on one's vision of the kind of society that one desires.

The Methodist religious settlers' vision of the society that they wanted began with evangelical hopes for a holy nation undergirded by a rigorous drive centered in Wesleyan perfectibility. This drive united them in the mission and cause that gave rise to hundreds of social institutions and the education of religious workers to run them. When they were forced by the overwhelming task that they had chosen to seek new ways of thinking and practice, they lost part of the religious underpinning that defined their vision. Despite these changes and the struggles behind them, the religious settlements survived and in many areas today are thriving. As such, they serve as reminders of what the church is capable of doing when the call for commitment, dedication, and sacrifice is answered, and when we seek "the recovery of our social ecology [that] would allow us to link interests with the common good" (Bellah et al. 1985: 287).

At the beginning of this century, Jane Addams wrote about the "thirst for righteousness" (1972: 139–61) in a reorganized society that was reeling from the effects of the "wrecked foundations of domesticity" (1972: 47). Many would agree that the same situation remains at the century's end. Family disorganization, massive international disruptions, tragic population shifts, and continuing disagreements over race, class, and gender create huge vacuums in cultural and value homogeneity. Our nation, like the church and other social service professions, seems to be searching for a renewed vision and mission.

There is some evidence that this vision has not been entirely lost. While the mission statements of today's religious settlements often reflect the nonsectarian orientation of agencies operating under governmental funding and policies, the sense of religious calling is evident in the voices of those who continue to serve in these institutions. Some staff members openly use biblical language as they describe their purpose "as feeding the sheep" (Robert Oliver, telephone interview, 6 September 1994). Others talk of "assisting in the balance of social reform with the good news" (George Sturdivand, telephone interview, 6 September 1994), while others simply talk of commitment to those less fortunate (Fred Mitchell, telephone interview, 7 September 1994). While many say that they resist the pressures of the church, now greatly diminished, to proselytize the people they serve, they nevertheless, as a group, believe strongly that the spiritual foundation on which their work rests is crucial in fostering the relationships and mutuality that have always been a part of the legacy of the settlements. As retired deaconess Nola Smee observed, "people sense it in the commitment and care one gives" (telephone interview, 22 July 1995). The sentiment among the group also is strong that the presence and support of the church connection is vital; both as a symbol of Christ's commandment to care for the disadvantaged and as a network for training, volunteers, and financial support. As one of the former directors now working for a nonsectarian agency said, "it is just so much harder to do [social work] without the church" (David Billings, telephone interview, 25 July 1995).

Many welfare activists are beginning to agree. They join a rising chorus of opinion makers who are calling for the same spirit of mutuality, neighborliness, egalitarian inclusiveness, consensus building, and genuine concern that carried earlier reformers beyond the comfort of their homes and communities into areas where the need seemed the greatest in the quest for a better society. Social settlement pioneer Robert Woods declared in his history of the settlement movement that the "true impetus" for the settlements "came out of the Wesleyan revival, which . . . wrought results so elemental in English life" (1922: 2). It is time to renew that impetus in ours.

References

Abell, Aaron Ignatius. 1962. *The Urban Impact on American Protestantism 1861–1900*. Hamden: Archon.

Addams, Jane. 1981. *Twenty Years at Hull House*. Phillips Publishing Co., 1910; Reprint, New York: Signet Classic.

———. 1972. *The Spirit of Youth and the City Streets*. New York: Macmillan, 1909; Reprint, Urbana: University of Chicago Press.

Ahlstrom, Sidney E. 1975. *A Religious History of the American People*. Vol. 2. Garden City, N.Y.: Image Books.

Alexander, Arabel Wilbur. 1898. *The Life and Work of Lucinda B. Helm, Founder of the Women's Parsonage and Home Mission Society of the Methodist Episcopal Church, South*. Nashville: Publishing House of the Methodist Episcopal Church, South.

Announcement of the Chicago Training School for City, Home and Foreign Missions. 1895.

Bancroft, Jane M. 1890. *Deaconesses in Europe and Their Lessons for America*. New York: Hunt & Eaton.

Barclay, Wade Crawford. 1957. *The Methodist Episcopal Church 1845–1939*. Vol. 3. New York: The Board of Missions of The Methodist Church.

Bellah, Robert N., et al. 1985. *Habits of the Heart: Individualism and Commitment in American Life*. Berkeley: University of California Press.

Bremner, Robert H. 1956. *From the Depths: The Discovery of Poverty in the United States*. New York: New York University Press.

Brown, Irva Calley. 1985. *"In Their Times": A History of the Chicago Training School on the Occasion of Its Centennial Celebration, 1885–1985*. Evanston: Garrett-Evangelical Theological Seminary.

Brown, Oswald Eugene, and Anna Muse Brown. 1904. *Life and Letters of Laura Askew Haygood*. Nashville: Methodist Episcopal Church, South Publishing House.

Bryan, Mary Lynn McCree, and Allen F. Davis, ed. 1990. *100 Years at Hull House*. Bloomington: Indiana University Press.

Bulletin of the Chicago Training School for City, Home and Foreign Missions 1905. Vol. 2, no. 3 (July).
1918. Vol. 15, no. 4 (December).

1945. Vol. 48, no. 1 (January-March).

Carson, Mina 1990. *Settlement Folk*. Chicago: University of Chicago Press.

Crist, Miriam. 1980. "Winifred Chappell: Everybody on the Left Knew Her." *Radical Religion* 5: 22–37.

Davis, Allen F. 1967. *Spearheads for Reform: The Social Settlements and the Progressive Movement 1890–1914*. New York: Oxford University Press.

———. 1973. *American Heroine: The Life and Legend of Jane Addams*. London: Oxford University Press.

Davis, Mrs. John. 1890. *Lucy Webb Hayes: A Memorial Sketch*. Cincinnati: Cranston & Stowe.

Deaconess Advocate. 1898–1914. Vols. 14–29.

  The Message. 1886–1892. Vols. 1–8.

  The Message and Deaconess Advocate. 1894–1897. Vols. 10–13.

  The Message and Deaconess World. 1893. Vol. 9.

Dewey, John. 1970. "The Development of American Pragmatism." In *Pragmatism: The Classical Writings*, ed. H. Standish Thayer. New York: New American Library.

Discipline of the Methodist Episcopal Church. 1880, 1884, 1888, 1898, 1904. New York: Phillips G. Hunt.

Dixon, Thomas, Jr. 1896. *The Failure of Protestantism in New York and Its Causes*. 2d. ed. New York: Strauss & Rehn.

Dougherty, Mary Agnes. 1979. "The Methodist Deaconess, 1885–1918: A Study in Religious Feminism." Ph.D. Diss., University of California, Davis.

Dubroca, Isabelle. 1955. *Good Neighbor Eleanor McMain of Kingsley House*. New Orleans: Pelican.

Farris, Buford. 1986. "Current Impact of the Settlement Movement on the Field of Social Action: Creating a Community of Participation." Paper Presentation. 17 October.

Fish, John Olen. 1969. "Southern Methodism in the Progressive Era: A Social History." PhD. diss., University of Georgia.

Gibson, Maria Layng. 1928. *Memories of Scarritt*. Nashville: Cokesbury.

Glidden, Elizabeth. 1988. "'For Jesus' Sake': A Century of Deaconess Service in the United Methodist Church." Paper Presentation. 16 June, 1988.

Golder, Christian. 1903. *History of the Deaconess Movement in the Christian Church*. Cincinnati: Jennings & Pye.

Hall, Jacquelyn Dowd. 1979. *Revolt Against Chivalry: Jessie Daniel Ames and the Women's Campaign Against Lynching*. New York: Columbia University Press.

Hardesty, Nancy, Lucille S. Dayton, and Donald W. Dayton. 1979. "Women in the Holiness Movement: Feminism in the Evangelical Tradition." Pp. 225–54 in *Women of Spirit*, ed. Rosemary Ruether and Eleanor McLaughlin. New York: Simon & Schuster.

Hardesty, Nancy. 1984. *Women Called to Witness*. Nashville: Abingdon.

Hardman, Keith J. 1983. *The Spiritual Awakeners*. Chicago: Moody.

Hofstadter, Richard. 1955. *The Age of Reform*. New York: Alfred A. Knopf.

Home Missions. 1930. Nashville: Woman's Missionary Council, Methodist Episcopal Church, South.

Hopkins, Charles Howard. 1940. *The Rise of the Social Gospel in American Protestantism 1865–1915*. New Haven: Yale University Press.

Horton, Isabelle. 1897. "What the Deaconess Says to the Churches." *Deaconess Advocate* 13 (March): 10.

———. 1904. *The Burden of the City*. New York: Fleming H. Revell.

———. 1928. *High Adventure - Life of Lucy Rider Meyer*. New York: Methodist Book Concern.

Hudson, Winthrop S. 1974. "The Methodist Age in America." *Methodist History* 13 (April): 3–15.

———. 1981. *Religion in America*. New York: Charles Scriber's Sons.

Hunter, Jane. 1984. *The Gospel of Gentility*. New Haven: Yale University Press.

Ingraham, Sarah R. 1844. *Walks of Usefulness or Reminiscences of Mrs. Margaret Prior*. New York: American Female Moral Reform Society.

James, William. 1987. "Pragmatism: A New Name for Some Old Ways of Thinking." Pp. 480–624 in *William James: Writings 1902–1910*, ed. Bruce Kuklick. N.p.: The Library of America.

Kearney, Belle. 1900. *A Slave Holder's Daughter*. 2d ed. St. Louis: St. Louis Christian Advocate Co.

Keller, Rosemary Skinner. 1981. "Creating a Sphere for Women: The Methodist Episcopal Church." Pp. 246–60 in *Women in New Worlds*, ed. Hilah Thomas and Rosemary Skinner Keller. Nashville: Abingdon.

————. 1984. "Women and the Nature of Ministry in the United Methodist Tradition." *Methodist History* 22 (January): 99–115.

Kreutziger, Sarah Sloan. 1991. "Going on to Perfection: The Contributions of the Wesleyan Doctrine of Entire Sanctification to Value Base of American Professional Social Work Through the Lives and Activities of Nineteenth-Century Evangelical Women Reformers." D.S.W. diss., Tulane University, New Orleans.

Ladies of the Mission. 1854. *The Old Brewery and the New Mission House at the Five Points.* New York: Stringer & Townsend.

Lee, Elizabeth Meredith. 1963. *As Among the Methodists: Deaconesses Yesterday Today and Tomorrow.* New York: Woman's Division of Christian Service, Board of Missions, Methodist Church.

Lee, Susan Dye. 1981. "Evangelical Domesticity: The Woman's Temperance Crusade of 1873–1874." Pp. 293-309 in *Women in New Worlds*, vol. 1, ed. Hilah Thomas and Rosemary Skinner Keller. Nashville: Abingdon.

Leiby, James. 1978. *A History of Social Welfare and Social Work in the United States.* New York: Columbia University Press.

Letzig, Betty J. 1987. *Expressions of Faith.* New York: National Program Division, General Board of Global Ministries, The United Methodist Church.

Lissak, Rivka Shpak. 1989. *Pluralism and Progressives: Hull-House and the New Immigrants, 1890–1919.* Chicago: University of Chicago Press.

Link, Arthur, et al. 1981. *The American People: A History.* Arlington Heights, Illinois: AHM Publishing.

Lloyd, Gary A. 1968. *A Study of Social Work Methods: 1890–1960. Part I: Charities and Settlements Methods of "Retail" and "Wholesale" Reform, 1890–1915.* New Orleans: Tulane University School of Social Work.

Lubove, Roy. 1965. *The Professional Altruist: The Emergence of Social Work as a Career 1880–1930.* Cambridge: Harvard University Press.

Lunn, Mary. 1895. "The Model Deaconess as Superintendent of a Home." *The Message and the Deaconess Advocate.* 10 (June): 5.

MacDonnell, (Mrs.) R. W. 1928. *Belle Harris Bennett: Her Life Work.* Nashville: Board of Missions, Methodist Episcopal Church, South.

Magalis, Elaine. 1973. *Conduct Becoming to a Woman.* New York: Women's Division, Board of Global Ministries, The United Methodist Church.

Magnuson, Norris. 1977. *Salvation in the Slum: Evangelical Social Work, 1965–1920*. Metuchen, N.J.: Scarecrow.

Marty, Martin E. 1986. *Modern American Religion*. Vol. 1.: *The Irony of It All, 1893–1919*. Chicago: University of Chicago Press.

Mason, Mary. 1870. *Consecrated Talents: Or the Life of Mrs. Mary W. Mason*. New York: Carlton & Lanahan.

Message, The. S.v. Mrs. John Davis.

McBride, Esther Barnhart. 1972. "Protestant Contributions to American Social Work, 1870–1912." PhD. diss., Tulane University.

———. 1983. *Open Church: History of an Idea*. N.p.: By the author.

McDowell, John Patrick. 1982. *The Social Gospel in the South*. Baton Rouge: Louisiana State University Press.

McLoughlin, William G., Jr. 1978. *Rivals, Awakenings, and Reform*. Chicago: University of Chicago Press.

Meyer, Lucy Rider. 1892. *Deaconesses, Biblical, Early Church, European, American, with the Story of How the Work Began in the Chicago Training School for City, Home, and Foreign Missions and the Chicago Deaconess Home*. Cincinnati: Cranston & Stowe.

Nelson, John. 1909. "City Missions." *Home Mission Fields of the Methodist Episcopal Church, South*. Home Department, Board of Missions, Methodist Episcopal Church, South.

North, Frank Mason. 1909. "The Socialized Church." Pp. 241–68 in *The Socialized Church*, ed. Worth M. Tippy. New York: Eaton & Mains.

Norwood, Frederick A. 1974. *The Story of American Methodism*. Nashville: Abingdon.

Palmer, Phoebe. 1985. *Promise of the Father*. 1859. Reprint, New York: Garland.

Rauschenbusch, Walter. 1911. *Christianity and the Social Crisis*. NewYork: Macmillan.

Richmond, May E. 1930. "Our Relation to the Churches." Pp. 115–19 in *The Long View*, ed. Joanna C. Calcord. New York: Russell Sage Foundation.

Riis, Jacob A. 1962. *How the Other Half Lives: Studies Among the Tenements of New York*. 1890. Reprint, American Century Series, New York: Hill & Wang.

Ruether, Rosemary Radford, and Eleanor McLaughlin, ed. 1979. *Women of Spirit*. New York: Simon & Schuster.

Ruether, Rosemary Radford, and Rosemary Skinner Keller. 1986. *Women & Religion in America*. Vol. 3. San Francisco: Harper & Row.

Schmidt, Martin. 1976. "Wesley's Place in Church History." Pp. 67–93 in *The Place of Wesley in the Christian Tradition*, ed. Kenneth E. Rowe. Metuchen: Scarecrow.

Scott, Anne Firor. 1970. *The Southern Lady: From Pedestal to Politics 1830–1930*. Chicago: University of Chicago Press.

———. 1984. *Making the Invisible Woman Visible*. Urbana: University of Illinois Press.

Seller, Maxine Schwartz, ed. 1981. *Immigrant Women*. Philadelphia: Temple University Press.

Sixth Annual Report of the Woman's Missionary Society of the Methodist Episcopal Church, South. 1884. (June). Nashville: Southern Methodist Publishing House.

Smith, Timothy L. 1980. *Revivalism and Social Reform in the Mid-Nineteenth Century America*. Nashville: Abingdon.

Smith-Rosenberg, Carroll. 1971. *Religion and the Rise of the American City: The New York City Mission Movement, 1812–1870*. Ithaca: Cornell University Press.

Sprecht, Harry, and Mark E. Courtney. 1994. *Unfaithful Angels: How Social Work Has Abandoned Its Mission*. New York: Free Press.

Stevens, Thelma. 1978. *Legacy for the Future: The History of Christian Social Relations in the Woman's Division of Christian Service, 1940–68*. Cincinnati: Women's Division, Board of Global Ministries, United Methodist Church.

Switzer, Elaine. N. D. "Hull-House in the Late 1940s." Pp. 245–49 in *100 Years at Hull House*, ed. Mary Lynn McCree and Allen F. Davis. Bloomington: Indiana University Press, 1990.

Strong, Josiah. 1893. *The New Era or the Coming Kingdom*. New York: Baker & Taylor.

Tatum, Noreen Dunn. 1960. *A Crown of Service: A Story of Women's Work in the Methodist Episcopal Church, South, from 1878–1940*. Nashville: Parthenon.

Taylor, Graham. 1936. *Chicago Commons Through Forty Years*. Chicago: Chicago Commons Association.

Thompson, Edgar. 1972. "God and the Southern Plantation System." Pp. 57–91 in *Religion and the Solid South*, ed. Samuel Hill. Nashville: Abingdon.

Trattner, Walter I. 1979. *From Poor Law to Welfare State*. 2d ed. New York: Free Press.

Trolander, Judith Ann. 1987. *Professionalism and Social Change*. New York: Columbia University Press.

Turner, James. 1985. *Without God, Without Creed.* Baltimore: John Hopkins University Press.

Wesley, John. 1986. *The Works of John Wesley*. Vol. 1–15. Grand Rapids: Baker Book House; Reprint of the 1872 ed. (London, Wesleyan Methodist Book Room).

Wheeler, Henry. 1889. *Deaconesses Ancient and Modern*. New York: Hunt & Eaton.

White, Charles Edward. 1986. *The Beauty of Holiness: Phoebe Palmer as Theologian, Revivalist, Feminist, and Humanitarian*. Grand Rapids: Francis Asbury.

Willard, Frances. 1889. *Glimpses of Fifty Years: The Autobiography of an American Woman*. Chicago: H. T. Smith.

Woman's Home Mission Society. N.d. *The Record of the Woman's Home Mission Society*. N.p.: Methodist Episcopal Church, South.

Woman's Home Mission Society. 1911. "The Early History of Deaconess Work and Training Schools for Women in American Methodism." N.p.: The Methodist Episcopal Church, South.

Woman's Home Missions. 1930. Vol. 47 (June): 1–36.

Woods, Robert. 1922. *The Settlement Horizon*. New York: Russell Sage Foundation.

Woods, Robert A., and Albert J. Kennedy, ed. 1911. *Handbook of Settlements*. New York: Charities Publication Committee.

Archives

Boston University School of Theology.
Special Collections, University Libraries, Boston, Massachusetts.
Garrett-Evangelical Theological Seminary Archives, Northwestern University, Chicago, Illinois.
  Lucy Rider Meyers Papers.
  Chicago Training School Papers.
  Methodist Deaconess Movement Papers.
Wesley Community Center. Atlanta, Georgia.
  Wesley Settlement Papers.

⌇ Robert C. Monk ⌇

The essays by Longfield, Rowe, Kreutziger, and Becker show how connectional endeavor takes local expression and how local initiative shapes the connection. Robert Monk explores both. He focuses on initiatives with respect to college youth, on their efforts to connect with one another in pursuit of a better world, on the importance of conference networks in the building of campus ministry. Over the middle third of the century the church established Wesley Foundations across American higher education, knit active students together through the Methodist Student Movement, inspired and resourced them through motive, deployed them in Youth Caravans, and gathered them in national, regional, and state conferences. Campus ministry became a connection in itself but also depended upon and contributed to the larger connection.

From that tension flowed a whole set of other tensions, not unlike those in any mission. Was this to be for students by the church or also by them to the church? How would it balance its prophetic, priestly, royal, and pastoral care roles? Should it make itself at home with the perspectives and the values of an increasingly secularized university or position itself critically and on the margins? Could the church's imagination, investment, and involvement be maintained for the long haul and particularly as students and the student world changed? How would the increasing professionalism of the campus ministry and the increasing peer pressures of collegiate life interplay? Should campus ministry help the church transcend its denominationalism while still seeking denominational support? And amid such tensions, could campus ministry be both a nursery for the ministry and the prophetic voice of the church on issues of war, labor, war again, race, poverty, war yet again? And if campus ministry could balance its "nursery," infrastructural, and prophetic roles, would it produce the ministry the church wanted?

As Monk indicates, the answers that campus ministry was giving by the 1960s did not please the church. Funding disappeared, and the program imploded. A new [U]MSM seems to be just now emerging and elements of the older program are re-emerging. The questions remain, as Monk's concluding reflections indicate.

United Methodist Campus Ministry and the Methodist Student Movement

Robert C. Monk

From the foundation of Harvard College until the post-Civil War establishment of land-grant colleges, American Protestant churches assumed that their students, including their ministerial students, would receive a strong grounding in the Christian faith along with a sound liberal arts education in their denominational schools. Rapid expansion of state-supported education in the last quarter of the nineteenth century, however, created a dramatically changed academic environment. For students enrolled in the state colleges, one element of this new climate was immediately evident; they no longer necessarily found the direct spiritual nurture previously available at denominational colleges.[1]

Removed from their traditional local churches, many students found spiritual challenge and sustentation in volunteer Christian student associations. They readily joined units of the YMCA and YWCA as these rapidly appeared on state and independent campuses in the 1870s and 1880s. An intercollegiate YMCA movement was formed in 1876 to coordinate the work on various campuses and give students occasions for regional and national interconnection. In 1886, spurred by student revivals in Great Britain and America, the Student Volunteer Movement for Foreign Missions organized and challenged students to enter into Christian missions around the world (some 11,000 responded to this call during the next thirty years). Established in 1895, the World Student Christian Federation coordinated student efforts on college and university campuses around the world.[2] In each of these developments and other similar volunteer organizations students, understanding their new setting to demand new patterns of Christian ministry to supplement traditional church models, responded by creating innovative forms of ministry at home and abroad as they experimented with early patterns of ecumenicity.

Although many Methodists students participated in and assumed significant leadership positions in these nineteenth-century volunteer student Christian associations, by the first decade of the twentieth century many church leaders began to envision a Methodist college ministry wherein the church would directly enlist participation from its own student and faculty members on state and independent campuses. The earliest formation of such a Methodist group occurred before 1890 on the University of Michigan campus, where the administration actively supported the creation of denominational student groups as well as sponsored a campus Christian association.[3] However, it was Bishop W. F. McDowell's 1907 selection of James C. Baker as pastor of Trinity Methodist Church adjacent to the University of Illinois (Urbana, Ill.) which initiated a campus ministry pattern that would become the standard for Methodist work on campuses throughout the nation. Bishop McDowell directed Baker to expand the nascent campus ministry for University of Illinois students already begun by the Trinity congregation. Baker quickly responded to the Bishop's instructions by attracting numerous faculty, staff, and students into Trinity's membership.[4] By 1913 the strength of the university portion of the church's work led Baker to incorporate the campus ministry under a separate Board of Trustees and to give it a new name—the Wesley Foundation.[5] Recognizing the statewide educational responsibilities of the university, Baker also formed a "Commission on Work Among Methodist Students at the University of Illinois" that included representatives from each of the Illinois conferences.[6] Through this "interconference" commission, the resources of Trinity church were supplemented and expanded to meet the demands of the campus ministry that could not be met by the local church. Baker's creative expansion of the work and his innovative patterns of ministry and organization began a Wesley Foundation "movement" across the church, and Baker is usually credited with being the "father" of Methodist campus ministry.

Through Baker's new ministry and similar ones that quickly followed his pioneering designs, the Methodist church "extended" itself onto the campus. That college campuses were understood as yet another Christian mission field is seen in the support the Illinois Foundation received from the church's Board of Home Missions and Church Extension.[7]

James Baker's explanation of why the word "foundation" was used as the name of this student ministry suggests that other elements were present in this new pattern:

> I suggested the name "Foundation" to my Board and it was chosen because it was clearly evident that no one could foretell how this work among students would develop. We wished a name with no limiting restrictions. We knew it should move out on an "open curve."[8]

In its Wesley Foundations Baker envisioned Methodism establishing a stable Christian "foundation" on which could be built unique experiments relating Christianity to independent university education—experiments that might well enlarge traditional ministries and their boundaries.

A half century later Kenneth Underwood in his monumental 1960s study of American campus ministry commented on Baker's work:

> This pioneer church statesman believed that the mission of organized religion and the meaning of the gospel in a new urban, technical society must be formed in close co-operation with the intellectual resources of the university. For him, we now realize, much more was at stake than a ministry to students which satisfied the home-town churches.[9]

Underwood was attracted to Baker's work because it exemplified what Underwood, studying the movement decades later, saw as the essential and interrelated elements of an adequate campus ministry. Relying on the early church's explanation of Jesus' ministry as falling into three distinct but interdependent modes—King (governance), Prophet, and Priest (pastor)—Underwood saw these modes of ministry, though historically modified by the church's experience, as the essential functions of every pattern of campus ministry.[10] Baker's work clearly exemplified these modes or patterns. Serving as the pastor/priest of a local congregation, Baker ministered to his local congregation but at the same time carried responsibility for that same role among all Methodist students on the University campus.[11] In addition, recognizing that the intellectual challenge of ministering in the university milieu would require new vistas, he opened avenues for the ministry to relate the gospel to the intellectual and social experimentation inherent in the life of every college and university—the prophetic role. Organizing the campus ministry so that it would enjoy functional and administrative independence Baker also pioneered new patterns of church governance and authority (the kingly role) which gave this specialized ministry the flexibility it needed to carry out its mission.

James Baker's ability to hold these distinct and often disparate features of campus ministry in creative balance significantly contributed to his ministry becoming a model for other Methodist student ministries. In his creative inclusion of differing elements Baker can perhaps be seen as emulating John Wesley's unique balancing of faith and works, reason and experience, scripture and tradition, etc. As our study will show us, when any one of campus ministry's modes was neglected or overshadowed the others, the ministry experienced difficulty.

Expanding Campus Ministries

While Baker's pioneering work at Illinois can be seen as initiating Methodist campus ministry on state and independent campuses, giving it distinctive characteristics as well as its enduring name, many of his contemporaries across the country shared his interests in students and their spiritual lives. By the first decades of the twentieth century it was obvious that more Methodist students would be attending state and independent colleges than would be able to attend Methodist colleges (some 40,000 at state schools by 1921).[12] Across the nation many annual conferences and local churches quickly followed the Illinois pattern. One prominent feature of these new ministries was the offering of Bible and other religion courses since the state universities, in view of the strictures laid down by the constitutional separation of church and state, did not often offer such courses. Bible chairs staffed by denominational ministers began student work at numerous campuses. For example, at the University of Texas, Methodists founded their first Bible chair in 1916 and a Wesley Foundation by 1922.[13]

Interestingly, since the needs of student ministry were distinct and yet universal, the traditional differences between the Methodist Episcopal Church and its southern counterpart, the Methodist Episcopal Church, South, were of little concern or no significant consequence for student work. Campus ministry spread quickly in both churches with little noticeable difference in pattern or purpose—the name Wesley Foundation was often adopted for student ministries in both churches as were many of its governance and support patterns.

Another form of campus ministry arose at a somewhat slower pace as college chaplaincies emerged on the campuses of Methodist-related colleges and universities. Methodist colleges in their early establishment were normally headed by pastors, while professors who taught religion courses were also most often pastors. In that climate the functions of spiritual guidance as we have noted them above were assumed to be the responsibility of these pastors serving in special educational roles—in reality, many times it was assumed that all faculty members carried responsibility for Christian nurture and example. As the church-related colleges and universities expanded and matured, college presidents and religion faculty members were often no longer available to carry the load of spiritual nurture in addition to their other responsibilities. While the transition was slow, by the mid-twentieth century most Methodist colleges had appointed chaplains whose duties among students paralleled in many ways those of Wesley Foundation campus ministers. As this pattern of campus ministry matured it took its place along with the Wesley Foundations as an important segment of the church's concern for its students spiritual life.[14]

By the early 1930s Methodist student ministries were established as distinctive ministries on numerous state and independent campuses and some Methodist college campuses. A prominent feature of these ministries was their interconnection with each other. Because college campuses formed distinctive social and intellectual contexts from the rest of society, students, faculty, and campus ministers, though separated geographically, often sought fellowship and support between campuses. Intercollegiate conferences, consultations, and organizations emerged as an important feature of student ministries. In Texas a Methodist Student Federation was formed in 1923 to meet several campus concerns, including "The need of a closer fellowship and a more real esprit de corps among the Methodist students of the State, . . . the need for more effective co-ordination and union of the agencies doing religious work among them, both in Church and State schools."[15]

In that same decade the Boards of Education of the major Methodist churches added staff positions designed to oversee and develop campus ministries throughout the nation. Although still often attached to local churches close to the campuses, these ministries had unique needs that made them the object of special attention and sustentation. By the end of the decade, campus ministry among Methodist students, wherever they might attend college, had clearly become a significant, specialized form of ministry.

Anticipating the union of the separate Methodist Churches by two years, the youth groups of each church met in a National Methodist Youth Conference in St. Louis, Missouri (1937). Students attending this meeting created a single student confederation to provide for student program needs and cooperation—the Methodist Student Movement. With elected student leadership and sustained by the cooperation of campus ministry staff from the three branches, the innovative organization launched a new era in Methodist campus ministry. Campus ministry now had a recognized organization and proceeded to develop programs, conferences, and publications that would attract innumerable students over the next several decades.[16]

When The Methodist Church formed out of the three previous major branches in 1939, its Board of Education established a

Department of Student Work whose staff cooperatively help direct and expand the work of the Methodist Student Movement, or MSM. The 1941 report of this Department documents the expansive nature of campus ministry at the beginning of World War II.[17] The Department staff consisted of three persons (Heil Bollinger, Harvey Brown, and Harold Ehrensperger) with four support personnel. By that time, 110 independent Wesley Foundations served 100,000 Methodist Students at state and independent colleges. When local churches serving students were included along with the Wesley Foundations and college chaplaincies, some 400 "preaching centers" served state, independent, and church-related campuses. Four regional leadership conferences annually trained student leaders as well as campus ministers. Summer graduate courses "for professional campus Christian leadership" were offered at Duke University, Lake Junaluska, and Garrett Biblical Institute. Four hundred college students also participated in 95 Youth Caravans rendering service to local church high school students. Numerous social service projects and mission programs were being carried out by local student groups. An MSM publication for university students, *motive* magazine, had been launched in the fall of 1940, gaining some 5000 subscriptions during its first year. A National Society of Wesley Players, with 25 chapters on college campuses, also published its own national magazine, *Footlight,* interpreting and encouraging Christian drama. Student loan funds administered by the Department provided financial help to some 3500 students. State MSMs and Inter-Conference Commissions on Student Work helped coordinate and promote the work. The feeling of students and staff that they were participating in a vibrant, growing, optimistic movement within the church is seen in the report's description of the ministry's contributions:

> The four regional conferences, the twenty-two state conferences and the national conference are *the organizational medium through which Methodist students give intercollegiate expression to a fast-developing consciousness of group.* This great host of student Christian leaders, with its own organization, designed to give maximum individual expression to Christian experience in campus and community, is developing a constructive consciousness of group in the building of the Kingdom of God. *Each year the Methodist Student Movement is pouring increasing thousands of consecrated and trained young men and women into the channels of the church's life.*[18]

The emphasis of the report was clearly on the pastoral mode of campus ministry—a church-related ministry to its own students. Cooperation with other national student and youth movements was mentioned and some interdenominational and ecumenical work noted, but the stress fell on campus ministry as a project of and service to the church, supplemented by prophetic concerns for peace and social justice. Campus ministry, begun only thirty years before, had obviously matured. Now it offered the church a vital, growing ministry among student members.

Campus Ministry as an Essential Ministry of the Church

The major renewal of the American society at the conclusion of World War II witnessed an unprecedented burgeoning of interest in education. The decision to provide each returning GI with the opportunity for a higher education permanently changed attitudes toward, and avenues of, higher education. America experienced in this post-war period greater expansion in higher education facilities, faculty, and students than any time in its history. In a very short time higher education was broadly embraced by the general population rather than being largely the privilege of an elite sector.

Expansion and change in perspective were accompanied by many other changes. The high demand for vocational training, with an emphasis on technology, quickly matched and ultimately threatened traditional liberal-arts models of education. The influx of veterans brought wives, children, supplementary jobs, and a vast host of changes in curriculum, student housing, student social patterns, and athletic emphases.[19]

In the same period the churches also welcomed their largest membership expansion in decades and moved to respond to the educational changes by expansion of their campus ministry. The Methodist Board of Education support for its office of student ministry enjoyed a 55% increase, growing from $97,574 in 1944 to $151,590 in 1947.[20] By 1952 Methodism could report 160 Wesley Foundations and 22 interdenominational units; a 58% increase in Wesley Foundations in a little over a decade.[21] The 1950s witnessed continuing expansion and a successful campaign in the last quadrennium of the decade to raise support for Methodist schools, colleges, and Wesley Foundations. Financial sustenance for Wesley Foundations rose from $777,984 in 1956 to $1,844,656 in 1959.[22] When it is remembered that much of this new money was expended in building new Methodist campus centers, a 137% rise in just three years is still phenomenal. By 1960 another 21 Wesley Foundations served the church, bringing the total number to 181.[23]

Expansion and strengthening called for better-prepared leadership. Regular conferences and workshops sponsored by the Department of Student Work helped train pastors and others serving in campus ministry. An Association of College and University Ministers of the Methodist Church formally organized in 1949. A Commission on Standards for Wesley Foundations began, in 1952, a procedure for officially certifying their work. To represent Wesley Foundation issues fully within the councils of the church, an Association of Wesley Foundations emerged in 1956.

Professionalization of the campus ministry reflected in these developments enlarged the attention given to the theological foundations of Christian ministry. Of particular concern was how Christian faith and commitment should impact the moral and ethical presuppositions expressed in the changing educational patterns and their social consequences. In 1949 such shifts in perspective were symbolized by the modification of the name of the Board of Education's "Department of Student Work" to a more universal title: "The Department of College and University Religious Life." In that same year the student section of the National Conference of Methodist Youth considered emphases such as "Christianizing the campus intellectually and morally" and "giving students a mature, intellectual and living religion." The Conference also requested that all state student conferences be interracial to conform to the MSM national policy—a policy predating by some years the civil rights movement's public moves toward desegregation.[24] The topic for the 1949 Methodist Student Convocation, "The Christian Use of Power in a Secular World," further suggests a clear shift among students and their leaders toward more emphasis on campus ministry's prophetic elements.

A suggestion from the student representative of the UCLA MSM that his group would prefer to donate directly to mission projects instead of having its money divided by the Methodist Student Fellowship Fund formula sounds very current but arose from subtly different motivations. In this case, it perhaps should be seen as an early example of the 1960s students demanding a larger voice in decisions of church and society.[25] Student Christian leaders generally were shifting their attention to the larger world and how they might be responsible players in the molding of its life.

The rising significance of the prophetic role in the minds of campus ministry staff as well as students is evident in the 1955 annual report of the Department of Campus and Religious Life:

The Department must look clearly to the future concerning the nature of the Christian witness in the university. This witness must at once be clear, pure, and disciplined.

. . . The Department envisions the need for a sound theological emphasis to lay the foundation for the spiritual trust that is in keeping with our Methodist heritage.

. . . Within the ten year period there should be great ecumenical developments. The witness is not only in the university but also in the Church of Jesus Christ, which Church must be one in Him.[26]

This report suggests Methodist Campus ministry leaders were convinced that by training Christian leaders whose duty it was to witness to the university, they would ultimately help remold the church and eventually the society. In many ways the statement anticipated Underwood's 1960s evaluation of campus ministry's significance in the life of the church and world.[27]

The strength of this shift is seen in a 1959 article authored by the campus minsters of Texas: "The church on campus, living in freedom from idolatrous dependence upon past structures, must continually face the real possibility that the previous structures are inadequate to the present situation and be ready to receive new, more adequate, structures."[28] The mood of the time was undoubtedly one which found the traditional patterns of campus ministry lacking and anticipated major change.

This philosophical shift escalated rapidly as the disturbances of the 1960s unfolded and campus ministry found itself inexorably identified with the student's critique of all traditional limitations. Understandings of and attitudes toward the campus ministry, particularly among those local pastors and laypersons who had been shaped by its traditional, nurturing, pastoral traditions, also changed substantially, as we shall see.

Student Revolution and the Campus Ministry

The traumas of the 1960s that resulted in permanent modification of social, political, and educational patterns in this country hardly need recounting here. Their role in remolding campus ministry has been recently analyzed by Don Shockley as well as Sam Portaro and Gary Peluso.[29] For purposes of this study we need only note a few of the changes in the academic context within which campus ministry labored.

Enrollments in American colleges doubled in the decade from 1963 to 1973.[30] Such numbers not only meant that there were more college students than ever before but that their needs required the universities and colleges to expand their facilities and assistance greatly. University student centers and counseling services were created, offering many "pastoral" and fellowship services previously provided through Methodist student centers. Consequently, however successful a particular campus ministry might be in attracting Methodist students, it almost inevitably found itself ministering to a smaller percentage of the total number of Methodist students. This inability to keep up contact with a large number of students was significant because one of the easier ways the general church used to evaluate their campus ministries was to note what percentage of Methodist students such a ministry might reach. Expanding university services and the constant need to design relevant ministries for ever-increasing numbers of highly diverse students tested every traditional campus ministry pattern but particularly affected the nurturing and pastorally-oriented ministry.

The theological thrust of the time demanded that every Christian believer, not simply pastors, take personal responsibility for living out the faith in the midst of their daily lives. Students were urged to act out their faith (and not wait until graduation!). Laity were also urged to take more responsible roles in the councils and decisions of the church.[31] As the decade advanced and students generally began to question everything on campus from curriculum requirements to college governance, it is not surprising they also became critical of what they judged to be inefficient and ineffective traditional church organization and ministry. Discovering, through their participation in the civil rights movement, new methods for expressing their critiques and effecting change in the society, students expected to redesign the society. Questioning most social institutions and conventions led student Christian leaders, as well as their peers, to seek justification for the diverse denominational groups of Christianity. If there was one gospel and one savior, why was it necessary to duplicate organizational structures and programs? One unified witness seemed not only practically sound but theologically mandated. Ecumenicity was not simply an attractive alternative but was demanded by their understanding of the gospel.

In this context Methodist campus ministers could not avoid facing the issues raised among students as college students generally took an active role in current societal problems. In 1964 the National Council of the MSM, the elected student officers of the Movement, publicly affirmed its support of the Freedom Democratic Party, SNCC, and CORE as these groups attempted to influence the political conventions of that year.[32] The 1965 annual report of the Department of College and University Religious Life noted the tensions present:

> The Methodist Student Movement obviously embodies both dimensions of "Christian presence," namely, the life of nurture [the pastoral ministry] and the life of involvement [the prophetic ministry]. Yet if a general tendency among our students can be detected, it is probably toward the latter dimension-involvement. The social lethargy of the fifties has gradually, and sometimes dramatically, lost hold as students have identified with the giant struggle for human rights in this country. Such a "scattered" kind of witness has pulled the student movement almost inexorably toward questions of social ethics, of the relation of the church to the world and of "sacred" to "secular." The search for a place "between" nurture and involvement is typified by a current debate in the National Council of the Methodist Student Movement concerning its responsibilities in and through the institutional church, and its mission to the secular order.[33]

The 1966 annual report further documented the rising tensions brought by student leaders: "state MSM organizations are choosing delegates to the national body who are intensely involved in the restless, searching mood of our time. . . . [T]hese leaders are creating painful pressures within the church."[34] This report also records the social involvements of MSM students which contributed to the pressures: 100 Methodist students accompanied by several campus ministers joined the Selma-Montgomery marches; Negro and white MSM representatives visited campuses throughout the south; national council members lived and worked in Negro housing projects; and several took part in an interdenominational political commission in Washington, D.C.

In 1963 the Board of Education commissioned Sam Gibson, an experienced Wesley Foundation director, to study the Wesley Foundations. Gibson's report, presuming that Wesley Foundations were not simply an "arm" of the church but the church itself on campus, found significant disparity between the understanding of the campus ministry among local church leaders, who continued to expect campus ministry to be primarily pastoral and nurturing, and many campus ministers, who embraced a campus ministry guided by the prophetic vision of the gospel. His study sought to discover ways to strengthen campus ministry relationships with the broader church and thereby guarantee that student work be supported as a full ministry of the church even in troubled times. However, other recommendations suggested changes that assumed an expanding emphasis on the prophetic role of campus ministry by both the national staff and local campus ministers. Methodist campus ministry was urged to join other denominations in ecumenical ministries by participating in several ecumenical structures taking shape at that time. Gibson further suggested that the staff of the Department of College and University Religious Life be deployed regionally and be given more direct supervision over the Wesley Foundations, essentially strengthening the national guidance of local units. This recommendation obviously called for substantial change in program orientation and, just as important, in governance of the ministry. In some senses it suggested reducing campus ministry's accountability to the local conferences. Regionalizing the national staff presence implied, whether recognized or not, a more independent, detached campus ministry, while other sections of the report sought greater understanding and support for campus ministry from the church.[35]

In an atmosphere where students demanded major change and campus ministers and national staff sought new patterns of ministry, it is not surprising that the latter half of the decade saw major shifts. A central goal in these changes was an ecumenically-based campus ministry. An United Ministries in Higher Education(UMHE) emerged in 1964 from the campus ministries of a previous ecumenical cooperative group which included students and staff from several churches: Disciples of Christ, Evangelical United Brethren, United Presbyterians, and the United Church of Christ. The next year a National Campus Ministry Association organized to coordinate the efforts of campus ministers from several denominations. The Methodist Association of College and University Ministers soon joined this ecumenical body, eliminating the denominational group traditionally responsible for fellowship and training among Methodist campus ministers. Students leaders of several denominational student organizations formed the University Christian Movement (UCM) in 1966, creating an independent ecumenical, student-led Christian movement. The organization included most major mainline Protestant student groups such as the Methodist Student Movement as well as Catholic, Orthodox, and Quaker student organizations; a truly ecumenical endeavor. By pooling the resources of staff from several denominations, the UMHE provided a staff structure coordinate with the student UCM. The Methodist Church became the eighth church to join the UMHE in 1968, completing the "ecumenicalization" of Methodist campus ministry.

While Methodist student and staff groups were by 1966 part of larger ecumenical ministries, the transition from traditional structures took some time. The National Conference of the Methodist Student Movement moved in June, 1967, to complete the transition by voting to dissolve the MSM. Their justification reads in part:

> If we are to be men of faith in the peculiar times in which we find ourselves, we must take with increased seriousness our missional tasks of service to the world. It has become increasingly evident that the old forms and structures through which we have labored have been rendered ineffectual and cumbersome. The University Christian Movement presents new possibilities for those who seek to be in mission. It is clear, however, that the UCM can live and thrive only if the discrete groups which originally formed it cease to perpetuate parallel structures and programs.[36]

While a National Council (student representatives) of the MSM continued through 1969, its task was to close the thirty-year ministry of the group. In joining these ecumenical organizations, the national student leaders and staff of the Methodist campus ministry were acting from their convictions that they were leading the church into a new day of unified witness to the oneness of the gospel and its mission in the university and "within the world."[37]

Transition periods which such moves require are always traumatic, and this one was compounded by events on campus and in the nation. The assassinations of Martin Luther King Jr. and Robert Kennedy in 1968, the escalation of the Vietnam war, and the use of police and military force against student protesters dampened the rather euphoric and idealistic optimism present when the ecumenical student movement formed in 1966. By 1969 the high hopes and dreams that had surrounded the creation of the UCM collapsed, causing the UCM council to dissolve the movement. The reasons for this decision were complex, reflecting the disturbance of the times. Among central issues were several spawned by the desire to take the gospel to the world. The UCM sought not only to be a union of denominational groups but to have an open door policy and actively pursued participation by campus groups with many concerns: groups representative of current student social movements such as those of black power, women's liberation, and often polarized political action groups. The result was an inability of the new group to focus, an identity crisis accompanied by attempts to do "too much too soon." A recent analysis by Paul Schrading, a Methodist who served on the UCM staff, suggests that the movement that had been created out of centripetal forces designed to unify, converge, and universalize found itself broken apart by centrifugal forces—those that forced divergence, particularization, and disruption. Schrading continues: "Part of the paralysis of the UCM in March, 1969, was precisely the effort to reduce the variety and riches of theological reflection to an ideology."[38]

If Schrading is correct in his analysis, then perhaps, in Underwood's categories, the intense appropriation of the prophetic, involvement voice among campus leaders and ministers had blinded them to the realities of ideology and the difficulties of giving their dreams truly practical applications. The necessary creative balance between prophetic, pastoral/priestly, and governance modes had by the close of the decade been lost.[39]

The consequences for Methodism of these ecumenical experiments in the closing years of the 1960s were far-reaching, even if largely unanticipated. It is clear that the actions of the national staff and national student officers to dissolve the MSM were generally supported among Methodist campus ministers and many students. The short life of the UCM, while discouraging, did not dampen the ecumenical convictions of many campus ministers, students, and the Departmental staff. The move toward ecumenical involvement is dramatically seen in the increase of Methodist support of ecumenical units: the 196 Wesley Foundation units of 1966 had fallen to 179 by 1975 as the 43 interdenominational units had risen to 247.[40] While many ecumenical units were added by simply expanding the Methodist relationship into UMHE units already existent, it is clear that ecumenicity strongly influenced Methodist campus ministry during the 1970s.[41] Staff changes also illustrate the strength of the movement toward ecumenicity. Responding to suggestions made in Gibson's earlier study and adapting to patterns already present in the UMHE, the Methodist Department of Campus Ministry assigned three of its five staff members to regional UMHE positions in the early 1970s.

The dissolution of a national Methodist student organization affected another important aspect of the traditional Methodist student connection. Perhaps it had been only natural, given Methodist governance structures that stressed the "connection" of local units to the church at large, that the earliest Methodist campus ministry patterns had appropriated the "interconnection" between its local campuses and its state and national student ministries. This unique sense of interconnection of students, evident in the nineteenth-century student volunteer movements, had even been incorporated into the name chosen to denote Methodism's student ministries—the Methodist student "movement." With no national or state MSM organizations and a reduced staff personnel to foster interconnection through conferences, training events, and service projects, the connectional aspect of campus ministry, traditionally so central to its life, quickly faded into memory. Don Shockley correctly suggests that this dismantling of the infrastructures which had supported the connection created a void "which had theological as well as practical dimensions, and it was simply going to take a long time to get to the place where new foundations could be laid."[42]

By the late sixties and early seventies the often latent, local-church distrust and lack of understanding of specialized ministries manifested itself by increased open criticism of the campus ministry. Sam Gibson's mid-sixties report found dissatisfaction at a number of levels, and these were elaborated in the '70s. Principal objections to campus ministry as it was practiced focused on the critical attitude of many students toward the traditional church, campus ministry's failure to reach large numbers of students, its "catering" to an elite intellectual group, its participation in and support of student social reform programs, the freedom with which the campus centers explored variant or radical ideas, and its experimentation with new worship patterns.[43] One state director of campus ministry pled in his 1968 report for the church at large to give campus ministers "at least the charity of Christian love" since these ministers lived "between" the worlds of the parish and the universities, receiving the criticism born out of the frustrations of both.[44] Don Shockley comments that as the age of the student radicals passed into history and students turned inward to find their academic interests again in vocationalism, campus ministers and their programs "reminded people (in our case church people) of something they were eager to forget."[45]

Perhaps it is not surprising, then, to find different governance patterns for campus ministry emerging from the general restructuring which accompanied the 1968 union of the Methodist Church and the Evangelical United Brethren.[46] In the new United Methodist Church each annual conference established a Board of Higher Education and Campus Ministry (paralleling the new General Board of Higher Education and Ministry). Designed to strengthen relationships between local conferences and their Methodist colleges and campus ministry units, these new boards generally assumed supervision and financial responsibility for local campus ministries, whether denominational or ecumenical. Effectively these boards replaced state interconference commissions and state campus ministry structures that were generally phased out over the next decade. Using Underwood's terms, the royal or kingly modes of Methodist campus ministry were being redefined to emphasize local campus concerns and not the traditional inter-connections of the work.

It is not surprising that by the mid-1970s campus ministers often found themselves struggling to understand their position and role within the church. Loss of the support of national and state infrastructure, accompanied by a distinct shift of accountability to local annual conference control and supervision, meant that they found themselves working in a new governance setting. Their traditional understanding of campus ministry as a distinctive, specialized ministry was also significantly diminished. Changing student attitudes and needs, combined with significant modification in college and university curriculums and programs, compounded their sense of working in a different world.

Nevertheless, in this changing campus milieu church support for the local units of campus ministry did not decrease but rather expanded. The number of ministries continued to rise in the early '70s as the church sought to serve the newly-established community colleges. In 1975 the GBHEM reported that quadrennial financial support for campus ministry across the church increased 15%, rising to a total of "over $5,000,000." Twenty Wesley Foundations and 200 ecumenical units had been added in the decade from 1966 to 1975. [47] By the late '70s some decline among numbers of Wesley Foundations was reported, while ecumenical units remained stable: in 1978 there were 179 Wesley Foundation units, 204 ecumenical units and 50 part-time units. By that year total financial support had increased to $6,099,983. [48]

Significantly, the changes that took place among national and state campus ministry personnel during the '70s presented a very different picture. At the national staff level, where five staff members continued well into the mid-seventies, only one was reported in the 1981 annual report. Two positions were evidently authorized, but only one was filled at the time of the report. The funds for the second position were used to support several campus ministers across the country who acted as regional part-time campus ministry consultants for the General Board of Higher Education and Ministry staff. [49] The program budget for the campus ministry section dramatically illustrated the changes: a budget of $17,600 as compared to a 1974 program budget item of $239,753. [50]

Similar reductions can be documented throughout the church. In 1970 the Interconference Commission, trustees for the Texas Methodist Student Movement, was dissolved and succeeded by a Texas Commission on Campus Ministry. In contrast to the responsibilities of the Interconference Commission, the new commission carried no responsibility for approval of campus ministers, distributed no conference funds, and quickly began to turn over campus properties to local Wesley Foundation boards. The student organization in the state had dissolved following the actions of the national MSM. Where two state staff persons operated through the '60s, only one was employed by the new commission. The state director's position was reduced in responsibility in 1972 to one of promotion rather than the supervisory roles it had traditionally carried. In the words of the Commission "His work is to evoke confidence and trust."[51] The state director's position was reduced to a part-time position served by one of the local campus ministers in 1976, and upon his resignation in 1979 the job became the unpaid responsibility of another local campus pastor.

The Slow Process of Renewal

In this period of unease and reduction subtle signs of change in the philosophy and understanding of campus ministry began to emerge. Conscious of the turmoil of the '60s and needing to assess the future of higher education, the 1972 General Conference established a National Commission on United Methodist Higher Education which, having surveyed the campus ministers, commented:

> In evaluating the importance of various aspects of campus ministry programs . . . campus ministers showed the concern for persons, for the community of faith, for values, for freedom of inquiry, and for global perspectives that should characterize campus—and indeed all—ministry. Their responses suggest, however, that the primary emphasis of campus ministry programs is pastoral, caring for the religious and personal needs of individual members of the campus community. Of the other three modes, the greatest emphasis was given to the prophetic activities of ministry. . . . They expressed the belief that their denominational constituency did not consider the prophetic ministry to be as important as did campus ministers, but believed they and their constituents agreed on the primacy of pastoral care.[52]

By the mid-'70s campus ministers were again acknowledging the basic role of the pastoral mode of ministry. At the same time, they sought to retain a significant emphasis on the prophetic mode. Balance between the two was returning. Recognition of this renewed balance, however, was not immediate among their ministerial peers and many laypersons. The popular image of much campus ministry remained under a cloud through the '70s and '80s.

The need for renewal of national as well as regional structures and events also began to be recognized by local campus ministers in the mid-seventies. Campus ministers surveyed by the national office in 1975 affirmed the need for a national conference of Methodist students (the last MSM conference had been held in 1964). Plans for such a conference to be held in 1978 were initiated, but the renewal of a Methodist national student conference was in fact delayed for another decade (1987) [53]

Calls were also being made to reestablish a national student movement. Joe Gibson, Associate Secretary for Campus Ministry, noted, however, that General Board of Higher Education and Ministry could not "create" a student movement: "It cannot come from the top down. What we can and will do is create the potential for it to happen and offer the resources of the church. I am in favor of a student movement." [54]

While detailed information on developments within the campus ministry during the decade of the eighties has not been readily available for this study, activities at the national level make it clear that Joe Gibson's desire to create the climate for renewal was the guiding principle in the national office. The appointment of Allan Burry as Assistant General Secretary for Campus Ministry in 1982 marked a turning point in the pace of change and the vision of renewal. Helen Neinast, appointed as an associate in the Campus Ministry Section at the same time as Burry, suggests that the two major tasks of the Section during the '80s were: (1) to change the public image of campus ministry among the local churches and conferences, and (2) to encourage campus ministers to understand their work as an important and productive ministry. [55] Renewal of interest in campus ministry at the national level was also attested to by the Section's program budget figures: a $50,000 budget in 1982 increased to $195,600 by 1987. Methodist campus ministers began to meet regularly in connection with the National Campus Ministry Association. Campus ministry training and continuing education events were again instituted to support the ministry. With the 1987 appointment of Richard Hicks to work with ethnic concerns, the Section on Campus Ministry staff was expanded to three positions.

In 1987 a "Jubilee Conference" celebrated the establishment of the MSM in 1937—the first time a national Methodist student conference had been held since 1964. National ecumenical student conferences in 1990 and 1994 included major denominational components, providing

Methodist students with continuing opportunities for denominational fellowship and programming on a national scale.

The renewal of intercollegiate programming and systems of support among students and campus ministers begun by Burry and Neinast has been sustained and substantially expanded under the leadership of Don Shockley, the present Assistant General Secretary for Campus Ministry, GBHEM. Beginning with a national student training event in 1989, the Campus Ministry Section established a Student Forum to provide annual opportunities for student fellowship, leadership training, theological education, education in social justice issues, and opportunities for voluntary Christian service.[56] Made up of student representatives from annual conferences, Forum also reestablished a national structure for Methodist student participation in ecumenical programs and organizations. Beginning in 1994 Forum incorporated international student representatives into its community.

This national effort has been supplemented in recent years by reorganization of student groups at conference, state, and regional levels. A United Methodist Southeastern Jurisdiction Student Movement now exists, as does a Southwest Texas Methodist Student Movement, and similar groups are present in several other states and annual conferences. Each of these groups regularly holds intercollegiate conferences.

Joe Gibson's mid-seventies vision of a new student movement arising from student need and commitment as the church provided the "potential" for its sustentation came to full fruition at the Student Forum's 1996 meeting. Student representatives from 60 of United Methodism's 68 annual conferences voted to create "The United Methodist Student Movement." Declaring the new movement to be a "real grassroots movement . . . that grew from the ground up," Christy Kniceley, student chairwoman, suggested that the grassroots dynamic present in the new UMSM made it different from the earlier MSM, which had united the separate, preexisting student movements of predecessor Methodist Churches.[57] Perhaps her statement also shows that the need for Christian fellowship, training, and service among students required the establishment of organizations and infrastructure to fill those needs even where such structures had earlier been abandoned.

Other initiatives have also significantly contributed to restoration of a more robust campus ministry. The 1992 General Conference established "Mission at the Center: a Campus Ministry Special Program" to provide grants for distinctive ministries among students and to encourage development of wider interests in social and international issues. Local campus ministry units are encouraged through these grants to develop racial/ethnic ministries as a part of their programs. Other grants of the program help raise student awareness of global issues present in the Christian mission today.

Perhaps as exciting for some who experienced the earlier Methodist Student Movement has been the "New Visions Summer Companies." In a program that "echoes" the Youth Caravans of the '40s and '50s the Summer Companies provide college-age leadership teams for local church youth programs, annual conference camps, and other leadership activities in various service programs.

The summer of 1995 saw the restoration of yet another important link in rebuilding a vital infrastructure to support campus ministry. Campus ministers reorganized their professional network which had not existed as a separate denominational group since the 1960s—United Methodists in Campus Ministry. Renewal of a denominational group permits direct attention to continuing education and training among Methodists and contributes to the "connection" with other campus ministers so vital to the support and encouragement of these ministers. The addition by several seminaries of courses in higher education ministries significantly contributes to the opportunity for campus ministers to receive specialized training.

In terms of statistical information the program budget for the Campus Ministry Section during the past quadrennium was $270,000 per year, only a $40,000 increase from the budgets of the early '70s. Ironically, while this is a great improvement over the early-'80s budgets, when inflation is factored into these figures the church continues to ask a reduced staff of three persons to effectively minister with diminished funds. Statistics on number of units are difficult to compare with early records since record-keeping methodologies have changed through the years. There are presently 696 campus ministers and chaplains related in some way to the United Methodist Church. One hundred thirty-eight of these are chaplains, others serve in dual capacities as local-church associates, and some serve as staff members in larger units. Units supported solely by the United Methodist Church, Wesley Foundations and college chaplaincies, number 296. Methodist participation in ecumenical units continues to expand, with 282 units being partially supported by Methodist funds in 1995.[58]

When we put this recent information together, there is every reason to be optimistic about the future of today's Methodist campus ministry. The rebuilding of infrastructure is clearly well underway;

student movement organizations are reemerging; and a new esprit de corps is felt among campus ministers, national staff personnel, and students.

Reflections

Many whose Christian commitment and dedication were positively affected by the campus ministry during its earlier successful days often wonder what happened to that strong movement. Why did the church seemingly abandon campus ministry during the sixties and seventies, and thereby lose a generation of students and pastors for the life of the church? This study suggests that such a question inadequately reflects the complex history of the ministry in the past few decades.

Clearly, the focus of the campus ministry shifted in the post-Second World War period in ways that allowed the prophetic mode of ministry to overshadow the traditional pastoral/priestly mode. This shift brought major changes in the ministry which were not always clearly understood or appreciated by many in the church. Modification in style of campus ministry was, however, not simply the result of a prophetic ministry being carried to its limit. Social revolutions, differing theological emphases, changing patterns of participation in organized religion, reorganization of the church, significant alteration in ministerial recruitment and education, and restructuring of the academic setting in which campus ministry worked must all be seen as contributing elements affecting the context in which effective campus ministry could take place. Combined, many of these elements had several significant, negative consequences for the ministry: (1) the dissolving of a viable denominational infrastructure at the student level and in state and national staff positions meant the loss of one of Methodist campus ministry's traditionally most significant features—its successful expression of Methodism's vital connectionalism; (2) loss of confidence in the campus ministry by many within the church during the 1960s and 1970s resulted in reduced dependence on the campus ministry for either nurture of its youth or solicitation of church leaders and pastors; (3) elimination of intercollegiate conferences, workshops, and missions often meant a lessened awareness of and emphasis on national and international concerns for social justice, peace, and theological involvement with the academy and the world at large—concerns which had earlier attracted student leadership; (4) the loss of a national student movement undoubtedly contributed to the decline in seminary enrollment among recent college graduates though its direct effect is difficult to assess because of the many other changes taking place in the church and the society during the period; and (5) the shift toward appointment of local pastors to Wesley Foundations, usually for a limited period, deemphasized the specialized nature of the campus ministry.

While these events clearly placed campus ministry of the late '60s, '70s and early '80s "under a cloud" we need to remember that the church did not abandon campus ministry during this period, for in spite of a widespread public distrust of the ministry, many local units continued strong pastoral and prophetic ministries on the nation's campuses. Following the demise of the national and state Methodist Student Movements and substantial restructuring in 1970, the church shifted its support and programming to the local conference level and concentrated solicitation of leadership at this level, but clearly continued to understand campus ministry to be a viable and significant ministry.

Understanding this history brings us to ask further questions. As the church moves toward another restructuring of itself, its ministries, and the agencies it has created to carry out those ministries, can the experience of campus ministry since the 1940s be used as a "case study" from which we may draw important lessons about change and renewal? I suggest it can.

First, the most obvious lesson is that every pattern of ministry demands creative balance, even when such balance results in vigorous, dynamic tension. From the experience of the campus ministry, the necessity of such balance between the pastoral (nurturing) role *and* the prophetic (involvement) role is clear. For meaningful symmetry to be achieved and sustained, the governance mode of ministry must also carefully incorporate the interests of local units *and* those of the larger connection. When any one element of ministry dominates the others, we lose the vitality which only comes through the interaction and connection of all. If that happens, as it did in campus ministry, we often fall into ideological accusation and defense. We play out our energies struggling to convince others of the truth of our position (and sometimes to maintain our own convictions!). The traumatic episodes in the life of the campus ministry that we have briefly reviewed teach again that as Methodists we need to recapture Mr. Wesley's ability to maintain a creative balance between many partial components of the truth if our ministries are to be relevant to ourselves and our world.

The second lesson is equally important. Viable "connection" between individual units (whether campus ministries or local churches) calls for those who can implement the interaction. If we take the role of state, regional, and national student conferences in the life of the campus ministry as our illustration, the point is obvious. Such MSM events expanded, challenged, and empowered local units, summoning them to experience a larger ministry than that possible at the local level. When the infrastructure of national and regional staff support was gone, student interaction, so often provided through state and national conferences, died—leaving the campus ministry without one of its most significant and attractive features. Such interaction simply could not occur without the dedicated service of leaders whose base and support were provided by the general connection of the churches. The experience of the campus ministry testifies that the leadership and support provided by some connectional staff and agencies is indispensable for vital ministries to be fully effective.

A third lesson is undoubtedly implied by the history of campus ministry. Recent calls for a restructuring of the Methodist Church have suggested that to achieve renewed vitality in our local churches all authority and responsibility must be returned to the local church level. Ministries should arise from the local church in the context of its local responsibilities. One effect of that suggestion would be to eliminate specialized ministries, including campus ministry, as we presently know them. Presumably local churches located close to college and university campuses would take responsibilities for campus ministry.[59] If that were to occur, this study suggests that those local churches would be forced to recreate a cooperative, "connectional" structure to meet those responsibilities and would discover that the needs of campus ministry significantly differ from those of the local parish. Local churches responsible for student ministries would again experience what James Baker discovered in 1913. He could not sustain a specialized ministry to students without outside financial help, but just as important he needed the support and insights of others working on similar campuses. Local churches serving campuses would be forced to reinvent the conference and national agencies that presently help empower campus ministry, or they would have to abandon an eighty-year history of significant ministry at academic institutions that substantially shape our students and their culture. Is either of these alternatives necessary in the name of local-church empowerment?

Finally, our study suggests that if the church chooses to *eliminate* rather than *reform* much of its present infrastructure, it may well repeat the experience of the campus ministry in the '70s and '80s on a church, wide basis. When campus ministry structures that were vital to a full and complete ministry were eliminated, they had to be recreated to regain a full ministry. One must wonder, however, if such actions were to be taken on a churchwide basis, whether the "connection" would not be lost and perhaps become irretrievable. There would be no viable interconnecting structure to support the church while it renewed itself, as was the case for campus ministry. Even at its lowest ebb and without the help of a healthy infrastructure, campus ministry had a foundational connection that continued to sustain it. If the church loses that connecting foundation, its survival, at least as a national and international witness to the gospel, will certainly be in question.

~ Robert W. Sledge ~

Denominations renegotiate their identity and reshape purpose or mission in a variety of ways. Sometimes such change comes by design and intention, as when commissions for self-study or reform movements or the admission of new constituencies put formal legislation before the church. At other time such change creeps up on the church, the result of living with new procedures or structures or adjusting to new patterns in American society or finding the religious ecology itself shifting or just growing (or shrinking). In both intentional and adventitious ways, divisions and mergers have altered Methodist connectionalism, identity, mission, and theological self-understanding. Methodist mergers, the topic of the following essay by Robert W. Sledge, have necessitated fraternal exchanges, formal dialogue, and then planning commissions. These processes, sustained over long periods, have sharpened awareness of connectional issues, issues separating the dialoguing churches, issues that were perhaps the reason for separation in the first place. Merger, if achieved, has typically dealt explicitly with those once-divisive issues, has brought to awareness the principles involved, has achieved some level of compromise or consensus, and has lodged that new self-understanding in Discipline, in structure, and in procedure. But merger also yields adventitious connectional change, change perhaps not immediately recognized, change away from the points of focus, change derived from putting different institutions and institutional cultures together, change occasioned by size differences in the merging partners, change produced by the merger process itself. Sledge explores both intentional and adventitious features of three twentieth-century mergers, commenting on positive and negative dimensions of both. By his analysis and reflection, he invites question about the compatibility of United Methodism's ecumenical commitments and strong connectional identity. Are United Methodism's interest in Christian unity in tension with its exploration of Methodist mergers? Is its embrace of COCU compatible with prospective unity with the African American Methodisms? And on a world level, are its commitment to multi-lateral and bi-lateral conversations and its investment in World Methodism in keeping with its efforts to understand itself as a global reality?

The Effect of Mergers
on American Wesleyan Denominations

Robert W. Sledge

The twentieth century has been the ecumenical century for the American followers of Wesley. It has also been the era when Methodist growth patterns in America slowed, stopped, and then declined. By contrast, American Wesleyans in the nineteenth century experienced schism coupled with phenomenal expansion in all respects.

Methodist ecumenicity appeared early in the century in the person of a man who was arguably the greatest ecumenist of the era, John R. Mott, a member of the Methodist Episcopal (M.E.) Church. Methodists of several stripes were in the forefront of the creation of the Federal Council of Churches and its successor, the National Council of Churches. These national movements were echoed on the local level by myriads of cooperative ventures between Methodist congregations and those of other denominations.

Methodist ecumenicity found more formal expression in several mergers, namely, the union of the Methodist Episcopal Church, the Methodist Episcopal Church, South, and the Methodist Protestant Church in 1939 to form The Methodist Church; the union between two groups often dubbed "German Methodists," the Church of the United Brethren in Christ and the Evangelical Church to form the Evangelical United Brethren Church in 1946; and the union of those two merged bodies in 1968 to become the United Methodist Church.

Further, the last year of the twentieth-century may see the completion of yet another church union. The 1996 General Conference created a unification commission looking to merger between the United Methodist Church and three predominantly black denominations, the African Methodist Episcopal Church, the African Methodist Episcopal Zion Church, and the Christian Methodist Episcopal Church. The Conference instructed the commission to come back in 2000 with a plan for debate and vote. In addition, there is a close international fellowship with other Wesleyan bodies in the World Methodist Council, and the church has held continuing talks with bodies from a broad range of traditions under the title "COCU."

Out of the broad array of twentieth-century Methodist ecumenism, this essay deals with the consummated unions of 1939, 1946, and 1968.

Reunions, as one of these was, would not have taken place without divisions to begin with. The Methodists in America splintered in the nineteenth century over race, polity, slavery, and holiness, among other things. The "mother" M.E. Church remained the largest of the resultant denominations. In addition, the Evangelical Association and the United Brethren in Christ, two independent bodies with strong Wesleyan ties, also experienced division in the latter part of the century. In 1900, there were two UBC churches (broken up over the issues of membership in secret societies and constitutional change) and two branches of the Evangelical group, a division which was subsequently healed. Thus there was a proliferation of Wesleyan bodies in the United States as the new century dawned. They began slowly to consider whether the Wesleyan tradition should be splintered in that fashion.

1. The Merger of 1939

The three churches which united in 1939 were weighted down with burdens from the past. The Methodist Protestant Church, a relatively small group, broke off from episcopal Methodism in 1830 over a perceived lack of democracy in the church. The dissenters opposed a strong episcopacy, episcopal selection of presiding elders, and the lack of lay representation in decision making at all levels.

The Methodist Episcopal Church and the Methodist Episcopal Church, South were Siamese twins surgically separated from one another in 1844. According the northern church, the cause of the separation was slavery, specifically, a slave-owning bishop. According to the southern church, the reason for the split was the overweening power of the General Conference. The division was exacerbated by subsequent events, particularly the northern repudiation of the agreed-on terms in 1848 and their post-Civil War attempts to recapture the property of the southern church under the slogan "disintegration and absorption." Overtures between the two in the post-reconstruction era were rebuffed. Early in the twentieth century, however, they prepared two separate plans of reunion, one of which came very close to consummation.

By the 1930s, all three groups were ready for another try at reunion. But there were major obstacles to be overcome. For the northern episcopal body, with its large black membership in the south, the principal obstacle lay in how their southern membership's geographical neighbors would relate to them in a merged church. Given southern intransigence on the racial issue, the outlook was not good for a true union. Likewise, the northerners were concerned about the southerners' weak position on clergy use of tobacco, southern theological conservatism, and the powerful southern episcopacy.

The concerns of the M.E. Church, South were the reverse of those: how to live in the same denomination and same region with black Methodists; how to cope with northern liberalism in theology and social concerns; and how to rein in the powerful northern General Conference. In short, north and south were still divided by many of the same issues that had caused the separation nearly a century before.

For the Methodist Protestants, the old issues still remained as well. Were there going to be sufficient safeguards for laity rights and sufficient freedom from episcopal tyranny? And perhaps more difficult, would they be swallowed up by the two much larger denominations, given that they were small minorities in both the North and the South? They would constitute only about 2% of the new denomination.

Nevertheless, strong forces compelled the reunion effort. Joint events in the early 1930s showed the three their common life and heritage. The three cooperated on a joint hymnal which appeared in 1935 as the official hymnbook for each. They celebrated together in 1934 in Baltimore the sesquicentennial of the founding of an American Methodist church. The sixth Ecumenical Conference of world Methodism was held in Atlanta in 1931, and all three groups acted as hosts. In these common ventures, the participants forged new relationships and came to trust one another. They found they were not so different as they had supposed.

Further, major structural changes, particularly in the M.E. Church, South, had brought the three closer together. The approval of a Judicial Council by the southern church in 1934 suggested that the north could find therein a check on a powerful episcopacy and that the south could find therein a check on a powerful General Conference. Likewise, the southern bishops had recently been restricted by a number of legislative acts, including the removal of their power over the Course of Study, the limitation of their appointive power over presiding elders, and a mandatory retirement age. In the hundred-plus years since the Methodist Protestant secession, both episcopal Methodisms had granted extensive laity rights at all levels. The Methodist Protestants, meanwhile, had moved toward centralized authority. Between them, these elements, transferred into a merged church, would make the new body much more palatable for all three groups.

As commissioners from the three bodies worked together toward unification, the place of Blacks in the final plan became the major point of debate. Southern commissioner Bishop John M. Moore, a tireless worker for union, produced a plan which became the basis for the merged church.

It called for the creation of six jurisdictional conferences, bodies intermediate between the General Conference and the annual conferences. Five of the jurisdictional conferences were regional, partially preserving sectional identities. The sixth jurisdiction contained the black annual conferences of the M.E. Church and overlapped the others geographically. This was acceptable to the South, because it assured them of face-to-face relations with Blacks only at the General Conference level.

Another inducement for accepting the plan was the name selected for the new church. It emphasized the historic themes the three churches had in common and avoided historic problems inherent in their old names. And it was simple—The Methodist Church.

However, the removal of the major objections to reunion is not, in itself, necessarily cause for merger. Positive forces had to be at work to impel the movement. Among them were calls from youth groups, who were impatient with old grudges and who felt a stigma attached to the separation in Methodism. Foreign missionaries found it difficult to explain to potential converts why they should choose one over the others. Many Methodists in all places and of all ages believed that a larger church would be more efficient and more influential. They believed it would grow faster.

Perhaps the most powerful force was the feeling in all branches that the splintered church was the result of sinfulness and sectional narrow-mindedness, and that continuation of the split placed an unnecessary burden of guilt on the current generation. The ecumenical movement held forth a shining vision of one single church, in which all Christians would some day be part of one body ("We are not divided, all one body we; one in hope and doctrine, one in charity"). Most Methodists, with their long tradition of theological tolerance, bought into that vision.

Thus, when the plan for union was placed before the three denominations in 1936, 1937, and 1938, it received affirmative votes from all three, and the uniting conference met in Kansas City in 1939 to complete the process. Though the margins of approval were decisive, the votes were not unanimous. Many persons who decided to enter union did so with regret and foreboding. Here and there, others resolved to leave, either quietly or not so quietly.[1]

Many M.E. black members seriously considered leaving rather than participate in the Central Jurisdiction. A meeting of ministers and bishops from across the country in 1938 concluded, "sentiment was divided as to whether this group should recommend to the colored conferences to withdraw from the Methodist Episcopal Church and set up a distinctive Negro church, or whether these Negro Methodists should now seek union with the Colored Methodist Church."[2] No block defections can be identified, but the new jurisdiction did not prosper. Between the years 1941 and 1948, in a period when The Methodist Church grew by a cumulative 12.9%, the Central Jurisdiction expanded by a total of only 0.3%.[3]

Minor withdrawals occurred from the former Methodist Protestant and Methodist Episcopal, South ranks. Rejectionists in the deep south, Ohio, and Missouri created a "continuing" Methodist Protestant Church. A former Methodist Protestant group in New Jersey formed the "Bible Protestant Church." A handful of dissenters from the M.E. Church, South, encouraged by Bishop Collins Denny, formed the "Southern Methodist Church" and unsuccessfully challenged the new denomination in the courts over property rights and the name. Centered in South Carolina and Mississippi, the denomination spent the next thirty years seeking converts principally among members of The Methodist Church. A holiness-oriented group split off in North Carolina, and a conservative group called the "Evangelical Methodist Church" withdrew in Texas. These withdrawals between them accounted for less than one percent of the former denominations.[4]

All three of the churches which formed The Methodist Church were growing slowly when they entered union, and the new church continued roughly those same growth trends. Redundancies were eliminated at the local, regional, and national levels. Several cases of "altar against altar" were resolved by merging small competing congregations. Small annual conferences became parts of larger, more viable, bodies. General boards and agencies were blended and streamlined. Further, the onus of sectional identity was removed, and a momentum toward further unity was established.

William K. Anderson surveyed church leaders soon after World War II, seeking their assessment of union to that point. Dissatisfaction was greatest in the Central Jurisdiction and least in the western, but even in the Central Jurisdiction, negative evaluations were below 20%.

Many thought that the churchwide Crusade for Christ had helped seal unity. Methodist Protestants, after Blacks the ones most likely to undergo significant change as a result of union, seemed to have found more virtues in the arrangement than they had supposed. The biggest hurdle remaining before the church was completion of the merger of the various denominational boards, a process which time would presumably handle.[5]

The principal benefit of this merger was that it was a *re*-union. It reconciled three denominations whose separations had been a cause of pain and guilt for over 100 years. The causes of the splits, in large part over polity, were now ironed out under changed circumstances. The three had drifted toward each other in matters of democracy and had never been very far apart in theology. Further, they now constituted a truly national church, free of sectional taint. Their polity was strengthened in the merger, particularly in the creation of the Judicial Council.

Two of the participating denominations were of comparable size. Neither would dominate the new structure. Further, they occupied (except for the Central Jurisdiction) different areas of the nation, and thus could get better acquainted from a respectful distance. The grace of the Methodist Protestants in accepting virtual absorption by episcopal Methodism went a long way toward making the union a success.

A major weakness was that they had not drifted all the way toward each other. In the short run, that matter was partially resolved by the jurisdictional system, allowing some sectional autonomy. In the long run, the cure came to be a cause of concern itself because it institutionalized regional differences. Perpetuated in the United Methodist Church, the regional jurisdictions seemed to many in the north to be an expensive structure which had outlived its usefulness. To many others, the jurisdictional structure had the value of permitting a wider range of options under the connectional "big tent."

A second weakness, the racial jurisdiction, became anachronistic as American society changed, and was abandoned by action of the Uniting Conference of 1968, just about paralleling the tide in the secular society. The Central Jurisdiction was always a symbol of failure, even though it did not actually change the segregated status of black Methodists much. Most Blacks and many northern Whites opposed it from the beginning because it appeared to change the motivation for having separate black and white annual conferences.[6]

Finally, although the theologies of the merging churches were close, they were not identical. Southern conservatives and northern liberals eyed one another with suspicion for many years. Yet they glossed over these differences in the name of denominational unity and in a spirit of tolerance.

2. The Merger of 1946

This union involved relatively small numbers of people. The participants went through very little friction during the process and had very few doubts after the fact. It seemed destined for success.

The Church of the United Brethren in Christ had its roots in a "German Methodist" movement headed by Philip William Otterbein and Martin Boehm in the late-eighteenth and early-nineteenth centuries. Its leaders had close personal ties with Bishop Asbury of the Methodist Episcopal Church, and its structures and doctrines mirrored those of the growing Methodist group. Except for the barrier of language (most UBCs did not speak English), the movement might well have become part of the Methodist structure.

By the middle of the nineteenth century, the denomination had grown westward into Ohio and Indiana and had left behind its German-language orientation. By the time of the Civil War, there were UBC churches in California and the northern west coast as well. Because the membership was concentrated north of the Mason-Dixon line, the issues of the Civil War did not split the denomination.

After the Civil War, however, sharp debates developed in the church over membership in secret societies. At the 1889 General Conference, the church moderated its absolute ban on such relationships. This angered a small segment of the church which, led by Bishop Milton Wright, promptly held a rump session and declared themselves to be the true UB Church. Both resultant bodies continued to claim the name. Wright's group remains as the Church of the United Brethren in Christ today, despite a serious overture at reconciliation by the main body in 1909.

The Evangelical Church derived from the Evangelical Association led by Jacob Albright, also stemming from eastern Pennsylvania in the late-eighteenth century among German-speaking citizens. It had Methodist polity and theology from the beginning, and, like the UBC, probably remained separate from the Methodist Episcopal Church only because of the language barrier. Also like the UBC, its German orientation faded, but by the time this had happened, the denomination had its own identity and felt no temptation to unite with the M.E. Church. It spread to Texas and California in the 1880s and subsequently to other areas.

The Evangelicals retained their Germanness longer than did the UBC. One of the principal Evangelical mission fields was Germany. Likewise, the Evangelicals were, on balance, more conservative than the UBC. They were not, however, less prone to division. In 1891, just two years after the UBC split, they divided into two groups. This proved to be temporary, and the two bodies reunited in 1922.

Both groups engaged in ecumenical conversations in the early-twentieth century, especially in the Interchurch World Movement. The two joined in serious discussions aimed at organic union with the Reformed Church in North America and the Evangelical Synod of North America, both of German origin with strength in Pennsylvania. After four years of discussion, the proposal fell apart. The other two joined to become the Evangelical and Reformed Church. With so much else in common, what finally distinguished the UBC and the Evangelical Church from their fellow conferees was the Wesleyan tradition of theology and polity. They had too much Methodism in them to make good partners for the E. and Rs. The question that then remained was whether they had enough in common to match with each other.

One catalyst that hurried union was the depression. Small churches like the UBC and the EC did not have the economic stamina to weather the storm in good health. The merger initiative came from the Evangelical Church. The UBC General Conference met in Akron in 1933 and heard fraternal messenger Bishop M. T. Maze announce, "the Evangelical Church is now ready to enter into negotiations with the UB Church looking toward merger."[7] The United Brethren were very receptive to this overture, and commissioners from the two denominations began meetings in 1934 and 1935, virtually contemporaneously with the Methodist discussions. A long courtship ended in 1942 with the preparation of a plan and a discipline. It was understood that there would be problems. As one participant put it, "A new machine does not always run smoothly. It must be broken in and lubricated quite well. So this ecclesiastical organization must be lubricated with the oil of patience, good will, and the grace of God."[8] Local church mergers were not expected; neither were they discouraged. Annual conference mergers would take place at the proper time, but only gradually. As late as 1964, a couple of conference mergers had still not taken place. After the Evangelical Church acquiesced to the UBC's choice of name, the

Evangelical United Brethren Church, the major obstacles to be overcome related to merging boards and agencies and staffing them.

The merger did not result from weakness. The UBC grew at an average rate of 0.6% per year through the 1930s, though not keeping pace with national population growth in most years. While membership numbers grew, however, Sunday-school and church attendance numbers were falling. The Evangelical Church at the end of the depression was outpacing national population growth patterns by a modest amount.

After union, the new church prospered, perhaps because of the merger but mostly because of the postwar growth experienced by many denominations. In 1947, growth was a modest 0.49%, but 1948 was 4.93% and 1949 was 6.34%.[9] Unification had certainly not hurt them. Further, there were practically no threats of withdrawal by the few dissenters. The church boards and agencies were merged gracefully. The annual conferences slowly blended with one another.

This union proceeded with great smoothness. There was no residue of bitterness and no fringe of rejectionists. Nearly everything worked as it should have, and the merged church grew substantially. The reasons for this appear to be: (1) the two groups were similar in size; (2) the two groups had parallel histories, and similar origins; (3) the two had similar polity, including term episcopacy, annual conferences, and appointment system; (4) the two had similar theology, with strong Wesleyan ties and a similar kind of warm-hearted conservatism; (5) the two were small enough for face-to-face relationships before merger, and still small enough to continue that fellowship after it; (6) the preparation for merger was slow, over the span of decade from first serious discussion to consummation; (7) the assimilation of the post-merger period was allowed to go at a comfortable pace, with congregations and annual conferences able to merge or not in their own good time.

3. The Merger of 1968

The Methodist Church and the Evangelical United Brethren Church both grew substantially in the years following their births, but that pattern had slowed by the end of the decade of the 1950s. There was, however, no feeling of panic that spurred the negotiations between the two looking toward merger. First conversations began while both churches were at the flood tide of their postwar expansion. After initial contacts in 1956, the two appointed a joint commission, which met for the first time in March, 1958. The EUB General Conference of 1958 and the 1960 Methodist General Conference both authorized preparation of a plan of union.

The problems included, first of all, the disparate sizes of the two. Any merger would have to result in the Methodist Church devouring the EUBs unless great care was exercised, and maybe even then. Complications of polity included the EUB term episcopacy and elective district superintendency, which differed from the Methodist lifetime episcopacy and appointive district superintendency. Eventually, the EUBs accepted the Methodist structure for both. Further, the EUBs were worried about the comparative liberalism of the Methodists (they felt they were not spiritual enough) and about the continued existence of the Central Jurisdiction. (While some Methodists, like W. T. Handy, feared merger might slow the dissolution of the Central Jurisdiction, the EUB pressure was for immediacy, and merger probably hastened the end of the black judicatory.)[10] They also understood that the familial intimacy of their denomination was ending as they were absorbed by the Methodists.

A plan was produced and voted on by the respective General Conferences meeting in Chicago in 1966. The Methodist General Conference of 1964 sat in adjourned session for the occasion. Messengers moved back and forth between the two bodies, which were meeting in the same building, bringing accounts of the debates. When the two voted, the Methodists approved easily. The EUB vote was much closer, but exceeded the constitutional minimum for approval.[11]

A Uniting Conference was set for Dallas in April, 1968. The conference faced enormous difficulties in structuring the new church, particularly at the national level. Merger of annual conferences was a concern in areas where the EUBs were strong. In other areas, they were simply absorbed by the 13–1 Methodist majority. The same thing happened over the next four years for Blacks, as the end of the Central Jurisdiction blotted out the black annual conferences and distributed the members, churches, and ministers to existing white annual conferences. While both EUBs and Blacks lost cherished institutions, there seemed to be little alternative since the two groups were statistical minorities in almost every region.

The plan stirred little Methodist opposition, but EUB rejectionism had been brewing in the northwest since the first rumors of possible merger surfaced. The old EUB churches in Canada were granted permission to leave, presumably to join the United Church of Canada, which had a large Methodist component.

Once merger was an accomplished fact, the majority of ministers, and congregations in the Pacific Northwest Conference left the church to form a new denomination, the Evangelical Church of North America. Eventually, the Canadian EUBs joined them.[12] In Montana, from about thirty churches and pastors, only three ministers and five churches remained after secessions took the rejectionists out.[13]

The new church had a membership just under eleven million members. It began to develop a new leadership structure, and after the 1972 General Conference had completed the process, emerged with a pattern at all levels based to some degree on the EUB conciliar polity. The Council on Ministries system, the new church believed, would streamline and democratize the decision-making process in local churches, districts, annual conferences, and at the general church level. The counterpart structures from the predecessor denominations underwent a period of blending. Former EUBs received their share of national staff positions, and the EUB bishops, along with the bishops from the former Central Jurisdiction, joined the five geographical jurisdiction colleges of bishops.

In spite of serious efforts to make the new church work, doubts cropped up almost at once. The Council on Ministries system, despite some successes, came under early criticism, especially in local churches. The denomination's overall membership declined consistently and rapidly, not from people leaving the church so much as from the failure to replace those lost by natural attrition. Minority caucuses began to demand increasing amounts of time and energy from the General Conference, and these issues, many of them worthy and heretofore ignored, nevertheless distracted the church's main deliberative body from other pressing issues. The pressure of the caucuses and the inevitable resistance they created troubled the church and blurred its focus, shattered its confidence, and may have repelled some potential converts.

Debate over this union continued to the end of the twentieth century. The merger had staunch defenders. A recent issue of *Circuit Rider* attempted an evaluation on the occasion of the twenty-fifth anniversary of the merger. Bishop James Ault, who served for four of the five quadrennia after union as episcopal leader in Pennsylvania where EUB work was strong, affirmed that "The Methodist Church Is A Better Church United." "The losses," he said, "have been minimal; the gains quite extraordinary."[14]

This could not apply to membership statistics. Since 1968, membership totals for the United Methodist Church have, as everybody knows, dropped dramatically. In addition to losing over 40,000 EUBs in Canada and the northwest immediately, the membership declined in 1969, in 1970 by 1.07%, in 1971 by 1.52%, in 1972 by 1.66% and so on, a hemorrhage that quickly became very serious. Lyle Schaller, in another 1993 *Circuit Rider* article, pointed out that the total membership dropped from 10,672,000 in 1960 to 8,853,000 in 1990, and that figure included some modest growth in the early 1960s. Relative to the cost of living, financial support was also substantially down. The numbers received on profession of faith and restored showed the 1990 totals to be about half what they were in 1960; the same was true for baptisms and Sunday-school attendance. Schaller concluded with the question, "Was the merger a success? It depends," he answered himself, "on what criteria you use to evaluate it."[15]

Bishop Ault, on the other hand, argued that the decline in membership "would have been experienced by both the EUB and the Methodist churches had they remained separate."[16] The trends of the mid-1960s showed both churches with declining memberships. Further, the fortunes of all "mainstream" denominations took a turn for the worse in the 1960s and have continued downward since then, so the United Methodist Church could well be seen a part of that trend.

Criticisms have been leveled at the Council on Ministries system that was introduced in the merger and subsequent restructuring over the next few years. Here the record was not so easily reduced to numbers. Many people argued that the GCOM was a flawed institution too far removed from the local church. Others have argued that the GCOM was fine, and that the *local* COMs were the real problem. Many local churches moved away from them in favor of an Administrative Council. Critics also charged that the COM system developed a parochial perspective in the minds of the participants.

The record was mixed regarding the missions of the EUBs under the new denominational umbrella. The EUB work in the Española Valley of New Mexico gained a larger support constituency at merger, but declined because the larger constituency supported it even less.[17] On the other hand, the EUB Red Bird Mission in eastern Kentucky has prospered under the new arrangement. Jim Morris, the first non-EUB superintendent of the mission, estimates that the mission is three times the size it was in 1968, even after losing some work to a neighboring annual conference.[18]

Twenty five years after merger, many former EUBs were disturbed about what had happened to "their" church since union. Despite attempts to make sure that they were well represented in all areas of the church, they felt left out. They consistently pointed, by way of example, to references to "the Methodist Church" by present day *United* Methodists. Part of the *Circuit Rider* colloquy was an article by Warren Hartman from the EUB point of view, subtitled, "The EUBs Had Reservations Then and Now." Hartman did not end by repudiating the merger, but he certainly had some serious criticisms of it from EUB perspective.[19]

4. Conclusion

Organic unions between Wesleyan bodies in the twentieth century has produced differing assessments of union's value. Some lessons seem clear. Unions are more likely to be successful when they are between groups of similar size. They do best when the merging bodies have similar polities and theologies. Participants are usually best satisfied when they change things least. Conversely, the more dissimilar the merging groups, the more likely there was to be discontent and secession.

For several generations, the ecumenical dream has been of one single body of Christians. The three mergers under consideration, once done, could not be undone and there was good reason to give thanks for them. But as the century ends, it may be possible to count the costs as well as the benefits of these unions and to forge other models of Christian unity. Such models of unity, alternatives to outright merger, could be based on 1 Corinthians 12–13, H. Richard Niebuhr's study of social class and denomination, Wesley's sermon on the Catholic Spirit, or perhaps some secular metaphor.

A connectional church must come to a decision about the levels of unity and diversity it seeks. Both are present and both must be accommodated. Organic union of the sort considered here is one possibility which emphasizes unity and deemphasizes diversity. Other models might place the balance point toward the other end of the continuum.

For example, recent actions by the United Methodist General Conference and the ruling bodies of several sister denominations lead in new directions. The new face of COCU is manifest in the cooperative ventures called "covenant communion," in which mutual recognition of baptism, the eucharist, ordination, and mission allow for the participants to share with each other while maintaining their denominational uniqueness.[20]

If we do in fact come to affirm our differences as useful, we must then work all the harder at affirming the matrix that holds us together as one holy Christian church. Christ's call to unity still resounds in our hearts; our problem is to find what shape that unity may take.

～ Mark W. Wethington ～

At its best, Methodist connectionalism has, as Heitzenrater's initial essay indicated, defined and oriented itself by its purpose and has been about mission. The connection served mission. The connection functioned to send, to prepare, to position, and to provision. Certainly that continued to be the case with the late-nineteenth-century restructuring that created the boards as denominational agencies. The church rebuilt itself, quite literally, to function efficiently and corporately for mission. What happens, though, when the church comes to new understanding of mission, its mission, itself? What happens to the structure that had been built around prior understandings? And what happens if the old structures do not flex and reshape themselves to suit the new understandings? To such questions Mark Wethington addresses himself, drawing on a decade of effort with Frederick Herzog and others to build more intimate and reciprocal covenantal bonds between United Methodism (and particularly the North Carolina Conference) and its former mission in Peru, now the Iglesia Metodista del Peru. His reflections draw also on reflection and writing that he and Herzog did together in the Lilly project before Herzog's untimely death. Wethington contends that a richer and theologically more adequate concept of mission, particularly a recognition of "missio Dei," i.e., of the idea that mission is God's, might lead United Methodism to fundamental reorientation of itself. He offers the North Carolina-Peru covenant as a model of such re-orientation, a relationship not mediated by a bureaucracy deploying North American saviors to benighted Latin Americans, but instead characterized by dialogue, mutuality, learning from one another, common profession of faith, unity in prayer and sacrament, joint discipleship, partnership in problem-solving, prophetic inquiry into social conditions and the church's implication therein, two-way travel, and close personal bonds between brothers and sisters, congregations, seminaries, and conference leadership of the two churches. What might it mean for United Methodism as a whole, and for its boards and agencies in particular, to reimagine Methodism for the missio Dei? How might United Methodism's global purposes look if conceived in covenantal and missio-Dei rather than structural terms? How does the missio Dei express itself in United Methodism's use of money?

God's Mission and United Methodism

Mark W. Wethington

The Missio Dei

**All authority in heaven and on earth has been given to me.
Go therefore and make disciples of all nations, baptizing
them in the name of the Father and of the Son and of the Holy
Spirit, teaching them to observe all that I have commanded
you; and lo, I am with you always, to the close of the age.
(Matthew 28:18-20)**

During the twentieth century there has been a slow awakening
within the Christian church regarding her understanding of the "Great
Commission." C. Stanley Smith has described the first great missionary
conference of the twentieth century, held in Edinburgh in 1910, as
"primarily a conference on missionary strategy. It was mainly occupied,
not in defining the missionary obligation, nor even the missionary
message, both of which it seemed to take for granted, but rather in
discussing ways for making the Christian message more effective
among the non-Christian nations of the world."[1]

Teaching at that time as a missionary at the Nanking Theological
Seminary in Nanking, China, Dr. Smith describes the decades before
World War I as a time when Christians in the West viewed the
Kingdom of God as very near and thus saw the world as sharply
divided between Christian and non-Christian nations and peoples. The
non-Christian peoples were seen as primarily outside of Europe and
the American continent. The 1910 Edinburgh Conference (which led to
the formation of the International Missionary Council in 1921) was a
meeting of personnel from mission boards and organizations who
gathered, in a kind of innocence, to program strategies for "going and
making disciples" within the non-Christian nations. Virtually absent
from this conference were Christians indigenous to countries outside of
North America and Europe.

Eighteen years later another great missionary conference was held in Jerusalem. Unlike the 1910 Edinburgh Conference, at this gathering there were many "nationals" represented from many parts of the world.[2] At this 1928 Jerusalem Conference charges were leveled that Christian missionaries were acting as agents of Western commercialism and political imperialism. While the "Western delegates" to the Jerusalem Conference sought to repudiate all charges of ulterior or imperialist mission motives, Smith notes that the conference once again failed to offer "any clearer statement of the theological basis of the church's missionary obligation than the command of Jesus to go into all the world making disciples of all men."[3]

In the 1930s and 40s segments of the church in North America and Europe became more self-critical about the nature of the church's mission as that mission was being defined and shaped primarily at a national church level. Some theologians and missionaries urged the church to recognize and confess that the church in North America and Europe was reflected in the following historical truth, namely, that as the early church's hope in the immediate return of the Lord faded away there came in its place "a more calculating mission of the church for the extension of its own glory and power, all too often with forces dominated by motives of cultural, political and economic imperialism."[4]

Emil Brunner is well known for his assertion that "the church exists by mission as fire exists by burning."[5] When the church "strategizes" or "programs" mission with the conscious, or sometimes innocent, motive of justifying the perpetuation of its own institutional structures (i.e., "for the extension of its own glory and power") then it ceases to burn with the fire of Christ's Spirit, its flame flickers, and it grows cold. At a time when many members and leaders of the church are looking for the rekindling of the fire of American Methodism, it is crucial that the church engage in critical self-examination of its understanding and focus of mission. Such critical self-examination, carried out both globally and ecumenically, will enable the denomination to develop a consciousness of connection primary to our Methodist heritage.

The continuing loss of church members in mainline North American churches, United Methodism included, has sparked a concerted interest in "church growth," with many strategies being marketed as solutions to reverse the decline. Even now, it is becoming clear that many of these strategies for increasing church membership are producing no long-lasting effect. When such strategies focus on an evangelism centered primarily on numerical growth, or, even worse, on growth as a means of financial development, a concern for discipleship formation (both personal and social holiness) is often peripheral. Jesus preached that the way is narrow and that those who enter are few. Can it not be the case, in fact, that a decline of membership may be the fruit of faithful discipleship? There are numerous examples of congregations who have battled courageously against racial injustice or other such issues and have lost members as a result. Numerical growth is frequently not the byproduct of faithful discipleship, at least not in the short term. The threshing of the chaff from the grain implies a decline in quantity.

In a time when our leaders appear to be desperately jumping from one lifeboat to another as a reaction to membership decline, the church in North America is in urgent need of a sound biblical and theological understanding and reclaiming of the church's raison d'être. At the same time, we are confounded that the churches in Latin America, Asia, and Africa that were "planted" by North American missionaries in past years now appear to be burning fervently with the Spirit's power while also experiencing remarkable membership growth. Where church growth is marked by faithful discipleship, we can agree that God, rather than a particular marketing strategy, has given the growth. That is not to imply that in these aforementioned places there is an all-pervading faithfulness in Christian discipleship. Furthermore, the church catholic does not always agree on universal standards for defining faithful discipleship.

Regardless of geographical location, this local pastor is confident that the church anywhere will gain new life and shape vital disciple-ship only as her people understand and incarnate the missio Dei, which is their raison d'etre.[6] The Acts of the Apostles clearly proclaims that when the disciples of Christ embody the missio Dei, God gives the growth. Growth of import, namely, maturation in discipleship, is first and foremost the byproduct of God's sanctifying grace rather than the byproduct of human strategies. Growth in discipleship, both personally and socially, is derived as an attribute of God.

David J. Bosch defines the concept of missio Dei as "not primarily an activity of the church, but an attribute of God."[7] Bosch goes on to say, "We cannot without ado claim that what we do is identical to the missio Dei; our missionary activities are only authentic insofar as they reflect participation in the mission of God. . . . The primary purpose of the missiones ecclesiae can therefore not simply be the planting of churches or the saving of souls; rather, it has to be service to the missio Dei."[8] It must be acknowledged that God's mission is indeed "larger than the mission of the church" and that the church is privileged to be a participant in it. We who are called into mission must constantly reassert the conviction that "neither the church nor any other human agent can ever be considered the author or bearer of mission. . . . Mission is, primarily and ultimately, the work of the Triune God. . . . Mission has its origin in the heart of God. God is a fountain of sending love. This is the deepest source of mission."[9] In recent years past and still today, the North American church, in the process of self-critical examination, has found it necessary to confess that the church's mission has much too often resulted in the usurpation of God's mission.

As early as 1932 Karl Barth offered a grounding for the church's theology in a theocentric understanding of mission.[10] A contemporary theologian, Letty Russell, notes how "this theocentric interpretation of mission had been largely forgotten in the development of the Western missionary movements until it began to be developed as a way of speaking about God's action and involvement in the world in the light of the crisis of World War II."[11] She suggests that the shift from an ecclesiocentric to a theocentric perspective meant that "the church became more modest in its claims to be the medium of God's action" and instead began to see itself once again as "an instrument of that action."[12]

The concept of the missio Dei underwent much study and development between its introduction at the the 1952 Willingen Conference and the 1961 New Delhi Conference (the conference at which the International Missionary Council and the World Council of Churches were integrated). In the July 1962 issue of *The International Review of Missions,* Donald McGavran reflects the popularity of this theme when he points out that central to Christian theology is the understanding that "Christian mission is not a man-initiated activity but is originated by God."[13]

Unfortunately, the embodiment of a theocentric understanding of mission has not been easy in a church like the United Methodist, which in the twentieth century has undergone such massive bureaucratic growth. Bulging ecclesiastical structures have tended to sidetrack church leaders from focusing on the mission of God. A large ecclesial structure brings about preoccupation with maintaining institutional viability. In addition, the church's splintering into interest groups leads to greater isolation for the protection of self-interests and a less cooperative vision.

In the midst of these realities, which surround and infiltrate the church, I believe that an understanding and incarnation of the missio Dei will be possible only when local congregations are willing to be fully engaged in mutuality-in-mission, i.e., in the forming of missional relationships in which Christians across contexts (e.g., cultural, economic, racial) accompany one another into the work and understanding of the missio Dei. Missions defined as a one-way strategy or program (e.g., North Americans sending mission personnel and resources to the "lost") must be jettisoned. We North American Christians must humbly confess that we ourselves also need to be "saved" from a web of cultural norms, values, and influences in which we are hopelessly entangled and from which we will never see clearly unless we humble ourselves and allow "the least" among us to be God's liberating instrument. Here is where encounter with the other becomes a channel of God's redemptive grace.

In an age of global communication and of global political and economic interdependence there is hardly a place on the face of this earth where the name of Christ has not been heard and his church planted. White middle- to upper-middle-class North Americans and Europeans no longer have "a market on the Gospel." In fact, many would argue that we have "lost the market" inasmuch as the kerygma has become mingled with a seductively economic and material market, which itself is the outgrowth of a very individualistic and narcissistic American psyche.[14] Honest analysis of our North American culture reveals ruling norms and values that function in sharp contrast to the missio Dei as that mission has been incarnated in the person and work of Jesus of Nazareth.[15] Entering into the missio Dei requires an understanding and acceptance of Christo-praxis.[16]

As a local pastor, I have witnessed that a sound biblical understanding of the missio Dei will more honestly arise only where there is dialogue (worship and Bible study) and mutual partnership with Christians in radically different cultural, racial, and economic contexts. In the sharing of faith between the rich and the poor; Latinos, African Americans, Asians, and Anglos; carried on both globally and ecumenically, the local and global church will uncover new insights into her nature as God's people in God's world, and there will be fostered more accountable and creative discipleship. If mission and unity are given by the Holy Spirit as the essence of the church, then it is critical that such contrasting communities of faith learn to walk together so that mutual understanding of the shape of Christ's ministry might foster transformation of individuals and congregations. Where dialogue centered on obedient and accountable discipleship is shared across contexts, there will emerge the reality of the gospel along with a more credible witness to the world.

Such an understanding of mutuality in mission might be compared to the class meeting of early Methodism, or to its retraditioning today in Covenant Discipleship.[17] In covenant relationship we are able to discern and do together what we are unable to perceive and carry out alone. The covenanting of Christians together in different contexts (cultural, ethnic, and economic) is an accompaniment which allows us "to watch over one another in love" by holding one another accountable in our discipleship; this is a particular necessity in a globally interdependent world where human relationships are tied together in a complex and illusive web. As a case in point, I have discovered in my own life and ministry that it is impossible for us North Americans to hold one another accountable, particularly with regard to our affluence. We deceive ourselves if we think that the rich are able to hold the rich accountable. We deceive ourselves if we neglect the reality that it is primarily the North American church's wealth which most hinders our faithful discipleship. For example, we must comprehend why dialogue about and understanding of the World Bank and the International Monetary Fund are critically important for Christian community.[18] From time to time we acknowledge the problem of affluence in the church. We even find at times that the guilt weighs heavy, but we fail to do anything about it either individually or corporately as the church. How the church ought to be about the missio Dei becomes confused in the midst of a national culture that promotes values of individualism, privatism, and capitalism, again, so aptly described by sociologists such as Robert Bellah. It is in the walking together, in the sharing of the pain of the world brought about by our inhumanity to each other (political, economic, environmental, etc.), that we begin to release the healing power of the missio Dei.

United Methodism and Mission

My interest in United Methodism and the church's mission is rooted in my own experience as the son of Methodist missionaries. I was five months old when my parents, my siblings, and I voyaged in 1954 from North Carolina to the Philippines. In that foreign land we were part of the "Great Commission." We lived the missionary life during a transitional period when specialists like professors were to "work themselves out of a job to make room for 'nationals.'" My memories of those first nine years of my life are vivid. During the past eight years of my own renewed and more direct involvement as a local pastor in the formation of a new paradigm of mission, my memories as a missionary child have taken on a peculiarly different appearance. What I once saw in a mirror dimly has now come more into focus.

After some thirty years, and having come out of a mission paradigm that has been the characteristic norm of the North American and European church over the past centuries, I have found myself engaged in what my friend Frederick Herzog liked to refer to as "the pioneering of a new paradigm for mission."[19] However, it is he who has been the forerunner of the mutuality-in-mission paradigm. I have followed in trying to embody this alternative vision within the local congregation and the annual conference. An alternative mission paradigm is essential in a time when it has become all the more clear that the paradigm under which the North American church has operated for so long has often undermined the missio Dei, and in doing so has lost its credibility in the global church. Even the unofficial alternative mission sending agency of United Methodism, the Mission Society, has not been able to offer the church any true alternative, but has simply continued to foster the same patterns of missional relationship defined too often by paternal superiority and capital advantage.

Within the past year I sat in a meeting with a former bishop of one of our Methodist churches in South America who observed that the General Board of Global Ministries "has become a bureaucracy that bleeds the church of power." United Methodists must scrutinize our *missiones ecclesia* to determine whether it is *God's* mission which gives life to the church rather than the church which creates mission programming as justification for its institutional survival. It is the burning that keeps the fire alive.

In a 1962 study paper on "The Central Conference of the Methodist Church" commissioned by the General Conference Commission on the Structure of Methodism Overseas, the author of that paper, my father, the Rev. Dr. L. Elbert Wethington, wrote that "recently in the U.S.A. many are complaining of getting so blinded by the glare of organization they are failing somewhat in holding forth the Light of the World." Concern across the church about a national mission agency with a bulging bureaucracy is not just a recent one, but has obviously been a growing angst for decades. The shaping and prioritizing of American Methodism's missional focus at primarily a general agency level has fostered an uneasiness that in recent years has led to further estrangement between local congregational visioning for mission and the general church's agenda. Perhaps nowhere is this more evident than in the increasing resistance among local churches to paying 100%

of their apportionment. Added to this is an obvious growth in interest among grassroots United Methodists to be engaged in hands-on mission (Volunteers in Mission, etc.).

The end result is that there is a kind of local church "tea party" which is forcing the general agencies of the church to be more self-critical. A case in point is the recent General Board of Global Ministries' Core Coordinating Task Force report entitled "Realizing a New Vision." In its introduction to the "new vision," the task force affirms that in its commitment to the whole church, the General Board of Global Ministries (hereafter referred to as "the Board') joins "God's mission" (the missio Dei) rather than being the determiner of what that mission is.[20]

This proposal of a "new vision" takes more seriously a need to reform how the Board enters into the missio Dei, indicating a desire to move away from a narrow, ecclesiocentric view of mission.[21] The report acknowledges the ever-increasing eagerness among grassroots United Methodists to be more directly engaged in mission, rather than simply financially supporting a missionary-sending agency. In a concept paper which was preliminary to the "new vision" report, the question is asked: "How can the Board work in a more cooperative fashion with those who wish to be directly, personally involved in mission and still afford opportunities for those who want the mission agency to represent them in witnessing to the love of Jesus Christ in word and deed?"[22] Herein the Board recognizes a need to connect with models of mission that have been initiated on the local church level. The report speaks of the need for the church to move from "having missions" to "being in mission" by enabling congregations to be more directly involved with Christian witness and communities of faith around the world. The report encourages "mutual witness" and the forming of "covenant relationships between missionaries and local churches and conferences."[23] The "new vision" demonstrates a sincere recognition of the need for reshaping the Board's understanding and involvement in the missio Dei, and it is a vision which one hopes will be radically and concretely realized.

The North Carolina/Peru Covenant As Model

The North Carolina/Peru Covenant is a model for mission that predates the Board's "new vision" by some five years. This is not to say that the Board has been unaware of the NC/Peru Covenant. The Board has known of this covenant model, but for the most part has been hindered from giving it much support because of the presumed obligation of sustaining programs and relationships of missions to which it is already committed.[24]

The nature of "covenant" as an example of mutuality-in-mission is today strongly modeled in the relationship between the North Carolina Annual Conference of the United Methodist Church and the Iglesia Metodista del Peru (the Methodist Church of Peru, hereafter referred to as the IMP). There is a lot of history behind this missional relationship that I cannot, in an essay such as this fully recount. Nevertheless, I will attempt a brief summary primarily so that this essay might serve the church not just as theory but as a paradigm in praxis.

Let it be said at the outset that leaders in the Peru church as well as the North Carolina participants recognized from the beginning that God was the primary mover in bringing us together. Every step of the way, we have sought to discern and understand the missio Dei as central to the kind of "connection" which this covenant very quickly became. The most reassuring aspect of the Peru covenant as a model for mission (and connectionalism) has been the obvious piloting of God. What appeared at first as an odd set of circumstances was soon recognized as God's gracious initiative. God's grace has not only initiated this relationship but has undoubtedly sustained it now for seven years. Communication has evolved from letters, which six or seven years ago took weeks to exchange, to fax and e-mail, which are now exchanged often daily and most certainly weekly.

It was in early 1987 that Professor Frederick Herzog of the Duke Divinity School (and a minister of the United Church of Christ) became interested in developing an educational contact with a South American country. For a number of reasons the country of Peru was selected, where he discovered there was a newly reorganized, Methodist-related seminary, the Comunidad Biblica Teologica (CBT) in Lima. During a visit of Frederick Herzog and his wife to Peru, conversations took place with Bishop Marco Ochoa, the bishop of the IMP at that time. Part of these conversations included the hope of strengthening ties between the Peru church and United Methodists in North America. There was mutual affirmation of Methodism as a global church and of the Wesleyan vision of a world parish. In this encounter was born the anticipation that there might be created a wider and global vision of accompaniment and theological reflection as our churches in both the north and south struggle to be faithful in their own particular contexts.

Prior to the Herzogs' visit to Lima, my wife and I had journeyed to Peru. We had gone in November 1986 for personal reasons, namely, to become acquainted with an orphaned baby who was to become our son through a channel of international adoption (we had been given the opportunity to adopt this Peruvian infant after our work toward completing an adoption in the Philippines was quickly terminated because of the Edsa Revolution and the overthrow of the Marcos dictatorship). Never before had I been in South America and little did I expect an adoption to give birth to a larger relationship. At this time I was pastoring a rural United Methodist charge. I had studied under Frederick Herzog at the Duke Divinity School and had also worked with him in developing a student exchange program between Duke and the theology department of the University of Bonn in Germany. By the grace of God, my mentor and I were brought together again in the forging of a new relationship.

In November 1988 Bishop Ochoa sent the Rev. Luis Reinoso, District Superintendent of the Lima-Callao District, to North Carolina as a spokesperson of the Methodist Church of Peru in the hope that some kind of relationship between the two church bodies might be further discussed. Bishop Ochoa stated by letter that the IMP was in crisis, not only because of its own internal issues, but also because of the ramifications of the crisis of the country as a whole (Peru at that time was faltering under seven years of terrorist activity by the Shining Path, with some 15,000 deaths due to the terrorism; inflation was running over 800%; and the infrastructure of the country was close to collapse). In closing his letter Ochoa wrote: "Our relationship of Church-Sisters is a two-way relationship and . . . we also would like to know more about your Conference and what ways we can support and help you. May God lead us in this relationship, bless us, and strengthen us all. Amen!"

When the Rev. Luis Reinoso[25] came to North Carolina, we brought together several pastors and lay people who represented a number of · congregations. In a letter dated 7 October 1988, Bishop C. P. Minnick, resident bishop of the North Carolina Annual Conference, wrote to me saying, "The event, to be held November 9–11, 1988, will afford us a good occasion to assess the implications of possible new relationships between the Methodist Church of Peru and the North Carolina Annual Conference." These conversations proved to be very fruitful and a strong interest in forming a covenant of mutuality between our two church bodies was affirmed.

At the close of these days with Reinoso, our annual conference study team issued a statement to the Council of Bishops regarding the crisis in Peru and of the Methodist Church of Peru in order to seek their awareness and support. In December, Bishop Minnick appointed a conference "Task Force on Global Covenant Community" with the purpose of further exploring this mutual desire for partnership in mission. A few months later, in February 1989, the task force submitted a proposal to the North Carolina Conference Council on Ministries seeking their support of the forming of a missional relationship between our annual conference and the IMP. The Council enthusiastically endorsed a plan for a team of clergy and lay people to go to Peru in order to further our conversation.

In May 1989 the first team of clergy and laity from the North Carolina Conference traveled to Lima, Peru, in order to become acquainted with a Methodist people about whom we knew virtually nothing. Our goal was to learn about each other, to fellowship together, to worship together, to share in the Eucharist together, to engage in Bible study together, to dialogue about personal, local, and global issues, etc. Our hope was to form a kind of "marital" relationship in which we would pledge to accompany one another for better or worse, for the richer and the poorer (and we knew who was which), in sickness and in health. After about a week of walking together in dialogue, prayer, and worship, we formed an informal covenant bond, "signed" in the sacrament of Holy Communion. During these days we discussed how the N.C. Conference might accompany the church in Peru during a critical time of crisis for them, but acknowledging that United Methodism in North America was also in crisis. We agreed to a comprehensive five-year plan entitled a "Discipleship Agreement," in which both sides pledged particular objectives and actions in the area of evangelism, social action, human rights, Christian education, liturgy, and worship. This Discipleship Agreement guided us in the years following.

This covenant relationship was ratified the following year by our respective judicatory bodies and has been reaffirmed by our church bodies at all subsequent sessions since its inception.[26] The covenant agreement ratified by the North Carolina Annual Conference reads as follows:

> We, the members of the North Carolina Annual Conference of the United Methodist Church, in session June 1990, hereby affirm our covenant in Christ with our sisters and brothers of the Iglesia Metodista del Peru. As an expression of that covenant bond, we will call upon the Cabinet and agencies of this Annual Conference to encourage and lead the Annual Conference, districts, and local congregations to enter into covenant/partner relationship with the Iglesia Metodista del Peru, for

prayer and other forms of mutual support, engagements, and communication as determined by and agreed upon by the communities of faith entering into such a covenant relationship.[27]

The covenant declaration of the IMP reads as follows:

The 12th General Assembly of the Methodist Church of Peru, meeting January 25–28, 1990, received with much joy in the Lord, the willingness to ratify the discipleship covenant between the North Carolina Annual Conference of the United Methodist Church of the USA and the Methodist Church of Peru. We recognize that you, as well as we, must pray together, support one another, get to know each other more, and exchange experiences in such a manner that with total trust in our Lord Jesus Christ we will walk together, striving for mutual growth and benefit of our churches. Thus, we affirm also the willingness to establish the discipleship covenant with the North Carolina Annual Conference. "We are partners in the work of service to our God . . ." (I Cor. 3:9).[28]

Whereas our visit of May 1989 was a new venture in forming mutuality in mission, the covenant which now binds our churches together has grown considerably in commitment on both sides. In a day when the definition and even history of "connectionalism" in Methodism have come under debate and question, "covenanting" between Methodists of various ethnic, cultural, and economic contexts offers hope for the clearer defining of connection; indeed, for a connection not defined by ecclesial structure, but rather by the missio Dei. The covenanting model is a model of missions that places primary emphasis upon "mutual witness" as that witness is lived out by walking with one another into the mission of God. Clarity of understanding of the missio Dei may only be derived out of worship, prayer, and Bible study that crosses lines of difference (trans-cultural, economic, and racial). Anything less than mutuality of relationship within such settings will likely result in *missiones ecclesia* taking precedence over the missio Dei. Anything less than a mutually derived understanding about the missio Dei (rooted in Christo-praxis) will likely result in mission that is predominantly and regionally ecclesiocentric rather than theocentric. In a time of global interdependence, it is critical that our heritage of "connectionalism" be reclaimed across contexts, as the mutuality of witness and accountability as disciples of Christ. Indeed, it was the mutuality of witness and accountability that shaped the early class meetings of Methodism.

The covenanting concept for the people of God is not new. We know that the making and keeping of covenants is at the very heart of Holy Scripture. In recent years, covenanting has been spoken of most frequently in the formation of ecumenical relationships. In 1989 the Consultation of Church Union issued a document entitled "Churches in Covenant Communion." In that document "covenanting" is defined as both an act and a process by which churches come into new relationship with one another. It is understood as a commitment to one another "in which the Spirit's gift of unity in Christ will be enabled to grow and to flower."[29] It is a way of being one. The commitment is not primarily expressed in ecclesial structure but rather in faith sacrament, ministry, and mission. Covenant communion assumes a new kind of ecclesial reality, an organic life in which there is unity of heart and mind, and unity in faith, in prayer, in the breaking of bread, in the word of the Gospel, in ministry, in sharing, and in witness and service to the world.

In his essay on "Connectionalism: End or Beginning?" Russell E. Richey points out that connectionalism has expressed itself in United Methodism in recent years in our "board and commission administrative order."[30] That is to say, connectionalism has been primarily marked by the denominational initiatives and programs "handed down" from the national agencies of the church to jurisdictional, conference, district, and local bodies. Criticism of the hierarchical bureaucracy by local churches who have felt burdened and controlled from above has brought this notion of connectionalism into serious question and produced calls for decentralization and local church empowerment.

Calling attention to the Council of Bishops' 1990 "Vision for the Church," Richey notes that the council insists on "a connectionalism of common discipline and holiness," a recognition that connectionalism might best be defined with reference to those who are "bound together in a connectional covenant of mission."[31]

I would point to the North Carolina/Peru covenant as an example of such a "connectional covenant of mission," one that is not defined by institutional structures but by a mutual commitment to worship and work together in cooperation with the missio Dei (working together to define and understand the missio Dei, together finding ways to give expression to and to glorify the missio Dei). Such a "connexion" (as Wesley referred to it) is rooted in Methodist history, most specifically, in Wesley's formation of classes (I have often referred to the N.C./Peru Covenant as a global class meeting, working together toward mutual witness and accountability). For Wesley the connection was primarily a reference to those who were joined together along their faith pilgrimage. Ecclesial authority and organizational structure were less defining of connection; more important were mutuality of support and accountability for one's discipleship. I am convinced that such a paradigm for mission will enable the global church, and American Methodism in particular, to understand and embody the missio Dei more faithfully.

The Missio Dei, Mutuality-in-Mission, and Money

The covenant mission paradigm is one that embodies mutuality. In the 1962 study paper on "The Central Conference," referred to above, it is asserted that the structure of Methodism overseas "has not been designed or retained to effect any ulterior motives of domination, possessiveness, or parasitism. . . ."[32] I suggest that American Methodism shared a common innocence of what detrimental effect its colonizing missional structure would have upon the churches in Asia, Latin America, etc. in the years to come—effects which are embarrassingly evident, for example, within Peruvian Methodism. As we work toward new paradigms for mission it is critically important that we look upon one another and ourselves in the mirror of our mission history, clearly interpreting the past years of missional relationship and confessing our naïveté and failures.

The North Carolina/Peru Covenant has enabled us to see ourselves more clearly as we have sought to understand our shared mission history in the context of worship, prayer, and Bible study, in the celebration of the sacraments, and in the bearing of our mutual burdens. In the mission covenant with Peru, we have been constantly and embarrassingly reminded of just how horribly American money has played a central role in the church's mission. Not only is the "dollar" the "core" of North American culture but it has also been the "soul" of the church's mission. The American dollar that has unquestionably shaped mission into being more paternalistic than mutual, more the mission of the church than the mission of God. It is something deeper than bureaucracy that has bled the church of its power; it is the North American church's money that has very frequently displaced the Spirit's power.

In an unpublished study written in conjunction with this essay, Frederick Herzog describes the transformation of the human being into the money-being of the consumer society and argues that this transformation belongs to the core of the Methodism-and-culture dynamics. This "outsider" to United Methodism (a pastor in the United Church of Christ) has walked beside us, and often in front of us, as

United Methodists of North Carolina have sought to fashion an alternative model of mission for the church. Herzog saw and felt painfully the clear relationship between missions, money, and the suffering of millions of God's children. More than once Herzog and I stood at the base of a statue which sits across from our Methodist seminary in Lima, in the median of Paseo Colon; it is a statue of Christopher Columbus, cross and sword in hand, subduing an Indian woman on her knees. It represented for the Catholic Church and the Spanish Crown the "mission" completed.

In his own case study of Methodist missions in Peru, Herzog discovered repeatedly how mission stations such as the IMP became almost totally dependent on money from the North American church. The issue was not money as such, but the mind-frame that goes along with money. In a major treatise written about the Methodist mission in Peru, Rosa del Carmen Bruno Jofre makes this summary point:

> In principle the Methodist teachings in Peru were addressed to everyone, without regard to social conditions, and within an atmosphere of "brotherhood." But the details of Mission practice show that the idea of "brotherhood" was not free from class distinctions and political choices. During the first thirty years of existence (1890 to 1920), the Mission, in its pursuit of prestige and influence, assiduously cultivated the dominant classes, including semi-feudal landowners.[33]

The question today, Herzog poignantly argues, is whether mission is still mission or whether it has turned into money-management.

In connection with the globalization efforts of the Association of Theological Schools, Jonathan J. Bonk quotes John Kenneth Galbraith as saying, "Nothing so gives the illusion of intelligence as personal association with large sums of money."[34] Herzog suggests a rephrasing of this quotation to say, "Nothing so gives the illusion of mission success as personal association with large sums of money." Money is something inside of us, a power that determines our identity and that defines our church's mission. It is for this very reason, i.e., the complex web of missions and money, that Frederick Herzog devoted so much of his energy and the latter years of his life doing courageous battle for salvation and liberation against the monetary structures that bring suffering to so many of God's children.

Herzog often pointed out that "the core of our culture is money; everything else is footnote." As culture has been shaped by money, so too has the church. Money and its multiplication turn everything in culture into a commodity, including human beings and God. Therefore, when Christians dialogue across contexts and engage in critical self-reflection the church is drawn into God's own missionizing work of destroying the idols, especially the idolatry of money.

Let it be said once more, therefore, that "the church does not 'undertake' mission; rather, the missio Dei constitutes the church."[35] And here it must be clearly understood that in our time the missio Dei, which needs to be constantly renewed and reconceived, is in large measure a war against the idolatry of money.

There is no denying that North American missionary agencies, United Methodism included, have exploited and marginalized indigenous populations with colonial power and politics, at the core of which is money. The marketing of missions long preceded the marketing that has now infiltrated most of the rest of the church as well. With regard to Latin American missions, David Martin states in his book, *Tongues of Fire*, the "arrival of American Methodism was . . . parallel to the arrival of capital."[36]

A mission history tightly intertwined with the growth of American capitalism is the greatest obstacle to the forming of new missional relationships centered on "mutual witness." It was a frustrating experience to be in conference with leaders of the church in Peru in March 1994, after some five years of forming this relationship, and for some Peruvian church leaders from marginal regions (who had not yet been as exposed to the covenant relationship) to bring to me a stack of some hundred pages of project proposals amounting to hundreds of thousands of U.S. dollars. They assumed that we were staff representatives from the General Board of Global Ministries, and they came from the exterior borders of Peru eagerly hoping that we would be able to fund their requests. Their appeals became a viewing of the history of American Methodist missions in a mirror, in which we have been seen by those to whom we have been sent not so much as witnesses to Jesus Christ but more as sources of revenue.

I explained to these representatives that we were not from "the Board in New York," but that we were just "little people" out of local congregations in North Carolina. At first they had difficulty comprehending the covenant of mutuality concept and were puzzled when they learned that money was not to become the primary focus of our accompaniment (although, because of our wealth and their poverty the talk about money absolutely cannot and should not be avoided).[37] In covenant with Peru, we have had to learn that we must honestly discuss the North American church's wealth and the sharing of it with Christians around the world who are poor.

In this particular encounter it again became so very apparent how difficult it is to establish a relationship of mutuality-in-mission, very different from the missional relationship to which many have become accustomed for over one hundred years.[38] It has been interesting to witness a kind of love/hate relationship with which the Peru church views "the Board in New York." There is an aspect of parental respect for the church from the north that gave her birth, and at other times there are feelings of "child neglect" or even "abuse."

On a number of occasions over the past couple of years, I have been in dialogue with Elton Watlington, a missionary to Peru from 1956 to 1978 who now resides in Memphis, Tennessee. He has shared with me how the Peruvian church experienced feelings of neglect when it became an autonomous church in January of 1970. It felt cut off suddenly from that which had been its life blood for so long, namely, North American Methodism. Watlington noted that Brazil was already autonomous at that time and that Chile, Argentina, and Uruguay were likewise ready and eager. But Bolivia, Panama, Costa Rica, and Peru felt uneasy about immediate autonomy. Nevertheless, the "push" from New York brought autonomy upon all the churches, ready or not.

Peru was not prepared for autonomy at that time, in part because its indigenous leaders were few in number. Added to the scarcity of trained clergy was the tragic death of three primary leaders of the IMP during the early years of autonomy.[39] These deaths left an additional vacuum that made it difficult from the very beginning to develop a self-sustaining church.

In addition to the issue of undeveloped indigenous leadership, Watlington also suggests that the large economic support of the North American church over many years created a dependence from which the Peru church had difficulty weaning itself. The gradual withdrawal of U.S. missionaries from Peru left fewer channels of contact and interpretation to the North American church, which might offer support from Advance Specials, etc. An article in the December 1970 *Peru Calling*, a publication of the IMP, anticipated this immediate time of independence as "a year of post-operative convalescence."[40] The "post-operative convalescence" stretched way beyond a year, and ramifications of the separation surgery continue drastically to affect the church into the present time.

This is not to say that anyone thought autonomy was not the right way to go.[41] It was. Bill Jones, in an article of *Peru Calling* a year prior to autonomy, wrote:

There comes a time in the life of each Church when the ways of thinking and the structures which it inherited from the Methodist Church in the United States must give way to truly national and indigenous forms. Dr. D. T. Niles has spoken of how the missionary church is like a potted plant brought by missionaries to a country. The plant grows through careful watering, and pruning until the pot can no longer contain it. It is necessary for the life of the plant to break the pot and put it in the ground. To assume autonomy means for the church to break the pot and to be planted deeply in the soil of each country so that it grows strong, "that the birds of the air can make nests in its shade."[42]

But many Peruvian leaders today believe that autonomy was forced upon the church too quickly and that the church has struggled over the past twenty years to recover from a dependent relationship. When we became acquainted with the church in Peru, her people were feeling very abandoned by those who had planted her some ninety-five years earlier. However, they were still willing to affirm that autonomy, with proper timing, is vital for allowing Christian faith to mature within a people's own indigenous context.

The North Carolina/Peru relationship has enabled us to uncover some of the pernicious assumptions which have so dominated the ecclesiocentric mission of American Methodism. Many of these assumptions have been well defined by Jonathan J. Bonk in his book, *Mi$$ion$ and Money: Affluence as a Western Missionary Problem.*[43] What Bonk so clearly describes is what we, who have been in covenant with the IMP, have so vividly experienced. These "leftovers" of an ecclesiocentric missionary enterprise remain our greatest obstacles to forming a model of mission centered on a mutual walk.

I recall a particular experience during our inaugural sojourn to Peru in 1989. Our team was being entertained by Quechua musicians from the highlands playing stringed instruments and pan flutes. As I heard the Condor Pasa played, it struck me that this melody had originated in the Peruvian highlands and was not original to Simon and Garfunkel! I was invited to dance by a young Quechua Indian woman who jokingly said to me, "When the first missionaries came to our country they showed us the 'right way' to dance, and, we almost forgot how our people danced. Now *I* want to show *you* the 'right way' to dance."

Beyond the cultural paternalism that has most often marked traditional mission paradigms of the North American and European Christian church, the question which Bonk so poignantly and painfully raises is a particularly critical one: "What influence does the material privilege of the missionary have on personal credibility and on global perceptions of the content and relevance of the good news itself?"[44] The affluence of North American missions has provided missionaries with insulation, cushioning them from the harsh realities of life (despite what church members back home are often led to believe); the affluence of North American missions, Bonk further points out, has provided missionaries with isolation from those they serve; economic disparity creates a social gulf that makes genuine fraternal friendship or reciprocity awkward and virtually impossible; affluence creates an illusion that money equals superior intelligence and creates among missionaries "secret" feelings of general superiority; affluence fosters relationships of mistrust and envy. Indeed, at the root of ecclesiocentric missions has been both the denial and the rationalizing of how much North American affluence directly contradicts the content of the good news.[45] How, in other words, have we been able to represent credibly a Lord who became poor for our sakes?

Mahatma Gandhi so perceptively commented upon the affluence of Christian missionaries in India when he said, "if they could refrain from 'telling' India about Christ and had merely lived the life enjoined upon them by the Sermon on the Mount, India, instead of suspecting them, would have appreciated their living in the midst of her children and directly profited by their presence. . . . Faith does not admit of telling. It has to be lived and then it becomes self-propagating."[46]

It is the mutual witness in covenant relationship that allows us to begin to understand and confess a mission history in which we have birthed a global church that is increasingly being held captive by greed, and in which it is difficult for persons from the affluent North American and European churches to be in missional relationship with Two-Thirds-World people without money as the primary link that binds and blinds. Money always has been and always will be a detriment to mutual witness between the rich and the poor. North American Methodism must acknowledge and confess that alone we will be unable to remove the albatross of money from around our necks and that without the help of the other we and the church will drown in greed. It is the mutual witness that has enabled us to be more honest and self-critical about the church and the obstacles to being Christian in North America.

Conclusion

A recent collection of Lesslie Newbigin's essays, sermons, and addresses summarizes his developing view of Christian world missions between 1960 and 1992. In an essay originally contributed to a Festschrift for Lukas Vischer and entitled "Mission in a Pluralist Society," Newbigin writes that "it is easy to talk about 'the Church' but to ignore or despise the ordinary local congregation, which can often be so slow moving and so inward looking." He goes on to say, "Yet [the local congregation] is where the Church actually exists. . . . It is in the local congregation of believing Christians that the courage is to be nurtured that will enable us to challenge our culture with the gospel."[47] Newbigin rightly contends that the mission of the church must be deeply rooted in the local congregation. The covenant between the North Carolina Conference and the IMP is based on this conviction. It is among clergy and lay people of local congregations that the North Carolina/Peru covenant both took form and continues to be sustained.

Ronda Lee, a United Methodist clergywoman who has been active with the NC/Peru covenant, spent part of 1995 and 1996 living and working as a short-term missionary in Peru. At the Peruvian church's request, she returned to Peru in July 1996 under endorsement and full-time appointment by the General Board of Global Ministries as the only North American United Methodist missionary in Peru. About five years ago all missionaries to Peru were withdrawn, in part because of the danger and violence of the Sendero Luminoso terrorism. One of her tasks will be to work alongside Christian educators in Peru to develop curriculum resources out of their context for use within congregations in North Carolina. The Peru Church is also presently using Spanish literature from Cokesbury that we have made available to them, resources that offer insights into our North American faith context. In addition, there is presently a project underway cooperatively between Latino Methodists and North Carolina United Methodists to translate the works of John Wesley into Spanish.[48] A covenant of mutuality affords opportunity for us to read the Bible and our Wesleyan resources through the eyes of the other's faith context and encourages walking together into the missio Dei.

The problem of the domestication of the gospel, so central to Newbigin's thesis, is an important one to understand if we are to foster the kind of mission that is needed in today's global church. Newbigin and others have clearly analyzed the present state of the gospel in American culture and have shown how the gospel of Jesus Christ has been domesticated within the thought-forms of our society in such a way that it has largely ceased to challenge the assumptions that govern our life and, in fact, has become simply part of the culture. In addition, our own American culture has so privatized and individualized religious faith that we fail to proclaim the gospel in fear that we will trample another's rights of faith.

Newbigin notes that "Christians coming to Europe from Asia and Africa are amazed and shocked to find Christians in the old Christendom so apologetic about their faith, so timid, so anxious to assure everyone that they do not want to impose their faith on anyone else."[49] This has to account, at least in part, for the decline of United Methodism and other denominations in North America as well, and makes more apparent the fervor of unabashed evangelism and religious growth in Asia, Africa, and Latin America.

Part of the irony, as Newbigin sees it, lies in the fact that we are embarrassed by the way we have introduced Christianity to other cultures around the world. Certainly there is reason for embarrassment, and even more reason for penance with regard to the authoritative ways we have used the Gospel to impose western culture. But the irony lies in the fact that now there are few places around this globe where the name of Jesus is not known. And furthermore, it is these very places, where the name of Jesus was taken via a colonial mission paradigm, that are now becoming vessels of conversion for the West through mutual dialogue in the context of Bible study, worship, and shared sacramental life. This remarkable "reversal" is itself testimony to the "Spirit-praxis"[50] in the missio Dei!

Because of the very fact that old Christendom aggressively took its Christian faith into all the world, mission can never again be a one-way flow from west to east or north to south. The Gospel is now shared by people around the globe and can no longer be proclaimed solely through one dominant cultural spectacle. A global church mission must be forever hereafter understood in the context of cross-cultural mutuality.

Only in a context of mutuality-in-missions can local Christians and congregations be freed from the domestication of the Gospel and more fully grasp the greater depth of God's activity of love in its varied dimensions and expressions. We are truly a global city where rapid travel, instant communication, economic oppression, and partnerships, etc. have bound humanity together all the more tightly into a single interdependent people. The activity of God's grace within this one global city must be viewed and interpreted through cross-cultural dialogue in a context of mutual trust and respect, with the dissolving of barriers of superiority due to education, culture, wealth, etc.

The nature of the global church and the reverse flow of missionaries from east to west and south to north are affirmations of the missio Dei; namely, that mission is not generated by the church but by God. Lesslie Newbigin states clearly the inherent mutuality of Christian mission:

> Here, in contrast to both the Indian and the modern Western views, there is no attempt to see the human person as an autonomous individual, and the human relation with God as the relation of the alone to the alone. From its very beginning the Bible sees human life in terms of relationships. . . . There can be no private salvation, no salvation which does not involve us with one another. Therefore, if I may venture to use a metaphor which I have used elsewhere, God's saving revelation . . . does not come to us straight down from above—through the skylight, as we may say. In order to receive God's saving revelation we have to open the door to the neighbor whom [God] sends as his appointed messenger, and—more-over—to receive that messenger not as a temporary teacher or guide whom we can dispense with when we ourselves have learned what is needed, but as one who will permanently share our home. There is no salvation except one in which we are saved together through the one whom God sends to be the bearer of his salvation.[51]

We who are in covenant with the Methodist people of Peru have come to see these saints as the "one whom God sends to be the bearer of salvation." Indeed, in our mutual witness lies the uncovering of God's saving Word. There is a power hidden in mutual witness that makes possible the conversion of people and churches. That power has been revealed to us through the North Carolina/Peru mission covenant, and we walk together in the hope that our mutual witness, although humble and small, might be another sign of Christ's coming Kingdom.

Newbigin so aptly states the juxtaposition between where we are and where we must be willing for Christ's Spirit to lead us:

> When the Church tries to embody the rule of God in the forms of earthly power it may achieve that power, but it is no longer a sign of the kingdom. But when it goes the way the Master went, unmasking and challenging the powers of darkness and bearing in its own life the cost of their onslaught, then there are given to the Church signs of the kingdom, powers of healing and blessing which, to eyes of faith, are recognizable as true signs that Jesus reigns.[52]

~ Charles E. Zech ~

Charles Zech picks up on the question with which Wethington left us, namely, that of mission and money. An economist, Zech focuses not on the theological but on the fiscal side of what he terms the "mission-funding crisis," commenting along the way on the implications that declining giving has for those employed in and by the General Board of Global Ministries and related agencies. He explores what Wethington hypothesized, namely, that the people and congregations no longer find United Methodism's missional self-expression engaging and compelling. (Zech notes that despite steadily eroding membership Methodists continue denominational financial support—if not for denominationally-sponsored mission—at a remarkable and increasing rate.) To test the notion of a mission-funding crisis, Zech isolates and discusses three hypotheses: local fiscal crises, preference for designated giving, and distrust of centralized and bureaucratic mission programs and system. Each hypothesis, he examines for its bearing on missions and mission-support in other mainline Protestant denominations and then tests by means of a questionnaire administered to the pastors and administrative board members of 1,000 randomly sampled United Methodist charges. It would seem a shame to divulge his findings here. We should, however, note that he frames his findings utilizing recent theory about denominational structure and process, and comparing denominations to corporations, a discussion that echoes points made by Frank and Everett but one that introduces yet another model for understanding denominational transactions, namely the franchise.

Zech's analysis, findings, recommendations, and conclusions point toward making the present connectional system work. The question remains whether funding the present mission system best serves our connectional mission.

Determinants of the
Denominational-Mission Funding Crisis:
An Evaluation of Three Hypotheses

Charles E. Zech[1]

The crisis facing the United Methodist Church in the United States is real. Declining membership and uncertain finances are eating away at the Church's historically solid base. One important element of the overall decline has been called the "mission-funding crisis," i.e., members' reluctance to finance denominational programs in general, and those supporting denominationally-sponsored missions in particular.

Since 1970, UMC membership has declined by one-sixth, at the same time as the overall U.S. population has grown by over 25%. During this same period mission giving did increase by over 37% (reaching a peak of $498 million in 1991).[2]

While the growth of mission funding in the face of a declining membership appears to be a positive development, it masks an underlying crisis since it includes benevolence contributions to all causes, not just denominationally-sponsored ones. In fact, denominational mission giving routinely fails to meet budget projections. The bulk of UMC mission budgets are supported by churchwide apportionments, for which every congregation is assessed a fair share. Yet in 1993, for example, the World Services Fund, one of the Church's keystone programs that supports worldwide and national agencies received only 85.7% of its apportioned amount.[3]

As a result, morale problems have developed within the Church. Herbert Mather, director of the section on stewardship, has observed,

> The funding crisis is reflected in a morale problem, both within congregations and with leaders of the denomination. Leaders of the local congregation feel in a bind. They have become convinced that mission is in the community as well as around the world. They see more to do than there are funds to do it with. They are angry about the money that goes away from the church and community. They are convinced that they can do a better job of using those funds for legitimate and faithful ministries than can be done by a distant bureaucracy.

The effect on the morale of denominational leaders is profound. They feel as if they are under siege. They wonder if they will have a job after the next financial report or after the next round in the denominational budget process. In the struggle to survive as a denomination and as employees of the system, the focus seems to change from giving as a spiritual discipline to giving to support a budget. With that shift, the joy of giving disappears.

I am not convinced that the funding crisis will ease until there is a radical reordering of the system. The system being used for cooperative funding was efficient and worked well in a previous era. It is not working in the present context. People are not willing to fund the old system, but we have not figured out what the new system needs to be like.[4]

The budgetary problems have had a dramatic impact on the Church's ability to support its missions. The United Methodist News Service reported in April 1994:

> As the average annual cost for maintaining an overseas missionary has increased during the past 20 years, direct financial support from UM's [United Methodists] has steadily dropped. So, while a $6,000-per-missionary cost in 1971 was fully funded through contributions to the advance giving program, only about 40% of the $31,541 salary-and-benefits cost in 1993 came from that channel of support. The World Division has been compensating for the difference by transferring money from reserve and program funds and special grants, according to Robert Harman, the division's top executive. But now even these sources of funding are being depleted. Only 3,500 of the 37,000 local UM congregations contributed to missionary support through the Advance in 1992. Last October [1993], Harman told the division that 20 current full-time missionaries had to retire or resign in order to balance the 1994 budget because of declining income. In 1994 there were 331 full-time missionaries, compared to 353 in 1993 and 376 in 1992.[5]

The mission funding crisis at the denominational level is not inevitable, nor is it irreversible. However, if it is to be corrected, its causes must be identified. While everyone seems to have a favorite explanation, the explanations typically fall into one of three categories:

1. Local churches face their own fiscal crisis, and are financially unable to maintain their support of denominational programs.

2. Local church members have a preference for designated giving (generally to local causes) rather than the undesignated giving that contributing to denominational missions entails.

3. Local church members are alienated from denominational mission programs because of both a distrust of denominational officials and a disagreement over mission priorities.

In the following sections of this paper, each of these will be described in detail. They will be tested empirically to determine which provides the best explanation for the existence of the mission funding crisis. Then, after a discussion of organizational models of the church, recommendations will be made as to how to address the denominational mission funding crisis. The reader should keep in mind that, while this study specifically deals only with the impact on denominationally-sponsored missions, this problem is symptomatic of a general rift in the relationship between local churches and the denomination, and therefore the recommendations could be generalized.

I. Hypotheses Regarding the Mission Funding Crisis

A. Local Church Financial Problems

One explanation for the reluctance of local churches to contribute to denominational missions is that they are experiencing financial pressures themselves. Supporters of this explanation cite the virtual explosion of local church labor costs in recent years. The desire for a more qualified and professional clergy and staff has led to a consequent increase in their salaries. There has been a proliferation of programs, which has combined with a decline in church volunteers (itself a consequence of the increased labor force participation rate of women) to necessitate an increase in the number of professional local church staff members. All of these labor cost increases, of course, have been accompanied by the enormous growth in the cost of fringe benefits, especially health care insurance. Local churches are facing pressure from non-labor cost increases as well, such as the need to maintain aging church buildings, and the earlier rise in energy costs. It is hypothesized that the combination of these factors has led some local churches to conclude that, as much as they would like to support denominational programs, their own local fiscal crisis must be addressed first.

This has been exacerbated by the free-rider effect. This refers to the penchant for local churches to assume that, since there are thousands of other local churches supporting denominational programs, reductions in their own contributions will not be missed. Naturally, the denomination faces a financial disaster when a large number of local churches reach that conclusion.

Other mainline denominations in the United States are in the same serious mission-funding straits as the UMC. Researchers have examined their plight. For example, Roger Nemeth and Donald Luidens[6] studied mission funding for the Presbyterian Church and the Reformed Church in America from the 1860s to the 1980s. Among their findings was that giving to the denomination in inflation-adjusted dollars per member had risen until about 1950, and then began to decline. Their statistical testing led them to conclude that virtually the entire decrease in mission funding since World War II can be explained by local church financial pressures caused by the increased cost of ministers' compensation and decreased volunteerism.[7]

In contrast, Gregory Krohn[8] studied a sample of Presbyterian Churches for the period 1973–88. He concluded that local church financial factors such as the cost of salaries, health insurance, and energy did not significantly affect congregation benevolences. He did discover a correlation between higher member income and lower benevolences' share of congregation revenues. He attributed the rising income to the increased female labor force participation rate, and he interpreted the corresponding decrease in volunteer hours as causing churches to decrease funding for benevolences in favor of congregation programs.

A third study of Presbyterian mission funding was conducted by Scott Cormode.[9] He analyzed the effect of pastor compensation on congregational mission giving. Noting that pastoral compensation had risen only 1.2% in inflation-adjusted terms since 1970, Cormode concluded that this change is too insignificant to have caused the dramatic change in budget priorities that resulted in decreased benevolences.[10]

Finally, Kenneth Innskeep[11] studied the Evangelical Lutheran Church in America. He observed that congregational giving to synods and church-wide organizations as a percentage of congregational revenue decreased by about one-third during the period 1979–91. Innskeep concluded that part of this decrease resulted from an 11.6% increase in congregational operating expenses over the same period.

In summary, the hypothesis that local church financial pressures have caused a decrease in their ability to fund denomination-sponsored missions is supported by the findings of Nemeth and Luidens, partially supported by Krohn, consistent with the data analyzed by Innskeep, but not supported by Cormode's analysis.

B. Local Church Preference for Designated Giving/Local Missions

The second hypothesis has, at its core, the issue of ownership. People feel ownership for causes, not for institutions. They are more likely to identify with causes that they select as opposed to causes selected for them. One important way that ownership is exhibited is in the preference for designated over undesignated giving.

Designated giving involves giving to specific causes. These are often local in nature, where the local church members have a good understanding of the organization's needs and accomplishments. The primary advantage of designated giving is that it allows donors some say as to how their contributions will be used. They take greater interest in the causes being supported. On the other hand, they may exhibit a short attention span. New, exciting causes may emerge, leading to a loss of interest in current ones. The resulting lack of reliable funding places a burden on the missions themselves, inhibiting their planning. They are forced to compete with other causes, which means that some of their income must be used merely to keep donors informed and to market themselves.

Churches engage in undesignated giving when they contribute to a centralized denominational board that is responsible for allocating resources collected denomination-wide to missions. The whole church is making the mission decision. This is a very efficient way to raise money since it only involves a single appeal. It provides mission projects the opportunity to plan, since they can anticipate a more stable funding source. Finally, it eliminates destructive competition among mission projects in their attempt to appeal directly to each local church. The downside is that contributors feel virtually no sense of ownership toward the projects they are funding.

In order for a denomination to employ designated giving successfully, it must demonstrate a linkage between the donors and its agenda. When mission boards fail to communicate their missionary vision and provide church members with a sense of ownership of that vision, local churches may prefer to support local social needs, where they see the impact of their giving. One pastor has described how the reduction in UMC missionaries has meant fewer personal visits by missionaries to local churches. He feels that such visits are a critical component of assisting members in identifying with denominational missions and maintaining their sense of ownership. Scott Brunger[12] has listed three organizational goals that could serve as the basis for evaluating mission funding programs.

1. Efficiency – raising and distributing funds at the lowest possible cost.
2. Transparency – the ability of donors and recipients to identify with each other and become aware of each others' needs.
3. Accountability – the ability to hold decision-makers responsible for the long-term effects of their actions.

Brunger has also identified four fund-raising models, each based on the relationship between the donor and the recipient.

1. Designated Giving with Dependent Partners

In the nineteenth century, mission societies existed as separate entities. Each society sponsored its own mission fields and appealed directly to the local churches for financial support. This made for a genuine sense of ownership among the donors. Unfortunately, over time donors' interests would waver as they became enamored of newer projects, forcing the mission societies into a competitive situation with each other. Even today mission societies exist, often at the local level, that provide local churches with an assortment of mission funding alternatives.

With respect to Brunger's mission-funding organizational goals, this model qualifies as transparent, since both parties are aware of each others' needs, but inefficient due to inadequate coordination among mission societies, and deficient in accountability because of the inability to make long-term plans.

2. Undesignated Giving with Dependent Partners

This model utilizes a centralized denominational board to dispense mission funds collected from local churches to a relatively few recipients. Besides generating economies of scale in fund-raising, it affords more continuity in funding. However, the fact that donors perceive little or no ownership may inhibit local churches' willingness to contribute. While this model is efficient and accountable, it is not transparent because barriers exist between the donors and beneficiaries.

3. Undesignated Giving with Independent Partners

The increased autonomy of mission fields in recent years has allowed them to negotiate with donor agencies on a virtually equal basis, giving them a degree of independence. This allows for a more stable, longer-term alliance in their dealings with mission boards, and enables them to plan for the future. There is more accountability between the partners. On the other hand, the large bureaucracies required on the part of both the denomination and the mission agency lead to high administrative costs. The lack of transparency means donors feel even less ownership than in the other models.

4. Designated Giving in a Decentralized Network

This model establishes horizontal attachments between donor associations and recipient associations. The mission field needs are presented directly to the donors, who are able to designate their gifts. The bureaucracy merely coordinates the relationship between the two sides. While transparent and efficient, this model tends not to be accountable.

Unlike the first hypothesis there has been relatively little testing of the hypothesis that a preference for designated giving over undesignated giving (or its variation, a preference for local missions) is a major cause of the mission funding crisis. Daniel Olson and David Caddell[13] analyzed a survey of 93,000 United Church of Christ members from 1199 congregations. They found a direct correlation between the proportion of a congregation's budget contributed to non-denominationally sponsored missions and members' contributions to the congregation. They concluded that members viewed undesignated giving to denominational missions as more a tax than a ministry and preferred the latitude that designated giving afforded them.

In his study of the ELCA cited above, Kenneth Innskeep[14] considered the relationship between giving to local missions and giving to churchwide organizations of the ELCA. He found no significant relationship between the two.

C. Alienation with the Denomination

Because of disagreements over mission priorities and a general mistrust of denomination officials, it is hypothesized, members have reduced their contributions to denominationally-sponsored missions. They resent the controls that the denomination has attempted to impose on local churches.

One explanation for this alienation is the changing relationship between the denomination and local churches that has been identified by Craig Dykstra and James Hudnut-Beumler.[15] They cite the emergence of the denomination as a regulatory agency, dominating not only denominational institutions but also local churches. They argue that denominations first adopted the regulatory role in response to their own fiscal crisis in order to gain control over a shrinking financial pie. Procedures and policies were developed and expanded as denominational leaders got carried away. Church members responded by not only resisting the required procedures but also becoming alienated from the goals that the regulations were intended to accomplish. The sense of loyalty that members had felt for their church, the foundation of congregation-denomination relations, was diminished if not entirely lost.

Loren Mead[16] has addressed the same issue from the perspective of the demise of the Christendom paradigm. Dating from the conversion of Constantine in 313 A.D., people identified with the congregation, the congregation was the church, and the church was the empire. Religion permeated all of society's institutions and social structures. While Mead believes that the Christendom paradigm has been deteriorating for some time, its swan song came with the unfolding of a new paradigm, the "ministry of the laity." This altered the relationship between the individual, the church, and society by conferring more freedom and responsibility on the individual. In brandishing their new-found freedom and responsibility, church members often found the denomination to be more of an obstacle than an asset. Mead believes that church leaders' usefulness has been diminished because of their inability to contend with this new model.

As with the second hypothesis, there has been relatively little empirical analysis of the alienation hypothesis. The Innskeep[17] study cited above found no significant relationship when testing for the effect of dissatisfaction with denominational organizations on church contributions. But he detected a troubling amount of indifference on the part of the laity. In his sample, 72% of the laity had no impression of churchwide organizations, and 74% had no impression of the synods. It is apparent that even if alienation was not at work, church organizations were doing a poor job of informing members of their activities.

II. Methodology

The method used to test the hypotheses involved surveying a group of United Methodist Church pastors and Administrative Board members with a questionnaire intended to elicit information on all three hypotheses. Responses from the survey were grouped by hypothesis. In order to reduce the independent variables to a workable number, they were tested in a stepwise multiple regression. Only those determinants that showed a significant relationship were included in the final hypothesis testing. The variables kept in the analysis, along with some selected background variables (technically known as control variables), are listed in Table 1 (located at end of chapter).

A. Data

The data were collected from a random sample of 1000 UMC local churches. Most UMC congregations are small, but most church members belong to larger congregations. To account for this the larger congregations (200 or more members) were oversampled, with two-thirds of the congregations selected from this group. Later, the sample was weighted to reflect the proper size distribution of UMC local churches.

The pastor of each local church in the sample received two types of surveys. One, which she/he was asked to complete, contained questions on local church background (size, ethnic makeup, age and income distribution of members, etc.) and questions of opinion concerning the denomination that related directly to the hypotheses. Each pastor also received eight surveys intended for members of the Administrative Board. These questionnaires contained the same opinion questions regarding the denomination as those on the pastor survey, as well as questions concerning the local church. No claim is made that the Administrative Board members in the sample were randomly selected; rather, pastors were merely requested to distribute the survey instrument to eight members of the Board. Presumably many pastors distributed them to those Board members whom they felt to be most supportive of their own positions. However, it is interesting to note that, of the 20 questions on the two surveys that were identical, correlation analysis revealed that for 14 questions no significant relationship existed between a pastor's responses and those of the Administrative Board members of her/his local church, for three questions there was a significantly positive relationship (i.e., agreement), and for three questions there was a significantly negative relationship (i.e., disagreement). In any event, all of the completed surveys were returned directly to the Principal Investigator so the pastor did not see individual responses. While this survey method is not perfect, it is a cost effective one that has been used elsewhere.[18] The survey of the pastors was random. The best that can be stated about the Board surveys is that they are probably representative. Survey packets sent to 8 local churches were undeliverable. A total of 316 pastor surveys (31.9%) and 2243 Board member surveys (28.3%) were returned. To ensure adequate representation, analysis was restricted to only those local churches where both the pastor survey and at least 5 Administrative Board surveys had been returned (n=198).

B. Empirical Results

The empirical results from testing the three hypotheses are shown in Table 2. The tool of multiple regression analysis was used to estimate the parameters of an equation relating denominational mission giving to a variety of variables that are believed to play a role in determining these contributions. Some of these are control variables, while the rest relate to the three hypotheses discussed earlier. In each equation, the dependent variable was derived by taking the portion of the local church's budget that went toward denominationally-sponsored mission programs.[19] Prior testing of the equations showed them to be affected by heteroscedasticity, a statistical problem in which the error terms are not independent. To resolve this problem, the equations were adjusted by means of the White correction.[20]

Table 2 actually shows the results from testing four separate equations—one including all of the variables, and the other three containing the control variables and the variables from different combinations of the hypotheses. The Table shows two types of information. The "Beta Coefficients" show the impact of each individual variable on the dependent variable, the portion of local church revenues contributed to denominationally-sponsored missions. The beta coefficients are the numbers in the body of the Table. An asterisk (*) next to a coefficient indicates that one can be 99% certain that the coeffient is different from zero, that is, that the variable has some effect on the local church's decision to contribute to denominationally sponsored missions. A negative sign indicates a factor that would cause a decrease in a local church's willingness to contribute to denominationally sponsored missions.

The focus of the analysis is on the other statistical measure shown in Table 2, the "Coefficient of Determination," also technically known as the adjusted R-squared. This tells how well the determinant variables as a group explain the dependent variable. These values are shown on the last line of Table 2. The higher the adjusted R-squared, the better the group of determinant variables are at explaining the level of local church denominational-mission funding.

The method used to ascertain which hypothesis best explains the mission funding crisis is to compare the adjusted R-squared for the equation employing all of the variables with that for the other equations, each of which is missing the group of variables from one of the hypotheses. The increase in the adjusted R-squared (i.e., the amount of explanatory power that is gained) when the group of variables from each hypothesis are included in the equation is then observed. The hypothesis which caused the greatest increase in explanatory power when its group of variables were included in the equation is deemed to be the most powerful in explaining the denominational-mission funding crisis.

As Table 2 indicates, including all of the variables from all the hypotheses along with the control variables explained 28.1% of local church denominational-mission funding. If the group of variables from hypothesis 3 are included, the explanatory power increased by 5.3 percentage points (from 22.8% to 28.1%). Including the group of variables from hypothesis 2 actually decreased the explanatory power of the remaining variables by 1.7 percentage points (from 29.8% to 28.1%). Finally, including the group of variables from hypothesis 1 increased the proportion explained by 11.3 percentage points (from 16.8% to 28.1%).

Since including the group of variables from hypothesis 2 (the one concerned with a preference for designated giving) actually decreased the explanatory power of the model, it can be concluded that the preference for designated/local giving is not a general explanation for the mission funding crisis, although for some local churches this may be a critical issue. The greatest increase in explanatory power occurred when the group of variables from hypothesis 1 (local church financial pressures) was included. This lends support to choosing this hypothesis as the primary cause of the mission funding crisis, with hypothesis 3 (alienation with denomination) a secondary cause.

Discussion

The empirical results lend support to two causes for the denominationally-sponsored-mission funding crisis: primarily, local church economic hardship, and secondarily, member alienation with the denomination. Solutions to the first of these are addressed in a paper appearing in another volume of this collection ("Patterns of Giving Among United Methodists: Member Contributions to the Local Church," in *The People(s) Called Methodist: Forms and Reforms of Their Life*). The remainder of this paper focuses on the secondary cause, member alienation from the denomination. Any policy analysis of these results must be performed within the context of an organizational structure model. The model serving as the basis for the discussion is the principal/agent model.

The principal/agent model views all economic transactions as a series of relationships between those who produce a good or service (agents) and those on behalf of whom the good or service is produced (principals). A good example is that of corporate managers who act as agents on behalf of corporate stockholders, the principals. The principals must protect their interests, given that their relationship with the agents is characterized by two tendencies:

1.   Agents prefer to pursue their own goals, rather than those of the principals.

2.   There exists asymmetric information. This means that agents commonly possess information that is unavailable to principals. These include factors concerning the agents' personal characteristics, such as work habits or integrity, and information affecting production, such as the range of strategic options available.

The principal/agent relationship in churches is compounded by the fact that, as Mark Chaves has argued, denominations comprise a dual, parallel structure.[21] The production of religious goods, however defined, is controlled by a "religious Authority structure," whose authority is derived from tradition and reference to the supernatural. However, today's denominations offer more than just basic religious goods. Other goods that the denomination provides are furnished by the "agency structure." As an example, the UMC sponsors a General Board of Publications, responsible for providing Sunday-school materials. Another part of the agency structure is the General Board of Global Ministries, the primary topic of this paper. Agency structure authority is legally, rather than supernaturally, based.

The dual structures differ in their relationship with the local church. Local churches are an object of control to the religious structure. In the principal/agent model terms, the religious structure is the principal and the local church is the agent. Control includes, but is not limited to, the ability to appoint pastors and, in the extreme, to discipline wayward members.

On the other hand, general boards tend to be the agents of the local churches, since they depend on them for their funding. This dependency may occur because the local churches are the primary customers of the agency's product (as in the case of the General Board of Publications) or because the local churches underwrite the agency's work through their contributions (as with the General Board of Global

Ministries). In either case, General Boards and Agencies are the agents of the local churches. With respect to the mission funding crisis, the principal/agent model acknowledges that the General Board of Global Ministries has information on a variety of elements of mission funding that is not available to the typical church member (the principal). Among these are: how missions are chosen to receive funding, how successful each has been, who the beneficiaries are, etc.—that is, information on the questions of transparency, efficiency, and accountability. Also, the staff of the General Board of Global Ministries have a natural tendency to pursue their own goals. These could be purely personal goals (e.g., personal prestige, power) or, more likely, professional in nature, such as setting priorities for the distribution of scarce mission resources that may differ from those of the church members.

In order for the system to work, it is imperative that principals have the ability to monitor the agents' performance and to establish a reward system that provides agents with the incentive to act on behalf of the principals. In the corporate-stockholder–corporate-manager example, stockholders can induce managers to work on their behalf (i.e., maximize profits) by establishing a reward system (e.g., profit sharing) that benefits managers when they act in the best interests of the stockholders. Corporate profits are both readily measured and linked to the goals of the principals, and they provide an ideal measure of the agents' performance, while profit-sharing encourages them to pursue that goal.

Churches do not have a single, clear measure of success like profits. Their principals have to develop some indirect (proxy) measures to monitor the performance of the agents. If the proxies fail to duplicate the principals' goals, the proxy measures become the agents' goals, a process known as goal displacement. When churches rely on undesignated giving, they aggravate mission measurement and monitoring problems. Special safeguards must be enacted to affirm that mission boards are acting on behalf of members. This requires a measure of mission output that is both easily monitored and compatible with members' goals. It also implies communication between the mission board and members so that principals are informed of agency activities. The current arrangement in the UMC is for the General Board of Global Missions to prepare a report for consideration at the General Conference. This process affords little opportunity for feedback, since there is a tendency to rubber-stamp the work of the general boards and agencies with a minimum of discussion. A new system must be devised that more adequately addresses the monitoring issue.

Rectifying the Church's principal/agent problem will entail an organizational structure that minimizes monitoring costs and goal displacement. Dykstra and Hudnut-Beumler[22] contend that the current structure is one where the denomination serves as a regulatory agency for local churches. This paper takes exception to that view, and depicts the relationship as one characterized by the franchise model of organization.

The franchise model of church organizations regards the denomination as a corporate entity with local churches as the franchisees. They are not mere branch offices but, rather, have some independence. But they are not free-standing, entrepreneurial enterprises.

The franchise relationship entails four characteristics. First, the franchise receives exclusive rights to the franchisor's trademark. In this context, the trademark is the UMC's name, which stands for a set of beliefs. People interested in joining a UMC local church would expect that church to express the doctrines of the denomination.

Second, the franchisee receives support, through training, materials, etc., from the franchisor. The UMC offers a variety of educational opportunity for both clergy and laity, and develops Sunday-school materials, hymnals, etc. One of the justifications for the franchise arrangement is that some tasks are best accomplished at the level (such as the local church) closest to the final customer while others should be performed by the level large enough to take advantage of economies of scale and scope.

A third characteristic is that the franchisor requires a high degree of control. This is critical, since the franchisor is aware that the entire organization's reputation can be diminished by the failings of just one franchise. The degree of control may differ from one franchise to another, as from one denomination to another. Orthodoxy of belief is the primary concern for churches, with some denominations more particular about standardization than others. Orthodoxy is enforced through many avenues, including the manner in which inquirers are admitted to the church, programs that are offered, and pastor qualifications and assignments.

The fourth characteristic of franchises is that franchisors require compensation from the franchisees to pay for the use of the trademark and the ongoing support. The compensation comes in two forms: an up-front, lump-sum fee and an ongoing, annual fee tied to the success of the franchise. The two-tiered payment can be interpreted in two ways. One approach is to treat up-front payment as reimbursement for the use of the trademark with the annual fee regarded as compensation for the continuing support supplied by the franchisor. Or, the financial relationship could be regarded as repayment of a loan from the franchisor to the franchisee. The lump-sum payment corresponds to a down payment, and the annual fee as the subsequent repayment of principal and interest. Today, many UMC local churches are questioning the high apportionments they are expected to pay, arguing that the denomination is not giving them their money's worth.

Recommendations

Loren Mead[23] has recognized three responses that churches can have to crisis situations like the denominationally-sponsored-mission funding crisis. They can hold fast and hope for the best, develop new programs in an attempt to conceal the basic problem, or move on to a new paradigm. Mead recognizes that many churches are at learning points, those instances when church members are anxious to act. By some accounts many UMC churches are at learning points in their overall relationship with the denominations, not just with respect to denominational-mission funding.

Church members have been voting with their feet (leaving the Church) and with their dollars (failing to support denominationally-sponsored missions) in an effort to alert denominational officials that holding fast and doing nothing is not a viable option. However, any solution developed by the Church is bound to alienate one or another faction. Many would be unhappy with changes that they perceive to be mere tinkering, since they feel the Church has done nothing but tinker in recent years. Others will view the development of a new paradigm as too radical. Since no single proposal is likely to satisfy all church members, this paper will list some possible alternatives suggested by the principal/agent model. There is no pretense that this list is complete; rather, it is an attempt to exemplify the scope of options available. The options are presented in order from least disruptive to the current system (i.e., tinkering) to most disruptive (i.e., new paradigm).

One of the elementary principles of the mission-funding principal/agent relationship is that monitoring mechanisms must be put in place. Currently the Council on Finance and Administration requires a periodic audit of all the agencies receiving funds from it, including the General Board of Global Ministries. One obvious approach to bolstering the monitoring function would be to require the General Board of Global Ministries (and for that matter, all the general boards) to undergo annual audits by external organizations, such as a big six accounting firm. Members would likely have more confidence in an externally-conducted audit.

A second recommendation is an outgrowth of the first. The Church could require the General Board of Global Ministries to distribute an annual report to every member of the Church. This report could take the form of a summary of the annual audit recommended above. Reports received directly by members would provide the principals with direct information on the activities of the agents and imbue them with a greater sense of ownership. The downside, of course, is the immense cost of printing and distributing even a brief report to every UMC household.

An extension of the first two recommendations would be to rule out dual membership on a general board and in the General Conference. Since the General Conference is charged with oversight on the boards, there is a conflict of interest when church members belong to both groups. Dual membership on the Judicial Council and General Conference is not permitted. The same standards should be applied to the general boards and General Conference. This would lead to more effective control by the principals over the agents.

A major step towards a new paradigm would be to abolish the guaranteed funding base that the General Board of Global Ministries currently enjoys, and force them to compete with non-denominationally-sponsored missions for their share of the local church mission budget. In recent years corporate conglomerates have permitted their divisions that use products produced by other of their divisions to solicit bids from vendors external to the conglomerate. The feeling is that introducing competition strengthens both divisions. Formally introducing competition into mission funding would enhance the local church's ability to monitor the General Board of Global Ministries' performance by forcing the board to market itself and keep the principals informed of its activities. Transparency and accountability would be increased. Enforcing the discipline of the market place on the mission board would enable local churches to establish reward systems that ensure that the agent acts on their behalf. The disadvantage of this proposal is that it would inhibit the mission board's ability to make long-term commitments. To some degree this could be alleviated if local churches and the General Board of Global Ministries negotiated, as equal partners, longer term agreements. The final solution proposed here is the most radical of all. The UMC might choose to divest itself of the mission-funding function altogether. Mission funding was not a charge of the early denominations in the United States. Instead, congregations contracted directly with independent mission agencies. Perhaps this "new" paradigm should be reconsidered. It would afford local churches the opportunity to structure the reward system so that the agents act on their behalf. Transparency would be increased, but to the detriment of efficiency. The greatest consequence, though, would be to the overall relationship with the connectional system. Once mission funding decisions are turned over completely to local churches, a Pandora's box would be opened with respect to the way local churches view their role within the connection. A new mission-funding paradigm might lead to a new paradigm of the connectional system.

Summary and Conclusions

This study has considered some reasons for the mission funding crisis faced by the United Methodist Church, along with some possible solutions. The causes for the mission funding crisis typically fall into one of three categories:

1. Local churches have their own financial pressures, and are financially unable to support denominational programs.
2. Local churches prefer to support mission projects that they themselves designate.
3. Local church members are alienated from the denomination because of a distrust of denominational officials and a disagreement over mission priorities.

To test these hypothesized causes, surveys were distributed to a sample of pastors and administrative board members. Both types of surveys contained questions pertinent to each of the hypotheses. Statistical testing using multiple regression analysis resulted in little or no support for the preference-for-designated-giving hypothesis. The hypothesis that mission funding has decreased because local churches are feeling their own financial pressures received the most support, followed by the denominational-alienation hypothesis.

Recommendations for dealing with local church financial pressures are contained elsewhere in this collection. The recommendations included in this paper for addressing the denominational alienation problem are based on an understanding of the principal/agent relationship. With regard to mission funding, the General Board of

Global Ministries is perceived as the agent working on behalf of the local churches and their members, the principals. This relationship is plagued by the fact that the mission board has information that is not available to the principals and has the tendency to pursue its own agenda. In order for the principals to be satisfied with this partnership, they must establish a means for monitoring the performance of the mission board and set goals for the board to achieve that correspond to their own goals.

Requiring more reporting from the General Board of Global Ministries is critical for the local churches and their members to conduct the monitoring process effectively. Incorporating a degree of competition within the relationship, either by discontinuing the mission board's guaranteed financial base or by abolishing denominationally-sponsored-mission boards altogether, are more radical steps but would result in an improvement in the ability of the local churches not only to monitor the agents' performance but also to establish goals for them.

In any event, it is clear that the United Methodist Church is at a learning point. Staying put and doing nothing is not an acceptable alternative. The Church must develop a new mission-funding system that goes beyond mere tinkering, yet is not so radical that it further alienates the membership.

Table 1
Variable Definition

I. Control Variables
   A. Membership – Number of full-time resident members
   B. Income – Pastor's estimate of member household median income
   C. Age – Pastor's estimate of percent of membership 25–39 years old
   D. Race – Pastor's estimate of percent membership white
   E. Education – Pastor's estimate of percent of adult members with college degrees

II. Hypothesis 1
   A. Labor – Number of full-time-equivalent staff working in areas of lay ministries
   B. Pastor – Number of full-time pastors assigned to local church
   C. Board perception of UMC financial need – Percent of board members agreeing that UMC has serious financial needs.
   D. Endowment – local church has endowment funds

III. Hypothesis 2
   A. Mission budget briority – Pastor – Believes other than denominational missions should have priority
   B. Denomination select – Pastor – Prefers denomination select projects
   C. Mission budget Priority – Board – Percent believing other than denominational missions should have priority

IV. Hypothesis 3
   A. Enough information – Pastor – Pastor believes he/she has enough information on denomination budgets
   B. Confidence in boards – Pastor – Pastor has confidence in General Boards and Agencies
   C. Boards affect giving – Pastor – Pastor believes programs of general boards and agencies affect local church giving
   D. Denomination out of touch – Pastor – Number of areas in which pastor believes denomination out of touch with members
   E. Enough Information – Board – Percent believing they have enough information on denomination budgets

Table 2
Empirical Results from Hypothesis Testing
Beta Coefficients and Adjusted R-Squared

Variables	All Variables	Hypotheses 1 and 2	Hypotheses 1 and 3	Hypotheses 2 and 3
Control				
Membership	-.11*	-.17*	-.10*	.04
Income	.09	.21*	.12*	.05
Age	-.13*	-.11*	-.14*	-.23*
Race	.15	-.37	.09	-.12
Education	-.14*	-.08	-.13*	-.13*
Hypothesis 1				
Labor	.16*	.16*	.15*	
Pastor	.44*	.60*	.44*	
Board Perception of UMC Financial Need	-.67*	-.95*	-.69*	
Endowment	.24*	.45*	.23*	
Hypothesis 2				
Mission Budget Priority - Pastor	-.05	-.03		.03
DenominationSelect - Pastor	-.10	.00		.03
Mission Budget Priority - Board	-.00	-.24*	.02	
Hypothesis 3				
Enough Information - Pastor	.03		.03	.20*
Confidence in Boards - Pastor	-.15		-.18	-.27*
Boards Affect Giving - Pastor	.36*		.32*	.40*
Denomination Out of Touch - Pastor	.19*		.16*	.23*
Enough Information - Board	.29*		.29*	.45*
Adjusted R2	.281	.228	.298	.168

* Denotes Beta Coefficient Significant at 99% Confidence Level

⌒ Penny Edgell Becker ⌒

Penny Edgell Becker takes up the question that McClain's essay posed in relation to Methodism and race, namely, how the denomination's formal and official self-conceptions (ecclesiology, vision and mission statements, views of connection, and prescriptions for order) compare with unarticulated but operative polities, priorities, styles of interaction, and modes of behavior. She focuses this question locally, studying twenty-three congregations (of various denominations) in one locale, and suggests that denominational or connectional ecclesiology, mission, and identity take local form, insofar as they do, in a congregational culture. The latter, she concedes, is partially expressive of the formal denominational self-understandings but partially defined by local factors— congregational size, context, history, makeup, and leadership. Local factors prove sufficiently determinative for Becker to elaborate four models of local Christian community, four internal ethics of leadership and conflict resolution, four distinctive styles of congregational culture, and four patterns that function across denominational lines. The four are a house of worship model, a family model, a community model, and a leader model. The two United Methodist congregations in her study fall into the first two models, models which orient members inward. The denomination and conference leaders who interact with those congregations, she argues, function with notions of mission more compatible with the other two local models. Community and leader models orient members to interest in and engagement with the world outside—the community, politics, social issues, the world—a public rather than simply private witness. Becker asks whether the denomination can respect and care for these several models, especially given the predilection of denominational leadership for the two more public styles. And what should United Methodists make of her finding that local churches in explicitly congregational polities more typically function with the two public religion models? Are the two more inward or private United Methodist congregations in her study and their counterparts across the nation simply going their own way? Are they expressing some rebellion against the denomination? Or are they relying on the connection to carry or express the needed public witness? Does the dependence of small congregations on the denomination—their connectionalism—ironically or paradoxically, lead them away from embodying connectional values of outreach and community service? And is such a paradox also at play in the connectional restiveness of the big local churches which so fully embody connectional missional values and so focus them on their immediate community that they have no time or money for denominational ventures? What premium should United Methodism put, then, on explicit commitment to denominational mission and culture, and on exercising that mission through denominational channels?

Understanding Local Mission: Congregational Models and Public Religion in United Methodist Churches

Penny Edgell Becker

When I walked into the United Methodist congregation one Sunday morning, I was greeted by a man who looked to be in his mid-40s. His dark hair was cut short, and he wore a dark suit with a carnation boutonniere. He smiled at me, said, "Welcome! How are you this morning?" and shook my hand. I replied that I was fine, and he handed me a bulletin. He told me to sit anywhere, to make myself at home. He asked, "Do you have any questions?" I said no, smiled, and went in to sit down.

It is a huge sanctuary, with gray heavy stonework, dark wood, and vaulted ceilings, with seating for about 500 on the main floor plus a large balcony. At one time several hundred people attended each Sunday morning. Now there were just over a hundred people in the sanctuary, typical for a Sunday service. Many of them were older, but there were also younger couples, some with children.

The small congregation was spread out through the first twenty pews. Taking a seat at the back edge of where the people were, I had half of a twenty-foot pew to myself. Nobody sat by me. When the time came for the passing of the peace, people turned to one another in their pews. The couple down in the other half of my pew looked at me and smiled. I smiled back. No one came over to speak to me, and I did not initiate contact.

At the end of the service, the pastor did not stand at the doors of the sanctuary to greet people on their way out. Most of the people left quickly, by the main door and side doors, hurrying to their cars in the chilly fall weather. The usher who had greeted me was still at the back of the sanctuary, so I asked him how to find the fellowship hall. The bulletin had said the coffee time would be held there.

He pointed out the adjoining fellowship hall, a cavernous room decorated with banners made with felt, the kind we used to make in Sunday-school and Bible-school classes when I was growing up a United Methodist church in Ohio; there were rainbows and Jesus as the Shepherd leading chunky white sheep. The pastor was standing at the entranceway to the fellowship hall, and since I had not yet made an appointment to talk with him about my research, I introduced myself simply as a visitor. He shook my hand, said, "Welcome!" and pointed out the information table over to the side that had brochures and flyers about the congregation's various committees and programs, and denominational mission activities.

There were perhaps 35 people there, standing with paper cups of coffee from the big urns. I introduced myself to several people, including a young woman in her late twenties standing at the information table. When I asked her how long she'd been coming here, she said she had just been a few times. When I asked what she liked about this church, she said she'd always been a Methodist, and that the pastor gave good sermons. And she liked Methodist mission activities. I stayed only 15 minutes, and by the time I left, perhaps 15 or 20 people were still there.[1]

* * * * * * * * * *

Introduction

In the UMC heritage, the idea of connectionalism is of central importance, signifying not only a formal relationship of church administration and governance, but also a strong doctrinal tradition of linking personal salvation and piety to compassionate outreach and social action in the world. Connectionalism implies a strong preference for public over private religion. As the *Book of Discipline* states:

> Scriptural holiness entails more than personal piety; love of God is always linked with love of neighbor, a passion for justice and renewal in the life of the world.[2]

Of course, denominational leaders are experts in the denomination's history and culture, with a sophisticated knowledge of how that fits into and flows from a larger religious tradition. Their job is to articulate a vision of and a mission for the church in relation to this historic tradition. They deal in formal ecclesiology. Like experts everywhere, they tend to privilege that about which they know the most. For religious leaders, that means privileging doctrine and concepts, highly articulated and systematic sets of beliefs and symbols.

"Official" or expert statements on mission emphasize theology, tradition, and doctrine.[3]

This study of congregations in and around one community demonstrates that "mission" in local congregations generally means something more pragmatic and less articulated and abstract. In local churches, mission is a practical linkage between local identity and some limited set of core tasks.[4] "Mission" may be an analytically separable category that experts can examine. But in local churches mission is embedded within and constitutive of local culture, something that is built up and negotiated over time and shaped by a variety of factors (see Fine 1987, 1984). Local cultures contain idiosyncratic elements but also conform to broad institutional patterns that make, for example, a local church readily distinguishable from a service club or a baseball team (Becker 1995, Powell and DiMaggio 1991).

Denominational culture is one resource for congregations in figuring out what tasks are central to their own local mission, but it is not the only resource. Other successful local churches, often belonging to different denominations, provide both models to emulate and specializations to avoid, shaping local mission "ecologically."[5] Mission ideas become institutionalized in local cultures in ways that are also shaped by formative events and leaders in the congregation's history and by the preferences of lay leaders that have been formed over a lifetime of diverse experiences—not all of them church-related. Mission is influenced by size and resources, and tends to be articulated in pragmatic and partial ways, not systematic, theological ways.[6]

A vital question for denominational leaders, then, is how to communicate effectively their tradition's most important or central ideas about mission to local congregations, which are also influenced by many other sources in forming their own local sense of identity ("who we are") and mission ("how we do things here"). The woman I spoke to at the coffee hour of the UMC profiled in the opening vignette had something specific in mind when she told me she'd been looking for a Methodist church. What was this? Was it the same thing that church leaders have in mind when they think of what makes the UMC distinctive?

I think that many UMC leaders would look for but not find the kind of connectionalism that the *Discipline* speaks about so eloquently in both of the UM churches that I studied in this community. They would look in vain for the "public religion" emphasis that links private piety to activism in the world. The church described above is primarily a place of worship, with relatively weak bonds between members and

270   *Connectionalism: Ecclesiology, Mission, and Identity*

no systematic outreach of its own, while the other UMC congregation is a place of close and family-like attachments between members that is internally focused on fellowship.

This paper will begin to address the question of why that is, and will suggest a tentative and somewhat paradoxical answer. UMC leaders, in trying to institute a "public religion" ecclesiology in local churches, may have a problem shared more generally by churches that have a formal polity that is connectional or hierarchical. Taking the two United Methodist congregations from my study, this paper discusses some typical difficulties in bringing local Methodist culture in line with larger Methodist mission priorities, noting the particular difficulty of fostering an idea of "public religion" in local Methodist churches. Comparing these two churches to other mainstream Protestant churches in the area, the paper concludes with some suggestions for how to foster this public religion orientation.

This Study[7]

For 18 months, from late 1991 to early 1993, I studied 23 congregations in and around Oak Park, Illinois. It is easy to give a facts-and-figures description of Oak Park. It has a population of just over 50,000. According to the latest (1990) census, 18% of the residents are black and 77% are white. It is predominantly a community of young professionals, particularly professional families. It is nine miles from the center of Chicago and has a village form of government.[8] It is harder, in a short description, to convey the character of the place. Although it is an urban area, with good restaurants and an active arts community, parts of it have a very suburban feel—houses with big front porches and backyards, moms (and some dads) walking the kids home from school in the afternoon.[9]

There are 77 congregations in and around Oak Park.[10] For this study, I collected data in two synagogues, two Catholic parishes, and 19 Protestant congregations.[11] These 23 congregations were chosen to achieve some scope for comparison along dimensions identified in the literature as relevant for conflict—size, polity type, and liberal or conservative religious orientation. The congregations were chosen to fit in the cells of Figure 1. I had planned to choose a total of 24 congregations, or three for each cell, but was able to find only two congregations in the community that were "large, conservative, and hierarchical" who would agree to be part of the study.[12]

Figure 1

	Liberal		Conservative	
	small	large	small	large
Congregational Polity				
Hierarchical Polity				

Congregations were labeled as liberal or conservative by how the head clergyperson and a majority of lay respondents categorized the congregation's religious orientation.[13] Polity type is divided into hierarchical and congregational, with "hierarchical" including both Presbyterian and Episcopal types as described by Moberg (1962). The two UMC congregations were coded as hierarchical. "Small" congregations correspond to Rothauge's (1990) family and pastoral categories, defined as congregations where the administrative structure revolves around the pastor and small group of lay leaders. "Large" congregations include what Rothauge (1990) terms program and corporation churches, roughly churches with more than 150 regular Sunday attendees, in which the administration is more formally divided into boards and committees. A short telephone survey administered to all 77 congregations in the three-community area indicates that these 23 are well-representative of the area in size, membership, and programs.

I interviewed 231 people from 23 congregations—203 lay members, and 28 clergy. Just over half the lay members were in leadership positions. In addition to interviews, I observed worship services and meetings, and analyzed mission statements, annual reports, constitutions, promotional brochures, written histories, and sermons.

The interview schedule facilitated a three-part, structured discussion, ranging from 45 minutes to an hour and a half. First I asked respondents to describe their feelings about their present congregation and their history of religious involvement. Second, I asked them to characterize their congregation on a variety of dimensions—the membership, the programs and activities, the goals and plans, the history and future trajectory. In the third and final part of the interview, I asked them to tell me about any conflicts in their congregation over the last five years. Members and clergy reported a total of 65 conflict events.

In addition to interviewing, I engaged in participant-observation of services and meetings. In observations, I focused not only on formal elements of process (what is the order of the service/meeting, who leads, who speaks, where are ideas or liturgical elements drawn from), but also on how members interacted with one another, and how they interacted with me, a visitor and stranger. Combined with the questions from the first and second part of the interviews, this yielded information not only about conflict, but also about the congregation's identity and history and members' style of commitment to the congregation and to one another.

Findings — Congregational Conflict and Congregational Models

While the study began as an investigation of how polity, size, and ideology (liberal/conservative) influenced congregational conflict, it generated a great deal of information about local congregational culture and decision-making more generally. In fact, an understanding of congregational culture proved to generate a better explanation of conflict than did the original factors I had targeted. It was "better" in that it explained more of the findings. But it was also better in that it allowed me to focus not only on conflict outcomes, but also on conflict processes, and to link conflict more broadly to "normal" styles of decision-making and interacting. And in turn, it allowed me to develop an understanding of why and how polity matters in local decision-making and conflict, an insight that will be explored below.

But first, it might be useful to summarize the "findings" in a concise way.[14] I found that congregations differ on several dimensions of conflict. They fight over different issues. Members frame and understand conflict differently. Some congregations have lots of conflict, and some have very little. Some have more compromise than others. In some, it is the pastor who "triggers" conflict by putting issues on the agenda; he or she will likely lead the congregation toward his or her desired outcome. In other congregations, the pastor's role is very different; members themselves put issues on the agenda, and the pastor exerts a more process-oriented leadership (telling people how to negotiate, but not what outcome he or she prefers). In a few congregations, there are serious, emotional conflicts that rage through a series of events and are resolved only through the exit of a large group of members, while other congregations may have many conflicts but none that is nearly so serious.

What I argue is that different congregations have different conflict patterns because they have different patterns of congregational culture. I find that there are four different sets or bundles or patterns of congregational culture. They can be distinguished by the *core tasks* that they emphasize.

* *All* congregations emphasize worship and religious education as core tasks.
* *Some* emphasize being a close-knit, supportive community for members.
* *Some* emphasize taking stands on social and political issues as an important part of their witness.
* *Some* congregations emphasize that activism beyond the congregation's own four walls is an important core task, and they adopt the role of *leader* in the community or in the denomination.

Which bundle of tasks a congregation institutionalizes has consequences not only for the setting of concrete mission goals, but also for the whole tenor of congregational life. Different bundles—different "models of and models for" the local congregation (Geertz 1973)—lead to different taken-for-granted ways of interacting with each other and with outsiders. They lead to different patterns of what sociologists have called "institutional culture"—not only norms and values, but also patterned sets of behaviors.[15] I call these different bundles "congregational models," and they can be understood as local, practical ecclesiologies. There are four distinct ones in the churches I studied.[16]

A house of worship model revolves around worship and education, core tasks shared with other congregations. There is no emphasis on community or on taking corporate stands on social and political issues. As a result, there is little intimate connection between people, and little issue-based conflict. House of worship congregations have virtually no conflict, and the conflicts they do have are small-scale, framed as administrative, and resolved by vote. The UMC congregation profiled at the beginning of this paper is a house of worship.

House of worship churches have an ongoing problem of organizational maintenance; they delegate so many tasks to professional clergy or staff that they have trouble mobilizing members widely for programs or initiatives that require high participation. Also, they face a problem of "mission creep," or the attempts by members and leaders to load more tasks onto the congregation's agenda. In the UMC congregation,[17] the pastor and a small group of lay leaders were always trying to get the congregation to be more activist on issues of race and poverty in the village, and also trying to foster more interpersonal connection and intimacy among members. But instituting a time of sharing in the worship service did not lead to a more intimate atmosphere here, where many people did not participate. And efforts to be more engaged in community affairs were resisted by the rest of the lay leadership.

A *family model* revolves around close-knit and supportive relations between members. Members know each other well and are involved in all aspects of each others' personal lives. Social times and worship are what bring them together—when they interacted with me, they asked about my personal life—was I married, did I have children?

Family congregations have few conflicts; mostly, they fight about the pastor, particularly over incorporating a new pastor into the ongoing life of the congregation. And they fight over the building and property, in conflicts that tend to pit arguments about efficiency against arguments about the value of preserving the congregations' history and status. Proposals to sell the rectory or rent the building cause great anxiety, and often drive a wedge between the pastor (who tends to make efficiency arguments) and the lay leaders (who tend to be offended by efficiency arguments). The other UMC congregation that I studied had a family model.

Family congregations have an ongoing problem of incorporating the pastor into the "family." This means that transitions in pastoral leadership are particularly difficult in family congregations. Also, in these churches, pastors tend to have a limited leadership role despite whatever formal power may be invested in their role. Confined to providing services like worship and counseling, they are often blocked from engaging in more fundamental leadership, like directing the congregation in a new sense of mission.

A *community model* emphasizes being close-knit and supportive, although in a different way than family congregations. Connection with others is achieved through small, interest-based groups, and members have more other commitments and are less involved as "whole persons." This model also emphasizes the importance of the congregation as a location for expressing the social and political beliefs of members, as a part of their witness. This tends to occur in an emergent and partial way, at the urging of individual committed members or small groups.

In community congregations, there is a great deal of conflict, most of it phrased in moral terms. Compromise is used in half of the conflicts, and members themselves trigger conflict by putting new issues on the agenda. The pastor takes a process-oriented role, adopting a stance of ensuring that the process itself is caring, open, consensual, and therefore moral. Conflict tends to be between well-defined groups of older and newer members.

Community congregations have an ongoing problem of balancing the contradictions inherent in two of their core tasks: nurturing and including members and providing a forum for strong and even conflictual debate on issues that members care about. Often, this is managed by instituting a series of small groups that are primarily locations for fellowship and support.

A *leader model* includes no emphasis on being close-knit and supportive. Like the community model, it includes an emphasis on the congregation as a location for members to express political and social stands as part of their witness. But the pastor is more likely to set the agenda and the congregation may take a stand on an issue—like ordaining women or being inclusive to lesbians and gays—before it affects its members personally.

Leader congregations are less likely to engage in compromise, (only half as likely as community congregations). The pastor takes a more substantive, and a less process-oriented, leadership role. This may be due to the fact that leader congregations are less oriented toward being a close-knit place, and less likely to view the congregation as expressive of members' particular interests and values. It also may be due to the increased legitimacy and moral authority that accrues to the pastor in his role as representative from the congregation to the wider community and other organizations.[18]

Leader congregations also face a problem of "mission creep," with some members expecting that the congregation will be more nurturing and develop more of an emphasis on providing members with experiences of closeness and fellowship. Also, it is possible that the relative unwillingness to compromise in leader congregations may make them more prone to schism if some event triggers a dispute that involves core doctrinal or religious issues.

Public Religion in Local Churches

The four models foster very different ideals of mission for the local church. Family and house of worship congregations think that worshiping together is their witness. One pastor of a family congregation told me that their role was to be "the believing community within the community" and referred to their physical presence—the building, the cars parked along the street on a Sunday morning, people coming in and out of the church—as their witness. The pastor of the UMC congregation with a house of worship model told me that the open and inclusive nature of their Sunday services is a large part of their witness; through this openness they become a church "for the whole community."

Community congregations believe that living their values is their witness. The fact that they engage in debate and provide a forum for members to voice and institutionalize their views on issues ranging from inclusive language to tolerance to race to abortion is their witness to their faith and their tradition (cf. Becker et al. 1993). Leaders live their values, too, but fundamentally, the members of these churches think that living their values is not enough. They want to change the world.[19]

Mainstream Protestantism tends to privilege a public religion model, one that would be compatible with a community or leader model of the local church, and to devalue or de-emphasize the "sanctuary" orientation and privatization implied by the house of worship and family models. This emphasis on public religion is communicated in everything from formal doctrinal statements to the training that pastors receive in seminaries to academic and professional writings of religious leaders. Leaders in many mainline denominations tend to view family and house of worship congregations as at best unenergetic and at worst as complacent and indulgent (Gilkey 1994, Carroll and Roof 1993, Dudley and Johnson 1993, Marty 1986, Roozen et al. 1984). The *UMC*, of course, recognizes the importance of providing fellowship and nurturing for members, but the emphasis on the articulation of religiously informed values and their implementation in outreach is similar to that in many mainstream Protestant groups.

Academicians follow this lead; those who would look to local churches as a source for communal ideology and a rationale for public activism that goes beyond individualism are upset by what they see as increasing trends toward privatization and an internal focus in local religious communities.[20] Many of the studies that support this interpretation are based on individual-level data, and the "culprit" in these tales is usually increasing voluntarism in member commitment.

However, this comparative study of local congregations makes clear that voluntarism does *not* lead to one single pattern of local participation and decision making, to one reaction to religious authority and tradition, or to one style of member commitment. It does not lead to one dominant congregational model, but to four different ones.

Voluntarism means, at the local level, the freedom to negotiate and implement a *limited range of local institutional cultures*, to figure out together, in an ongoing way, different sets of answers to the fundamental questions of identity and mission—"who are we" and "how do we do things here?"

And these different answers have different implications both for the nature of member commitment and the structure of religious authority. In the congregations in and around Oak Park, it is not the case that public religion has disappeared, or that all is rampant individualism. Rather, the private/public dichotomy is reproduced in the split between family and house of worship models on the one hand and community and leader models on the other. The former are privatized models that focus on the nurturing of individual members through worship and fellowship and reject a focus on social issues. The latter incorporate an emphasis on individual spiritual nurture and religious education but combine that with the idea that the local church is, indeed, the place where stands on issues ranging from race to gender roles to sexuality and civil rights are to be debated and institutionalized. Further, embodying the congregation's values on social issues is seen as part of the congregation's witness to the local community. Leader congregations go farther, not merely adopting internal policies on social issues but conducting active, issue-based outreach in the local community.

The real question, then, for denominational leaders who want to foster public models of local mission, is what factors tend to push a congregation toward a community or a leader model. In the congregations that I studied, official denominational ideology, doctrine, or tradition do not seem to be determinative. In one way, this makes perfect sense. Religious traditions are large, and provide a multiplicity of rationales for local leaders to use in constructing local identity and mission (Swidler 1986).

Anecdotal evidence indicates that formative events and leaders play a part in determining local identity and mission. For the UMC profiled in the opening vignette, this was an experience of extreme conflict that began with the activism of a former pastor in the 1960s Civil Rights Movement. The current pastor told me that all his efforts to get the church to take a stand on local community issues, be they racial justice or gay rights or the homeless shelter or developing AIDS awareness, had been met with indifference. His interpretation was that the congregation was so worn out from the earlier conflicts that longer-term members simply refuse to engage in anything potentially controversial; lay leaders agreed.

However, local history is only one factor. Size also plays some role. While not every small congregation in my sample had institutionalized a "family" model, all of the congregations with a family model were small. Larger size and the resources that that brings do not guarantee that a congregation will have a public orientation, but they do seem to facilitate this orientation, perhaps by providing a kind of plausibility structure for thinking of the church as an effective public "player" in the community.

Also, it was common for congregations with a congregational polity to exhibit either a community or a leader model.[21] This is true even if outreach is not a strong part of the denomination's heritage. For example, this was true for City Baptist,[22] an independent fundamentalist Baptist church on the border of Oak Park and Austin, which had instituted a community model. This congregation provided forums, in the small age-based fellowship groups, in the meetings of elders and deacons, and in the Sunday service, for discussion of such issues as race, racism, violence, and poverty. Its leaders urged people to go beyond tolerance to genuine acceptance, and they were able to institutionalize a multicultural ministry that embraced members spanning not only racial but also extreme economic and educational divides.

This congregation also engaged in some forms of outreach, the most visible being the participation of the pastor and lay leaders in a march, organized by black pastors in the neighboring poor black section of Chicago, to protest urban violence, and held after two gang-related shootings near the church. When I completed fieldwork, the church was considering joining a revolving homeless shelter and starting a project to help unemployed members of the church find work.

When I asked this pastor where he had looked in developing his rationale for multicultural ministry, he told me that evangelical and fundamentalist churches are only now beginning to draw upon their experience in mission settings abroad to form ideas for multicultural ministry at home. He pointed to the congregation's own lay leadership as the main impetus for their current mission focus, crediting a longer-term group of older leaders who did not want to abandon their church as the composition of the surrounding community changed, and who resisted the pattern of closing up and moving further west to the whiter suburbs. These leaders wanted their church to remain rooted in the changing local community and called a pastor with the commitment to helping them achieve this goal.

Likewise, the five congregations with a leader model did not all come from denominational families that emphasize activism or outreach.[23] And one of them did not even have the advantages of large size. Of all the congregations I studied, the most "atypical" in this sense was a small Disciples of Christ congregation.[24] It also had had an experience in the 1960s with a pastor who was an outspoken activist in the Civil Rights movement, with completely different results. This period of activism awakened the congregation and has become a valued part of their identity and mission. When their last pastor left, they called a man whose main interest is in social justice and activism, and the church has gone on both to be a leader in the local community on issues of racial and economic justice, and to participate in compassionate ministries.

When I asked the pastor what part of his Disciples heritage he drew upon for his ministry rationale, he told me that the strongest element was the history of local autonomy and a de-emphasis on doctrine. Local congregations within this tradition are free, he told me, to come up with their own mission emphasis, and for him and this congregation that has meant an ability to respond energetically to crucial local issues.

In the examples of these four congregations, as in the rest of the study, it is clear that denominational culture and official ecclesiologies are not adopted by local congregations in any straightforward way. This research shows that structural factors like size and polity, while not strictly determining of local culture and mission, have some influence apart from doctrine or religious tradition. Likewise, formative events and leaders can push a congregation in a direction that is either confirming or disconfirming of central denominational mission priorities.

There are several possible interpretations of the finding that congregational polity stimulates a public-religion orientation. One interpretation is that, at the local level, members of hierarchical congregations are more willing to think of public religion as something *for which someone else is responsible.* That is, they are likely to delegate the taking of stands on social issues to religious professionals and, perhaps more important, to other levels or kinds of organizations. For example, some members of the Methodist congregation with a family model sympathized with the idea of granting more legal protections to homosexuals, but they did not see the local church as the appropriate place for that kind of issue-based activism.

Another possible explanation is that these are not only institutional models of the congregation, but institutional models of religion more generally. That is, a privatized model of mission at the local level could indicate a broader rejection of public religion. This was the case for a Presbyterian congregation in my sample. The members of this church were divided on political issues like abortion and the legal rights of homosexuals. But they see their religion as having little to do with these issues, and they were and are annoyed when their denomination takes a stand on such an issue. They tend to think that that is not what religion in general is about. This is not quite the same thing as delegating stands on social issues to another level of the organization. Rather, this is rejecting the idea of "public religion" more broadly.

To put it another way, a local ecclesiology that limits the congregational mission to privatized matters may or may not stem from a more generally privatized ecclesiology; it may simply mean that members of local churches think that social activism is someone else's responsibility. Evidence from the two UMC congregations I studied indicates that the latter is more likely the case. Both of these churches are members of the Community of Congregations and support its outreach programs, including a rotating community homeless shelter and a pulpit exchange designed to increase tolerance across all kinds of boundaries (racial and denominational, liberal and conservative). They also support denominational outreach and service programs with donations of money, if not time. That is, these UMC congregations were not against the idea of public religion in general, but they were reluctant to make themselves into forums for the discussion and debate of social issues, and they were not willing to incorporate an activist idea of mission into the tasks for which they took responsibility at the local level.

Conclusions

For denominational leaders, the term "ecclesiology" implies something both systematic and theological. However, it is fairly clear that the cultural patterns that influence conflict (and, I think, decision-making more generally) in local congregations *are not the same thing as the set of espoused beliefs that members have*. Rather, the patterns vary by the nature of the affective or emotional ties between members, and the bundle of tasks singled out as what their local congregation ought to be engaged in. This becomes the bundle of things that people are loyal to in their particular local context. These are not just patterns of norms and values, *but they are institutionalized in routines of behavior that become a whole style of congregational interaction*.

In fact, the patterns I found operate at a taken-for-granted level, and remain, in normal times, *unarticulated*.[25] For example, the imperative to be a close and supportive community could have a theological rationale applied to it, but many members could not and did not articulate a theological or religious reason for their desire for close connections with other people in their congregation. Also, these patterns of culture are not terribly systematic, but are organized around fairly broad and general ideas about what the core tasks of the local congregation should be. This is, in one sense, "mission," but it is not *necessarily* theological. And the same ideas about the "mission" of the local church can be found in churches with widely divergent theological backgrounds.

While polity does not determine congregational culture, it does seem to be easier for members of congregations with a hierarchical or connectional polity to view outreach, taking stands on social and political issues or being a leader, as *someone else's task*—a task of denominational leaders, ecumenical organizations, or religious professionals, perhaps, but not something that they seek out in their local congregations. Likewise, members of a congregational-polity congregation seem more able to use the local church as a forum to express their deeply held social, religious, and political values.

This generates two kinds of practical insights for UMC leaders in fostering the aspect of connectionalism that links private piety to an engaged concern for the world. The first has to do with size. It seems that supra-congregational structures, particularly confederations of local churches, are the venues through which smaller congregations engage in local mission and outreach; such venues should be strengthened wherever possible.

The second insight has to do with fostering, as much as possible, a kind of de-facto congregationalism that leads members to feel ownership of and commitment to the local church as a public space to articulate public values and through which to take public action. A first step here might be to identify "model" UMC congregations in various settings that have been successful in institutionalizing community or leader models of the local church, with an eye to identifying the key programs, events, and structural factors that allowed leaders to move successfully in this direction.

What must be emphasized is that any attempt to recast the nature of the connectional tie in a way that affects local congregational culture and ministry must take into account the role of the local institutionalized understandings of congregational mission and identity if it is to have any hope of success. This research suggests that local taken-for-granted patterns of interaction and norms of behavior have a formative impact on processes like decision-making, goal-setting and conflict in local congregations. Without some understanding of how congregational cultures work, it will be difficult to forge meaningful and effective links between denominational goals and local congregational ministry.

References

Ammerman, Nancy Tatom. 1987. *Bible Believers: Fundamentalists, in the Modern World*. New Brunswick, N.J.: Rutgers University Press.

———. 1990. *Baptist Battles*. New Brunswick: Rutgers University Press.

———. 1994. "Telling Congregational Stories." *Review of Religious Research* 35, no. 4 (June): 289–301.

———. 1996. *Congregation and Community*. New Brunswick, N.J.: Rutgers University Press.

Becker, Penny Edgell. 1996. "Congregational Models and Conflict: A Study of How Institutions Shape Organizational Process." In *Sacred Companies: Organized Aspects of Religion and Religious Aspects of Organization*, ed. Jay Demerath et al. New York: Oxford University Press.

Becker, Penny Edgell. 1995. *"How We Do Things Here": Culture and Conflict in Local Congregations*. Dissertation, University of Chicago.

Bellah, Robert N., et al. 1985. *Habits of the Heart*. Berkeley: University of California Press.

Blau, Joseph L. 1976. *Judaism in America: From Curiosity to Third Faith*. Chicago History of American Religion Series. Chicago: University of Chicago Press.

Cantrell, Randolph, et al. 1983. "Parish Autonomy: Measuring Denominational Differences." *Journal for the Scientific Study of Religion* 22 (3): 276–87.

Caplow, Theodore, Howard M. Bahr, and Bruce A. Chadwick. 1983. *All Faithful People: Change and Continuity in Middletown's Religion*. Minneapolis, University of Minnesota Press.

Carroll, Jackson, and Wade Clark Roof. 1993. *Beyond Establishment*. Louisville: Westminster/John Knox.

Davidman, Lynn. 1991. *Tradition in a Rootless World*. Berkeley and Los Angeles: University of California Press.

Dudley, Carl, and Sally A. Johnson. 1993. *Energizing the Congregation*. Louisville: Westminster/John Knox.

Eiesland, Nancy. 1995. *A Particular Place: Exurbanization and Religious Response in a Southern Town*. Doctoral thesis, Emory University, Department of Sociology and Graduate Division of Religion.

Fine, Gary Alan. 1984. "Negotiated Orders and Organizational Cultures." *Annual Review of Sociology* 10:239–62.

———. 1987. *With The Boys*. Chicago: University of Chicago Press.

Furman, Frida Kerner. 1987. *Beyond Yiddishkeit: A Struggle for Jewish Identity in a Reform Synagogue*. Albany: State University of New York Press.

Geertz, Clifford. 1973. *The Interpretation of Cultures*. New York: Basic Books.

Gilkey, Langdon. 1994. "The Christian Congregation as Religious Community." Pp. 100–32 in *American Congregations*, vol. 2, ed. James Wind and James Lewis. Chicago: University of Chicago Press.

Glock, Charles. 1993. "The Churches and Social Change in Twentieth-Century America." *The Annals of the American Academy of Political and Social Science* 527:67–83.

Greenhouse, Carol J. 1986. *Praying for Justice*. Ithaca: Cornell University Press.

Gremillion, Joseph, and Jim Castelli. 1987. *The Emerging Parish: The Notre Dame Study of Catholic Parish Life Since Vatican II*. San Francisco: Harper and Row.

Hammond, Philip. 1988. "Religion and the Persistence of Identity." *Journal for the Scientific Study of Religion*, Presidential Address, 27 (1): 1–11.

Hunter, James Davison. 1991. *Culture Wars*. New York: Basic Books.

Marty, Martin. 1994. "Public and Private: Congregation as Meeting Place." Pp. 133–68 in *American Congregations*, vol. 2, ed. James Wind and James Lewis. Chicago: University of Chicago Press.

Marty, Martin. 1986. *Protestantism in the United States*. New York: Scribners.

Moberg, D. 1962. *The Church as a Social Institution*. Englewood Cliffs, N.J.: Prentice-Hall.

Mock, Alan. 1992. "Congregation Religious Styles and Orientations to Society." *Review of Religious Research* 34 (1): 20–33.

Neitz, Mary Jo. 1987. *Charisma and Community: A Study of Religious Commitment within the Charismatic Renewal*. New Brunswick: Transaction Books.

Powell, Walter W., and Paul J. DiMaggio, ed. 1991. *The New Institutionalism in Organizational Analysis*. Chicago: University of Chicago Press.

Prell, Riv-Ellen. 1989. *Prayer and Community*. Detroit: Wayne State University Press.

Roof, Wade Clark. 1993. *A Generation of Seekers*. San Francisco: HarperCollins.

Roof, Wade Clark, and William McKinney. 1987. *American Mainline Religion*. New Brunswick: Rutgers University Press.

Roozen, David A., William McKinney, and Jackson W. Carroll. 1984. *Varieties of Religious Presence: Mission in Public Life*. New York: Pilgrim.

Rothauge, Arlin J. 1990. *Sizing up a Congregation for New Member Ministry*. Washington, D.C.: Alban Institute, On Demand Publications.

Seidler, John, and Katherine Meyer. 1989. *Conflict and Change in The Catholic Church*. New Brunswick, N.J.: Rutgers University Press.

Swatos, William. 1981. "Beyond Denominationalism." *Journal for the Scientific Study of Religion* 20:217–27.

Swidler, Ann. 1986. "Culture in Action: 'Symbols and Strategies.'" *American Sociological Review* 51:273–86.

United Methodist Church. 1992. *The Book of Discipline*. Nashville: United Methodist Publishing House. http://www.netins.net/showcase/umsource/umdoct.html#basic (6–5–96).

Warner, R. Stephen. 1993. "Toward a New Paradigm for the Sociological Study of Religion in the United States." *American Journal of Sociology* 98 (5): 1044–93.

Wertheimer, Jack, ed. 1987. *The American Synagogue: Sanctuary Transformed*. New York: Cambridge University Press.

Wind, James, and James Lewis. 1994. *American Congregations*, vols. 1 and 2. Chicago: University of Chicago Press.

Wuthnow, Robert. 1994. *Sharing the Journey*. New York: Free Press.

———. 1995. *Learning to Care*. New York: Oxford University Press.

∽ Penny Long Marler and C. Kirk Hadaway ∽

In the following essay, Penny Long Marler and C. Kirk Hadaway study the health of the connection, focusing especially on religious identity—on the person in the pew and particularly on the person not in the pew. Here and in a larger study of American Protestantism using polls, telephone surveys, and personal interviews, they examine the population of unchurched who nonetheless continue to identify themselves denominationally. Such marginals constitute half of self-identified Protestants and are disproportionately young Americans and baby boomers. Among such moderns, they suggest, identity is often achieved, "self-authored," a life style, rather than attributed, communally given, defined by tradition, ascribed by family of origin. They compare churched and churched Methodists and then isolate and characterize four groups or types of marginal Methodists—disenfranchised pragmatists, disaffected skeptics, dislocated idealists, and disengaged seekers. Obviously, these groups lack what characterizes churched Methodists, namely a high degree of institutional and/or ideological loyalty. Yet, they represent populations with intellectual strengths and ethical commitments from which the church could well benefit. Marler and Hadaway's study returns us to the question raised by Heitzenrater, namely what, after all, really defines our connectionalism. To whom or to what do we connect ourselves? Is the genius of Wesleyan connectionalism best and fully captured by an organization demanding brand loyalty?

Methodists on the Margins: "Self-Authoring" Religious Identity[1]

Penny Long Marler
and
C. Kirk Hadaway

If there were no such thing as churches, I would be the perfect Christian
—marginal Protestant, Connecticut

Many Americans retain a denominational affiliation and often a personal memory of active involvement in a church. Yet they find themselves outside congregational life, either by active choice or simple neglect. They remain "marginal Methodists" or "lapsed Lutherans," and feel no compelling reason to attend church worship.

Despite its popular image of strength and robustness, religion in the United States is characterized by the steady erosion of associational life—what Robert Putnam calls "social capital." In a recent article in the *Journal of Democracy* tellingly entitled, "Bowling Alone," Putnam (1995) catalogues rather dramatic post-War membership decline in many "secondary associations"—that is, social organizations that generate "dense networks of civic engagement" and that "broaden the participants' sense of self, developing the 'I' into the 'we.'" Such groups include labor unions, PTAs, the League of Women Voters, the Red Cross, the Jaycees, the Boy Scouts, and of course, bowling leagues. And while most polls do show a "modest" decline in rates of church membership over the same period, the self-reports of all mainline denominations in the United States for the last 30 years reveal more serious losses (Putnam 1995: 68–70).

A recent study of church attendance suggests that the *gap* between polls (self-reported attendance) and rolls (actual counts of worship attendance) is very close to the decline in participation reported by labor unions and PTAs (Hadaway, Marler, and Chaves 1993). In fact, our research on marginal Protestants indicates that almost half of all self-identified Protestants are functionally unchurched, attending worship a few times a year or not at all. Regular weekly church attendance is restricted increasingly to evangelicals and older mainline Protestants. Young Americans and Baby Boomers—and particularly those with mainline Protestant backgrounds—are disproportionally represented among the ranks of the unchurched (Marler and Hadaway 1993).

The thesis of this paper is that the conditions of late modernity pose particular epistemological and practical problems for the nature and shape of religious self-identity—and that these problems have reciprocal effects on religious institutions and may explain, for instance, declining church membership and attendance. We examine this thesis through analysis of an extensive data set on American Protestants. Within this larger sample, Methodists (and secondarily, other mainline Protestants) are the research focus because of their historic and current "mainstream" socio-demographic and attitudinal characteristics.

Our research strategy is to explore the attitudes and lifestyles of mainline unchurched Protestants. We show how Methodist churched and unchurched persons differ from one another and from other churched and unchurched Protestants (conservative and mainline). We also compare the dominant "adaptive strategies" of unchurched mainline Protestants (including Methodists) in order to explain how unchurched persons are making sense out of their spiritual lives, personal struggles, conceptions of Deity, religious identities, and current behavior in the context of an increasingly "unsettled" culture.

The data for this analysis are drawn from a three-stage research effort focused on marginal Protestants. Stage one was a 2,010-respondent poll conducted in four states: Connecticut, Georgia, Ohio, and Arizona. The states were chosen based on their demographic representativeness in each respective U.S. Census region. The sample was randomly selected and stratified, using known proportions of Protestants in the four states. A fifteen-minute telephone survey was conducted among the adult (21 and over) Protestant population in 1991. Stage two was a longer interview conducted among over 500 Protestants who attend church infrequently (several times a year or less). This phase of the research was completed in 1992. Stage three consisted of fifty, two-hour, face-to-face interviews with selected marginal Protestants who represent the dominant adaptive strategies that unchurched persons use to interpret their lives and connection to religion. The tape-recorded personal interviews were conducted in 1993, with several follow-up contacts in 1994 and 1995.

Religion in Late Modernity

Anthony Giddens describes the late modern period as a "runaway world." He observes that "not only is the pace of social change much faster than in any prior system, so also is its scope and the profoundness with which it affects pre-existing social practices and modes of behaviour" (Giddens 1991: 16). It is, according to Giddens, a "post-traditional" order "in which the question, 'How shall I live?' has to be answered in day-to-day decisions about how to behave, what to wear and what to eat—and many other things—as well as interpreted within the temporal unfolding of self-identity." In a period of great dynamism, relationships that are time-and-space bound (local, anchored by tradition), embedded (ascribed, institutionalized), and taken-for-granted (habitual, internalized) are increasingly disembedded and unsettled. In this setting, the self-making or "authoring" project shifts from traditional institutions like the family, community, and local church to the individual.

Does this mean that traditional ways of believing and being are completely ineffectual and unimportant for interpreting the modern situation? Quite the contrary. Again, as Giddens argues, the issue is not whether we find ourselves outside the influence of tradition and its accouterments, adrift in a community-less sea (as, for example, with Bellah's Sheilaism), or safe inside some new kind of community harbor (as, for example, with neo-fundamentalistic sectarianism). The issue in the present era is that we are somewhere in between: some adrift and at the mercy of the sea; some clinging desperately to once-friendly shores resisting the force and lure of "the beyond"; some anchored obstinately at the harbor's mouth arguing over what to do or whether to go; and some intentionally setting out in search of whatever may be just over the horizon. It is a time of great *unsettlement*.

For denominations and most congregations, the difficulty of the present situation is that most religious institutions were organized to meet the needs of individuals experiencing, in Ann Swidler's words, more "settled lives" (Swidler 1986). Here Swidler provides a helpful image for understanding the complex relationship between individuals and institutions: she suggests that culture influences individual action by providing the ultimate "tool kit" of habits, skills, and styles from which people construct "strategies of action" (Swidler 1986: 273). As Peter Berger (1977) observed, the traditional mediating structures in more settled times were the family and the church. They served as the primary "outfitters" for individuals' cultural toolkits; and they also provided the "user's manuals"—whether explicitly through instruction or implicitly through experience—for guiding individuals in the use of those tools.

Settled cultures and institutions that operate within them tend to be *all-encompassing*. As Swidler argues, this is primarily because "they are not in open competition with alternative models for organizing experience." Consequently, "they have the undisputed authority of habit, normality, and common sense" (Swidler 1986: 281). They shape traditions—that is, "articulated cultural beliefs and practices, but ones taken for granted so that they seem inevitable parts of life" (279), and they build what Giddens calls "face commitments" that are necessary for building social trust or, in Putnam's words, "social capital" (Giddens 1990; Putnam 1995). Thus, institutions like the family and the church in more settled cultures become the arbiters of individual action by establishing and reinforcing traditions. The result is a relatively high level of security and comfort for the individual, and increasingly, a high level of taken-for-granted routine for institutions.

In more settled cultures, an individual's cultural toolkit is composed of a relatively limited set of tools, and one person's toolkit looks a lot like another's. Over time, however, the habitual use of inherited cultural tools leads to a decrease in the perceived need explicitly to discuss the values and beliefs that underlie action. In this way, social practices tend to become disconnected from values and beliefs. So, Swidler concludes, in the transition from settled to more unsettled cultures, action persists—sometimes even when the underlying values and beliefs have changed. The "user's manuals" fall into disuse and eventually may be lost—a situation that typically presages or accompanies the transition to unsettlement.

In *unsettled* times once-established cultural values and beliefs are "jettisoned with apparent ease," and more explicitly articulated cultural models begin to play a powerful role in organizing social life. The problem in the context of *transition* from a more settled to an unsettled culture is, who does the work of "outfitting" the individual's cultural toolkit? And who prepares, teaches, and reinforces strategies of action—that is, where does a new or revised "user's manual" come from? The problem is particularly acute in a time of cultural flux—which we would argue is the precise condition of late modernity—because traditional institutions have been:

1) relativized by change in the face of ethnic and religious pluralism and globalizing technologies—resulting in the "separation of time and place" (Giddens 1991: 16–17);

2) disabled by change in the face of dramatic shifts in role and function of traditional structures like the family and the local community (Drucker 1992: 95–98; Marler 1995); and

3) paralyzed by change in the face of ideological and economic cross-pressures to maintain the old, "retrench," *and* to make way for the new, "retool" (Abelson 1991: 172–76; Giddens 1991: 2, 146; Berger 1992: 9–11, 18, 41; Beyer 1994: 90–94; Marler 1994).

When traditions no longer provide the answers for the problems of everyday life *or* when traditional institutions provide no clear guidance for understanding what Giddens calls "counterfactual information" and how it relates to the old tools, then individuals are, for the most part, on their own to create functional strategies of action and meaningful self-identities. The self—each person's understanding of who she is and what he does—becomes a "reflexive project for which the individual is responsible" (Giddens 1991). Identity is "self-authored," and actions are oriented increasingly to the self-authorship process as individuals try to maintain the integrity of their own self-project.

In unsettled or *unsettling* cultures, then, the individual becomes the arbiter of strategies of action. In times of increasing unsettlement, even individuals who were once—and still may be—part of the taken-for-granted constituencies of the church begin to feel the stresses and opportunities of choice. And as Swidler argues, the more dynamic the culture becomes, the more alternative cultural "outfitters" arise with new tools and new rules to offer for organizing social life. Individuals caught in the fray lean first on traditional social resources in reorganizing their cultural toolkits and updating their user's manuals. Typically, however, traditional institutions are not tooled to help individuals sort out truth and choose among options. They are more in the business of handing down a particular subcultural version of truth as the only (or best) option (Duck 1993: 109). So in the absence of any real help from traditional institutions, individuals are forced to lean more on their own understanding in an attempt to construct functional strategies of action.

Identity, once the province of traditional institutions, is increasingly the responsibility of the individual. And institutional culture, once a more coherent and taken-for-granted "pedagogue" or teacher, becomes something more like a full (and in the process of unsettlement), somewhat disorganized "toolkit." The individual is less the object of institutional pedagogy and more often an active subject reflexively engaged in cultural action (Hirschhorn and Gilmore 1992: 104–15). By the same token, culture is not simply the subject (respected "pedagogue") but also the object of individual action.

One outcome of this process is stress on the individual. As Berger (1992) observes, it takes the form of a nagging sense of uncertainty and impermanence which human beings naturally seek to resolve. Ultimate questions remain to be answered and, in fact, become more cogent and troubling in a world where doubt permeates everyday life (Giddens 1991: 3). The cultural tools that religious institutions traditionally provided—a scheme of values, a myth of immortality, an attitude toward death, a connection to a greater whole (society or cosmos), and a sense of mystery and wonder—might be of great value in combating personal meaninglessness (Moore 1992: 204–8). But in late modernity, such institutions no longer have the force of authority that allows their answers to be taken for granted. In the face of many alternative ways of doing and being, they seem less anchored and permanent. It is, again, up to the individual—to accept/reject, believe/doubt, experience/ignore the "provisions" (content and community) offered by religious institutions (Giddens 1994: 74–76).

In many ways, institutions in dynamic cultures are in the same position as individuals: no longer able to count on all-encompassing cultural values and beliefs and associated taken-for-granted strategies of action, churches also begin to feel very much "on their own." As the individual becomes disconnected from the church, churches become disconnected from denominations. Strategies of action handed down from denominational hierarchies that once "worked" in one place no longer seem to help, or at least they don't seem to work the way they once did. Old tools and old rules are at odds, simultaneously, with the new tools and new rules that alternative institutions and movements forming in the breach have to offer and with the new strategies for action (competencies) that individuals are busily acquiring to survive.

According to Anthony Giddens (1990: 134–37), the dangers and opportunities of unsettlement—this "risk profile" of modernity—lead to four typical, adaptive reactions on the part of individuals. These strategies of action, if you will, for dealing with the juggernaut of the modern world are strikingly similar to the four kinds of self-authoring projects we have uncovered in our surveys of and conversations with marginal Protestants. The first strategy is characterized by *pragmatic acceptance*, in which the actor "maintains a focus on day-to-day problems and tasks" and attempts to avoid thinking about much of what goes on in the modern world, because it is seen as beyond anyone's control. Another typical response to modernity is that of *skepticism* (or what Giddens calls, *cynical pessimism*) in which one deals directly with the emotional impact of anxieties arising from modern life and attempts to dampen their impact, sometimes through a humorous or a world-weary response to them or, most often, through persistent intellectualizing. A third reaction is marked by a stubborn (counterfactual) *idealism.* This strategy ignores or redefines the problems and dangers of modern life in order to maintain a continued faith in providential reason. A final response is marked neither by fatalistic detachment, cynical skepticism, nor rigid idealism but by *radical engagement.* In this case, the individual actively contests the problems of modernity by mobilizing resources to reduce their impact or, in the case of our *seekers,* to transcend them (Giddens 1990: 134–37).

These strategies of action each provoke a unique relationship to the institutional church. In order to describe the character of that connection (or disconnection), we will talk about them as *disenfranchised pragmatists, disaffected skeptics, dislocated idealists,* and in relation to the church (particularly mainline churches), *disengaged seekers*—although they are clearly *engaged* with alternative "outfitters" like the parachurch and new religious movements. At bottom, the lifestyles of increasing numbers of mainline Protestants no longer seem compatible with active participation in the church, but this was not always the case— particularly for a denomination that defined the mainline for many generations, United Methodism.

Methodism and American Society

Church historian Frederick Norwood wrote in 1974 that "Methodism became in many ways the most American of the churches. Not only in its inception but throughout its development it was most in tune with the American song." He goes on to ask, "Does this mean that America was Methodized or that Methodism was Americanized? Probably some of both. . . . [There was] a close and continuing love affair, for better or worse, between the Methodist Church and the United States" (Norwood 1974: 17).

One indicator of the close link between Methodism and American culture is the geographic distribution of the United Methodist Church. This denomination has at least one church in 2,965 out of the 3,105 counties (or county equivalents) that comprise the United States—more than any other Protestant body and equal to the Catholic Church. In addition, the United Methodist Church is not concentrated primarily in any region of the nation. Unlike other denominations which also have churches in large numbers of U.S. counties (the Assemblies of God, the Southern Baptist Convention, the Churches of Christ and the Presbyterian Church [USA]), the United Methodist Church is unique in that it has a major presence in all nine U.S. Census Regions. Methodists are the largest Protestant denomination in the Middle Atlantic states and the East North Central region; they are the second largest Protestant denomination in four other Census Regions (West North Central, South Atlantic, East South Central, and West South Central). And even where Methodists are less strong (New England, the Mountain states, and the Pacific region) they are among the five largest Protestant denominations or denominational groups (Bradley et al. 1992: ix, 5–11).

The manner in which Methodism became "the most American of churches" is well-documented, and has become part of the history and folklore of the settling of the North American continent. Methodism arrived in the United States during the 1760s in the form of a missionary movement, rather than as a church or denomination (Hudson 1981: 122). Methodist preachers, some official and some not, organized religious societies that were only nominally related to the Church of England. This activity continued even during the American Revolution as native lay preachers took the place of English itinerants (most of whom returned to England). And unlike most other religious groups in America, the Methodists continued to grow, more than tripling in size during the war years (Hudson 1961: 58).

American Methodists became independent of England and the Church of England in 1784, but retained John Wesley's system of circuits, societies, and classes. This system, which remained more movement-like than church-like for many years, facilitated the rapid deployment of Methodist preachers and the mobilization of lay leadership, while maintaining centralized control by church officials. According to Winthrop Hudson (1981: 124), "no system could have been more admirably designed for moving quickly into new territory, whether that territory was in older settled regions of the seaboard or over the mountains into the new communities of the frontier. In both areas Methodists met with equal success." The Methodist churches achieved their remarkable national distribution primarily by following the population in its westward migration. Circuit riders "went everywhere—to mountain cabins, prairie churches, schoolhouses, and camp meetings—preaching free grace and individual responsibility and the need for conversion and regeneration" (Mead and Hill 1990: 157).

By following the population "everywhere" and through the heavy use of lay leadership, Methodism spread throughout all regions of the nation and among remarkably diverse groups of constituents. This diversity continues and helps explain why the United Methodist Church does not fit easily into a single denominational category. Some survey researchers have placed Methodists into the "Liberal Protestant" group, along with the Episcopalians, Presbyterians and members of the United Church of Christ (Stark and Glock 1968). More recently, the trend is to include Methodists along with other "moderate" Protestant bodies, such as the Christian Church and Lutherans (Roof and McKinney 1987).

A closer look at survey data on self-identified white Methodists reveals the reason for classification problems: in some ways Methodists are similar to Liberal Protestants; in some ways they are similar to Moderate Protestants; and in some ways Methodists are actually closer to Southern Baptists and other conservative evangelicals. In terms of education, income, and occupational prestige, white Methodists are similar to Moderate Protestants (lower than liberals and higher than conservatives on these SES measures). The same is true for most issues related to religious belief—Methodists are more "orthodox" than liberal Protestants and less conservative than white Southern Baptists and other evangelicals. On the other hand, white Methodists are closer to white Southern Baptists and other evangelicals than to Moderate or Liberal Protestants in terms of their political ideology and views on certain moral issues (such as premarital sex). Furthermore, white Methodists, Moderate Protestants and white Southern Baptists are all more concentrated in smaller towns and rural areas than are Liberal Protestants (Davis and Smith 1988; 1990). The picture, then, is of a denomination that is at the center of white American culture. However, that central position apparently results as much from the fact that extremes "average out" in a very diverse denomination as from the tendency of Methodists to represent "middle America" in a precise way.

Churched vs Unchurched Methodists

Not all who use the name "Methodist" to describe their current religious identity or denominational heritage are active members of a United Methodist, African Methodist Episcopal, African Methodist Episcopal Zion, or Christian Methodist Episcopal church. Indeed, many self-identified Methodists can be considered "unchurched" by virtue of infrequent or no participation in churches of any kind. The focus of this research is on the emerging lifeways of these marginal Methodists (and other marginal mainline Protestants), and as a first step to understanding why the church does not seem to fit their self-authored strategies, we examine a number of factors that discriminate "unchurched" Methodists from "churched" Methodists.[2] In survey results displayed in Table 1 (located at end of chapter), the unchurched are defined as persons who say they attend church "several times a year" or less. Churched persons attend church more frequently—nearly once a month to more than once a week.

In the first section of the table we compare the *Religious Heritage* of persons who are now unchurched with that of persons who remain in the church. This allows us to determine if certain differences in religious background may have "predisposed" unchurched persons to adopt a lifestyle that does not include active church participation. Not surprisingly, differences do exist. Churched Methodists were more likely to grow up in homes where grace was said before meals, to have attended youth programs or church camps when they were adolescents, and to say that their mother attended church every week. Conversely, *unchurched* Methodists were more likely to report that their father *never* attended church.

Churched Methodists report particularly *high* levels of religious exposure during their formative years, whereas for unchurched Methodists the amount of exposure provided by the example of mother and father is particularly *low*. These findings suggest that childhood religious experience is a very important factor that affects whether or not individuals incorporate active church participation as part of their lifestyle later in life. Furthermore, the influence of religious background appears to be stronger for Methodists than for other denominations— liberal or conservative.

The *Reactions and Attitudes* of Methodists to the church and to church participation (second section) are also important to an understanding of the unchurched. Although we do not know if present attitudes of unchurched respondents were formed *before* a drop-off in attendance, they still tell us a great deal about why unchurched Methodists do not return to the church now. For instance, most unchurched Methodists (74%) and other unchurched mainline Protestants (74%) do not feel guilty when they miss church. By contrast, only 40% of churched Methodists report not feeling guilty about their lack of attendance. The difference between the churched and unchurched in response to this question about guilt is considerably greater for Methodists (34 percentage points) than it is for the other two groups, indicating that a sense of "oughtness" about church attendance is a particularly important factor in determining whether or not a Methodist is likely to be an active church participant.

Methodists react more strongly to the church as an *institution* than do other Protestants. Unchurched Methodists are the most likely of all groups to say church worship is boring and the least likely to say that churches help provide meaning. Perhaps as a consequence, a large percentage of unchurched Methodists (40%) say they have attended church enough in their lifetime and they don't need to attend anymore. Churched Methodists, by contrast, tend to have a very positive image of the church. They are, for instance, particularly likely to say that churches help provide meaning (73% agree).

Churched and unchurched Protestants differ in how they relate to God, how they view the authority of the Bible, and how they understand their institutional responsibilities as Christians. Unchurched persons (and particularly unchurched mainliners) are less likely than the churched to use the traditional term "Father" for God or to say they feel "extremely close to God." Also, unchurched *Methodists* and unchurched mainliners are least likely among all groups in Table 1 to believe that "the Bible is God's Word and all it says is true." Churched Methodists are more likely to give traditional responses to these questions, but in all cases they are closer to other churched mainline Protestants than they are to conservatives. The clear exception to this rule is a question about giving to the church as a requirement to be a good Christian. As can be seen in Table 1, Methodists appear to see giving as an integral part of being a Christian—even in the absence of attending. Unchurched Methodists are, of course, more likely than churched Methodists to say giving is unnecessary, but a surprisingly small percentage of unchurched Methodists hold this view.

Finally, it is clear from Table 1 that an unchurched lifestyle tends to mitigate against other traditional forms of religious expression. Unchurched Methodists (as well as unchurched mainliners and conservative Protestants) are much less likely than the churched to say grace before meals now, read liturgical prayers aloud, engage in a regular discipline of prayer or meditation, and read devotional literature. These are resources or "tools" that the church uses to "equip" its clients and thus are seen more as church resources than as general cultural resources. On the other hand, the final line of Table 1 shows that unchurched persons are *more* likely to engage in what might be considered non-traditional forms of religious expression, such as experimentation with astrology or crystals. The same difference was found for questions dealing with prayer through nature, belief in reincarnation, and exposure to Native American spirituality. Personal interviews with unchurched mainline Protestants confirm this suggestion. Unchurched Methodists and unchurched mainliners show the highest frequency of religious experimentation, whereas churched Methodists and conservative Protestants show the lowest level of such involvement.

Self-Authoring Religious Identity: Four Adaptations

Although unchurched Protestants are distinct from churched Protestants in many ways, not all of the differences seen in Table 1 are large. This lack of consistent variation can be explained by the fact that people reject the church as a lifestyle option for very different reasons. And most of these reasons are not unidimensional. For instance, we found people in a single denominational tradition who rejected the church because it was too restrictive and others who rejected the church because it was not restrictive enough. Following Giddens (1990), we noted earlier that there seem to be four dominant "adaptive reactions" to modernity through which individuals "self-author" a lifestyle and a religious identity. Although one or two of these strategies do not seem necessarily corrosive of church participation (because of certain nostalgic or providential elements), none of the adaptive reactions represents a truly traditionalistic approach to life. Even when tradition is chosen as a response to modernity, it is still a choice, rather than part of a taken-for-granted life course. Modernity creates problems for institutions that are dependent on tradition—as the church, by nature, is. Therefore, it is not surprising that the adaptive reactions described by Giddens were apparent among unchurched persons generally, and particularly apparent among unchurched persons in the cultural center—unchurched Methodists and other mainline Protestants.

As part of our research procedure, a cluster analysis was conducted among unchurched Protestants using items (criterion variables) related to God, the church, social attitudes, and personal demographic characteristics. Four dominant clusters emerged independent of, yet very like, Giddens' theoretical description. They are labeled: *disenfranchised pragmatists, disaffected skeptics, dislocated idealists, and disengaged seekers*. In Table 2, we show how persons representing the four orientations answer a series of survey questions. In addition to numerical data, the types are explored through fifty personal interview narratives, with special emphasis on individuals with Methodist backgrounds.

Finally, in Table 3, we examine the degree to which Methodism and other denominational groups "hold" (keep as churched) or "lose" (to unchurched status) disproportionate numbers of persons who share similar orientations. This is accomplished by comparing the percentage of currently unchurched individuals in each type with the proportion of persons with similar characteristics who remain active in each denominational group.

Disenfranchised pragmatists are our youngest group: the vast majority, in fact, are under 45 years of age. They are predominantly single or divorced, highly educated, disproportionately male, and extremely mobile. They hold very liberal beliefs concerning sexuality and other social issues. Barely eight percent ever feel guilty when they miss church, and they are much more likely than any other group to respond: "I don't have anything against churches, I just don't feel the need to attend very often." So why do they continue to identify?

Many pragmatists had inconsistent exposure to religion and the church while growing up, and even for those who went "nearly every Sunday," the typical pattern was to drop out, usually by their early-teen years. For this reason, they tend to have a "Sunday-school faith," that is very literalistic, anthropomorphic, and draws very heavily on "Bible stories" from the Old Testament. This characterization seems particularly apt for Pragmatists, who were far more interested in social aspects of the church when they were children than they were in the religious content. They frequently use traditional words and images that they learned in church (47% prefer to call God "Father"), but they express little confidence in what they learned (none of the mainline unchurched Pragmatists said the Bible is "all true"). Instead, they lean more on their own common sense interpretations of what is to be believed.

Robert Parks is a twenty-something Methodist pragmatist whose parents divorced when he was in his early teens and who, consequently, had inconsistent church exposure. Nearly everything Robert says about God is phrased in anthropomorphic terms, "I just don't believe there is a Heaven and a Hell. I don't believe there is some place up there in the sky with God sitting up in a chair. . . . I don't believe there is a big inferno and there is a guy with a pitchfork, stabbing people in the ass, saying get on down the line." But a large part of Robert's doubt rests in the fact that he can't get a clearer image of what God looks like. He says, "In the Bible they don't really paint pictures of God. You don't see that. And everybody, I guess would have their own image of what he would look like, if there was a God. I sure wish I could see it though. It's like I can't even close my eyes and picture it, you know."

Most pragmatists didn't particularly enjoy attending church when they were growing up. It was a "charade," according to Robert, "and I didn't feel like I was missing anything due to the fact that I wasn't going to church. I had a busy life. I had a good time and I was enjoying life and learning new things every day." And when Robert does speak appreciatively of church participation, it is the social aspects that he remembers, "When I was a kid we went on retreats . . . and it was great because they didn't power religion into me. You were just kind of going along with your peers and having a good time." So it is not surprising that when Robert is asked if he'd take his own children, he responds, "when I have children I would like for them to do that too." Nevertheless, different from parents of the previous generation, Robert stops and thinks, then adds, "but then again, I wouldn't like to feel that I had to go to church just because of my kids."

Indeed, for many pragmatists it seems that "to go or not to go" boils down to personal convenience. John Simon, a young, single medical technician with a Congregational background, says, "I know that you really probably should go but it's more convenient not to go. What I mean by convenience is that I have the freedom not to go, so I can 'not go' because to go is inconvenient. And if you can 'not go' and get away with it, and still be okay, why deal with the inconvenience?"

John and Robert, like other pragmatists, learned that attendance was optional from the example of parents and/or from the rather lax norms for church attendance promoted by their mainline Protestant churches. John observes that unlike the Catholic church, which tells people, "you better come back or you're going to fry," the Congregationalists "allow you to get away with it," even though they "don't actually say 'it's okay to stop.' I don't think they taught that."

Pragmatists have a very diversified cultural toolkit: and they are adding new tools all the time. Their "user's manuals"—their rules—are clearly pragmatic and calculating. Like Doug Walrath's "calculators" they were raised in a world of diminishing resources (Walrath 1987). They aren't that hopeful for the future, and they know they'll have to work harder (and compete) to match or surpass the living standards of their parents.

Pragmatists' strategies of action follow consumerist rules. They are pretty picky about what they give their time and energy to (if it's work) and can be very extravagant in their play (splurging more than indulging). Their religious tools are largely inherited—and, through lack of parental modeling, consistent use, or perceived relevancy to their daily lives, virtually unused. In this sense, pragmatists are "disenfranchised."

The "user's manual" of disenfranchised pragmatists does contain a few moral axioms about "right and wrong" that many attribute to the church. Robert says he enjoyed Bible stories because "they have a good moral to them: be kind"; and John talks about being a Christian almost exclusively in terms of being a "good person" and living "somewhat by those rules." However, they rarely consciously use biblical or theological principles and are as likely to employ the rules of the market—fair advertising; getting the most for your money; cutting a good deal—to settle matters of moral and religious importance. John Simon, for example, sums up his position on church attendance and its value in relating to God: "you can deal direct if you have to. You can skip the middleman and go right to the boss."

Like all denominational groups, Methodists tend to lose disproportionate numbers of persons who reflect a pragmatic strategy for dealing with modern life. Disenfranchised pragmatists are not heavily represented among unchurched Methodists, however, making up only 15% of the total (see Table 3).

Disaffected skeptics do not form a demographically identifiable group. Instead, what they share is a skeptical or cynical orientation toward religion. They claim to be Protestant, but less than half call themselves Christian. Very few say they are "close to God," that religious faith is important to them, or that they have had a religious experience. The vast majority are neither religious nor spiritual. They almost never attend church, even on holidays. Likewise, they are not involved in religious experimentation.

Skeptics are "irreligious" by nearly any measure, but irreligion does not capture the essence of this group. Skeptics are very articulate about religious issues because most have given such issues a lot of thought. Many are agnostics and a few are even atheists. Most keep an open mind about God, but because they cannot prove the existence of God, and since few have ever had a religious experience, they have difficulty believing in a personal God.

Charles Bridges, an older Boomer who grew up in a small southern town that "probably had more churches than it had grocery stores" was raised in a Methodist family and attended a Methodist church. Now he categorizes himself as a "little to the left" of an agnostic. A self-confessed "science fiction nut," Charles says he can't believe in God for the same reason he can't believe in UFOs: "they've got to show me first."

Charles says that he has no personal "proof" of God's existence and he does not trust the Bible, "because it was written by men." He explains that the King James Bible was completely rewritten "to fit the tenets of the English Church at the time. If he didn't want something, he just struck it out." Charles wonders, "how many thousands of times over the years has this been done?" and suggests that we have no real idea what was said "in the original Bible."

Charles also has logical problems with the theological tools he has been given to understand God. He says, "I can't imagine an all-omnipotent being that creates an entire universe, down to the microns and atoms, who is so concerned and worried about whether you worshipped him or not." For Nelson, a retired chemist and an unchurched Presbyterian from Ohio, the reasoning is even more complex, as is his conception of God. Nelson reflects, "do I believe in God? That's an awful hard question. Yeah. Lots of times I have said, 'yes, I do.' And then other times I have said, 'well, what do I mean by that?' What do I mean by 'God?' Are we talking about a personal God? Are we talking about a universal force? Are we talking about the order of law in the universe? Are we talking about a moral superlative? You know? If I put all of those together I would say I probably believe in that, except as the personal God, as the individual who sent Christ to earth to die on the cross to save our sins. I suppose I could go along with almost everything except that. I would say, 'yeah, I see the position for that type of force.'"

Many skeptics say they would like to believe in some kind of higher power or supernatural, guiding force. Charles admits, "I like the idea that there is a God, because then the cosmos is a very orderly place. I like the idea, the thought, that there is something up there that understands all of this. . . . I like the idea of there being somebody in control of all this. I hate to think it's just totally chaos. I would like to believe that there is something bigger out there." He confesses that "I [have] said to myself, 'boy, it would be nice if the spirit moved me,' you know. But I would feel like I was cheating if I said that I felt the spirit and I didn't. I just didn't feel it. The closest I might get is an emotional high."

Gayle, a college-educated, Midwestern businesswoman, says, "I've thought about it a lot. Religion makes so many people so happy. To believe in something other than themselves. And sometimes I think, 'gee, am I missing out just on a real selfish, shallow level?' Am I missing out on having someone to help me?" But she cannot believe because of what she sees "in the world." According to Gayle, "I just really don't think there could be a God when all this awful stuff happens."

The tension and struggle between an affinity toward religion and an intellectual inability to believe is also clear in the remarks of Nelson, "even though I am not religious, in that I don't practice religion now, I have a lot of religious overtones and background in my thinking." He rejects "much of Christian doctrine" for intellectual reasons and yet says "I can't run away from [Christ] even if I wanted to, and I have an adherence to many of the things that he taught." Nelson even calls himself a skeptic, but indicates with some wistfulness, that "I think skepticism has its place, but I don't think it's good as a steady diet."

Skeptics have a full and carefully organized cultural toolkit. Most were religiously "tooled" in the context of a traditional church. And whereas they may retain an appreciation for (if not the practice of) strategies of action dictated by the church, they are clearly operating with a revised "user's manual." The new rules of skeptics are not the taken-for-granted rules of the traditional church; they are rational, scientific canons. Still it is important to remember that skeptics are not questioning out of a firm position that there is no God; they are really not sure, and at bottom, most would like to be convinced otherwise. Therefore, it would be misleading to describe skeptics as not "musical" in a religious sense or as the polar opposite of seekers. To the contrary, skeptics are a "left-brained" version of seekers. In fact, they could be called rational or intellectual seekers.

Methodists and conservative Protestants tend to lose disproportionate numbers of persons with a skeptical/rational orientation toward truth. Other mainline denominations also tend to lose these individuals, but such losses are negligible.

Dislocated idealists include a wide range of ages. Many are baby boomers, some are busters, and a disproportionate number are in their 70s or over. Few are college-educated. They live disproportionately in the South, and few have moved in recent years. Most were active in the church as children, and a distinct majority identify with a conservative denomination.

Dislocated idealists hold very conservative beliefs. As opposed to seekers and pragmatists, they categorized very few moral issues as "gray"—most issues, like premarital sex, abortion, and homosexuality, were rejected as "wrong." They tend to call God "Father" rather than "higher power" or "creator," and they are not involved in any sort of religious experimentation. They talk about being saved, following the Lord, and believing in the Bible. So why are they not active church members? Idealists are temporarily (or permanently) "dislocated" because they have an idealized image of the church or an idealized image of the type of person one must be in order to be a "good Christian." Either the church is not "good enough" for them or they are not "good enough" for the church.

For idealists, life is less a struggle than it is an effort to find the "right way" to believe and behave—to identify the correct rules and follow them without regard to competing alternatives. The problem for idealists is that life circumstances create problems that may not allow strict adherence to the rules. The tension that results may prompt a transformation of one sort or another, in which the individual adopts a new course of action that is designed to "make things right." Alternatively, the idealist may engage in a subtle reinterpretation of the unchanging rule book in order to justify behavior that may seem to violate some of its rules.

Helen Myers is fifty-seven years old and a marginal Methodist from northern Georgia. She was brought up a Baptist, and her first break from the church occurred in her early twenties when she left home, moved to St. Louis, and met a man who she said "literally, one night just simply drove me to a motel" and had sex with her. She never married the man or lived with him, but continued to sleep with him for 14 years, "because I thought I was already ruined." This difficult situation ended when Helen moved to Miami, where she started a new life. She married a Methodist man who was not a regular church-goer himself, had a daughter, and joined a Methodist church. She was very active and "regularly went out on visitation on Wednesday nights." But she quit going when her daughter was still a small child. Helen says, "I will tell you why we quit going to church. Because my husband would berate me every single Sunday . . . like get the daughter ready, make sure the house was ready to leave. Everything. Everything was left on me, and all he had to do was get himself ready and yell at me. So I just thought, forget it." Helen has not returned to active church participation.

For Rhoda, a very devout young woman who was reared in the Assemblies of God, the problem is not personal moral failure or a difficult spouse. Rhoda has a serious problem with—not her own unrighteousness, but—the hypocrisy of church people. She says, "I feel very uncomfortable praying in front of other people, and especially when a majority of those people are doing things that aren't so

Christian-like." Rhoda knows her user's manual well and chooses to stress certain parts of it rather than others. She observes, "the ideal church for me would be here in my home. You see, that's what church is. It's not the building. It's the group of people. It says so in the Bible, or at least that's what I was taught. The church is the congregation, not the building . . . so why not stay at home and pray when you want to pray, believe what you want to believe, and teach your children what you really think is important for them to know."

Idealists from mainline denominations rarely talk about the specific content of their strongly held belief. Helen, for example, trusts in what she calls "blind faith." She says "if I didn't believe in just blind faith in God I wouldn't be able to be anywhere or do anything. It's just blind faith. . . . He is my source of faith and comfort. He is my source of living basically." Truth is permanent; truth is given; truth is exogenous for the idealist. The nature of that truth is determined, therefore, by the authoritative source that handed it down. Idealists are very suspicious of anything that is new or novel. And this is particularly true for idealists with evangelical or fundamentalist church backgrounds. John, a Church of Christ idealist living in Arizona, remarks, "I already believe in God. I already believe in Jesus Christ. I already believe in the Holy Ghost. So when you start introducing some other concept into that I go, wait a minute, this came after."

Idealists have bought the old church rules for belief and conduct to the letter—and they have followed the strategy of action that they believe those rules allow. As might be expected, idealists have a relatively limited set of tools in their cultural toolkits—and one that is included is a big, active religious hammer. Rigid rules about faith and practice get pounded home through their more traditional subcultural worlds. Many are rural; isolated in urban enclaves; or simply "retrenched" in the face of change. As noted above, idealists are not innovators; innovation, in fact, would be heresy.

Persons with a conservative, idealistic, traditional orientation are overrepresented among the *churched* rather than the unchurched. Individuals with this orientation tend to remain in the church. Conservative Protestants tend to have more of them (both among the churched and unchurched), whereas Methodists have proportionately more than other mainline Protestants.

Disengaged seekers are disproportionately from the baby boom generation, but are found among all age groups. They tend to be highly educated and hold fairly liberal social and political values and beliefs. They are typically married, settled, and disproportionately female.

Seekers have a fairly strong religious biography: most went to church at least up until high school. Many tell stories of very vivid religious experiences. Janice Jones, a widow living in a high-priced condominium in Scottsdale, Arizona, described a spiritual awakening in which "I had a flash go through my body." On an Easter morning, she woke up and she says, "the words to the Lord's prayer came rushing out and I had no control." Another, a female lumberjack from rural Georgia, recalls: "I have always believed in God. As a child, very little, I can remember having conversations with God." Her bookcase is literally filled with a variety of volumes on world religions, native American spirituality, numerology, and Edgar Cayce.

Melissa Hayes, a housewife and mother of three children, explains that her first exposure to the "knowledge of God" came through Methodist Sunday school but her "Damascus Road" experience did not occur until years later. In college, she read the Bible while she was taking heavy doses of crystal methamphetamine, and "under the influence of this high vibrational drug . . . the Bible came alive. I mean I was an instant believer because it literally created revelations. Granted, they were drug revelations, and they [came] too soon for the rest of me to handle, but the revelations were real. They were your basic, universal truths." Melissa says that it was "the beginning of the real substance-building, the beginning of the real healing."

Not all seekers experience supernatural visitations or had drug-induced spiritual revelations, of course, but they do speak of new insights and understandings that allowed them to make sense of their lives. For instance, Sarah Becker, a long-time Congregationalist who rarely attends church, talks about the fact that "I have seen the light in many ways." And Robin, a high-school-educated secretary for a union hall in Connecticut, developed a her own theory of transformations, in which a person moves from one "zone" to another. She says, "there are different areas, different realms, different zones in closeness to God . . . and you can go one way and forget it, or you can go another and stay with it . . . [and move to] a big zone where every adult should be."

Seekers are intolerant only of intolerance. They abhor judgment, condemnation, and any type of guilt-motivated religion. According to Sarah, "original sin is original crock." Their open, liberal attitudes when combined with a strong attraction toward a holistic faith produce an unusual social profile. Seekers say they are *both* spiritual and religious persons (67%); they believe in life after death (78%), and they commune through God through nature (98%). At the same time, seekers tend to believe that abortion is right, that homosexuality is right or morally gray, and that the Bible has errors. They are spiritually-oriented, but liberal minded people who in Melissa's terms are interested in something "beyond dualistic kinds of beliefs."

Seekers like Melissa, and women seekers in general, seem to have little trouble finding ways to practice their spirituality outside a traditional mainline or evangelical church. Melissa attends the Unity church now and then, engages in discussions with a woman friend she calls her "metaphysical Avon lady," and is a voracious reader of New Age literature. And Sarah Becker, for instance, remains "involved in the church in a non-Sunday-morning way. I designed T-shirts for the [church's] peace award." Sarah and her husband are also very involved in local community politics. She adds, "to think globally, act locally, that's a slogan that I take to heart. And I think that doing things that follow a way of life that the faith suggests [is]at least as important as showing up and hearing a sermon about it."

Seekers have a cultural toolkit with an unlimited variety of tools—including religious tools. Their interest in religious tools is largely due to their baseline church experience. So in a sense, you could say that spiritual seekers have retained at least some portion of the "user's manual" from their mostly mainline and Pentecostal church traditions. Those cultural "outfitters" taught them to appreciate and value religious experience and the power and presence of the supernatural. And now, the pluralization of social life has presented them with a host of religious and spiritual possibilities to explore. And to the extent that they are not permitted or encouraged to do so in the church, they have sought new religious tools elsewhere. And with new tools come permutations of older rules: seekers are innovators. They are armchair philosophers and creators of homemade theologies. And most are still seeking.

Interestingly, Methodists are the only denominational group that keeps a disproportionate number of its seeker-types. Mainline Protestants, on the other hand, have proportionately more seekers but also lose more to unchurched status.

Conclusions

More than any other denominational group, *churched* Methodists are characterized by their enduring sense of institutional and/or ideological loyalty. Not surprisingly, then, the largest groups among churched Methodists in our sample (and the groups they are most likely to keep)—the seeker and idealist types—both have a lot of baseline church experience and a positive orientation to religion. On the other hand, those who tend to stray from the Methodist fold (the *unchurched* or marginally churched Methodists) are strikingly anti-institutional: either because they lack much baseline exposure or because of a generalized skepticism (if not cynicism) about the answers that their Methodist churches/upbringing purported to give for the problems of daily living. In the context of cultural and institutional unsettlement, churched Methodists are religious loyalists. But they are loyalists who are dramatically divided on their stance toward modernity. Seeker-types are innovators and future-oriented; they want to engage and incorporate social change. Idealist-types are conservative and past-oriented; they want to cling to tradition, particularly Methodist tradition. The self-projects of these types are on two different trajectories, which makes for intra-denominational conflict.

Our research indicates that Methodists who are outside the church tend to be the wayward children of marginally churched parents. Disenfranchised pragmatists don't really know the church very well and, consequently, don't see where it could fit into their busy, career and leisure-oriented lives. And if institutional loyalty marks "stayers" (or churched Methodists) then a generation of less active youth is a significant problem for Methodism. But unchurched Methodists also include serious, analytical questioners—disaffected skeptics—whom, interestingly enough, Presbyterians and Congregationalists tend to retain. Should both groups of "missing Methodists" simply be written off? Probably not. They tell us a lot about what the denomination has been, but at the same time they may hold important clues to what institutional religion might (yet) become. In fact, the practical, present-orientation of currently disenfranchised pragmatists and the self-reflective, sober (and ironic) orientation of disaffected skeptics might be just the kind of leavening influence needed in the Methodist church's present negotiation with change—a struggle between future and past.

In the dynamic context of late modernity, then, how can institutions begin to think about members and potential members in different ways? The real challenge in any process of retooling is getting "employees" (clergy, laity) to think in different ways (Abelson 1991: 176). Let us suggest that knowing what is going on in the minds and lives of the people is crucial. What cultural resources are individuals drawing on? What strategies of action are they building? Only by understanding these complex, but very adaptive, processes can traditional institutions reach individuals and begin to fill what we think is the "new role" for traditional institutions in a very nontraditional world, namely, helping individuals go about their project of cultural "outfitting" by supporting them in building strategies of action or competencies. Again, it is no longer a case of telling persons *what* to believe and what to do but helping them figure out in the face of a dizzying array of options *how* to choose their beliefs and live authentically (Marler 1994; Hirschhorn and Gilmore 1992:105).

TABLE 1
CHURCHED AND UNCHURCHED PROTESTANTS

	Churched			Unchurched		
	Conserv. (N=681)	Methodist (N=196)	Mainline (N=303)	Conserv. (N=271)	Methodist (N=88)	Mainline (N=186)
Religious Heritage						
Said grace at home as child (%)	81	82	74	77	72	68
Attended youth programs; church camps (%)	42	55	47	27	31	31
Father never attended church (%)	23	18	24	37	45	38
Mother attended every week (%)	58	63	57	47	25	41
Religious Reactions						
Church worship is not boring (%)	70	63	56	46	31	44
Churches help provide meaning (%)	70	73	68	66	54	64
Do not feel guilty when miss church (%)	35	40	51	51	74	75
Attended enough in lifetime (%)	9	11	18	22	40	23
Religious Orientation						
Extremely close to God (%)	56	45	45	31	25	18
Call God "Father" (%)	76	66	64	58	52	44
Say Bible is all true (%)	80	48	41	62	24	20
Don't have to attend to be good Christian (%)	53	76	74	86	96	96
Don't have to give to be good Christian (%)	44	48	56	72	67	82
Religious Practice						
Say grace before meals now (%)	92	90	80	69	60	53
Read liturgical prayers aloud (%)	30	44	48	23	16	19
Regular discipline of prayer (%)	65	54	54	29	25	23
Read devotional literature (%)	71	67	57	48	30	27
Experimented w/ astrology; crystals (%)	6	6	9	8	15	15

TABLE 2
DISTRIBUTION OF MAINLINE UNCHURCHED BY SELECTED VALUES

	Pragmatists (N=55)	Skeptics (N=40)	Idealists (N=27)	Seekers (N=38)	Prob.
		Unchurched Styles			
Religious Heritage					
Enjoyed church when growing up	39%	68%	89%	72%	.01
Prayed alone in teens (some or often)	55%	35%	80%	69%	.00
Attitudes and Social Background					
Homosexuality is right or morally gray	87%	42%	30%	69%	.00
Abortion is right	47%	59%	33%	62%	.00
Did not call any issue morally gray	8%	40%	56%	16%	.00
Divorced or never married	76%	20%	48%	27%	.00
College Graduate or more	58%	25%	7%	53%	.00
4+ moves in past decade	55%	8%	27%	15%	.00
Religious Orientation					
Religious & Spiritual	39%	25%	56%	67%	.00
Had a religious experience	13%	10%	56%	53%	.00
Say religious faith is very important	22%	20%	70%	47%	.00
Religious Belief/Traditionalism					
Believe in life after death	55%	27%	78%	78%	.00
Call God "Father"	47%	43%	74%	26%	.00
Say Bible is all true	0%	24%	56%	7%	.00
Say can't just believe in something greater	18%	25%	70%	11%	.00
Feel guilty when miss church	8%	17%	70%	16%	.00
Religious Practice					
Read Bible at home in past year	33%	16%	63%	47%	.01
Watch religious TV (some or often)	37%	30%	89%	46%	.00
Commune with God through nature	42%	32%	59%	98%	.00
Explored Native American spirituality	27%	5%	15%	64%	.00

TABLE 3
DISTRIBUTION OF UNCHURCHED PROTESTANTS

	Pragmatists (N=46)	Skeptics (N=86)	Idealists (N=112)	Seekers (N=74)
Percent of Unchurched				
Conservative Protestants	8	20	63	9
Methodists	15	27	29	29
Mainline Protestants	23	25	13	39
Difference Between Churched and Unchurched Proportion				
Conservative Protestants	+5	+16	-24	+3
Methodists	+6	+16	-19	-4
Mainline Protestants	+13	+2	-21	+6

References

Abelson, Reed. 1991. "Retooled." *Forbes*, 28 May 1991, 172–76.

Berger, Peter. 1977. "In Praise of Particularity: The Concept of Mediating Structures." Pp. 130–47 in *Facing Up to Modernity*. New York: Basic Books.

———.1992. *A Far Glory: The Quest for Faith in an Age of Credulity*. New York: Anchor Books.

Beyer, Peter. 1994. *Religion and Globalization*. London: Sage Publications.

Bradley, Martin B., et al. 1992. *Churches and Church Membership in the United States 1990*. Atlanta: Glenmary Research Center.

Davis, James A., and Tom W. Smith. 1988. *General Social Survey, 1988* [MRDF]. Chicago: National Opinion Research Center.

———. 1990. *General Social Surveys, 1972–1990* [MRDF]. Chicago: National Opinion Research Center.

Drucker, Peter. 1992. "The New Society of Organizations." *Harvard Business Review*, September-October, 95–104.

Duck, Jeannie Daniel. 1993. "Managing Change: The Art of Balancing." *Harvard Business Review*, November-December, 109–14.

Giddens, Anthony. 1990. *The Consequences of Modernity*. Stanford, CA: Stanford University Press.

———. 1991. *Modernity and Self-Identity: Self and Society in the Modern Age*. Stanford, CA: Stanford University Press.

———. 1994. "Living in a Post-Traditional Society." In *Reflexive Modernization,* by Ulrich Beck, Anthony Giddens, and Scott Lash. Stanford: Stanford University Press.

Hadaway, C. Kirk, Penny Long Marler, and Mark Chaves. 1993. "What the Polls Don't Show: A Closer Look at U.S. Church Attendance." *American Sociological Review* 58:741–752.

Hirschhorn, Larry, and Thomas Gilmore. 1992. "The New Boundaries of the 'Boundaryless' Company." *Harvard Business Review*, May-June, 104–15.

Hudson, Winthrop. 1961. *American Protestantism*. Chicago: University of Chicago Press.

———. 1981. *Religion in America, Third Edition*. New York: Charles Scribner's Sons.

Marler, Penny Long. 1995. "Lost in the Fifties: The Changing Family and the Nostalgic Church." In *Work, Family and Religion in Contemporary Society,* ed. Nancy T. Ammerman and Wade Clark Roof. New York: Routledge.

———. 1994. "Rethinking the Unchurched." David O. Moberg Lectureship, Bethel Theological Seminary.

Marler, Penny Long, and C. Kirk Hadaway. 1993. "Toward a Typology of Protestant Marginal Members." *Review of Religious Research* 35:53–73.

Mead, Frank S., and Samuel S. Hill. 1990. *Handbook of Denominations in the United States, New Ninth Edition.* Nashville: Abingdon.

Moore, Thomas. 1992. *Care of the Soul.* New York: HarperCollins.

Norwood, Frederick A. 1974. *The Story of American Methodism.* Nashville: Abingdon.

Putnam, Robert. 1995. "Bowling Alone: America's Declining Social Capital." *Journal of Democracy* 6:65–78.

Roof, Wade Clark, and William McKinney. 1987. *American Mainline Religion.* New Brunswick, NJ: Rutgers University Press.

Stark, Rodney, and Charles Y. Glock. 1968. *American Piety.* Berkeley: University of California Press.

Swidler, Ann. 1986. "Culture in Action: Symbols and Strategies." *American Sociological Review* 51:273–86.

Walrath, Douglas. 1987. *Frameworks.* New York: Pilgrim.

Contributors

Penny Edgell Becker is Assistant Professor in the Department of Sociology at Cornell University, in Ithaca, New York. Her most recent publication was "Congregational Models and Conflict: A Study of How Institutions Shape Organizational Process," in *Sacred Companies: Organized Aspects of Religion and Religious Aspects of Organization*, edited by Jay Demerath, Peter Dobkin Hall, Terry Schmitt, and Rhys H. Williams (Oxford University Press, 1996). A forthcoming book is entitled *How We Do Things Here: Culture and Conflict in Local Congregations* (Cambridge University Press, 1997). Dr. Becker's fields of interests are in the sociology of religion, the sociology of culture, organizational theory, and gender.

William J. Everett is the Herbert Gezork Professor of Christian Social Ethics at Andover Newton Theological School, in Newton Centre, Massachusetts. He has taught ethics and ecclesiology in Roman Catholic and Protestant seminaries in Milwaukee, Atlanta, Heidelberg, and Bangalore. He has also been a consultant to Methodist, Baptist, Lutheran, Catholic, and ecumenical organizations on political ethics, ecology, church mission, and organization. Parts of his co-authored essay in this volume will appear in his latest book, *Religion, Federalism, and the Struggle for Public Life: Cases from Germany, India, and America* (Oxford University Press, 1997).

Thomas E. Frank is Associate Professor of Church Administration and Congregational Life at Candler School of Theology, Emory University, in Atlanta, Georgia. He directs the Rollins Center for Church Ministries, conducting research and consultations on the identity and mission of local church congregations. Dr. Frank's primary interest is the history, congregational life, and organizational culture of mainstream Protestant denominations. His most recent book is *Polity, Practice, and the Mission of the United Methodist Church*. He also authored *Theology, Ethics, and the Nineteenth Century American College Ideal: Conserving a Rational World*.

C. Kirk Hadaway is Minister for Research and Evaluation for the United Church Board of Homeland Ministries (UCC). A sociologist, he is based in Cleveland, Ohio. He formerly conducted research for the Southern Baptist Convention. His previous publications include articles in *American Sociological Review*, in the *Journal for the Scientific Study of*

Religion, and in many other journals. He is the author of *What Can We Do About Church Drop-Outs?* and he is co-author of *Re-routing the Protestant Mainstream: Sources of Growth and Opportunities for Change.*

Richard P. Heitzenrater is Professor of Church History and Wesley Studies at The Divinity School, Duke University, in Durham, North Carolina. He chaired the writing committee of the Committee on Our Theological Task that wrote the present doctrinal statement in Part II of *The Book of Discipline.* Dr. Heitzenrater's published works include *Wesley and the People Called Methodists* and *The Elusive Mr. Wesley.* He is the general editor of the Wesley Works project.

Sarah Sloan Kreutziger serves as the Director of Continuing Education and Assistant Professor for the Tulane School of Social Work, in New Orleans, Louisiana. Her research and teaching interests are the impact of women's spirituality and religious beliefs on American values, ethics, and social institutions. She provides crisis intervention and therapy for individuals and families in the areas of health care and substance abuse. Dr. Kreutziger's most recent publication was an article entitled "Spirituality in Faith," in *Reflections* 1, no. 4, (Fall 1995).

Bradley James Longfield is Associate Professor of Church History at the University of Dubuque Theological Seminary, in Dubuque, Iowa. His teaching interests are the history of Christianity, American church history, and historical theology. Dr. Longfield's most recent publication was *The Secularization of the Academy,* coedited with George M. Marsden.

Penny Long Marler is Assistant Professor of Religion and Philosophy at Samford University, in Birmingham, Alabama. She is co-principal investigator in a study, "Church Attendance and Membership in Four Nations: A Comparative, Historical Study of 'Gaps,' Discrepancies and Change," funded by the Lilly Endowment, Inc. Dr. Marler's most recent publication was "Four Styles of Religious Marginality" in *Mobilizing Community Ministry: Case Studies of Caring Congregations,* edited by Gary Tobin and Amy Sales.

William B. McClain is Professor of Homiletics and Worship at Wesley Theological Seminary, in Washington, D.C. His areas of interest are Western studies in homiletics, African American church history, and Wesleyan studies. Dr. McClain conceived and wrote much of the introductory material for *Songs of Zion,* a book of religious songs from the African American tradition. He subsequently published its liturgical companion, *Come Sunday: The Liturgy of Zion.* He also coedited *Heritage and Hope: The African American Presence in Methodism* with Grant S. Shockley and Karen Y. Collier.

Robert C. Monk began his career as a United Methodist campus minister and has served as Professor of Religion at McMurry University, in Abilene, Texas since 1964. Dr. Monk's most recent publications were two articles in *The Historical Dictionary of Methodism* (1995). His special interests are in church history and the history of Christian thought, with a concentration in seventeenth- and eighteenth-century British and American church history. Dr. Monk is an ordained Methodist minister in the Northwest Texas Conference.

Kenneth E. Rowe is Professor of Church History and Librarian at the Methodist Archives and History Center, Drew University, in Madison, New Jersey. His latest book is *The Methodists*, coauthored with James Kirby and Russell Richey. He is also the general editor of the American Theological Library Association monograph series.

Robert W. Sledge is a professor of history at McMurry University, in Abilene, Texas. He served as president of the Historical Society of the United Methodist Church from 1989 to 1993. Dr. Sledge presently serves as chair of the Texas United Methodist Historical Society. He is the author of *Hands on the Ark* and most recently coauthored and edited *Pride of Our Western Prairies*.

Mark W. Wethington is Pastor of Duke Memorial United Methodist Church, in Durham, North Carolina, and Adjunct Instructor at Duke University Divinity School, where he teaches on the nature and mission of the church. He chairs the North Carolina-Peru Covenant Task Force, which is developing a new paradigm for missions, and he leads teams of lay and clergy to Peru, as well as preaches and teaches among the Methodists of Peru.

Charles E. Zech is a professor of economics at Villanova University, in Villanova, Pennsylvania. His area of expertise is the economics of religious organizations. He has published many articles on the subject, and is coauthor of *The Mainline Church's Funding Crisis: Issues and Possibilities* and *Money Matters: Personal Giving in American Churches*.

Editors

Russell E. Richey is Professor of Church History at The Divinity School, Duke University, in Durham, North Carolina. Dr. Richey is a member of the Historical Society of the United Methodist Church and the American Society of Church History. He is the author of *The Methodist Conference in America* and coauthor with James Kirby and Kenneth Rowe of *The Methodists*. Dr. Richey is codirector of United Methodism and American Culture.

Dennis M. Campbell was Dean of The Divinity School and is Professor of Theology, Duke University. Dr. Campbell has served as President of the Association of United Methodist Theological Schools since 1992. He is the author of *Who Will Go For Us? An Invitation to Ordained Ministry* and *The Yoke of Obedience*. Dr. Campbell is co-director of United Methodism and American Culture.

William B. Lawrence is a professor of the practice of Christian ministry and Associate Director of the J. M. Ormond Center for Research, Planning, and Development at The Divinity School, Duke University. He has served as Project Associate for this study of United Methodism and American Culture. He is the author of *Sundays in New York: Pulpit Theology at the Crest of the Protestant Mainstream, 1930–1955*.

Notes

Notes to "INTRODUCTION"

1. See Donald T. Kauffman, *The Dictionary of Religious Terms* (Westwood, N.J.: Fleming H. Revell, 1967).

2. Certainly one important exception is the UCC, which, on its Puritan or Congregational side, combined elements of the Radical and Magisterial Reformations in complex fashion. American Puritanism sought to be both congregational and established. Until well after the Revolution, the Congregational Churches were established in New England.

3. One would need to concede that these distinctions are handy and somewhat arbitrary. No church now behaves in a more centralized, coercive, connectional way than the Southern Baptist Convention. And all connectional churches have had to come to terms with localism and a congregationalist mentality, particularly within the flock.

4. The connectional background for the Evangelical and United Brethren traditions is more complex, showing some indebtedness to Wesley; having deeper roots in the Magisterial Reformation (Lutheran and Reformed respectively); but betraying as well the critiques mounted by Pietism and Anabaptism.

5. The essays devoted to the Evangelical and United Brethren heritages appear in other volumes.

6. They titled the minutes of the first conference thus: "Minutes of Some Conversations between the Preachers in Connexion with The Reverend Mr. John Wesley. Philadelphia, June, 1773," *Minutes of the Methodist Conferences, Annually Held in America; From 1773 to 1813, Inclusive* (New York: Daniel Hitt and Thomas Ware for the Methodist Connexion in the United States, 1813), 5–6.

7. Article XIII.—Of the Church, *The Book of Discipline of The United Methodist Church, 1992* (Nashville: The United Methodist Publishing House, 1992), 61. Thankfully that is now buttressed by the richer and more Wesleyan article from "The Confession of Faith of the Evangelical United Brethren Church," Article V.—The Church, 66, and by the other Disciplinary renderings that bear on ecclesiology, "Historical Statement," 9–20; "Our Doctrinal Heritage," 40–49; "Our Doctrinal History," 49–58; "The General Rules," 71–73; "Our Theological Task," 74–84; "Mission Statement," 85–86; "Social Principles," 87–107; and "The Ministry of all Christians," 108–15.

Given this rich theological array in the Discipline, we could and ought to recognize connectionalism's ecclesiological force. The resources are at hand and readily combined.

8. John Miley, one of American Methodism's early systematic theologians, positioned his discussion of the church under soteriology, affirming:

> As the Church is divinely constituted for the work of evangelization and the spiritual edification of believers, and also contains the divinely instituted means for the attainment of these ends, it may properly be treated in connection with soteriology.

John Miley, *Systematic Theology*, 2 vols. (New York: Hunt & Eaton, 1892; reprint, Peabody, Mass.: Hendrickson, 1989), II, 385.

9. For assessments of Methodism's working, see Nathan O. Hatch, *The Democratization of American Christianity* (New Haven and London: Yale University Press, 1989) and Roger Finke and Rodney Stark, *The Churching of America, 1776–1990* (New Brunswick: Rutgers University Press, 1992). The latter measures Methodist success by the numbers, by membership statistics, a mode of assessment to which Methodists themselves inclined. A more appropriate gauge of the success or fidelity of connectionalism, we suggest, would draw on each of these eight points. After all, the period of greatest and fastest Methodist growth came as it embraced slavery and was not expressive of Methodism's better self-understanding, mission, ideals and commitment—a point made eloquently here by William B. McClain.

10. A different statement of the argument of this paragraph can be found in "The Legacy of Francis Asbury: The Teaching Office in Episcopal Methodism," *Quarterly Review*. The section as a whole depends on *The Methodist Conference in America: A History* (Nashville: Kingswood Books 1996) and *Early American Methodism* (Bloomington and Indianapolis: Indiana University Press, 1991).

11. For the levels of dependence upon and independence from the Methodist Episcopal pattern in the United Brethren and Evangelical Association, see J. Bruce Behney and Paul H. Eller, *The History of the Evangelical United Brethren Church*, ed. Kenneth W. Krueger (Nashville: Abingdon, 1979).

12. Minton Thrift, *Memoir of the Rev. Jesse Lee. With Extracts from his Journals* (New York: N. Bangs and T. Mason for the Methodist Episcopal Church, 1823), 48–60. From the itinerant's angle, his own "liberty" keyed the process. Hence the constant assessment of whether the word was preached and heard:

> "Sunday 7th of March, I preached at Robert Jones', to a serious congregation, and blessed be God, it was a happy time, and the Lord was among us of a truth."

> "I continued to preach with much liberty. . . ."

> "Sunday 4th, I preached at Robert Jones', to a serious company of people, and had liberty among them. . . ." (Ibid., 59–60).

> [June] "Sunday 20th, I preached at Coles, but [as] the congregation was so large, that the house would not hold them, of course we had to look for another

place; we got under the shade of some trees, where I spoke with great freedom, and with a heart drawn out in love to the souls of the people; and I felt a longing desire to be instrumental in bringing their souls to God. When I met the class, the friends wept greatly, while they heard each other tell of the goodness of God to their souls" (Ibid., 65–66).

13. The second edition of the *Discipline*, printed with *The Sunday Service of the Methodist in North America* (London, 1786), ran to twenty-nine pages.

14. See the extended discussion and documentation in *Early American Methodism* [n. 10 above].

15. "Minutes for 1780," *Minutes of the Methodist Conferences, Annually Held in America; From 1773 to 1813, Inclusive* [n. 6 above], 26.

16. John Ffirth, *The Experience and Gospel Labours of the Rev. Benjamin Abbott*, published by Ezekiel Cooper (Philadelphia: Solomon W. Conrad, 1802), 164–66.

17. George Coles, *My First Seven Years in America*, ed. D. P. Kidder (New York: Carlton & Phillips, 1852), 49–52.

18. George Peck, ed., *Sketches & Incidents; or A Budget from the Saddle-Bags of a Superannuated Itinerant* (New York: G. Lane and P. P. Sandford for the MEC, 1844–45; reprint, Salem, Ohio: Schmul, 1988), 101. The reflection is attributed to Abel Stevens. Compare another retrospective, also reported by Peck:

> His quarterly meeting was on Lycoming circuit. It was held in a barn, and the meeting was highly favored of the Lord. In those days there was seldom a quarterly meeting held where there were not souls converted. The Methodists would attend from every part of the circuit. Twenty, or thirty, and even fifty miles was not so far off but they would make an effort to attend, and look upon it as a great privilege to go to quarterly meeting. They would come on horseback through the woods, and from the settlements and towns in their great old-fashioned wagons, drawn by oxen very often, and crowded full; sometimes they would come down the river in canoes. They came with hearts alive to God, and every one was ambitious of excelling in getting nearest to, and in doing most for God and truth.
>
> Consequently many sinners were converted before the meeting closed. Such exhortations and prayers, such shouting, for old-fashioned Methodists would shout. Their thorough enjoyment, their genuine tokens of holy delight, their ready responses, always expressed in a hearty manner, bore the preacher onward to success. To preach tamely before such an audience would be an impossibility. No Christian could slumber in such a vivifying atmosphere, no aspirations became weary, no ardor grow cold. (George Peck, *Early Methodism Within the Bounds of the Old Genesee Conference from 1788 to 1828* [New York: Carlton & Porter, 1860], 419–20)

This account was of a quarterly meeting in 1814 at Painted Post, on the northern Pennsylvania border, for George Harmon, p.e. on Susquehanna District, and was rendered by Harmon's daughter.

19. The representative, delegative, republican, political style of connection might well be introduced and developed here. It clearly has early origins, indeed, roots in typically American patterns of political behavior that Methodists began drawing into their religious life from the 1760s onward. I choose to focus on this style of conference not in this early "republican" stage or during the formative phases of the Methodist Protestant movement, but in the twentieth century. A good case can be made, I concede, for introducing what Frank and Everett term the "federal" style at this point.

20. Nathan Bangs, *An Original Church of Christ: Or, A Scriptural Vindication of the Orders and Powers of the Ministry of the Methodist Episcopal Church,* published by T. Mason and G. Lane (New York: J. Collord, 1837), 348–51. Bangs continued:

> This is a general outline of the system, the different parts of which have grown out of the exigencies of the times, suiting itself to the mental, moral, and spiritual wants of men, and expanding itself so as to embrace the largest possible number of individuals as objects of its benevolence. I may well be suspected of partiality to a system, to the benign operation of which I am so much indebted, and which has exerted such a beneficial influence upon the best interests of mankind; but I cannot avoid thinking that I see in it that "perfection of beauty, out of which God hath shined," and that emanation of divine truth and light, which is destined, unless it should unhappily degenerate from its primitive beauty and simplicity "into a plant of a strange vine," and thus lose its original energy of character, to do its full share in enlightening and converting the world.

21. A. J. Kynett, "Report of the General Board of Church Extension." *Journal of the General Conference of the Methodist Episcopal Church,* 1876, 602–4.

22. "Report of Committee on Benevolent Societies," *Journal of the General Conference of the Methodist Episcopal Church,* 1872, 295–98.

23. In very recent years, the Council of Bishops has begun to take important leadership initiatives as a council, a point I wish to acknowledge here and that I treat more fully in the *QR* essay previously mentioned [n. 10 above].

24. See *The Methodist Conference in America: A History* [n. 10 above], 145–74.

25. For discussion of changes in denominational life see Milton J. Coalter, John M. Mulder and Louis B. Weeks, *The Re-forming Tradition: Presbyterians and Mainstream Protestantism* (Louisville: Westminster/John Knox, 1992), *Reimagining Denominationalism: Interpretive Essays,* ed. Robert Bruce Mullin and Russell E. Richey (New York: Oxford University Press, 1994), and especially Richey, "Denominations and Denominationalism: An American Morphology."

Notes to "CONNECTIONALISM AND ITINERANCY"

1. In addition to my own research, I have benefited from using the "word list" prepared on tens of thousands of slips of paper by George Lawton, which he used as the basis for his study, *John Wesley's English: A Study of his Literary*

Style (London: Allen & Unwin, 1962). The entries on the slips represent a virtual concordance of the Wesleyan corpus. I have also used another extensive collection of note slips (numbering also in the tens of thousands) prepared by Albert Outler and Wanda Smith during the last thirty years of his lifetime, arranged by topic, phrase, person, etc.

2. See his letter to Vincent Perronet, published as "A Plain Account of the People Called Methodists" (1748); in *The Methodist Societies* (hereinafter *Societies*), vol. 9 of *The Bicentennial Edition of the Works of John Wesley* (Nashville: Abingdon, 1989), 259. Wesley defines his understanding of Christian fellowship (or "connexion") in the sentences immediately preceding these: "Which of those true Christians had any such fellowship with these? Who watched over them in love? Who marked their growth in grace? Who advised and exhorted them from time to time? Who prayed with them and for them as they had need? This, and this alone, is Christian fellowship; but, alas! where is it to be found?" This intentional nurturing, especially by leaders, became the hallmark of the Methodist fellowship.

3. This projected program was the result of a chance meeting of three Johns—Wesley, Robson, Gambold (all Oxford Methodists) on November 12, 1739. At that time, Wesley himself was active only in the Bristol, London, and Oxford areas. Their quarterly meetings were to be on the second Tuesday in July, October, and January. The list of recruits included Westley Hall, Benjamin Ingham, John Hutchings, Kinchin, Stonehouse, Sympson (all Oxford Methodists), as well as Jacob Rogers, John Cennick, William Oxlee, John Browne, and other spiritual friends who were able and willing to join with them.

4. See, for instance, his comments in "A Short History of Methodism," in *Societies* 9:370–72.

5. He understood these "outward ordinances" to be specific means by which not only "the inward grace of God is ordinarily conveyed to man" but also means by which "the faith that brings salvation is conveyed to them who before had it not." See Sermon 16, "The Means of Grace," in *Sermons*, vols. 1–4 of *The Works of John Wesley* (Bicentennial ed.; Nashville: Abingdon, 1984–1987), 1:376–97. See also *Minutes of the Methodist Conferences* (London: Conference Office, 1862), 1:549–57, on "instituted" and "prudential" means of grace.

6. *Journal and Diaries* (hereafter *J&D*), in *Works* (Bicentennial ed.), 19:332–33 for the text of this memorandum.

7. These included Richard Viney, a Moravian layman from Oxford, and Thomas Meriton, a clergyman from the Isle of Man who had Calvinist leanings.

8. See *J&D* 19:116–18, 220–24 (Extract 4, preface and epilogue).

9. The sermon on "Catholic Spirit" represents one of Wesley's better known attempts to deal with the question of diversity within the body of Christ, entailing the necessity to distinguish between "essentials" and matters of "opinion." While the occasion for the writing of the sermon and the "Letter to a

Roman Catholic" may have been the problem of theological differences with Catholicism, the principles stated there seem also to be applicable to the issue of diversity within any segment of the Church, including Methodism itself, where the identification and reinforcement of the essentials was crucial.

10. For many years, nearly all of the leaders as well as preachers were personally appointed by Wesley himself.

11. An interesting example of Wesley's enforcement of discipline involved an attendance rule—members must attend a certain number of class meetings each quarter (at one time eleven), otherwise they were liable to expulsion, *and* the preacher was liable for expulsion if he did not enforce this rule.

12. Most of the uses of this terminology in his writings refer to the preachers as being in connection with him. At times, it is stated as "in connection with us," usually implying the inclusion of Charles. A few times, the phrase "in the connection" is used, implying the whole movement.

13. *The Journal of the Rev. Charles Wesley*, ed. by Thomas Jackson, 2 vols. (London: John Mason, 1849), 2:86 (hereafter *CWJ*).

14. *Minutes* 1:203; *JWL* 8:190.

15. *The Letters of the Rev. John Wesley*, ed. John Telford, 8 vols. (London: Epworth, 1931), 7:204 (January 10, 1784); hereafter *JWL*.

16. Charles Wesley's version of this covenant of the preachers in 1752 said that the signers would not speak ill of each other, and would abide in union with each other and the Church. The latter stipulation is based on Charles's expressed view that "there is no salvation out of the Church," *CWJ*, 2:116. The covenant was reaffirmed nearly every year for several years and fostered both unity and discipline.

17. Also signed in 1773 (49 of them), 1774 (72), 1775 (81).

18. The connectional collections and funds included the "penny subscriptions" at various times, based on the early ones such as that in 1741 in London for the relief of the poor and sick of the society and that in 1742 at Bristol to help JW pay the debt on New Room; the Circuit Fund (later Yearly Subscription) that helped with preachers' expenses; the Connectional Fund, for the relief of common debt or for relief of persecuted societies; the Kingswood Fund, for the education of the poor (both boys and girls) and children of preachers; the General Fund, to which every Methodist in England was to contribute something, primarily for the payment of debts on preaching-houses; the Preachers' Fund, to provide pensions for worn-out preachers, their widows and children; the Yearly Subscription (by 1767), the Methodist internal revenue system, based on a penny a week from everyone (those who could pay were expected to pay for those who could not) for the preachers' expenses; and the Contingent Fund, started in 1787 as a means of taking up the slack in supporting preachers' wives (this fund was supplemented by contributions from JW and Thomas Coke).

19. Sermon 88, "On Dress" (1786), ¶28: half-Methodists, "you that trim between us and the world, or that frequently, perhaps constantly, hear our preaching, but are in no farther connexion with us; yea, and all you that were once in full connexion with us but are not so now." *Sermons* 3:261.

20. *JWL* 8:205 (March 3, 1790), to friends in Trowbridge. The letter goes on, "But this can't be done unless the Conference, not the trustees, appoint all their preachers." He enclosed a copy of the Model Deed.

21. *Minutes* 1:608–10.

22. *J&D* 19:472. JW's interview with the Bishop of Bristol elicited this principle, best remembered by the phrase he used in a contemporary letter to John Clayton: "I look upon all the world as my parish." *Letters I*, in *Works* (Bicentennial ed.) 25:616 (March 28, 1739? see also his letter to his father, Dec. 1734).

23. See *Minutes* 1:28 (1745): "Go always, not only to those who want [need] you, but to those who want you most."

24. Half-itinerants were first listed as such in the 1753 *Minutes*; twelve were listed in 1755. They either traveled half the year (as William Shent, barber), or had another job (as Matthew Lowes, who sold veterinary medicine).

25. See his dispute with Charles over controlling the preachers by controlling or limiting their income, thus making them totally dependent. Charles sent a note to Lady Huntingdon (that was diverted first to JW), saying that if the preachers did not have to depend on John for bread, they stood a better chance of breaking his power and reducing his authority within due bounds, as well as helping to "guard against that rashness and credulity of his, which has kept me in continual awe and bondage for many years," *Letters II*, in *Works* (Bicentennial ed.) 26:479.

26. *JWL* 3:192 (Sept. 3, 1756), to J. Smith: "as the persons so qualified were few and those who wanted their assistance very many, it followed that most of these were obliged to travel continually from place to place; and this occasioned several regulations from time to time, which were chiefly made in our Conferences" (N.B.: *in*, not *by*).

27. *JWL* 8:83 (August 8, 1788), to Lady Maxwell; followed by, "But we cannot forsake the plan of acting which we have followed from the beginning. For fifty years God has been pleased to bless the itinerant plan."

28. *JWL* 7:86 (October 20, 1781), to C. Atmore: "But you must not stay there too long at a time. That is not the Methodist plan. I expect, therefore, Brother Johnson and you constantly to change once a quarter."

29. *J&D* 22:229 (May 12, 1770). See also *J&D* 22:408 (May 17, 1774): "How is it that there is no increase in this [Greenock] society? It is exceeding easy to answer. One preacher stays here two and three months at a time, preaching on Sunday mornings and three or four evenings in a week. Can a Methodist preacher preserve either bodily health or spiritual life with this exercise? And if

he is but half alive, what will the people be? Just so it is at Greenock too." See also *J&D* 23:306 (May 5, 1784): "In the evening, I talked largely with the preachers, and showed them the hurt it did both to them and the people for any one preacher to stay six or eight weeks together in one place. Neither can he find matter for preaching every morning and evening, nor will the people come to hear him. Hence he grows cold by lying in bed, and so do the people." (Twice a day for six to eight weeks equals 84 to 112 sermons, about the equivalent of two years of preaching once a week.)

30. *JWL*, 7:294 (Sept. 30, 1785), to Francis Asbury, on the question of whether or not preachers should stay in one place three years together: "I startle at this. It is a vehement alteration in the Methodist discipline. We have no such custom in England, Scotland, or Ireland. We except the Assistant, who stays a second, to stay more than [one year]." See *JWL* 3:194–95 (Sept. 3, 1756), to Samuel Walker: "Peter Jaco and Thomas Johnson have settled. Be their talents ever so great, they will ere long grow dead themselves, and so will most of those that hear them. I know, were I myself to preach one whole year in one place, I should preach both myself and most of my congregation asleep." See also *JWL* 5:94 (May 27, 1770), to Mrs. Bennis: "the preachers must change regularly. It would never do to let one man sit down for six months with a small society; he would soon preach himself and them as lifeless as stones."

31. *Minutes* 1:452 (1753 "Large" *Minutes*).

32. *Minutes* 1:37. See also the occasional heavy emphasis on field-preaching.

33. Sermon 107, "On God's Vineyard" (1787) II.6, in *Sermons* 3:510–11. After talking about the Conference and quoting Eph. 4:16 ["The whole body being fitly framed together, and compacted by that which every joint supplieth, maketh increase of the body, to the edifying of itself in love"], Wesley says, "That this may be the more effectually done, [the Methodists] have another excellent help in the constant change of preachers; it being their rule that no preacher shall remain in the same circuit more than two years together, and few of them more than one year. Some indeed have imagined that this was a hindrance to the work of God. But long experience in every part of the kingdom proves the contrary. This has always shown that the people profit less by any one person than by a variety of preachers; while they 'used the gifts on each bestowed, / Tempered by the art of God'" (*Hymns and Sacred Poems* [1740], 195).

34. *JWL* 8:337 (July 30, 1786), to Mr. Torry.

35. *JWL* 3:194–95 (Sept. 3, 1756), to Samuel Walker.

36. "Large" *Minutes* (1780), in *Minutes* 1:613.

37. *JWL* 8:161 (August 23, 1789). This was in the context of a dispute at Dewsbury; this letter calls for everyone "that wishes well to Methodism, especially to the itinerant plan, to exert himself on this important occasion."

38. *JWL* 8:52 (April 4, 1788), Printed Notice: "Great are the advantages we have reaped for many years from the continual change of preachers, but this

cannot subsist any longer than the places of all the preachers are appointed by one man or body of men. Therefore wherever trustees are to place and displace the preachers, this change, which we call itinerancy, is at an end. It is for your sakes, not my own, that I wish this may continue, and the appointment of preachers, which now lies upon me, be afterwards executed by the Conference, not the trustees of any of the houses. Is it possible that itinerancy should be continued by any other means?"

39. *JWL* 8:169 (Sept. 11, 1789), to the Methodist People.

40. *Societies*, 9:507–9 (The Case of Birstall House).

41. See his "Thoughts on Liberty," "Some Observations on Liberty," and "Thoughts Concerning the Origin of Power," in *The Works of John Wesley*, ed. Thomas Jackson (London, 1872), 11:34–53, 89–118.

42. Ibid., 11:41.

43. "You have nothing to do but to save souls. Therefore spend and be spent in this work," *Minutes* (1745) 1:28.

44. "Thoughts upon Methodism," ¶1, in *Societies*, 9:527.

Notes to "CONSTITUTIONAL ORDER"

1. See *The COCU Consensus. In Quest of a Church of Christ Uniting*, ed. Gerald F. Moede (Princeton: Consultation on Church Union, 1985).

2. Nathan O. Hatch, "The Puzzle of American Methodism," *Church History* 63:2 (June 1994) 187.

3. *Doctrines and Discipline of The Methodist Church 1939* (New York: Methodist Publishing House, 1939) 1–2.

4. For the problem of constitutionalizing public assemblies see Hannah Arendt, *On Revolution* (New York: Viking, 1965), 241–44.

5. *The Federalist Papers* (1788), Nos. 10, 51.

6. For an examination of the biblical sources from a political theory standpoint, see Daniel Elazar, *Covenant and Polity in Biblical Israel* (New Brunswick, N.J.: Transaction Books, 1994). For a constructive theological appropriation of the federalist tradition, see William Johnson Everett, *God's Federal Republic* (New York: Paulist, 1988).

7. See Donald S. Lutz, *Documents of Political Foundation Written by Colonial Americans: From Covenant to Constitution* (Philadelphia: Institute for the Study of Human Issues, 1986), and Charles S. McCoy and J. Wayne Baker, *The Fountainhead of Federalism: Heinrich Bullinger and the Covenantal Tradition* (Philadelphia: Westminster, 1991).

8. Predecessor bodies had also written constitutions, beginning with the Methodist Episcopal Church in 1900. The Commission on the Constitution of the MEC, which worked from 1888 to 1900 to formalize a constitution for the church for the first time, defined it this way:

> A constitution is an instrument containing a recital of principles of organization and of declarations of power, permissions, and limitations which cannot be taken from, added to, or changed in any particular without the consent of the power which originally created the instrument, or by the legal process determined by the body possessing original power.
>
> (General Conference *Journal*, Methodist Episcopal Church, 1896, 338.)

The Methodist Episcopal Church South was content with its historic understanding that the Restrictive Rules, including a rule on representation in General Conference, comprised the church's constitution (though it was not so titled). Prior to the 1968 union the Evangelical United Brethren Church had a considerably longer Disciplinary section titled "constitutional law," including the basic units and powers of all conferences, local churches, and forms of ministry.

The following discussion of the 1968 Constitution draws upon a fuller analysis in Thomas Edward Frank, *Polity, Practice, and the Mission of The United Methodist Church* (Nashville: Abingdon, 1997), Chap. 3.

9. John J. Tigert, *A Constitutional History of American Episcopal Methodism*, 6th ed., rev. and enl. (Nashville: Publishing House of the M. E. Church, South, 1916), 15.

10. *The Book of Discipline of The United Methodist Church 1996* (Nashville: The United Methodist Publishing House, 1996) ¶ 38. Unless otherwise indicated, all Disciplinary references are to the 1996 *Discipline*.

11. *Discipline*, ¶ 57. Tigert, *Constitutional History*, 323–24, 403.

12. *Discipline*, ¶ 15.

13. *Discipline*, ¶ 16–20.

14. *Discipline*, ¶ 17.

15. John L. Nuelsen, *Die Ordination in Methodismus* (1935), quoted in Gerald F. Moede, "Bishops in the Methodist Tradition: Historical Perspectives," in Jack M. Tuell and Roger W. Fjeld, *Episcopacy. Lutheran—United Methodist Dialogue II* (Minneapolis: Augsburg, 1991), 59.

16. *Discipline*, ¶ 45.

17. *Discipline*, ¶ 52.

18. *Discipline*, ¶ 415.

19. James K. Mathews, *Set Apart to Serve. The Meaning and Role of Episcopacy in the Wesleyan Tradition* (Nashville: Abingdon, 1985), 47.

20. *Discipline*, ¶¶ 403–4. For further discussion see James M. Buckley, *Constitutional and Parliamentary History of the Methodist Episcopal Church* (New York: Methodist Book Concern, 1912), 187–88.

21. *Discipline*, ¶ 414.1

22. Murray H. Leiffer, "The Episcopacy in the Present Day," in *The Study of the General Superintendency of the Methodist Church. A Report to the General Conference*

of 1964. (The Co-ordinating Council of the Methodist Church, January 1964), 169.

23. *Discipline,* ¶ 31.

24. *Discipline,* ¶ 15.

25. *Discipline,* ¶ 604.2.

26. John M. Moore, the MECS bishop who worked tirelessly for this plan, put the argument best in 1943:

> The Jurisdictional Conference is the essential, vital, and principal administrative and promotional unit of the Church, with legislative power limited to regulations on regional affairs. . . . [It] is the key and core of the entire system. . . . The Plan of Union [1939] sets up a commonwealth of balancing bodies wherein no one shall be supreme, except in its own field.

John M. Moore, *The Long Road to Methodist Union* (New York: Abingdon-Cokesbury, 1943), 192–93.

27. Already in 1958 James H. Straughn complained that the Northeast in particular was not taking the jurisdiction seriously as a programmatic unit; see *Inside Methodist Union* (Nashville: Methodist Publishing House, 1958), 141.

28. *Discipline,* ¶ 15.10.

29. *Discipline,* ¶ 29.5.

30. *Discipline,* ¶ 537.9.

31. *Discipline,* ¶ 45.

32. *Discipline,* ¶ 54.

33. *Discipline,* ¶¶ 12–14.

34. *Discipline,* ¶ 324.

35. Thus some United Methodists argue that church membership numbers should be given more weight in figuring representation.

36. *Discipline,* ¶ 216.

37. See Max L. Stackhouse, *Public Theology and Political Economy: Christian Stewardship and Modern Society* (Lanham, Md.: University Press of America, 1991), 113–37.

38. The modern theory of corporation begins with Max Weber. See *From Max Weber: Essays in Sociology,* transl. and ed. H. H. Gerth and C. Wright Mills (New York: Oxford/Galaxy, 1958), 196–244. For more recent developments in organizational theory see Gareth Morgan, *Images of Organization* (Newbury Park and London: Sage Publications, 1986).

39. William McGuire King, "Denominational Modernization and Religious Identity: The Case of the Methodist Episcopal Church," *Perspectives on American Methodism: Interpretive Essays,* ed. Russell Richey, Kenneth Rowe, Jean M. Schmidt (Nashville: Abingdon, 1993), 343–55.

40. Margaret Wheatley, *Leadership and the New Science* (San Francisco: Berrett-Koehler, 1992); Peter Senge, *The Fifth Discipline. The Art and Practice of the Learning Organization* (New York: Doubleday, Currency, 1990); Ezra Earl Jones, *Quest for Quality in the Church. A New Paradigm* (Nashville: Discipleship Resources, 1993).

41. Information for this section draws on Edward McGlynn Gaffney Jr., Philip C. Sorenson, and Howard R. Griffin, *Ascending Liability in Religious and Other Nonprofit Organizations* (Macon: Mercer University Press, 1984); Jean Caffey Lyles, "Methodist Litigations and Public Relations," *The Christian Century*, December 19, 1979, 1256–57; "Report to the 1980 General Conference Regarding the Pacific Homes Litigation," Exhibit C, No. 17, pp. 42–48 in Conference Proceedings; official court documents; and materials graciously provided by the General Council on Finance and Administration, United Methodist Church, Evanston, Illinois.

42. *Barr v. United Methodist Church*, 90 Cal. App. 3d 266, 153 Cal. Rep. 328 (1979) [cited hereafter as "Barr"]. For discussion of liability of unincorporated associations see Gaffney et al., *Ascending Liability*, 20–40.

43. "Minute Order" of the Superior Court of California, County of San Diego, No. 40-4611 (1978).

44. Barr at 328, 333.

45. Barr at 329, quoting the *Discipline* 1976, ¶ 525.2. Ironically the 1976 *Discipline* was the first to include such language. The 1972 General Conference authorized a "Study of the Offices of Bishop and District Superintendent" during the 1972–76 quadrennium, which resulted in a Chapter Five of legislation on "The Superintendency," now separated from the chapter on "The Ordained Ministry." Section VII on "Corporate Expressions of the Superintendency," and in particular ¶ 525.2, represented the first legislative efforts in Methodist history to define the Council of Bishops ecclesiologically.

46. Barr at 328 (internal quotation from *Carnes v. Smith* [1976], 236 Ga. 30).

47. See "The Methodist Approach," by Kent M. Weeks, in Gaffney et al., *Ascending Liability*, 133–37, for some examples. Some Lutheran organizational adjustments are described by Philip Draheim in the same volume at 137–42.

48. *Discipline* (1984), ¶ 526.2. In addition, the 1984 *Discipline* added specific language denying that either "master-servant" or "principal-agent" relationships—both with legal precedent—defined the relationship of general agencies and the General Conference (¶¶ 801, 802). General agencies are amenable to the General Conference, but the General Conference—which has no continuing executive body between sessions—is not liable for the actions of general agencies. 1996 *Discipline* ¶ 112. This statement was greatly condensed in the 1996 *Discipline*, ¶ 109.

49. See Gaffney et al., *Ascending Liability*, 103–32.

50. However, in two Georgia cases involving Presbyterian churches in 1969 and 1979 the Court developed the concept of "neutral principles" by which to approach church property disputes without entangling itself in doctrinal matters. In fact, however, "neutrality" simply means formulations familiar to civil law. See Gaffney et al., *Ascending Liability*, 60–75; Douglas Laycock, "The Right to Church Autonomy as Part of Free Exercise of Religion," in *Government Intervention in Religious Affairs*, ed. Dean Kelley (New York: Pilgrim, 1986), 28–39.

51. A separate appeal by the General Council on Finance and Administration of the United Methodist Church was rebuffed by the United States Supreme Court with Justice Rehnquist's claim that "the First and Fourteenth Amendments [cannot] prevent a civil court from independently examining, and making the ultimate decision regarding, the structure and actual operation of a hierarchical church and its constituent units in an action such as this." 439 U.S. 1355 (1979). Cited with comment in Gaffney et al., *Ascending Liability*, 75.

52. *Discipline* 1976, 1980, ¶ 525.2.

53. *Watson v. Jones*, U.S. (13 Wall) 679 (1872).

54. *Discipline*, ¶¶ 2501, 2503.

55. In the Georgia case of *Carnes v. Smith* (1976) the state courts did use trust doctrine, but the United States Supreme Court never reviewed the case.

56. For a detailed examination of this point see Kendall O. White, "Constitutional Norms and the Formal Organization of American Churches," *Journal of Sociological Analysis* 33:2 (1972), 95–109.

57. *Kedroff v. St. Nicholas Cathedral*, 344 U.S. 94 (1952) and *Serbian Orthodox Diocese v. Milivojevich*, 426 U.S. 696 (1976) involved matters of ecclesiastical appointment and related control of church property.

58. "Memorandum . . . to Dismiss . . ." by attorneys representing persons served as representing the United Methodist Church in *Trigg et al. v. Pacific Methodist Investment Fund et al.*, before the United States District Court for the Southern District of California, No. 78-0198-S (1978), 5.

59. Affadavit of Murray H. Leiffer to California Superior Court, San Diego, in case of *Barr v. United Methodist Church*, January 6, 1978, also used in other Pacific Homes cases. References are to pp. 4, 20, 21.

60. Emile Durkheim's characterization of those moments of collective enthusiasm that create new forms of legitimate social order, in *The Elementary Forms of the Religious Life*, tr. J. W. Swain (New York: Free Press, 1965), 474–75. See also Arendt, *On Revolution*, chaps. 3 and 6.

61. *Discipline* 1992, ¶ 112. This statement was greatly condensed in the 1996 *Discipline*, ¶ 109.

Notes to "AFRICAN AMERICAN METHODISTS"

1. Richard Allen, *The Life Experience and Gospel Labors of the Rt. Rev. Richard Allen* (Nashville: Abingdon, 1960; repr. of 2d ed.), 15–16.

2. Allen, ibid., 29.

3. Ibid. Italics added.

4. It should be noted that there were five other, smaller African American groups who were associated with Methodism. The Union American Episcopal Church (originally called "the Union Church of Africans"), which is actually the oldest of all Black Methodist denominations, was founded by Peter Spencer in Wilmington, Delaware in 1813. Other groups separated themselves from the AME and the AME Zion Churches. They include the Reformed Methodist Union Episcopal Church (1885), the Reformed Zion Union Apostolic Church (1881), and the Independent African Methodist Episcopal Church (1907). Finally, the African Union First Colored Methodist Protestant Church (commonly known as AUMP), was a merger of the Union Church of Africans, a split-off from the original Union Church of Africans, and the First Colored Methodist Protestant Church. See C. Eric Lincoln and Lawrence Mamiya, *The Black Church and The African American Experience* (Durham: Duke University Press, 1990), 48ff., and several of the writings of Professor Lewis V. Baldwin, especially his doctoral dissertation published as *"Invisible" Strands in African Methodism: A History of the African Union Methodist Protestant and Union American Methodist Episcopal Churches, 1805–1980* (Metuchen, N.J.: Scarecrow, 1993).

5. See William B. McClain, *Black People in the Methodist Church: Whither Thou Goest?* 2d ed. (Nashville: Abingdon, 1989), 7ff.

6. Frederick A. Norwood, *The Story of American Methodism: A History of the United Methodists and Their Relations* (Nashville: Abingdon, 1974), 166; and Harry V. Richardson, *Dark Salvation: The Story of Methodism as It Developed Among Blacks in America* (New York: Doubleday, 1976), 35. In the official history, *The African Methodist Episcopal Zion Church: Reality of the Black Church,* by William J. Walls (Charlotte, N.C.: A.M.E. Zion Publishing House, 1974), the author points out that of the 360 members of the John Street Church in 1789, seventy were African Americans.

7. Joshua E. Licorish, *Harry Hoosier, African Pioneer Preacher* (Philadelphia: Afro-Methodist Associates, 1967). The Rev. Joshua E. Licorish, now deceased, was for many years the pastor of African Zoar United Methodist Church in Philadelphia, and a fine historian in his own right. He credits Hoosier as founding the African Zoar Church (the first lot was purchased, and the first edifice was constructed in 1794) around the time when Allen and others left St. George's M.E. Church to form Bethel African Methodist Episcopal Church (under the leadership of Allen) and African St. Thomas Episcopal Church (under the leadership of Absalom Jones). Licorish devoted many years to collecting material on Hoosier—some of which he published, but much if not most of which he died without making available to scholars and the general

public. If ever found and made available, these materials would be valuable sources for additional information and insights into Harry Hoosier.

8. Abel Stevens, *History of the Methodist Church* (New York: Carlton and Porter, 1866), 174. See also Warren Thomas Smith, *Harry Hoosier: Circuit Rider* (Nashville: The Upper Room, 1981), 18; cf. my discussion of "'Black Harry' Hoosier: A Horseman for the Lord" in McClain, *Black People in the Methodist Church" Whither Thou Goest?* [n. 5 above], 41–46.

9. McClain, *Black People in the Methodist Church . . .* , 43, as quoted in Stevens, *History*, 176.

10. Quoted by Matthew Simpson Davage, "Methodism: Our Heritage and Hope," *The Daily Christian Advocate*, 11 May 1939, 474.

11. Lewis Baldwin, "Early African American Methodism: Founders and Foundation," in Grant Shockley, *Heritage and Hope: African American Presence in United Methodism* (Nashville: Abingdon, 1991), 24ff. See also Baldwin, "New Directions for the Study of Blacks in Methodism,' in *Rethinking Methodist History: A Bicentennial Consultation*, ed. Russell E. Richey and Kenneth E. Rowe (Nashville: Kingswood Books, 1985), 185ff. Of the list given, Harry Hoosier and Henry Evans remained in the predominantly white Methodist Episcopal Church, or what is now the United Methodist Church. The others who remained Methodists gave outstanding pastoral and administrative leadership to the founding and development of the independent African Methodist Churches (AME and AME Zion Churches). (Jones, it will be remembered, broke away and became the first African Episcopal priest in America.)

12. John Thompson, *The Life of John Thompson, A Fugitive Slave* (Worcester, Massachusetts, 1856), 18–19. Quoted in Albert J. Raboteau, *Slave Religion* (New York: Oxford University Press, 1980), 133.

13. Donald G. Mathews, "Evangelical America—The Methodist Ideology," in *Rethinking Methodist History: A Bicentennial Historical Consultation,* ed. Russell E. Richey and Kenneth E. Rowe (Nashville: Kingswood Books, 1985), 92.

14. Ibid., 92 (italics added).

15. Clarence C. Goen, *Broken Churches, Broken Nation* (Atlanta: Mercer University Press, 1987).

16. *The Journals and Letters of Francis Asbury*, ed. Elmer E. Clark, 3 vols. (London: Epworth; Nashville: Abindgon, 1958), vol. 2, 151, 284, 591. Cited by Lewis V. Baldwin in his chapter, "Early African American Methodism: Founders and Foundations" in *Heritage and Hope: The African American Presence in United Methodism,* ed. Grant S. Shockley (Nashville: Abingdon, 1991), 27.

17. William H. Williams, "The Attraction of Methodism: The Delmarva Peninsula as a Case Study, 1769–1802," in Shockley, *Heritage and Hope*, 107. See his endnotes for sources for other such anecdotes.

18. The many works of Martin E. Marty, *A Nation of Behavers: Mapping the Religions in the United States* (Chicago: University of Chicago Press, 1976), *The*

Public Church (New York: Crossroads, 1981), and (with R. S. Appleby) *The Glory and the Power: The Fundamentalist Challenge to the Modern World* (Boston: Beacon, 1993), are good places for starters. See also Wade Clark Roof, *A Generation of Seekers* (San Francisco: Harper Collins, 1993); William Strauss and Neil Howe, *Generations: The History of America's Future, 1584–2069* (New York: William Morrow, 1991); and Dean R. Hoge, Benton Johnson, and Donald A. Luidens, *Vanishing Boundaries: The Religion of Mainline Protestant Baby Boomers* (Louisville: Westminster/John Knox, 1994).

19. William Capers was his successor at Fayetteville, and later bishop of the southern Methodist church. Cf. William M. Wightman, *William Capers, Including an Autobiography* (Nashville: Southern Methodist Publishing House, 1858), 124.

20. *Ibid.*, 139.

21. Shockley, *Heritage and Hope . . .* [n. 11 above], 40.

22. Justo L. González, ed., *Out of Every Tribe and Nation: Christian Theology at the Ethnic Roundtable* (Nashville: Abingdon, 1992).

23. Shockley, *Heritage and Hope*, 41.

Notes to "METHODIST IDENTITIES"

1. See for example, Nathan Bangs, *A History of the Methodist Episcopal Church*, vol. 2 (New York: T. Mason & G. Lane, 1839), 320–22; Arlo Ayres Brown, "Methodism's Educational Activities," in *Methodism*, ed. William K. Anderson (Nashville: Methodist Publishing House, 1947), 179–80; William R. Cannon, "Education, Publication, Benevolent Work, and Missions," in *The History of American Methodism*, vol. 1, ed. Emory S. Bucke (New York: Abingdon, 1964), 549–50; John O. Gross, *The Beginnings of American Methodism* (Nashville: Abingdon, 1974), 217; William W. Sweet, *Methodism in American History* (New York: Abingdon, 1954), 210–11; and William W. Sweet, *Religion on the American Frontier: 1783–1840*, vol. 4, *The Methodists* (Chicago: University of Chicago Press, 1946), 65–68.

2. Sweet, *Methodism in American History*, 208–10; quotation, 208.

3. Ibid., 211–24; Cannon, "Education, Publication, Benevolent Work, and Missions," 549–61; Donald B. Marti, "Rich Methodists: The Rise and Consequences of Lay Philanthrophy in the Mid-Nineteenth Century," in *Perspectives on American Methodism: Interpretive Essays*, ed. Russell E. Richey, Kenneth E. Rowe, and Jean Miller Schmidt (Nashville: Kingswood Books, 1993), 268; Donald G. Tewksbury, *The Founding of American Colleges and Universities Before the Civil War* (New York: Teachers College, Columbia University, 1932; reprint, New York: Arno Press and the New York Times, 1969), 69, 103–11.

4. For a listing of Methodist universities and colleges see Gwen Colvin, *The 1993 United Methodist Directory and Index of Resources* (Nashville: Cokesbury, 1993), 104–9. The University Senate of the United Methodist Church, using the criteria of the Carnegie Foundation, recognizes nine universities related to the church: American, Boston, Clark Atlanta, Duke, Emory, Southern Methodist,

Syracuse, University of Denver, and the University of the Pacific. ("UM-Related Colleges and Universities by Carnegie Classification" [typed manuscript, General Board of Higher Education and Ministry, The United Methodist Church, 1996]).

5. George Marsden suggests this as one reason for the plethora of Methodist universities in *The Soul of the American University: From Protestant Establishment to Established Nonbelief* (New York: Oxford University Press, 1994), 276.

6. Sydney Ahlstrom, *A Religious History of the American People* (New Haven: Yale University Press, 1972), 437; Wade C. Barclay, *The Methodist Episcopal Church, 1845–1939*, vol. 3, *Widening Horizons, 1849–95* (New York: Board of Missions of the Methodist Church, 1957), 49.

7. Barclay, *The Methodist Episcopal Church*, 50; Aaron I. Abell, *The Urban Impact on American Protestantism, 1865–1900* (Cambridge: Harvard University Press, 1943), 4; Ensign M'Chesney, "The Effect of Increased Wealth Upon American Methodism," in *The Present State of the Methodist Episcopal Church: A Symposium,* ed. George R. Crooks (Syracuse: Hunt and Eaton, 1891), 53–64; David B. Potts, *Wesleyan University, 1831–1910: Collegiate Enterprise in New England* (New Haven: Yale University Press, 1992), 85.

8. On this see Marti, "Rich Methodists," 265–76. Marti notes (267) that Matthew Simpson, in his *Cyclopaedia of Methodism* published in 1878, listed almost 350 laymen notable largely for their business success.

9. George Marsden suggests this in *The Soul of the American University*, 276.

10. Marti, "Rich Methodists," 268. See also Robert D. Clark, *The Life of Matthew Simpson* (New York: Macmillan, 1956), 72–73.

11. On Presbyterian dominance of higher education see William W. Sweet, *Indiana Asbury-DePauw University: 1837–1937, A Hundred Years of Higher Education in the Middle West* (New York: Abingdon, 1937), 17–20.

12. It was in this era, as E. Digby Baltzell has claimed, that "the proper college degree became the main criterion for potential elite status" (E. Digby Baltzell, *The Protestant Establishment: Aristocracy and Caste in America* [New York: Vintage, 1964], 209). This quest for respectability was not new in the post-Civil War years. See, e.g., Nathan O. Hatch, *The Democratization of American Christianity* (New Haven: Yale University Press, 1989), 201–6.

13. Henry A. Buttz, "The Obligations of a Great Church," in *The Present State of the Methodist Episcopal Church: A Symposium*, ed. George R. Crooks (Syracuse: Hunt and Eaton, 1891), 7. Ironically, as Baltzell has argued, as mainline Protestants began building universities, they also began a simultaneous, gradual loss of cultural authority (Baltzell, *Protestant Establishment*, esp. chap. 9).

14. Richard L. Bushman, *The Refinement of America: Persons, Houses, Cities* (New York: Alfred A. Knopf, 1992), 346–47.

15. Marti, "Rich Methodists," 272; Donald Marti, "Laymen Bring Your Money: Lee Claflin, Methodist Philanthropist, 1791–1871," *Methodist History* XIV (April

1976) 176–77. A neat symbol of the Methodist rise to prominence in this era is that William Claflin, Lee Claflin's son, was the governor in 1869 and signed the charter for Boston University (Marti, "Laymen Bring Your Money," 177; E. Ray Speare, *Interesting Happenings in Boston University's History: 1839–1951* [Boston: Boston University Press, 1957], 34; James Mudge, *History of the New England Conference of the Methodist Episcopal Church 1796–1910* [Boston: By the Conference, 1910], 263).

16. Baltzell, *Protestant Establishment*, 20.

17. Oscar Handlin, *Boston's Immigrants: A Study in Acculturation* (Cambridge: Harvard University Press, 1959), 219–20.

18. Thompson's Emory History Scrapbook, Emory University Library; quoted in Alfred M. Pierce, *Giant Against the Sky: The Life of Bishop Warren Akin Candler* (New York: Abingdon-Cokesbury, 1948), 131. On the Vanderbilt controversy see Paul K. Conkin, *Gone With the Ivy: A Biography of Vanderbilt University* (Knoxville: University of Tennessee Press, 1985), 147–222.

19. Charles H. Payne, "The American University and the Educational Institutions of the Church," in *The American University and the General Conference of the Methodist Episcopal Church* (Omaha: Rees Printing, 1892), 15. As Baltzell has noted, the early-twentieth century witnessed "the passing of intellectual and spiritual leadership in America from the church to the university, from the preacher in the pulpit to the professor in the classroom" (*Protestant Establishment*, 181).

20. Estelle F. Ward, *The Story of Northwestern University* (New York: Dodd, Mead & Co., 1924), 5–10, 170–71. Congregationalists had 1/413. The percentage of individuals attending college increased dramatically in the course of the first half of the twentieth century. In 1900 only about 4% of all college-age Americans attended college, while by 1940, 16% attended (Ernest Havemann and Patricia Salter West, *They Went to College: The College Graduate in America Today* [New York: Harcourt, Brace, 1952], 12).

21. Richard Hofstadter, *Anti-Intellectualism in American Life* (New York: Vintage, 1962), 95.

22. Ibid., 100–103.

23. Ibid., 98–99.

24. Thomas H. English, *Emory University, 1915–1965: A Semicentennial History* (Atlanta: Emory University Press, 1966), 11–13; Charles H. Candler, *Asa Griggs Candler* ([Atlanta]: Emory University, 1950), 389–409.

25. On Asa G. Candler and his support of Emory see Candler, *Candler*, esp. 375–421; English, *Emory University*, 12–15; Henry M. Bullock, *A History of Emory University* (Nashville: Parthenon, 1936), 291.

26. Quoted in Pierce, *Giant Against the Sky*, 154.

27. Mary Thomas, *Southern Methodist University: Founding and Early Years* (Dallas: SMU Press, 1974), 40–41.

28. Quoted in Hiram A. Boaz, *Eighty-Four Golden Years: An Autobiography of Bishop Hiram Abiff Boaz* (Nashville: Parthenon, 1951), 89.

29. Robert F. Durden, *The Dukes of Durham: 1865–1929* (Durham: Duke University Press, 1975), 94–95, 109–11, 229.

30. Bruce Leslie, *Gentlemen and Scholars: College and Community in the "Age of the University," 1865–1917* (University Park: Pennsylvania State University Press, 1992), 1. See also David O. Levine, *The American College and the Culture of Aspiration: 1915–1940* (Ithaca: Cornell University Press, 1986).

31. Levine, *The American College*, 126–27, 132.

32. Ibid., 132.

33. Ferdinand Lundberg, *America's 60 Families* (New York: Vanguard, 1937), 377.

34. Dewey W. Grantham, *Southern Progressivism: The Reconciliation of Progress and Tradition* (Knoxville: University of Tennessee Press, 1983), 9.

35. H. Richard Niebuhr, *The Social Sources of Denominationalism* (New York: Henry Holt, 1929), 70–72.

36. English, *Emory University*, 13–14; Candler, *Candler*, 397–99. Atlanta grew from a population of under 90,000 to over 200,000 in the first twenty years of the twentieth century (Grantham, *Southern Progressivism*, 5).

37. Levine, *American College*, 78.

38. Kevin J. Christiano, *Religious Diversity and Social Change: American Cities, 1890–1906* (Cambridge: Cambridge University Press, 1987), 13. See also Arthur M. Schlesinger Sr., *A Critical Period in American Religion: 1875–1900* (Philadelphia: Fortress, 1967).

39. A Vanderbilt professor wrote in 1909 of Southern life that "the city is more and more setting the pace of and dominating Southern life and Southern thought" (Gus W. Dyer, "Social Tendencies in the South," in *The South in the Building of the Nation*, vol. 10, ed. Julian A. C. Chandler et al. [Richmond, 1909–13], 665–66; quoted in Grantham, *Southern Progressivism*, 5).

40. Bushman, *Refinement of America*, 353–54.

41. Quoted in Harvey B. Hurd and Robert D. Sheppard, eds., *Historical Encyclopedia of Illinois and History of Evanston*, vol. II, (Chicago: Munsell, 1906), 54; and Ward, *The Story of Northwestern University*, 7. See also James F. Bundy, *Fall from Grace: Religion and the Communal Ideal in Two Suburban Villages, 1870–1917* (Brooklyn: Carlson, 1991), 41–42.

42. Gordon Melton, *Log Cabins to Steeples* (N.p.: Commissions on Archives and History of the Northern, Central, and Southern Illinois Conferences, 1974), 185.

43. Melton, *Log Cabins*, 186, 190.

44. Ward, *The Story of Northwestern University*, 13, 19.

45. Bundy, *Fall from Grace*, 42; Hurd, *Historical Encyclopedia*, 20.

46. Durden, *Dukes of Durham*, 91–94.

47. Ibid., 92. See also Earl W. Porter, *Trinity and Duke, 1892–1924: Foundations of Duke University* (Durham: Duke University Press, 1964), 19–21.

48. Durden, *Dukes of Durham*, 82–83.

49. Ibid., 15–24, 92.

50. Porter, *Trinity and Duke*, 20–23.

51. Ibid., 23–24. See also William K. Boyd, *The Story of Durham: City of the New South* (Durham: Duke University Press, 1925), 167–74.

52. Durden, *Dukes of Durham*, 124–25. For the same concerns at Emory see Levine, *American College*, 82.

53. Porter, *Trinity and Duke*, 64.

54. Durden, *Dukes of Durham*, 171, 226–27.

55. Ibid., 241.

56. Robert F. Durden, *The Launching of Duke University: 1924–1949* (Durham: Duke University Press, 1993), 33. Paul V. Turner, *Campus: An American Planning Tradition* (Cambridge: MIT Press, 1984), 196.

57. William H. Wilson, *The City Beautiful Movement* (Baltimore: Johns Hopkins University Press, 1989), 1; Turner, *Campus*, 167. On the link, or lack thereof, between the Columbian exposition and the City Beautiful movement see Wilson, *City Beautiful Movement*, chap. 3.

58. Turner, *Campus*, 167, 169, 196.

59. Freeman Galpin, *Syracuse University*, vol. 1: *The Pioneer Days* ([Syracuse]: Syracuse University Press, 1952), 12–30.

60. Thomas, *Southern Methodist University*, 13–14.

61. Ibid., 14–19.

62. Walter N. Vernon, *Methodism Moves Across North Texas* (Dallas: The North Texas Conference of the Methodist Church, 1967), 220, 228, 230. The population of Dallas more than tripled in the first two decades of the twentieth century (Grantham, *Southern Progressivism*, 277).

63. Olin Nail, ed., *History of Texas Methodism: 1900–1960* (Austin: Capital Printing Co., 1961), 164–66; Thomas, *Southern Methodist University*, 15–23, 30–31.

64. Thomas, *Southern Methodist University*, 23–24, 30–31. On the controversy over moving Southwestern see also Boaz, *Eighty-Four Golden Years*, 81–86.

65. Elizabeth Turner, "Episcopal Women as Community Leaders: Galveston, 1900–1989," in *Episcopal Women*, ed. Catherine Prelinger (New York: Oxford University Press, 1992), 79. In 1906, 86% of all Methodists lived outside of principal cities (Niebuhr, *Social Sources of Denominationalism*, 183).

66. Quoted in Nail, *History of Texas Methodism*, 330.

67. Joseph R. Gusfield, *Symbolic Crusade: Status Politics and the American Temperance Movement* (Urbana: University of Illinois Press, 1963), 7.

68. Bushman, *Refinement of America*, 400. Though Bushman's study focuses on antebellum America, the categories and attitudes still fit in the era under consideration here.

69. Grantham, *Southern Progressivism*, 277.

70. See, e.g., David B. Potts, "American Colleges in the Nineteenth Century: From Localism to Denominationalism," *History of Education Quarterly* 11 (winter 1971): 363–80; David B. Potts, "'College Enthusiasm!' As Public Response, 1800–1860," *Harvard Educational Review* 47 (Feb. 1977): 28–42; Potts, *Wesleyan University* [n. 7 above], esp. chap. 1.

71. See Bradley J. Longfield, "'Denominational' Colleges in Antebellum America? A Case Study of Presbyterians and Methodists in the South," in *Reimagining Denominationalism: Interpretive Essays*, ed. Robert Bruce Mullin and Russell E. Richey (New York: Oxford University Press, 1994), 295.

72. Potts, *Wesleyan University*, 56–57. Warren Candler, Chancellor of Emory and chair of the Educational Commission of the Methodist Episcopal Church, South, advised against advertising Emory in a denominational periodical west of the Mississippi for fear of infringing on SMU's territory (Pierce, *Giant Against the Sky*, 133).

73. Ward, *The Story of Northwestern University*, 20–21, 238–39.

74. Hurd, *Historical Encyclopedia*, 65.

75. Thomas, *Southern Methodist University*, 44–45. Lundberg has noted that "Class lines in the United States . . . are to some extent obscured by regional particularism, so that where an individual does not perceive himself as exploited by another class, he often sees himself as exploited by another region. . . . It is all too obvious in studying school gifts and endowments that the rich have largely passed over the people of the South" (*America's 60 Families*, 402).

76. Thomas, *Southern Methodist University*, 32.

77. Ibid., 33.

78. Conkin, *Gone with the Ivy*, 3–12.

79. William E. Ross, "A Methodist Experiment in Graduate Education: John Fletcher Hurst and the Founding of American University, 1889–1914," (Ph.D. diss., American University, 1992), 3–4; Payne, "The American University," 14.

80. Ross, "Methodist Experiment," 6–7, 10.

81. Ibid., 80–81, 101–2, 114–15, 144–47.

82. Ibid., 107 n. 42. See 148ff. on Day and Hurst. On Hurst see Albert Osborn, *John Fletcher Hurst: A Biography* (New York: Eaton & Mains, 1905). Thomas Langford has claimed that "Boston University, during this period, was the major contributor to the growth of Methodist theology" (Thomas Langford,

Practical Divinity: Theology in the Wesleyan Tradition [Nashville: Abingdon, 1983], 124).

83. Ross, "Methodist Experiment," 148.

84. Ross, "Methodist Experiment," 105–7.

85. Ibid., ii-iii.

86. On the University Senate see Beth Adams Bowser, *Living the Vision: The University Senate of the Methodist Episcopal Church, the Methodist Church, and the United Methodist Church, 1892–1991* (Nashville: Board of Higher Education and Ministry of the United Methodist Church, 1992). In 1898 the Southern Methodist Church created an Educational Commission to fix admission and graduation requirements for its colleges (C. Vann Woodward, *Origins of the New South: 1877–1913* [N.p.: Louisiana State University Press, 1951], 439).

87. Bowser, *Living the Vision*, i, xi.

88. Ibid., 128–30.

89. On growing bureaucratization in mainline denominations see, e.g., Ben Primer, *Protestants and American Business Methods* (N.p.: UMI Research, 1979); and James H. Moorhead, "Presbyterians and the Mystique of Organizational Efficiency, 1870–1936," in *Reimagining Denominationalism* [n. 71 above], 264–87.

90. On these see Norwood, *Story of American Methodism*, 91–93, 127–29, 181–84, 197–205. This does not deny a hierarchical vs. democratic interpretation of these struggles.

91. Andy Langford, "A New Connectionalism?" *Leadership Letters from the Duke Divinity School Project*, 15 July 1995, 1–5.

92. Quoted in Candler, *Candler*, 397–99.

93. Quoted in Candler, *Candler*, 398–99. See also 392.

94. See Longfield, "'Denominational' Colleges," 297.

95. Sidney E. Mead, "Denominationalism: The Shape of Protestantism in America," in *Denominationalism*, ed. Russell E. Richey (Nashville: Abingdon, 1977), 102–5. See Longfield, "'Denominational' Colleges," 295–98 as a comparison with the early Emory.

96. See, e.g., Potts, "American Colleges," 373.

97. On efforts in the Southern Church to tighten church-college relations see Porter, *Trinity and Duke*, 193–98 and n. 86 above.

98. Ward, *The Story of Northwestern University*, 29; Bundy, *Fall from Grace*, 43, 243 n. 36; Arthur H. Wilde, *Northwestern University: A History, 1855–1905* (New York: The University Publishing Society, 1905), vol. 1, 414–16; vol. 3, 152. Bishop Matthew Simpson moved to Evanston in 1859 and lived there until 1863. In 1855 Evanston became a dry town due to a stipulation in Northwestern's charter that liquor would not be sold within four miles of the campus (Clark, *Simpson*, 210, 237; Bundy, *Fall from Grace*, 43; Frances E. Willard, *A Classic Town:*

The Story of Evanston [Chicago: Woman's Temperance Publishing Association, 1891], 166).

99. Bundy, *Fall from Grace*, 184; Robert Moats Miller, *How Shall they Hear without a Preacher: The Life of Ernest Fremont Tittle* (Chapel Hill: University of North Carolina Press, 1971), 246–47; Hurd, *Historical Encyclopedia*, 19, 311; Willard, *Classic Town*, 88. See also Melton, *Log Cabins*, 198, 200.

100. Willard, *Classic Town*, 6; Ruth Bordin, *Frances Willard: A Biography* (Chapel Hill: University of North Carolina Press, 1986), 24, 54–55.

101. Potts, *Wesleyan University*, 101–3; Durden, *Dukes of Durham*, 110. The Northwestern Female College had been opened in 1855 (Willard, *A Classic Town*, 57–58).

102. Potts, *Wesleyan University, 101.*

103. Quoted in W. Freeman Galpin, *Syracuse University*, vol. 2, *The Growing Years* (Syracuse: Syracuse University Press, 1960), 488.

104. Quoted in Galpin, Syracuse University: Pioneer Days, xi.

105. Ross, "Methodist Experiment," 3–4, 10.

106. Ibid., 87.

107. *The American University and the General Conference of the Methodist Episcopal Church* (Omaha: Rees Printing, 1892), facing title page.

108. Ibid.

109. Marsden, *Soul of the American University*, 287.

110. Sidney Mead, *The Lively Experiment: The Shaping of Christianity in America* (New York: Harper & Row, 1963), 134, 141, 157.

111. Russell E. Richey, *Early American Methodism* (Bloomington: Indiana University Press, 1991), 96.

112. I am grateful for the comments of Elmer Colyer, Shannon Jung, George Marsden, and Russell Richey on an earlier version of this essay.

Notes to "REDESIGNING METHODIST CHURCHES"

1. Abel Stevens, *The Centenary of American Methodism* (New York: Carlton & Porter, 1865), 233–34.

2. Jeanne H. Kilde, *Spiritual Armories: A Social and Architectural History of Neo-Medieval Auditorium Churches in the U.S., 1869–1910* (Ph.D. diss., University of Minnesota, 1991), 30.

3. Resources of the homeless congregation were so large and the congregation so scattered throughout the city that the congregation divided the proceeds equally between members living in the east end of Pittsburgh and in Allegheny, a western suburb. The western portion of the congregation built an equally grand new church, Calvary Church, though in Gothic style. Cornerstones of the twin churches were laid on the same day, 18 May 1893.

4. For detailed descriptions of the church when dedicated, see *Remembering 1893–1993, Celebrating the Centennial of the First United Methodist Church Building* (Pittsburgh: First UMC, 1993). In 1946 Christ Church merged with First Methodist Church, and the united congregation took the name of the First Methodist Church. Christ, now First United Methodist Church, is a designated historical landmark of the Pittsburgh History & Landmarks Foundation.

5. Kramer aimed to outdo his mentor Richardson. The steel-reinforced, 100-foot-wide transept arches support a dome span of 50 feet, exceeding Trinity Church's dome by four feet.

6. The divided organ, built by Farrand and Votey of New York, was one of the very few in America at the time with a detached keyboard.

7. Three large windows were created by Louis C. Tiffany Co. of New York City: the great nave window, "The Sermon on the Mount"; the east transept window, "Miracle at the Marriage in Cana"; and the west transept window, "Christ Commissioning his Disciples." Playful angelic figures occupy the twenty-four lantern windows high above the heads of the congregation. In each of these windows the dark and handsome greens and reds, so effectively employed by the best American artists in glass, are used in the draperies, relieved by smoky grays and golden yellows, the soft olives and russet tones of the architectural background and of the landscape. Alastair Duncan, *Tiffany Windows* (New York: Simon and Schuster, 1980), 221.

8. Kilde does not include Kramer's favorite, Christ Church, Pittsburgh, in her list of "Neo-Medieval Auditorium Churches in the U.S." (see *Spiritual Armories,* Appendix A, 218–25).

9. The Methodist Episcopal Church formed a department of architecture in its Board of Church Extension as early as 1875. Within a decade the M.E. Church, South and the Church of the United Brethren in Christ had formed similar offices in their church-extension agencies.

10. For historical context and social analysis, this study relies heavily on three studies: A. Robert Jaeger's *The Auditorium and Akron Plans: Reflections on Half a Century of American Protestantism* (M.A. thesis, Syracuse University, 1984), the first serious study of Auditorium/Akron plans so popular in the late-Victorian era; Jeanne Halgren Kilde's sophisticated study, *Spiritual Armories* [n. 2 above]; and James F. White's *Protestant Worship and Church Architecture: Theological and Historical Considerations* (New York: Oxford, 1964).

11. Jaeger, *The Auditorium and Akron Plans*, chap. 2.

12. "The plan of the interior of [Broadway Temple] was my own. I had observed the defects of churches in regard to sound; and was sure that I could give the plan of a church in which I could easily speak to a much larger congregation than any house would hold that I had ever seen. An architect was consulted [Joseph Ditto], and I gave him my plan. But he objected to it that it would not appear well, and feared that it would injure his reputation to build a church with such an interior as that. However I insisted on it, and told him that

if he would not build it on that plan he was not the man to superintend its construction at all. It was finally built in accordance with my ideas; and it was altogether the most spacious, commodious, and comfortable place to speak in that I have ever seen of its size" (Charles Finney, *Memoirs of Charles G. Finney, the Complete Restored Text*, ed. Garth M. Rosell & Richard A. G. Dupuis [Grand Rapids: Zondervan, Academie Books, 1989], 367). See also Keith J. Hardman, *Charles Grandison Finney 1792–1875, Revivalist and Reformer* (Syracuse, N.Y.: Syracuse University Press, 1987), 313–14; Susan Hayes Ward, *History of the Broadway Tabernacle Church* (New York: Trow Print, 1940), 28–31; L. Nelson Nichols, *History of the Broadway Tabernacle of New York City* (New Haven, Conn.: Tuttle, Morehouse and Taylor, 1940), 58–73.

13. Beecher himself drew up the first design, which was completed by J. C. Wells, an English architect. The first service was held on 6 January 1850. The 2,000-seat church broke new ground by being joined to a two-story structure which contained rooms for the Sunday school, parlor, and library. Plymouth Church of the Pilgrims, Brooklyn, N.Y., *A Church In History: The Story of Plymouth's First Hundred Years* (Brooklyn, N.Y.: Plymouth Church of the Pilgrims, 1949), 16–24. Kilde traces auditorium churches to Beecher's Plymouth church only (p. 100). She does not mention Finney's, Spurgeon's, or Moody's churches as models.

14. As Spurgeon was resolutely opposed to Gothic architecture, his church was Grecian in style, with six massive Corinthian columns forming an imposing porch, designed by W. W. Pocock. Beneath the auditorium was a large Sunday-school room seating 900. Ernest W. Bacon, *Spurgeon, Heir of the Puritans* (London: George Allen & Unwin Ltd, 1967), chap. 6 "Metropolitan Tabernacle," 63–74.

15. For a contemporary description and line drawing of Moody's church, see W. H. Daniels, "The New Revival Hall," *Northwestern Christian Advocate* [Chicago] 24/39 (September 27, 1876), 1; see also Darrell M. Robertson, *The Chicago Revival, 1876: Society and Revivalism in a Nineteenth-Century City* (Metuchen, N.J.: Scarecrow, 1989), 49–51.

16. For an insightful analysis of sanctuary as performance space, see Kilde, *Spiritual Armories*, chap. 2, 77–136.

17. George W. Kramer, *The What, How and Why of Church Building* (New York: G. W. Kramer, 1897), 111. To meet continuing demand, Kramer's book was reprinted in 1901. Typical of his later designs was Plan no. 4 in a pamphlet he wrote for the Board of Church Extension of the Methodist Episcopal Church, South around 1910; see George W. Kramer, *The Departmental Sunday School Building, the Materialization of an Ideal* (Louisville: Board of Church Extension of the M.E. Church, South, [ca. 1910]) 9.

18. Obituary, *New York Times*, 21 October 1938, 2:23. See also *The National Cyclopaedia of American Biography* IX (1899), 331–32. In addition, Kramer received commissions for great numbers of public buildings and private residences.

19. Sofa pews from 1860 have been recently restored for use in historic Washington Square United Methodist Church in New York City. Nancy A. Carter, *Ark of Refuge: A History of the Washington Square United Methodist Church, 1820–1927* (M.Div. thesis, Union Theological Seminary, New York, 1987).

20. Karen Westerfield Tucker, *"Till Death Us Do Part": John Wesley's Services of Marriage and Burial and Their Development in the Methodist Episcopal Church* (Ph.D. dissertation, University of Notre Dame, 1992).

21. Beginning in 1880 paper applique imitation stained glass was manufactured and sold by Benjamin D. Price of Philadelphia, who in 1876 became the chief architect of the Methodist Episcopal Church. Price boasted that his product, which sold for 6 cents per square foot, was "more durable and better in every respect than cheap stained glass" (advertisement in *Manual of the Methodist Episcopal Church* 8/1 [January 1888], inserted between pp. 48 and 49). Chief executive Kynett favored its use, though shied away from directly associating the Board of Church Extension in its manufacture and sale; see Alpha J. Kynett, "Paper Imitation of Stained Glass," *Manual of the Methodist Episcopal Church* 5/3 (1885): 213–14.

22. For Tiffany's figure and landscape windows see Alastair Duncan, *Tiffany Windows* (New York: Simon and Schuster, 1980), 135–48, 163–78. Thirty-five Methodist churches around the country with Tiffany windows are documented in an appendix that lists windows commissioned between 1877 and 1910, pp. 201–24. Methodist and other churches continued to commission Tiffany windows between 1910 and the firm's closure in 1932, but they are not listed in Duncan's book.

23. Upscale Christ Church, Pittsburgh, had its own electrical plant with a fifty horsepower engine until the city provided electrical power for its residents.

24. First United Methodist Church, Birmingham, Al., *Cornerstone & Spire: Celebrating the First Century of the Sanctuary of First UMC.* (Birmingham, Al.: First U.M.C., 1991) 10. Cleveland's Epworth Memorial M.E. Church, erected in 1893, also boasted a primitive air-conditioning by forcing air through a system of pipe coils filled with cold water in the summer; see *Epworth Memorial Church: A Monument and a Movement, Published on the Tenth Anniversary of the Dedication of the Church.* (Cleveland: Epworth Memorial M.E. Church, 1903) 23.

25. Kramer, *The What, How and Why of Church Building*, 221.

26. "Our Architectural Plans," *Manual of the Methodist Episcopal Church* 5/3 (July 1885), 210–11; see also Paul Neff Garber, *Methodist Meeting House* (New York: Board of Home Missions and Church Extension, The Methodist Church, 1941), 76.

27. Methodist Episcopal Church Board of Church Extension, *Catalogue of Architectural Plans for Churches and Parsonages* (Philadelphia: Board of Church Extension, M.E. Church, 1885). This new plan, which cost $10,000 to $16,000 to build, was featured in the *Manual of the Methodist Episcopal Church* 5/3 (July 1885), 208–9. The same plan appeared as number 35 in Methodist Episcopal

Church, South, Board of Church Extension, *Catalogue of Architectural Plans for Churches, Parsonages and Dwellings* (Louisville: Board of Church Extension, M.E. Church, South, 1885), 48.

28. Methodist Episcopal Church Board of Church Extension, *Catalogue of Architectural Plans for Churches and Parsonages* (Philadelphia: M.E. Church, Board of Church Extension, 1889) 35, 72, and 74. The plans were first featured in the *Manual of the Methodist Episcopal Church* a year earlier, 1888. Plan 54 was also featured in the *Catalogue of Architectural Designs for Churches and Parsonages furnished by the Church-Erection Society of the United Brethren in Christ for the year 1889–90* (Dayton, Ohio: Church Erection Office, United Brethren Church, 1889), 17.

29. Beginning in 1877 the majority of plans drawn by Benjamin Price for catalogues issued by the Methodist Episcopal Church, the Methodist Episcopal Church South, and the United Brethren churches gave the Sunday school space adjoining the sanctuary. The area would often be located in a single rectangular space to one side of the sanctuary or a pair of rooms to either side (see plans no. 54 and 55). Other designs crowded the classrooms in the front or back of the sanctuary. More popular with building committees were Price's two-story designs which gave an entire floor to the Sunday school, allowing a greater freedom and flexibility for educational functions, though he had a "decided preference" for one story churches where sufficient ground could be obtained (Methodist Episcopal Church, Board of Church Extension, *Catalogue of Architectural Plans*, 1889, 75).

30. The best study of the Akron-plan Sunday school is Jaeger, *The Auditorium and Akron Plans* chap. IV, 139–80. See also Lewis Miller's essay, "The Akron Plan," in *Seven Graded Sunday Schools*, ed. Jesse L. Hurlbut (New York: Hunt & Eaton, 1893), 11–32. An older and briefer study is Marion Lawrance's "The Akron Plan—its Genesis, History and Development," in his *Housing the Sunday School; or, A Practical Study of Sunday School Buildings* (New York: Eaton & Mains, 1911), VIII: 83–92. An abbreviated version of Lawrance's chapter on the Akron plan was reprinted by the Methodist Episcopal Church, South, Board of Church Extension in its *Thirty-Second Annual Report, 1913–1914*, 268–71.

31. Ellwood Hendrick, *Lewis Miller* (New York: G. P. Putnam's Sons, 1925). See also Lewis Miller, "The Akron Plan," in *Seven Graded Sunday Schools*, ed. Jesse L. Hurlbut (New York: Hunt & Eaton, 1893), 11–32.

32. Hendrick, *Lewis Miller* 144–47.

33. Vincent's oft-quoted maxim became almost as famous as the architecture it inspired. Quoted from Marion Lawrance, *Housing the Sunday School*, 84.

34. The Sunday-school wing cost the 400-member congregation $20,000; the sanctuary cost $100,000, not including the half block of land on which the buildings stood. Miller was a heavy contributor to the building fund. The entire church plant was destroyed by fire in 1914, and a new church in classical revival style with a large multi-roomed Sunday-school wing was erected on the same site.

35. The open rotunda was huge, forty-one by sixty-four feet, reaching up to a domed ceiling sixty-four feet high (Jaeger, 151).

36. A brief contemporary description of the Sunday-school interior can be found in Matthew Simpson's 1877 *Cyclopedia*, 18. A fuller description appears in First M.E. Church's 70th anniversary booklet, 1907. Jaeger, *The Auditorium and Akron Plans*, 155f., gives fullest description.

37. For early description and floor plan see "The Model Sunday-School Room," *Sunday School Journal* n.s. 2/1 (October 1869), 11. Jeager's detailed description is based on a description of the building in the *Akron Daily Beacon* at the time of the dedication, 1870 (Jaeger, *The Auditorium and Akron Plans*, 150–54).

38. John H. Vincent, "The Model Sunday-School Room," *Sunday School Journal* n.s. 2/1 (October 1869): 11; idem, *The Modern Sunday-School* (New York: Hunt & Eaton; Cincinnati: Cranston & Curts, 1887), 160–61.

39. Architect Oscar S. Teale was also secretary of the Sunday-school. See "A Model Sunday School Room" in *Seven Graded Sunday Schools*, ed. Jesse L. Hurlbut (New York: Hunt & Eaton, 1893), 113–20, and "Building of Vincent Chapel," in First Methodist Episcopal Church, Plainfield, N.J., *Program of the 100th Anniversary Exercises October 16–23, 1932 and Historical Sketch* (Plainfield, N.J.: First M.E. Church, 1932), 8–9. For description and floor plan, see Lawrance, *Housing the Sunday School*, 59–63.

40. For a detailed description of the Sunday-school building see George S. Bennett, "The Wilkes-Barre Plan," in *Seven Graded Sunday Schools*, ed. Jesse Lyman Hurlbut (New York: Hunt & Eaton, 1893), 36–38. The church as built survives and has been lovingly restored.

41. *Epworth Memorial Church: A Monument and a Movement, Published on the Tenth Anniversary of the Dedication of the Church* (Cleveland: Epworth Memorial M.C. Church, 1903), 23.

42. Marion Lawrance, *Housing the Sunday School; or, A Practical Study of Sunday School Buildings* (New York: Eaton & Mains; Cincinnati: Jennings & Graham; and Philadelphia: Westminster, 1911) [Modern Sunday Schools Manuals series]. After a thirty-one year stint as Sunday-school superintendent of the Washington St. Congregational Church in Toledo, Ohio, Lawrance was general secretary of the Ohio State Sunday School Association and later general secretary of the International Sunday School Association.

43. *The Bushwick Avenue Methodist Episcopal Church, Brooklyn, N.Y., Kramer & Simonson, Architects, 1 Madison Avenue, New York* (Brooklyn, N.Y.: Bushwick Ave. M.E. Church, [1894]), a 12-page brochure. For description see Lawrance, *Housing the Sunday School*, 64–67.

44. A notable Auditorium/Akron-plan church clothed in Gothic costume is Trinity Methodist Episcopal Church, Denver, designed by Robert S. Roeschlaub and completed 1888, highlighted by Kilde, *Spiritual Armories*, 115–20.

45. Bad acoustics later forced the introduction of a pulpit and sounding board set to one side against one of the four tower piers.

46. For an extended treatment of the meaning of Neo-Medieval, i.e., Romanesque, exteriors, see Kilde, *Spiritual Armories*, 62–70. See also Henry Russell Hitchcock, *The Architecture of H. H. Richardson and His Times*, rev. ed. (Hamden, Conn.: Archon Books, 1961).

47. David G. Wright, *The Restoration of the Lovely Lane Church, Part I, Conception to Realization: A Historic Building Statemen* (Baltimore: Architectory, 1980); Calvin Corell, *The Restoration of the Lovely Lane Church, Part II, Perpetuation: A Restoration Feasibility Study* (Baltimore: Architectory, 1980).

48. First United Methodist Church, Birmingham, *Cornerstone & Spire, Celebrating the First Century of the Sanctuary of First United Methodist Church* (Birmingham, Ala.: First United Methodist Church, 1991).

Note to Kreutziger introduction

1. *Minutes of Several Conversations between The Rev. Thomas Coke, LL.D., The Rev. Francis Asbury and Others . . . in the Year 1784. Composing a Form of Discipline* (Philadelphia, 1785). Reprinted by Jno. J. Tigert in *A Constitutional History of American Episcopal Methodism*, 3rd ed. (Nashville: Publishing House of the Methodist Episcopal Church, South, 1908), 533–602, in parallel columns with "The Large Minutes."; see 535.

Notes to "UNITED METHODIST CAMPUS MINISTRY"

1. George Marsden has shown that in the beginning these new universities often incorporated Christian patterns of teaching and even worship since many of their faculty and administrators came from the traditional Christian colleges. This was to change with time but opened the state colleges and universities to Christian ministries on and surrounding their campuses (*The Soul of the American University* [New York: Oxford University Press, 1994], 167ff.).

2. For detailed discussions of these nineteenth-century student ministries see Charles Shedd, *The Church Follows Its Students* (New Haven, Conn.: Yale University Press, 1938) and Donald Shockley, *Campus Ministry; The Church Beyond Itself* (Louisville: Westminster/John Knox, 1989), Chap. 1.

3. Shockley, *Campus Ministry*, 33; Marsden, *The Soul*, 171.

4. James C. Baker, *The First Wesley Foundation* (Nashville: Parthenon, 1960), 10.

5. Ibid., 14–15.

6. Ibid., 12.

7. Ibid., 14.

8. Ibid., 15. See also pp. 108–9 for further comment on the expansive nature of the ministry.

9. Kenneth Underwood, *The Church, The University, and Social Policy* (Middletown, Conn.: Wesleyan University Press, 1969), I, 67.

10. Underwood, I, 83ff. For a current reinterpretation of Underwood's terms for present day campus ministry see Sam Portaro and Gary Peluso, *Inquiring Minds and Discerning Hearts* (Atlanta: Scholars Press, 1993).

11. Underwood maintains that American Protestantism so expanded the pastoral care aspect of a minister's priestly/pastoral role that it became a distinct fourth mode of ministry. Consequently his analysis incorporates four modes of campus ministry rather than the traditional three (Underwood, *The Church*, I, 89 and the Table of Contents). The distinction is an important one since pastoral care stresses the most common image of campus ministry among Methodists, yet most campus ministers carry varying degrees of priestly responsibility within their pastoral duties. For purposes of the present study, references to the pastoral mode will include those traditional priestly functions of ministry.

12. Baker, *The First Wesley Foundation*, 21–22.

13. Glenn Flinn, "The Wesley Foundation Work in Texas," in *History of Texas Methodism: 1900–1960*, ed. Olin W. Nail (Austin: Capitol Printing Co., 1961), 212.

14. Don Shockley discusses campus chaplaincy in significant detail. (Shockley, *Campus Ministry*, 27–28.) See also Underwood, *The Church*, 56ff.

15. "Constitution and By-Laws of The Methodist Student Federation of Texas" (Special Collections, Bridwell Library, SMU).

16. The name "Methodist Student Movement" had been used earlier to designate the student work of the Methodist Episcopal Church, South (Neien C. McPherson, ed., *Being a Christian on Campus: A Report of The First Methodist Student Leadership Training Conference* [Nashville, Tenn.: General Board of Education, 1939] 2).

17. *The Methodist Student Movement: Report to the Board of Education*, May, 1941 (Special Collections, Bridwell Library, SMU).

18. Ibid., 6.

19. For an instructive examination of the these changes and the church's response see Portaro and Peluso, Chap. 1.

20. *1948 Yearbook*, Board of Education, The Methodist Church, 731.

21. Portaro and Peluso, *Inquiring Minds*, 17.

22. *Journal of The Methodist Church* (1960), ed. Leon T. Moore, 1567. Cited by Portaro and Peluso, *Inquiring Minds* 38.

23. *1960 Yearbook*, Board of Education, The Methodist Church, 85.

24. *Minutes*, National Methodist Student Commission, 4 Sept. 1949 (Records of the General Board of Higher Education and Ministry, United Methodist Archives). Hereafter the Board will be cited as GBHEM.

25. *Ibid.* The 1951 United Student Christian Council's proposal for a "study department" within the SCM (Student Christian Movement) organization based their proposal on the "freedom and radicalism which is eternally in Jesus Christ." Their statement further suggested that the department:

> may determine priority in its projects and shift from one to another area of study as the Holy Spirit and the needs of the students so demand. Only in this way can the Study Department develop a tradition which will avoid the besetting ills of institutionalism and which will be a continual inspiration to the SCM and the church. (Records of GBHEM, United Methodist Archives).

26. *1955 Yearbook*, Board of Education. Cited in *Historical Material of the Methodist Student Movement* [1963] (Records of GBHEM, United Methodist Archives).

27. Underwood, *The Church*, I, 3.

28. *The Life and Mission of the Church on the University Campus: A Working Paper Written by a Group of Directors of Wesley Foundations, TMSM* (Special Collections, Bridwell Library, SMU).

29. Shockley, *Campus Ministry*, Chap. 8; Portaro and Peluso, *Inquiring Minds*, Chaps. 2, 3, & 4.

30. Shockley, *Campus Ministry*, 90.

31. Portaro and Peluso, *Inquiring Minds* 32–34.

32. *Minutes*, National Council, MSM, 5 Sept. 1964 (Records of the GBHEM, United Methodist Archives).

33. *1965 Yearbook*, Board of Education, The Methodist Church, 80. Bracketed phrases have been added to indicate identification with the terms used in this study.

34. *1966 Yearbook*, Board of Education, The Methodist Church, 23–24.

35. Gibson's report was the basis for Woodrow A. Geier's *The Campus Ministry of The Methodist Church* (Nashville: The Board of Education, The Methodist Church, 1967). Recommendations of the report are found on pages 53–60 of this work.

36. Proposal for the Phasing out of the National Structures of the Methodist Student Movement (Records of GBHEM, United Methodist Archives, Madison, N.J.).

37. William Corzine, in an article written to help campus ministers and others understand the "new look," suggests that theological reconstruction underlying these actions had been molded by the intense study among campus groups of the works of Tillich, Bonhoeffer, Harvey Cox and others (William Corzine, "The UCM and the MSM: Toward a United Mission," 2 [Records of GBHEM, United Methodist Archives]).

38. Paul E. Schrading, "The University Christian Movement; A Personal Remembrance," *Journal of Ecumenical Studies* 32 (summer 1995), 352.

39. Don Shockley suggests that while Underwood's study creatively designates the various patterns of ministry, the report tends to favor the prophetic voice even in the discussion of pastoral, priestly and governance modes (Shockley, *Campus Ministry*, 98–99.)

40. *1966 Yearbook*, Board of Education, The Methodist Church; "Memo to the United Methodist Campus Ministers," 28 June 1975 (Records of GBHEM, United Methodist Archives).

41. *Ibid.*

42. Shockley, *Campus Ministry*, 97–98.

43. Geier, *The Campus Ministry*, 10–11.

44. "State Director's Report," Annual Report of the Texas Methodist Student Movement, 1967–68.

45. Shockley, *Campus Ministry*, 100.

46. In the 1970 reorganization of the church, the Department of Campus Ministry became the "Campus Ministry Section" of the General Board of Higher Education and Ministry.

47. "Memo to United Methodist Campus Ministers," 28 June 1975 (Records of GBHEM, United Methodist Archives).

48. *Report on Campus Ministry* [1978] (Records of GBHEM, United Methodist Archives)

49. Author's interview with Helen Neinast, 15 September 1995.

50. *1974 Yearbook* and *1981 Yearbook*, General Board of Higher Education and Ministry, The United Methodist Church.

51. *Minutes*, The Executive Committee, TCCM, 4 March 1972 (Special Collections, Bridwell Library, SMU).

52. *Ministry on Campus: A United Methodist Mission Statement and Survey Report* (Nashville: National Commission on United Methodist Higher Education, 1977), 65. Among the campus ministers themselves, Wesley Foundation directors tended to be more concerned with pastoral roles while ecumenical campus pastors and college chaplains tended to be more conscious of the prophetic (*Ibid.*, 41).

53. "Memo to United Methodist Campus Ministers," 28 July 1975 (Records of GBHEM, United Methodist Archives).

54. Clyde Chesnutt, "U.M. Collegians to Organize Again?" *Texas Methodist Reporter*, July, 1976.

55. Author's interview of Helen Neinast, 15 September 1995.

56. "Progress in Campus Ministry Programs," Report of Section of Campus Ministry, GBHEM, 1993.

57. *United Methodist Daily News*, United Methodist News Service, Nashville, Tenn., 4 June 1996.

58. I am dependent, for this information and most of the material on the current status of the campus ministry, on conversations and materials provided by Don Shockley.

59. Andy Langford, "A New Connection," *Leadership Letters*, Duke Divinity School Project on United Methodism and American Culture, 15 July 1995, 5. For a more generalized discussion of the empowerment of the local church see Andy Langford and William H. Willimon, *A New Connection* (Nashville: Abingdon, 1995).

Notes to "THE EFFECTS OF MERGERS"

1. Many books tell this story. Among them are Harry E. Woolever, *The Highroad of Methodism* (Washington, D.C.: Commission on Methodist Union, 1939), John M. Moore, *The Long Road to Methodist Union* (New York and Nashville: Abingdon Cokesbury, 1943), and James H. Straughn, *Inside Methodist Union* (Nashville: Methodist Publishing House, 1958). All three authors were members of the unification commissions. Later studies include Frederick E. Maser, "The Story of Unification," in Emory S. Bucke, ed., *The History of American Methodism* (New York and Nashville: Abingdon, 1964), III, 407–78, Frederick A. Norwood, *The Story of American Methodism* (Nashville: Abingdon, 1974), and Robert W. Sledge, *Hands on the Ark* (Lake Junaluska, N.C.: General Commission on Archives and History, 1975).

2. Dwight Culver, *Negro Segregation in the Methodist Church* (New Haven: Yale University Press, 1953), 75–76.

3. Data from The Methodist Church, *General Minutes and Yearbook* annual editions for the period.

4. Gordon Melton, ed., *Encyclopedia of American Religion,* 4th ed. (Detroit, Washington, London: Gate Research, Inc. 1993), 239–41.

5. William K. Anderson, *Methodism* (Nashville: Methodist Publishing House, 1947), 276–82.

6. Methodist Episcopal General Conference *Daily Christian Advocate*, 1936. Delegate David Jones argued that "this plan turns its back on the historical attitude of the Methodist Episcopal Church. All through the years we have had interracial fellowship. . . . [I]f we have made progress it has been in a measure due to the kind of fellowship and the kind of leadership we have had" (87–88). Delegate George W. Lewis noted that "What we have now [segregated annual conferences and separate election for Negro bishops] is from choice, but what you are about to give us is from law, and there is a tremendous difference between choice and force" (89).

7. United Brethren in Christ General Conference *Journal* (1946), 33.

8. Ibid., 333.

9. See EUB *Yearbooks* for statistical data on this period. The EUB story is told in J. Bruce Behney and Paul H. Eller, *The History of the EUB Church* (Nashville: Abingdon, 1979).

10. See his speech to the Methodist Church General Conference of 1966 in *Daily Christian Advocate* (November 12, 1966), 989.

11. James M. Ault, "The Methodist Church Is A Better Church United," *Circuit Rider* 16, no. 10 (December 1992–January 1993), 7. See also the respective 1966 General Conference *Journals* and the Methodist *Daily Christian Advocate* for details.

12. The story of the EUBs in the Pacific Northwest Conference is told best by Theodore R. Buzzard, the leader of the group in the conference that vigorously opposed unification but entered the United Methodist Church when unification came. His book is *Lest We Forget: A History of the Evangelical United Brethren Church in the Pacific Northwest* (Portland, Oreg.: by the author, 1988.)

13. Rev. R. L. Dunn, one of the three ministers who entered the United Methodist Church, telephone conversation with the author, 23 August 1995.

14. James M. Ault, "The Methodist Church Is Better United," *Circuit Rider* 16, no. 10 (December 1992–January 1993), 7.

15. Lyle E. Schaller, "A Statistical View of the 1968 Union," *Circuit Rider* 17, no. 6 (July–August, 1993), 11.

16. James M. Ault, "Jim Ault's Final Comment," *Circuit Rider* 16, no. 10 (December 1992–January 1993), 11.

17. Rodney Roberts, conversation with author, Dallas, Tex., 10 August 1994.

18. James Morris, conversation with author, Madison, N.J., 13 August 1994.

19. Warren J. Hartman, "The EUBs Had Reservations Then and Now," *Circuit Rider* 16, no. 10 (December 1992-January 1993), 4–6.

20. Ann Whiting, "COCU: Faith and Order Ecumenism," *Circuit Rider* 20, no. 5 (June 1996), in "Roundup Edition" insert of the *Daily Christian Advocate*, 1996, 7.

Notes to "GOD'S MISSION AND UNITED METHODISM"

1. C. Stanley Smith, "An Exploratory Attempt to Define the Theological Basis of the Church's Missionary Obligation," Part I, *International Missionary Council: A New Study of The Missionary Obligation of the Church* (National Council of Churches, 1952), 1.

2. "Nationals" has been a term used over the years to refer to indigenous persons in the countries to which North American missionaries have been sent.

3. Smith, Part I: 4.

4. Ibid., Part II: 2.

5. Emil Brunner, *The Word and the World* (New York: Charles Scribner's Sons, 1931), 108.

6. Missio Dei, or the mission of God, is a concept which became prominent at the 1952 International Missionary Conference in Willingen, Germany. The 1961 New Delphi Assembly of the World Council of Churches adopted missio Dei as a foundational principle in its study, "Missionary Structure of the Congregation."

7. David J. Bosch, *Transforming Mission* (New York: Obis Books, 1993), 390.

8. Ibid., 391.

9. Ibid., 392.

10. Karl Barth, "Die Theologie und die Mission in der Gegenwart," *Theologische Fragen und Antworten* 5:3 (Zollikon: Evangelischer Verlag, 1957), 100–26.

11. Letty M. Russell, *Church in the Round* (Louisville: Westminister/John Knox, 1993), 88.

12. Ibid., 89.

13. Donald McGavran, "The God Who Finds and His Mission," *International Review of Missions*, Vol. 51 (London: Oxford University Press, 1962), 303.

14. The church can be assisted in its theological anthropology and cultural analysis by sociologists Robert Bellah and others who help us to understand our culture self-critically. See Bellah's *Habits of the Heart* (Berkeley & Los Angeles: University of California Press, 1985, 1996) and Christopher Lasch's *The Culture of Narcissism* (New York: Norton, 1979). Such diagnoses have revealed us to be a people who are very narcissistic, individualistic, and materialistic. These are values which run counter to the shape of Christ's ministry.

15. Congregations must be encouraged to engage in serious and honest study of the Gospels which portray for us the shape of Jesus' ministry, particularly defined by a life and ministry of self-denial, of association with and seeking after justice for the poor and all others living on the margins of societies. Many congregations are content to "set aside" these stories because they challenge the contradictions between what we profess and how we live. I highly recommend such works as Frederick Herzog's *Justice Church* (Maryknoll, N.Y.: Orbis, 1980) and *God-Walk* (Maryknoll: Orbis Books, 1988), as well as Letty M. Russell's *Church in the Round* (see n. 11 above) and Leonardo Boff's *Ecclesiogenesis (Maryknoll, N.Y.: Orbis, 1986).*

16. Christo-praxis is a term used by Frederick Herzog to talk about "the shape of the ministry of Jesus of Nazareth." See his book *God-Walk*, 90–167.

17. See the work of David Lowes Watson in his trilogy *Covenant Discipleship, Forming Christian Disciples,* and *Class Leaders* (Nashville: Discipleship Resources, 1991).

18. I recommend *50 Years is Enough: The Case Against the World Bank and the International Monetary Fund*, ed. Kevin Danaher (Boston: South End Press, 1994).

19. I shall forever be indebted to my mentor and friend of twenty years, Frederick Herzog, who died 9 October 1995 during the completion of this project, and who over the years taught by example the grace of "God-walk."

20. "Realizing a New Vision," Proposal for the Structure of the General Board of Global Ministries, Report of the Core Coordinating Task Force, 17–21 October 1994, 1.

21. I mean by ecclesiocentric the tendency to place the missio Dei as a secondary consideration to the maintenance of the institutional structures (e.g., general agencies) of the church.

22. Preliminary Proposal, 1993, Proposal for the Structure of the General Board of Global Ministries.

23. Ibid., 12.

24. The language of the Board in this vision is to shift from "the programming of mission" to "the facilitating of mission" on behalf of the conference and local ministries of the church. This will indeed be a formidable challenge.

25. Luis Reinoso is presently serving as a pastor in the North Carolina Annual Conference. His presence and ministry among us has offered important interpretation, which has greatly enhanced the mutuality of the covenant.

26. The covenant was unanimously endorsed by the 1990 annual conference of the North Carolina Conference with a representative of the IMP present. A similar statement of covenant was endorsed unanimously by the IMP at their 1990 General Assembly with representatives from North Carolina present.

27. *1990 Journal of the North Carolina Annual Conference* (Raleigh: Derreth Printing Co.), 375–76.

28. Ibid., 376.

29. "Churches in Covenant Communion: The Church of Christ Uniting," approved and recommended by the Seventeenth Plenary of the Consultation on Church Union, 9 December 1988, New Orleans, Louisiana, 9.

30. Russell E. Richey, "Connectionalism: End or New Beginning," *Leadership Letters*, from the Duke Divinity School Project on United Methodist and American Culture, 15 February 1995, vol. 1, no. 2, p. 1.

31. Ibid., 2.

32. Wethington, COSMOS Study Paper on The Central Conference, 1962.

33. Rosa del Carmen Bruno-Jofre, *Methodist Education in Peru: Social Gospel, Politics, and American Ideological Penetration, 1888–1930* (Waterloo: Wilfrid Laurier University Press, 1988), 102.

34. Jonathan J. Bonk, "Globalization and Mission Education, in *Theological Education* 33, no. 1 (autumn 1993): 51.

35. Bosch, 519.

36. David Martin, *Tongues of Fire* (Cambridge: Blackwell, 1990), 86.

37. In our walking together, money is obviously one thing that the North American church has to offer. But we have been very cautious about the way in which this has been done. It has been obvious from the beginning that a key point of divisiveness in the Peru church has been the scarcity of resources, which creates factions and unhealthy elements of secrecy.

38. The IMP was given birth by Methodist missionaries from the United States in the late 1880s. The Rev. Thomas Wood, who came to Peru in August of 1891, is credited with primary leadership in the founding of Methodism in Peru. He worked primarily in the establishment of a school system. In April 1970 the IMP separated from the Central Conference and became an autonomous church.

39. Within a short period of time, Wenceslao Bahamonde, the first bishop of Peru, died in a car accident, Hector Laporte Sr. died of heart failure, and Rose Savala succumbed to a parasite infection.

40. Bill Jones, "Seeing it Whole: The First Year of Autonomy," *Peru Calling* 32 (Methodist Church of Peru, December 1970): 1.

41. While the Peruvian church and other Latin American Methodist churches might not have been prepared for autonomy at that time, there was general agreement among all that autonomy was the best thing. It was recognized that the Central Conference often becomes the facade of connection and not true connection. Tinkering with ecclesial structures will not promote intimacy of relationship. With autonomy there is a sense in which all are freer to find new models of connection.

42. Bill Jones, "The Meaning of Autonomy," *Peru Calling* No. 28 (Methodist Church of Peru, April 1969).

43. Jonathan J. Bonk, *Mi$$ion$ and Money: Affluence as a Western Missionary Problem* (New York: Orbis, 1992).

44. Ibid., 43.

45. Ibid., 45–58.

46. Mahatma Gandhi, "Young India," 20 October 1927: 45.

47. Lesslie Newbigin, *A Word in Season: Perspectives on Christian World Mission* (Grand Rapids: Eerdmans, 1994), 175.

48. The Wesley Heritage Project was begun in 1990 by the Wesley Heritage Foundation, a nonprofit foundation established by United Methodists in North Carolina. In cooperation with Latinos, and with Justo González as chief editor, this project is producing fourteen volumes of Wesley's works in Spanish.

49. Newbigin, *A Word in Season* (Grand Rapids: Eerdmans, 1994), 178.

50. See Frederick Herzog's *God-Walk* [n. 16 above], in which he uses the term Spirit-praxis to refer to the Spirit of God working sometimes through us and sometimes independently of us and in spite of us.

51. Lesslie Newbigin, *The Gospel in a Pluralist Society* (Grand Rapids: Eerdmans, 1989), 83.

52. Ibid.

Notes to "Determinants of the Denominational-Mission Funding Crisis"

1. Some of the analysis in this paper is based on material that has appeared in Ronald A. Vallet and Charles E. Zech, *The Mainline Church's Funding Crisis* (Grand Rapids: Eerdmans, 1995). The author acknowledges his gratitude to Mr. Stan Sager, Rev. Jere Martin, Rev. David High, Mr. Robert Doughterty, Ms. Barbara Wynn, Mr. Dale Owens, the members of the United Methodism and American Culture Study, and the Lilly Endowment for their support of the subject.

2. Vallet and Zech, *The Mainline Church's Funding Crisis*, 36.

3. Ibid., 39.

4. Ibid., 37.

5. Ibid, 39.

6. Roger J. Nemeth and Donald A. Luidens, "Congregational versus Denominational Giving: An Analysis of Giving Patterns in the Presbyterian Church in The United States and the Reformed Church in America," *Review of Religious Research* 36, no. 2 (December 1994): 111–22.

7. Ibid., 188.

8. Gregory A. Krohn, "The Receipts and Benevolences of Presbyterian Congregations, 1973–1988," *Journal for the Scientific Study of Religion* 34, no. 1 (March 1995), 17–34.

9. D. Scott Cormode, "A Financial History of Presbyterian Congregations Since World War II," in *The Organizational Revolution: Presbyterians and American Denominationalism*, ed. Milton J. Coalter, John W. Mulder, and Louis B. Weeks, (Louisville: Westminster/John Knox, 1992), 171–98.

10. Ibid., 188.

11. Kenneth W. Innskeep, "Giving in the Evangelical Lutheran Church in America: A Test of Seven Hypotheses," unpublished paper presented to the Catholic University Seminar on Religious Giving, March 1993.

12. Scott Brunger, "Designated and Undesignated Giving in Four American Denominations," unpublished paper presented at the Atlantic Economics Association Annual Meetings, October 1993.

13. Daniel V. A. Olson and David Caddell, "Causes of Financial Giving to United Church of Christ Congregations," unpublished paper presented to The Catholic University Seminar on Religious Giving, March 1993.

14. Innskeep, "Giving in the Evangelical Lutheran Church in America."

15. Craig Dykstra and James Hudnut-Beumler, "The National Organizational Structures of Protestant Denominations: An Invitation to a Conversation," *The Organizational Revolution* [n. 9 above], 307–31.

16. Loren B. Mead, *The Once and Future Church* (Washington, D.C.: The Alban Institute, 1991).

17. Innskeep, "Giving in the Evangelical Lutheran Church in America."

18. Jackson W. Carroll and David A. Roozen, "Congregational Identities in the Presbyterian Church," *Review of Religious Research* 31 (June 1990), 351–69.

19. Most previous studies have shown the relationship between mission funding and its determinants to be curvilinear. By this is meant that changes in the determinant variables change mission funding at either an increasing or decreasing rate, rather than at a constant rate. To put this relationship into an equation form, the square root of the portion of the local church's budget going towards denominational mission was taken. Taking the square root is one of the techniques that results in the estimation of a curvilinear relationship.

20. See G. S. Maddala, *Econometrics* (New York: McGraw-Hill, 1977), 265–67.

21. Mark Chaves, "Intraorganizational Power and Internal Secularization in Protestant Denominations," *American Journal of Sociology* 99, no. 1 (July 1993): 1–48.

22. Dykstra and Hudnut-Beumler, "The National Organizational Structures of Protestant Denominations."

23. Mead, *The Once and Future Church*, 5–6.

Notes to "UNDERSTANDING LOCAL MISSION"

1. Taken from Becker 1995, pp. 164ff.

2. This statement was taken from a web-page posting of the *Book of Discipline*, copyright 1992 by The United Methodist Publishing House, http://www.netins.net/showcase/umsource/umdoct.html#basic, visited 5 June 1996. The quotation is from ¶ 65.1 "Our Doctrinal Heritage" (the text appears in a section on "Distinctive Wesleyan Emphases, ¶ 60 [p. 45] of the *Book of Discipline of the United Methodist Church 1996* [Nashville: The United Methodist Publishing House]). Several paragraphs later, under "General Rules and Social Principles," the *Discipline* adds:

> In asserting the connection between doctrine and ethics, the General Rules provide an early signal of Methodist social consciousness. The Social Principles . . . provide our most recent official summary of stated convictions that seek to apply the Christian vision of righteousness to social, economic, and political issues. . . . Our struggles for human dignity and social reform have been a response to God's demand for love, mercy, and justice in the light of the Kingdom. *We proclaim no personal gospel that fails to express itself in relevant social concerns;* we proclaim no social gospel that does not include the personal transformation of sinners. (emphasis altered; cf. the *Book of Discipline . . . 1996,* ¶ 60, p. 47)

3. This is true for official documents like the *Discipline*, for policies on specific issues, and for more general or scholarly treatments. For just one example of the latter, see Gilkey 1994.

4. This study also included two Catholic parishes and two synagogues; the ideas developed here are meant to be broadly applicable to the institutional field of American congregational religion, but this discussion will draw out some more limited implications for mainstream Protestantism, with a specific focus on the UMC.

5. Congregations of the same denomination in one community often specialize. For example, in this community, there was the Unitarian-Universalist church known for social activism and the one known for fellowship. Likewise, congregations often model themselves on other congregations that match them in size and resources, not denominational affiliation; for example, the members and pastor of a large Presbyterian church told me they judged themselves against the other large, affluent, activist churches in the area—one fundamentalist Protestant, one a "United" UCC and Presbyterian congregation—not against other congregations of their own denomination. And members of several congregations of various denominations told me that they were trying to copy the programs of the local Lutheran church that had led it to grow from just over 50 to just under 200 people in the space of a few years.

6. This insight developed not only from my own fieldwork but also from a body of work sometimes referred to as "congregational studies." This consists of a wealth of case studies and some more general synthesizing or theoretical accounts. See, for example, Eiesland 1995, Wind and Lewis 1994, Olson 1989, Prell 1989, Hammond 1988, Warner 1988, Ammerman 1987, 1990, and 1994, Gremillion and Castelli 1987, Neitz 1987, Furman 1987, Wertheimer 1987, Greenhouse 1986, Caplow et al. 1983, Swatos 1981, Blau 1976. These accounts differ a great deal, but most emphasize the pragmatic, partial, emergent nature of local identity and mission.

7. Longer introductions available in Becker 1995.

8. The two adjacent communities, River Forest and Forest Park, were also included. River Forest is economically and demographically similar to northern Oak Park, and Forest Park is economically and demographically similar to south Oak Park (1990 Census). They both share community organizations with Oak Park; there is a joint River Forest/Oak Park high school, and the Community of Congregations spans all three villages; there are also joint business and development associations. In 1991 I developed a profile of all three villages based on census data, archival sources, and interviews with leaders in local business, politics, the local press, and education. While each village is distinct in governance and in history, considering them all together as a "community" is plausible for my limited purposes. It captures not only economic and demographic similarities, but also some sense of how people who live in these villages see their own identity as in part a common one, and their future trajectories as interdependent.

9. Most people have never heard of Oak Park, but in some academic and policy circles it is rather famous for achieving stable racial integration in the early 1970s, resisting the trend of rapid black in-migration and white flight that characterized many West Side neighborhoods and near-western suburbs. It is known for being progressive. This reputation is deserved, and yet there are many conservative people remaining. They vote Republican, some go to the community's evangelical and fundamentalist churches, and they report feeling very outside the current power structure.

10. Or there were as of 1992, based on phone book listings and a driving street survey.

11. For a discussion of similarities and differences between congregations in these three traditions, see Blau 1976, Cantrell et al. 1983, Gremillion and Castelli 1987, Wertheimer 1987, Seidler and Meyer 1989, Davidman 1991, Hunter 1991, Swatos 1991, Carroll and Roof 1993, Glock 1993, Warner 1993.

12. I approached a Catholic church associated with Bishop LeFevre's sect, but was refused permission to study them.

13. While it is certainly possible that there would be disagreement among laity or between the pastor and the laity on this classification, in fact in all twenty-three of these congregations there was general consensus. Moreover, most people who were asked this question displayed some understanding of these as larger orientations that encompassed theology and stands on social issues (revealed through prompts to the initial question). While most people could classify their congregation, many were either uncomfortable doing so or expressed the opinion that this was not the important aspect of their congregation's identity, while others expressed that it was highly important. Again, within a given congregation, there was some agreement on how central liberal or conservative ideology was to the congregation's overall identity and reputation.

14. For a more extended discussion of conflict, see Becker 1995 and Becker 1996.

15. There is a large literature on institutional analysis; a good introduction is Powell and DiMaggio 1991.

16. These categories draw upon mission orientation categories used by Mock (1992). The major difference is that Mock concentrates on mission as orientation to the external world, while these models encompass all of the core tasks, both internal and external, that are most highly valued and best institutionalized in local churches. For discussions of different ways of classifying mission orientation, see Dudley and Johnson 1993, Gilkey 1994, Carroll and Roof 1993, Dudley 1988, Roozen et al. 1984. All these authors preserve a basic distinction between inward and outward oriented groups. It is common to acknowledge the difference between a "civic" orientation which is concerned with the local community and an "activist" orientation that actively seeks to change the world. Some authors also make the distinction between those that see their primary mission as saving individual souls (an evangelistic orientation) and

those that see the changing of societal institutions as their goal (see Dudley and Johnson 1983, Roozen et al. 1984).

17. The characteristics of the two UMC congregations I studied are listed below:

United Methodist Congregation #1.

Membership: over 400.

Average Sunday morning attendance: 140.

People present the morning I attended: 100–110.

Largely residents of Oak Park. Mostly middle-class professionals.

80–85% White, rest African American or Asian; some mixed-race couples.

Model: **House of Worship**

Conflicts: —over whether to raise pastor's salary
          —over staff, replacing secretary, firing custodian
          —over how to stem decline, several years ago; disagreements centered mostly around issues of budget/programming, but some members also disliked the former pastor.

United Methodist Congregation #2

Membership: 56

Average Sunday morning attendance: 40–50

People present the morning I attended: 45–50

Most are residents of Forest Park and Oak Park. There is a gap in the 45–65 age range. Maybe 45% have a college education, but that is the growing group.

Over 90% White, rest Hispanic and Asian.

Model: **Family**

Conflicts: —sell parsonage
          —what to do after fire (rent/buy/merge with another congregation?)

18. *Mixed congregations.* There were four churches undergoing a transition from one congregational model to another. These congregations show the most severe pattern of conflict. Conflict is frequent, widespread, and highly emotional. Formal rules are invoked, but voting and other routine procedures are unable to contain the conflict. Rather, conflict is likely to rage through a series of events, encompass a wide variety of issues, and see multiple frames and arguments. The pastor is quickly implicated, but these are different from the pastor conflicts in family congregations. In these transitional congregations, the pastor is championed by one faction and disliked by another, because he is seen as favoring one congregational model over another.

In such conflicts, competing claims and arguments cannot be resolved by an organizational routine or by religious authority—which have both been called into question along with the rest of the congregational model. They also cannot be subsumed by a larger set of understandings, since participants are operating with two such larger sets. Rather, they are often resolved only by the exit of losers and the institutionalization by the winners of a new, dominant model. These are "winner take all" conflicts, and that is why they are so bitter. These are the only congregations where the conflict ends with the exit, en masse, of a large group of congregation members. An example is a series of conflicts in a Unitarian Universalist congregation about whether to become more a leader congregation, or to remain a family congregation, focusing on fellowship, worship, and the education of members. This conflict was only resolved when the pastor resigned, after a large group of the congregation (over 20%) had left.

19. This is akin to the difference between a person who feels that she is a good citizen because she is informed on the issues and votes regularly (living her values), versus the one who thinks that it is incumbent upon her to be a political activist, to try to persuade others to vote a certain way and to change public opinion or public policy (changing the world).

20. Robert Bellah and his co-authors, in *Habits of the Heart* (1985), have developed the most extended treatment of this theme. This work has been very influential and has spawned a host of other studies that confirm the trend toward individualism, and, in many cases, critical of it. Thus, even Wuthnow (1994, 1995), who describes a healthy voluntary sector, is nevertheless worried that some forms of religious organization (small groups) are fostering a "domestication" of religion, concentrating on love and personal needs at the expense of discipline, outreach, and social justice. For good reviews of this literature, see Warner 1993 and Ammerman 1996.

21. Five out of the six family congregations and both of the houses of worship had a hierarchical polity. All told, seven of the hierarchical congregations (out of 11) had either a family or a house of worship model; one had a community model, one a leader model, and two were "mixed."

22. This congregation is described in much more detail in Ammerman 1996. Basic information on this congregation is:
Independent Baptist Church #1
    Membership: 255.
    Average Sunday morning attendance: 155.
    People present the morning I attended: ca. 155.
    60–65% White; 35–40% African American.
    Most are residents of Oak Park and Austin.
    There is a core group of black and white professionals from Oak Park that provide much of the leadership, although there is great economic and educational diversity in the congregation as a whole.
    There is a small gap in the 35–55 age group.
    Model: **Community**
    Conflicts: —over funding a missionary
                —over worship style (music)
                —over fundraising

23. Although some did. The five congregations belonged to these traditions: Reform Judaism, independent Baptist, Disciples of Christ, United (UCC/Presbyterian Church USA), Presbyterian USA.

24. *Disciples of Christ*

Baptized members: about 130.

Average Sunday morning attendance: 70 or 80.

People present the morning I attended: 60–65.

60–65% White, and at least 30% African American. Some Asian Americans attend.

The members mostly come from Oak Park and from Austin (Chicago). The dominant group is middle-class professionals, but members cover a fairly broad range of occupation and income.

Model: **Leader**

Conflict: —over whether to install elevator
            —over the last pastor's mission activity
            —over baptism/communion rituals

25. They were well-articulated only in the mixed congregations that were in the throes of much more serious conflict.

Notes to "METHODISTS ON THE MARGINS"

1. Survey results include respondents 21 years of age or older who claim a religious preference. In the case of this subsample, respondents claimed a "Methodist" preference.

2. A separate cluster analysis was performed among churched persons using the same criterion variables with initial cluster centers "seeded" from the final cluster centers produced by the unchurched cluster analysis. The relative proportion of each unchurched type was then subtracted from the relative proportion of each churched type.